Choosing Among
the Options

ACTFL Review, *published annually in conjunction with The American Council on the Teaching of Foreign Languages*

An Integrative Approach to Foreign Language Teaching: Choosing Among the Options, ed. Jarvis, Vol. 8 (1976)

Perspective: A New Freedom, ed. Jarvis, Vol. 7 (1975)

The Challenge of Communication, ed. Jarvis, Vol. 6 (1974)

Responding to New Realities, ed. Jarvis, Vol. 5 (1973)

Foreign Language Education: A Reappraisal, ed. Lange, Vol. 4 (1972)

Pluralism in Foreign Language Education, ed. Lange, Vol. 3 (1971)

Individualization of Instruction, ed. Lange, Vol. 2 (1970)

Foreign Language Education: An Overview, ed. Birkmaier, Vol. 1 (1969)

Other books *published in conjunction with The American Council on the Teaching of Foreign Languages*

Teaching Culture: Strategies for Foreign Language Educators, Seelye

Living in Latin America: A Case Study in Cross-Cultural Communication, Gorden

An Integrative Approach to Foreign Language Teaching:

Choosing Among the Options

Edited by Gilbert A. Jarvis

In conjunction with the American Council on the Teaching of Foreign Languages

NTC National Textbook Company, *Skokie, Illinois 60076*

Foreword

Volume 8 of the ACTFL Foreign Language Education Series continues the purposes of the former Review of Foreign Language Education—the annual collection, analysis, synthesis, and interpretation of the work of the profession. The elimination of the term *Review* from the designation is intended to reflect the utility of the *Series* to the classroom teacher as well as to the scholar/researcher.

The creation of a volume such as this within the necessary time constraints is dependent upon the assistance and cooperation of many persons beyond the editor and authors. At ACTFL Headquarters, support and expert help came from C. Edward Scebold and Warren Born. At the National Textbook Company Marcia Seidletz and Karla Heuer planned and guided the production of the Volume. At The Ohio State University Cathy Kaiser and Ronna Turner provided skillful clerical assistance. Alice Omaggio, in the role of Assistant to the Editor, contributed expertly and extensively to all phases of the preparation of the Volume.

The Advisory Committee should be credited with planning the volume. The members are Walter Bartz, Warren Born, Donald Greenham, Alice Omaggio, June Phillips, C. Edward Scebold, Lorraine Strasheim, and Barbara Wing.

A very special acknowledgement is in order for the sensitivity, patience, and support of Carol, Vicki, and Mark Jarvis throughout the preparation of this volume as well as earlier volumes.

Contents

1

Introduction: Teachers, options, and the future

Gilbert A. Jarvis
Alice C. Omaggio
The Ohio State University

Examining the state of any living art is bound to be difficult simply because that which is vital will not stand still for inspection. In presenting a contemporary perspective of foreign language education, however, the authors of a publication such as this Series must attempt to examine the state of the art while it is in motion, capturing and documenting the year-to-year development of the profession. To record fully that dynamic process the lens through which the profession is viewed must be adjusted to the widest possible angle, expanding the field of vision to include all the diverse components of the total picture. The picture thus presented to an observer from outside the profession would probably be judged favorably. The profession would probably be perceived as a vibrantly alive organism, changing and adapting to a fluid, and sometimes even hostile, environment. Intellectual fascination with change and the future shock it produces has given way to concrete innovations that are purposely divergent. Pluralism and individuality are increasingly valued; terms like *diversification, new roles, new*

A dynamic profession

Gilbert A. Jarvis (Ph.D., Purdue University) is Professor of Foreign Language Education at The Ohio State University, where he teaches courses in second language learning, research, and measurement in the graduate foreign language education program. He has taught French at the elementary, secondary, and college levels and has directed teacher workshops and spoken to teacher groups throughout the country. Dr. Jarvis is Associate Editor of the Psychology Section of the ACTFL *Annual Bibliography*. He has coauthored a series of *French Readers for Communication* (Holt, Rinehart & Winston) and has edited Volumes 5, 6, and 7 of the ACTFL Review of Foreign Language Education Series. His articles have appeared in many professional journals.

Alice C. Omaggio (A.B.D., The Ohio State University) is Research Associate in Foreign Language Education at The Ohio State University. She has taught French at the university level, has supervised teaching assistants, and has conducted demonstration classes. She has contributed to foreign language education publications such as *Foreign Language Annals*, the *Canadian Modern Language Review*, and the ACTFL Review of Foreign Language Education Series. She has developed workshop materials and has made presentations to various teacher groups. Affiliations include ACTFL and OMLTA.

goals, relevance, individualization, self-expression, and *openness* echo throughout the profession. Conferences, workshops, and publications clarion one "new" idea after another. Such vigorous innovative activity clearly creates the external impression of a vitally healthy profession—and indeed, this impression may be very accurate.

There are, however, several important implications of our having transformed ourselves into a brainstorming—rather than a deliberating—profession. From a vantage point from within, for example, the perception of what is occurring can be very different from that obtained from an external perspective. There is growing evidence that a significant number of language teachers have a negative impression of what is happening in their own profession. They see themselves at the center of a whirlwind of dizzying confusion. Little in which they once believed is secure, stable, or sacred. The wide-angle vigor and vibrancy becomes at close range a blur—a whirl of controversial (even irreconcilable) strategies, ideas, theories, societal pressures, curricula, methods, goals, and philosophies. For many of these educators, blurred vision leads to a sense of threat and a loss of equilibrium. The problem is compounded by the fact that this very real disorientation frequently gives way to a devastating feeling of helplessness, which in turn undermines motivation to respond, inhibits the ability to see that responding really does help, and results in emotional dysfunctions such as anxiety and depression. Thus, a divergently thinking profession is at the same time generating feelings of excitement and discomfort.

Dizzying confusion

Whenever the total of work in a field is comprised of many fragments produced by the creative energy of individuals, the relationships among these parts may sometimes be unclear. Wisdom would seem to demand that we clarify those relationships. Having accentuated the creation of new alternatives—both in ideas and practice—it is time to devote energy to integrating those alternatives. The goal is certainly not to recreate a monolithic profession but rather to evaluate and synthesize the work of recent years. Surely some of our new creations should be discarded and others modified.

A need for integration and synthesis

Other facts also militate for an integration of our knowledge. We are gradually coming to recognize and acknowledge the multivariate nature of the teaching/learning process. There is

A multivariate world

need to understand better the relationships among hundreds of variables in the foreign language classroom. Simplistic comparisons between Method A and Method B are anachronistic because of the myriad forces that affect learning at any given time. The methodology, for example, may influence as little as 5 percent of the learning that occurs (Stephens, 3, p. 84). Thus, from a research point of view, we do not need new curricula and programs; we do not yet know how to use what has already been created. We must learn more about the factors that make a particular technique or program work in a particular context.

Integrating teaching and research

The relationship between teaching and research continues to be problematic. Yet, an optimistic view of the future has to include hope that a closer relationship will slowly evolve. The professional literature through many years contains regular reminders that there is much that researchers can learn from effective teachers and much teachers can learn from effective researchers. This observation is all the more important at a time when integration of our work is essential to ensure further progress. There is, however, less research now in foreign language education than in the past several years. In a recent listing of major research studies (written for those outside foreign language education), Arendt (1) included no items published since 1972. While many researchers would undoubtedly disagree with the selection of studies, the bulk of our research is now done for dissertations. Moreover, the quality of this research is probably inferior to other educational research—already rated as substandard (Ward, Hall, and Schramm, 4). Coordination of effort is done only by individual dissertation advisors or within single graduate programs.

Thus, the need for integration, coordination, and communication can be readily documented. The achievement of this goal is not within easy reach; it cannot be accomplished in the space of one year or even several years. It requires a commitment that has a remarkable affinity to the concept of lifelong learning.

Lifelong learning

In the late 1970s the concept of lifelong learning is growing in intellectual respectability throughout the world. Because it is an integrational movement *par excellence,* it has implications for the current condition of foreign language education. Just as the individual teacher feels the need to sift and sort among the fragments to build a viable curriculum, this movement views man as an integrated whole—a being who learns throughout the entire span of his lifetime and who selects from that learning the materials with which to build his own life structure. Formal education or schooling is an important but not dominant portion of one's education. All that a person does between birth and death involves learning, and his total well-being is in many ways dependent upon an integration of thinking, feeling, and behavior. We have too long indoctrinated ourselves with the notion that education occurs only in schools. "Finish your education before you get married," parents tell their children. In an interdependent rapidly changing world where man has a prospect for a greatly increased lifespan, there is a direct need for every educator to consider all the implications of that prospect.

Lifelong learning for a profession

The concept of lifelong learning provides, furthermore, a model for the profession, if we personify foreign language education and view it as an organism that must grow and develop steadily. That growth must come from within. The need to integrate the bits and pieces requires of every foreign language educator a particular participant role. Today's (and tomorrow's) teacher must be an active creator of the future rather than a passive recipient of prepackaged knowledge and problem solutions. There will be no more prophets; there will be few absolutes; there will not be a definitive direction in which to turn. There will instead be options, each of which has its own unique consequences and implications and each of which must be far better understood than it is today.

Believing in ourselves

The work of the profession cannot, however, be delayed until the time when we have succeeded in pulling together the many pieces of the teaching/learning process. Teachers must teach today; students are waiting in classrooms for immediate and competent help. We must, therefore, come to believe in our capability to make intelligent informed decisions. Believing must precede being. Only by believing can we move closer to the status of a true profession.

Teacher as integrator

Professionalism presupposes that one has a command of a substantial core of knowledge about effective teaching and learning—that one knows what lies within the parameters of one's field of specialization. Beyond this fundamental knowledge, the professional possesses vital coping skills. He or she has the capacity to integrate knowledge, to take the pieces and build meaningful patterns of instruction. A teacher functioning as an integrator may be, for example, one who has read the literature about individual differences in second language learning, recognized the value of small-group instruction, and therefore decides to use small-group work in his or her overall pattern of teaching to accommodate better the needs of the students. Another teacher may integrate the knowledge that it is important to provide students with relevancy, give them opportunities for making meaningful contributions to the classroom, furnish them with individual attention, and therefore decide to enlist upper-level students as aides in lower-level classes.

As well as possessing integrative skills, the teacher of the future must have the perceptivity that enables him or her to sort the good from the bad—to read books, articles, and research reports with a critical eye, detecting flaws in reasoning and research methodology where they exist. Furthermore, the teacher of the future must recognize the complexity of any body of knowledge (especially in the behavioral sciences) and have the humility to recognize that no one answer exists for any problem. He or she has, in effect, outgrown the cookbook. In addition, this teacher is a person who can choose intelligently among the options, who can decide "what kinds of interventions by what kinds of interveners in what contexts elicit what response from what subjects" (Fuller and Brown, 2, p. 26).

A vision of professionalism

The vision of the future in which educators make intelligent and informed decisions requires that every foreign language teacher be a model of lifelong learning and self-renewal. We must be comfortable with continually modifying and integrating our approaches. The vision is ambitious, but there is no acceptable alternative. A Chinese proverb reminds us that even a journey of 1,000 miles must begin with a single step. The chapter authors of this volume have taken more than the first step. They have taken very seriously their charge to attempt to integrate knowledge within their topical domains and to attempt to assist the practitioner with the task of choosing among the options.

Overview of the volume

Floyd Coppedge sets the tone for the volume by providing a thoughtful explication of the lifelong learning movement. He describes both the issues that are involved and the development of the concept up to this time.

Reid Baker carefully examines available research and information about grouping and creates a compelling rationale for integrating it into foreign language instruction. He combines theory and practice to provide very practical suggestions for the instructor.

Robert Lafayette has collected all accessible data on the minicourse. He too has integrated theory and practice to provide a description of the many options available to the teacher in terms of both content and format.

John Walker emphasizes the importance of taking the student viewpoint into account—particularly in curriculum development. He also summarizes the results of various surveys of student attitudes.

R. Marshall Brannon and David Cox delineate problems that are faced by every secondary teacher. Their synthesis of strategies for coping with these problems should be useful to teachers of all levels.

Beverly Galyean describes the options available in the area of humanistic education. She analyzes and synthesizes the many movements and provides a clarification of the relationships among them. Sample activities illustrating the kinds of techniques currently in use are given so that the instructor can choose and implement those that are compatible with his or her teaching style.

Edith Allouche and Gerard Ervin have gathered the many fragments of information available about instruction in languages other than French, German, and Spanish in order to build a better composite image of the profession. They describe some of the problems faced by teachers of these languages and show the relationships among them.

Dwayne Adcock has surveyed societal trends, developments in general curriculum, and factors within foreign language education. The result is a compelling rationale for a rebirth of foreign languages in the elementary school. He also describes current successful FLES programs.

Roland Goddu elucidates the unique characteristics of foreign language teachers and their resulting needs for continuing education. He provides an overview of the options for pursuing lifelong learning as an educator.

Ernest Frechette has sorted through hundreds of research

studies published since 1970 and has classified them in terms of content and research methodology. His synthesis provides a new perspective on critical issues such as the role of research in the profession, the implications of the types of research being done, and areas in need of research.

Thus, these chapters contain information that is important to everyone involved in foreign language education. They reflect a direction that seems likely to influence our future—a future we are constantly creating.

References, Introduction: Teachers, options, and the future

1 Arendt, Jermaine D. "Research in Foreign Languages." *NN&Q* 20,vi(1976). [Newsletter of Phi Delta Kappa.]

2 Fuller, Frances W., and Oliver Brown. "Becoming a Teacher," 25–52 in Kevin Ryan,ed., *Teacher Education.* The Seventy-Fourth Yearbook of the National Society for the Study of Education. Chicago: National Society for the Study of Education, 1975.

3 Stephens, J. M. *The Process of Schooling: A Psychological Examination.* New York: Holt, Rinehart & Winston, 1967.

4 Ward, Annie W., Bruce W. Hall, and Charles F. Schramm. "Evaluation of Published Educational Research: A National Survey." *American Educational Research Journal* 12,ii(1975):109–28.

2

Lifelong learning

An historical perspective

Floyd L. Coppedge
University of Science and Arts of Oklahoma

That public education should shoulder major responsibility for the education of all the nation's youth has been an increasing expectation for several generations. The fast-paced changes of the past two decades have led to awareness of the complexity of meeting this responsibility and of the impact universal education for five to eighteen year olds has on the rest of society. Increased interdependence of peoples, which transcends local boundaries and often extends to global levels; awareness of limitations in educational methodology; enlarged enrollments at postsecondary levels; awakening sensitivity to inequalities within our pluralistic society; and the future shock of rapid change have all served to place a strain on the existing models for public education. The result is an acceleration of efforts at many levels to develop new and more comprehensive models to meet the challenges of formal education. Phrases such as *the learning continuum, the seamless curriculum,* and *lifelong learning* have appeared in the education literature. Each in its own way suggests the need for a new model or models that will move beyond existing conceptualizations of formal schooling.

New models to meet challenges

Knowles (18), referring to criticisms of recent years, notes

Floyd L. Coppedge (Ph.D., Oklahoma University) is Academic Dean at the University of Science and Arts of Oklahoma. He received his B.S. and M.T. from Northeastern Oklahoma State University with a major in mathematics; his doctorate is in secondary education and administration. His experience includes teaching mathematics and serving as principal at the junior high and high school levels; university teaching in math education, secondary education, school administration, curriculum, and individualized instruction. He has served on the faculty of Kansas State University and Indiana University and as a visiting professor at Northeastern Oklahoma State University and the State University of New York at Plattsburgh.

Dr. Coppedge, a specialist in individualized instruction, has written numerous articles on this subject and has served widely as a consultant. He has also published works in math education, instruction, and administration. He is currently serving on the editorial board of a national journal and is a member of the Phi Delta Kappa Commission on Curriculum Models for Lifelong Learning.

that "the heart of much of the criticism is that the schools are out of touch with the reality of both human nature and the nature of a changing world. . . . Therefore new models of education as a lifelong process must be developed" (p. 2). Although the call for new models has been characterized by generalizations rather than specifics, models that will provide options are required. Such models will have to integrate currently successful patterns with a degree of flexibility so that the result is a broadening of the options rather than a restriction of choices. What is a clearly successful learning model for one individual or a particular group will not be presupposed to be good for all.

Schools out of touch

Integration of the options

Efforts to focus on lifelong learning have resulted in either attempts to correct individual flaws or broadly conceived plans with minimal details. Proponents of widely diverse emphases as early childhood education and education for retirement, career or vocational education and leisure-time education, or educational technology and humanistic education have tried to capture the imagination and support of the education community. While American education is one of the most malleable in existence and has endeavored to incorporate all ends of the various spectrums, it has typically responded without adequate reflection or evaluation to initial tentative proposals that often involve contradictory ends and means.

That the complexity of the present and anticipated future requires reasoned systematic alternatives to meet the needs of an ever-changing society is now obvious to many Americans, including educators. Change, a threat to some persons, is a reality that presents challenges that require deliberate and often swift action. No longer can educators permit a lag of two to five decades between the formulation and implementation of needed improvements.

Swift action

Relationship to other movements

Although the deliberate study of lifelong learning is new, most persons have always engaged in some form of lifelong learning. In the simpler days of earlier centuries when changes within the life span of an individual were slowly paced, fostering lifelong learning was less critical. The normal course of life included contact with sufficient situations for the development of skills and resources adequate to the tasks of coping with existence. With the increase in industrialization, mobility, and development of democratic government ideals, however, came an increasing dependence upon formal education and institutionalized learning. Postindustrial developments have resulted in demands that cannot be sufficiently met by the present system of formal education.

Aim for learner independence

The present system possibly never really developed learners who are generally capable of individual goal setting and active pursuit of learning. Far too many students developed a dependency on their teachers and the system and did not develop the qualities that characterize a lifelong learner. This may be the fault of the system. Many teachers have taught for dependence of the learner, whereas the aim of a good teacher should be to develop the learner so that a teacher is no longer necessary.

Individualized instruction

The lifelong learning movement is not the first to recognize the problem and call for revisions in the system. No sooner had American education developed the beginnings of the current grade-standard method of offering educational opportunities than many were beginning to point out the shortcomings of group-oriented and group-paced instruction. The encouragement for individualized or nongraded education began in the last quarter of the nineteenth century and has been strongest since the 1960s. Emphasis is placed on the individual and "learning to learn."

Alternative schools

Another movement that has grown rapidly during the 1970s and has many ideas that are supportive of lifelong learning is the alternative school movement. Smith (25) notes that more than 1,000 such schools are now in operation. He defines an alternative public school as one that "provides alternative learning experiences to those provided by the conventional schools within its community and that is available by choice to every family at no extra cost" (pp. 14–15). The terms *alternative*, *available*, and *choice* in this definition are common to the lifelong learning movement.

Career education

A more recent movement, career education, has a similar thrust. Career education also recognizes that the emphasis must be placed on the individual, his learning needs, and the developing nature of these needs. Much of what the individual needs to know will best be served, and in some cases, can be served only by a combination of formal and informal learning opportunities.

Where the action is today

A review of the literature reveals that the term *lifelong learning* was not widely used until very recently. Instead, various terms that suggest an *extension* of the public school—upward, downward, and outward—have been employed. *Adult education, career education, leisure education, early childhood* and *preschool education* are examples of terms most frequently used to describe such extensions.

An exception to the above is a work by Hesburgh et al. (15). This work contains 67 recommendations for colleges and universities within the realm of continuing education and lifelong learning, terms that the authors tend to use interchangeably. They make the important point that we should no longer be satisfied with lifelong learning as an extension of the university or the public school; lifelong learning means something more than schooling. The authors emphasize the need for Americans to develop a learning society and point out that our youth-oriented school system is ill equipped to bring this about. The discontinuous relationship between learning and living must be changed. Their recommendations support the establishment of an emphasis on lifelong learning in every undergraduate's curriculum, changes in public policy toward continuous learning, the creation of a consortia of institutions, or possibly the formation of a commission or center that would promote the aims of lifelong learning.

Extension and adult education

Universities and high schools have developed extension programs, adult branches, and night schools. Agricultural agencies of various levels of government have designed extension and adult leader programs. Industries have conducted large training and inservice programs for their administrators and employees. All the military branches and most of the major government units have entered the field of continuing education. Churches have developed some widespread programs for educating both the professionals and the laity within their memberships.

Industry, military, and church programs

Little can be reported regarding fully developed models for promoting lifelong learning in the school setting. Work is underway in this area by a Commission on Lifelong Learning under the auspices of Phi Delta Kappa. Some of the best conceptualization is Shane's (22) model of the "Seamless Curriculum." It represents the most comprehensive model for all levels, though it is expressed in a chronological age/grade pattern rather than a sequence based on learning needs and aspirations. He points out the need to depart from the "night school" tradition for adults in order to make better use of the "paracurriculum" and to reverse the present drop-out phenomenon. He does use the term *lifelong* as in lifelong postsecondary education.

No state legislation

While no state has comprehensive legislation-making provision for continuing education, a good deal of attention and debate centers around career education. In addition to the interest in career and continuing education, numerous curriculum models for early childhood education have been developed.

Adult learning for literacy, for leisure, for enrichment; early childhood education for a headstart; career education to help the young person enter the world of work; industrial programs to improve the worker; programs to make it easier for the serviceman to reenter civilian life—all give support to a broadening of the interest in making learning opportunities more accessible to larger numbers. This interest is doing much to contribute to the development and expansion of the concept of lifelong learning.

Definition of lifelong learning

The better part of wisdom dictates against stating a definition of lifelong learning that in any way would restrict a more detailed study of the concept. What is attempted in this section, therefore, is definition by description rather than prescription, definition that is as open for alteration as is the lifelong learner, definition that invites further refinement rather than serves to restrict thought.

What is it that makes definition so difficult? The concept "appears to be very complex and comprehensive. The functions of lifelong education, its relationship with the existing stages and types of education, its coverage, scope, and prerequisites—all these have to be viewed in an analytico-integrative manner in order to unfold the multidimensional meaning of the idea" (Dave, 5, pp. 8–9).

Contrasting simplicity and complexity of lifelong learning

On the surface the concept is characterized by simplicity and at the same time possesses a contrasting complexity.

Lifelong learning is simple and self-explanatory in that it de-

> scribes the involvement of an individual in one aspect of his natural human activity from birth until death. However, this definition, although simple, is deceiving; for lifelong learning is much more than simply learning throughout the lifespan. Lifelong learning is a complex concept involving, at the very least, an actor [the learner], an activity [the learning process], and a delivery system [an environment conducive to learning] (28, p. 10).

Limitation of well-conceived programs

Third, definition is difficult because of the serious scarcity of well-conceived programs promoting the concept. At best it is a concept whose "time has come," according to Strasheim's (26) analysis. Lifelong learning is now at the point where its mention and study are sufficiently developed that we can expect models of lifelong learning to begin being implemented, much as we have seen with other movements—for example, individualized instruction.

The following sections should be considered with the above points clearly in mind. The reader's analysis, contemplation, and contribution to further clarification of the concept are encouraged.

Clearing up the vocabulary: Difference between learning and schooling

Learning not schooling

Often the terms *schooling* and *learning* are equated and used interchangeably. As used here, however, *lifelong learning* must be differentiated from schooling.

> Lifelong learning is a descriptive phrase for a process which is usually perceived as including informal family and community education prior to nursery or kindergarten, a period of formal education beginning about five years af age and continuing through age sixteen or longer, and the balance of life which includes exposure to many informal and a few formal learning opportunities of diminishing frequency (Overly, Coppedge, and McQuigg, 20, p. 16).

Learning throughout the lifespan

In somewhat simpler terms, *lifelong learning* has reference to all learning occurring from the moment of birth until death. *Learning* must not be used interchangeably with *schooling;* for no one looks with favor on a lifetime of continuous formal school. I do not want to discount the value of schooling, only to place it in proper perspective. A discussion by Shane and Weaver (23) of what they call the "paracurriculum" illustrates what must occur to permit structures that support learning and that go beyond the conventional school setting at the secondary and postsecondary levels.

> As a rule, between the ages of 13–15, an adolescent for whom a nonschool experience would be deemed appropriate, could engage in one of several out-of-school activities. The primary responsibility of the educational institutions to which the student was associated would be to provide a psychological support system; that is, to develop a close working relationship with the student to assure ongoing in-depth counseling, to maintain communication with the student's parents, to assist in identifying cooperative businesses and social service agencies within the community, and to arrange meaningful travel experiences. Specific activities might include work in libraries, hospitals, welfare agencies, and preschools, or "with-pay" employment when proper safeguards are insured to avoid exploitation of child labor. . . . Education continues as a seamless continuum in which both paracurricular and curricular offerings are intertwined and linked administratively by infinite entry-exit-reentry opportunities. . . . At the same time, postsecondary education as envisioned by the writers would encourage persons of an increased age span to participate on a continuing or continual basis in what traditionally has been termed adult education (p. 3).

Seamless continuum

What it is: Concept-characteristics

Dave (5) provides a most useful list of "concept-characteristics" which to him represents an analytico-integrative treatment in defining lifelong learning. While not an exhaustive list, it does represent a broad coverage and is used here as a means of adding to the definition. It is significant to note that Dave arrived at this list through a study of the literature, through interpretation of the material, and through personal consultation. Therefore, the list does represent collective thinking about lifelong learning.

Analytico-integrative treatment

1 The three basic terms upon which the meaning of the concept is based are *life, lifelong,* and *education.* The meaning attached to these terms and the interpretation given to them largely determine the scope and meaning of lifelong education.
2 Education does not terminate at the end of formal schooling, but it is a lifelong process. Lifelong education covers the entire lifespan of an individual.
3 Lifelong education is not confined to adult education, but it encompasses and unifies all stages of education—preprimary, primary, secondary, and so forth. Thus, it seeks to view education in its totality.
4 Lifelong education includes both formal and nonformal patterns of education, planned as well as incidental learning.
5 The home plays the first, most subtle, and crucial role in initiating the process of lifelong learning. This continues throughout the entire lifespan of an individual through a process of family learning.
6 The community also plays an important role in the system of lifelong education right from the time the child begins to interact with it and continues its educative function both in professional and general areas throughout life.
7 The institutions of education like schools, universities, and training centers are of course important, but only as one of the agencies for lifelong education. They no longer enjoy the monopoly for educating the people and can no longer exist in isolation from other educative agencies in the society.
8 Lifelong education seeks continuity and articulation along its vertical or longitudinal dimension.
9 Lifelong education also seeks integration in its horizontal and vertical dimensions at every stage in life.
10 Contrary to the elitist form of education, lifelong education is universal in character. It represents democratization of education.
11 Lifelong education is characterized by its flexibility and diversity in content, learning tools and techniques, and time of learning.
12 Lifelong education is a dynamic approach to education

which allows adaptation of materials and media of learning as and when new developments take place.

13 Lifelong education allows alternative patterns and forms of acquiring education.
14 Lifelong education has two broad components: general and professional. These are not completely different from each other but are interrelated and interactive in nature.
15 The adaptive and innovative functions of the individual and the society are fulfilled through lifelong education.
16 Lifelong education carries out a corrective function: to take care of the shortcomings of the existing system of education.
17 The ultimate goal of lifelong education is to maintain and improve the quality of life.
18 There are three major prerequisites for lifelong education, namely, opportunity, motivation, and educability.
19 Lifelong education is an organizing principle for all education.
20 At the operational level, lifelong education provides a total system of all education (pp. 14–24).

What it is not: Some exclusions

In delineating some of the ideas that are not consistent with the concept of lifelong learning, no attempt has been made to be exhaustive, only to reach a level of specificity sufficient to communicate clearly. Lifelong learning is not:

What lifelong learning is not

1 The same as schooling
2 Merely adult education
3 Limited to career training or retraining
4 Something that should be available only to the economically favored
5 Time restricted
6 Limited in content
7 An unarticulated set of ad hoc learning activities
8 Something engaged in only after having mastered basic skills or literacy training
9 Dependent upon typical credentialing—credit hours, diplomas, and certificates
10 The province of "professional educators"

11 Restrictive where options and flexibility can be provided to meet the needs of the learner

Characteristics of the lifelong learner

An individual act

In the final analysis learning is an individual act. The instructional program (teaching), the system (school), and the resources (materials) are all valuable and sometimes essential aids to learning, but the changes that occur within the individual (learning) are the critical test.

A number of legitimate questions may be asked in our attempt to focus on the lifelong learner. What is a lifelong learner like? What are his characteristics? How does a lifelong learner differ from a person who is not a lifelong learner? What is known about how people learn that has some bearing on the development of lifelong learners? How does a lifelong learner learn? Responses to these questions are related to perceptions of the learner.

More than products

Learners are more than products. To think of the learner merely as a product of a formal educational institution is both myopic and degrading because the individual was a learner long before being influenced by a formal educational institution and has inherent worth as a human being–worth that is not dependent on an institution to shape him as a product. An individual is more than a thing on which to perform various functions or apply certain forces. Being human has inherent value that is not predicated on how much one knows. Human uniqueness is evidenced in the ability to know and to add to this ability.

Goethe is credited with saying, "Treat people as if they were what they ought to be and you help them to become what they are capable of being" (Hillson and Bongo, 16, p. 7). The anticipation of and striving for individual fulfillment characterize human beings who require unique treatment as they develop. Faure et al. (9) noted the lifelong nature of the process of becoming what one is capable of being. "We should no longer assiduously acquire knowledge once and for all, but learn how to build up a continually evolving body of knowledge all through life–'learn to be' " (p. vi).

Learning to be

Although viewing students as products may be useful to examine the effect of a given institution or instructional sequence on them, such an analysis seems totally inadequate. To view persons only as products will probably lead to the further perpetuation of systems whose primary aim is to reduce the individual to a member of a class group, thus giving little heed to his uniqueness and his capacity to become. American educators must begin to view their task as one of providing the structures within which the uniqueness of individuals can be expressed and nurtured.

From the beginning of our nation the ideals of democracy and the influence of the Judeo-Christian beliefs have been instrumental in encouraging a commitment to individual uniqueness. The fact that our nation has often fallen short of making provisions for individual worth does not alter her ideals. Principal among the ideals that support America's moral commitment to respect and honor the uniqueness of the individual are the regard for:

Moral commitment to individual uniqueness

1 The worth and dignity of the individual
2 The exercise of self-determination by individual citizens and pursuit of their interests
3 The right to participate in shaping the general welfare
4 Equality and universality of opportunity
5 The application of reason to the solution of problems (3; Coppedge, 4; Everett, 8; Fraenkel, 10).

What are the characteristics which, if developed, are most likely to nurture *individuals who are capable of learning at any point in life and likely to continue learning at many points in life?* No priority ranking is intended in the characteristics discussed. Even though development of the characteristics will vary from person to person, each one is mutually supportive of all; therefore, thinking in terms of total development of learners is better than isolating one characteristic as more worthy than another.

Lifelong learners are goal-directed. To sustain the interest in and maintain the motivation for continued learning the learner must begin to see clearly the direction his development is taking him. He must see his goals in sufficient depth so that he may perceive alternatives or options. The development of this characteristic cannot be left to chance but must be provided for by

Characteristics for nurturing learning

all institutions that offer learning opportunities. Obviously this must include the family because much learning takes place prior to entry into a formal educational institution. Equally obvious is that for the present and the forseeable future the school will continue to lead in the development of this characteristic. This development is most likely to take place in an environment that provides learners with both specific (immediate) and general (long-range) goals that they may pursue, assists students in diagnosing individual strengths and deficiencies, encourages the implementation of learning activities designed for individual growth, and encourages individuals to begin to assume more responsibility for making judgments about their learning. Admittedly, the level of responsibility that can be assumed by the learner is in direct relationship to his maturity and level of learning. Experienced teachers have long observed that merely growing a year older does not appear to be the most critical factor. To the contrary, the experiences gained appear to make the difference.

Developing goal-directedness

Lifelong learners assume increasing responsibility for being self-directed. This means that the individual has learned to move toward the attainment of goals and the pursuit of learning in such a way that options are open to him and adjustments are made as needed. It does not mean that the learner must be highly skilled as an independent learner, though this would be advantageous. It does mean that the learner has sufficient command of his learning to enable him to pursue various appropriate learning modes, whether learning in a group or working independently. It also includes the capacity of the learner to select from a variety of materials those that offer him more efficient learning opportunities.

Teaching as a deterrent to self-directedness

A deterrent to developing self-directed learners is the current overemphasis placed on the function of teaching. In no way should this statement be taken to mean that teachers should be eliminated; but it does mean that a need is seen to diminish the dependence students have on teachers as fonts of knowledge, purveyors of information, and custodians of student time and all respectable learning strategies. The dependence of pupils upon teachers, even to the point of domination by teachers, has become the accepted mode of formal education. But if one of the conditions or goals of good education is increasing self-directedness on the part of the learner, a long-range goal for a teacher must be to become unnecessary for the student. Showmanship and ego involvement, however, often work to subvert efforts to develop self-directedness in students. Thus, the student maintains a level of performance that ends in too much dependency on the teacher. Such over-emphasis on teaching rather than learning leads to spoon-feeding which may result in intellectual health and growth for some while the feeder is available, but ultimately leads to intellectual stagnation and crippling once the support system is removed. Too often we hear, "Don't read ahead of the class assignment"; "Wait until everyone is ready to go on"; "The teacher will tell you where to find the information you need"; "Look up every word you aren't absolutely sure of." Self-directedness is impaired by such a narrow conceptualization of teaching.

Intellectual stagnation

Becoming skilled at learning is essential for lifelong learners. Learners must "know how to learn" or "possess the skills essential for learning." Often such statements are made when contrasts are being drawn between content and method in the instructional program. The conclusion that is frequently reached is that individuals cannot be taught everything they must know; therefore, they should become skilled at learning so that they can continue to learn as needed. On first thought this statement seems perfectly reasonable; however, its lack of refinement and clarity of meaning leaves far too much to chance. For example, in a school situation a well-meaning teacher might develop a sequence of learning for students that would captivate their interests for the moment, but when viewed more thoroughly would reveal that very little had been accomplished that could be said to contribute to the process of learning how to learn.

How to learn

Educational practice is replete with such examples. The problem with this approach is one of confusion regarding the intent and outcome of learning experiences. Activity can easily be confused with learning. An example of this is in the highly regimented classroom where the teacher has mastered the management of a class group. Students can be kept busy, but a more thorough analysis will often reveal that relatively little choice is given the student; he makes very few decisions; his work must conform to a set pattern (oftentimes a pattern that has evolved over a number of years); much of what he does is at the lowest

Confusion between intent and outcome

level of the cognitive operation; in short, he is being managed rather than learning to manage.

In contrast to the above, but equally ineffective in terms of helping individuals learn how to learn, is the totally unstructured classroom. This setting is characterized by a naive approach to learning. The assumption is made that learning is so simple that no planning is necessary. While this approach might have some merit for those learnings that occur as a result of maturation, it is obviously insufficient to meet the complex demands of today and the future.

Planning for flexibility

The resolution of the above is not simply to seek a middle ground between management and nonmanagement of learning and learners. The solution is to be found in a procedure where the learner is cast into an active role and is supported by professional teachers and others serving as facilitators. Sometimes this will mean that the facilitator is a presenter, at other times an inquirer with the student, and at times a learner. Recent attention focusing on individual teaching style and the value of matching teaching style with learning style may serve to facilitate development of skills for learning. The learner in this kind of environment is guided in an ever-increasing comprehension of the relationships between what is being learned (content) and how the learning occurs (method or mode). Learning how to learn becomes a reality as the learner becomes both goal-directed and self-directed. Such an environment provides opportunity for the learner to inquire through use of the scientific approach, to use a variety of resources, and to function more frequently at the more complex cognitive levels. Learning is seen as a formative process rather than a summative activity as the learner shares in the management activities rather than being totally managed.

Learning as a formative process

Although the above approach may pertain to a formal educational setting—a school—the more one becomes actively involved in learning how to learn, the less one is restricted to a school setting. The total environment becomes the base for learning. Those who facilitate and direct the learning will not all be holders of teaching certificates, nor will learning necessarily be measured in units or credits.

Learning from desire, not compulsion

Lifelong learners are active rather than passive. The entire society, possibly spearheaded by educators, must move away from the concept that learners are supposed to be "made to learn." According to Trump and Georgiades (29), Quintilian wrote almost 2,000 years ago: "Moreover, by far the larger proportion of the learner's time ought to be devoted to private study. The teacher does not stand over him while he is writing or thinking or learning by heart, while he is so occupied, the intervention of anyone, be he who he may, is a hindrance" (p. 108). Indeed, learning is ultimately an individual activity, though not necessarily an independent activity.

The importance of the active role that must be assumed by the learner is implied in previous characteristics dealing with goal-directedness and self-directedness; yet even more is required. To be an active learner means that the individual accepts an obligation for learning, shares the responsibility for learning, and begins to learn more because of desire and less because of compulsion. Frequently, skills must be taught before the learner sees the benefits. In the study of a language, for example, the learner may see benefits after beginning to learn rather than before. This will certainly be true if the language proves personally useful. To say, therefore, that the learner learns because of desire rather than compulsion does not ignore some *delayed* benefits in much of the learning that occurs.

Delayed benefits

Developing active learners is not an easy task for American society. In fact, some of the policies that have shaped American education and were appropriate in the past now seem inconsistent with demands. Compulsory school attendance, restricted enrollment boundaries, and limited entry and exit points are among the policies that may require revision.

Positive-directed motivation is essential for lifelong learners. One of the most meaningful descriptions of motivation for this discussion is Frymier's (11) contention that "motivation to learn is that which gives direction and intensity to human behavior in an educational context" (p. 16). The characteristics of lifelong learners and this type of motivation are mutually supportive in the sense that "direction" refers to the goal orientation of the learner, and "intensity" to the nature of the effort put forth to attain the goal.

The learner is encouraged to develop yet another quality of motivation: approaching learning in a positive rather than negative manner. There are abundant examples in educational

Avoiding learning

practice of learners who spend more time and effort in avoiding learning than they spend in learning. This practice must be attacked from all directions until it is destroyed; for where this tendency exists, little learning will occur.

Perceiving the options

As learners are provided an environment where they are encouraged to learn and where ample options in goals and resources are available, the stage is readied for nurturing a higher degree of internal motivation. However, lifelong learners need the support of internal motivation if they are to be capable of learning at all times and likely to continue learning in a relatively consistent pattern.

Lifelong learners are perceptive. To say that an individual is perceptive is to say that he is "tuned in" to his environment and able to see alternatives or options in that environment. In many ways perception appears to be a mental process that some possess in full measure but in which others seem to be dismally deficient. A direct relationship between the development and practice of this characteristic and goal- and self-direction is clearly evident. Perception of one's environment demands an awareness that is enhanced by goal clarification and a comprehension of options. "What options do you see?" may well be the stem to many investigations as the lifelong learner takes command of his environment.

The lifelong learner has a developed self-concept that supports self-confidence. A self-concept that is relatively free from feelings of insecurity and defeatism has long been recognized as a valuable individual asset. It exists not merely on the surface level of liking oneself, but in a deeper sense that involves a willingness to take chances and to explore the uncertain. An ability to be at ease when faced with ambiguity and to be functional in exploring options is very much a part of positive self-concept as viewed here. A positive self-concept aids the individual in being able to view failure as a step toward success rather than the end product of a learning sequence. Self-assessment as well as evaluations by others serve as means to improvement, not merely as proof of a level of weakness or strength.

Failure as a step toward success

Observation, experimentation, and the satisfaction of curiosity characterize the lifelong learner's attitude toward learning. An open mind, ever seeking a higher level of knowledge and appreciation, is a passport to sustaining a positive self-concept and appreciating the fluid nature of his future focused life (Singer, 24).

Human potential for learning throughout the lifespan

Full range of uniqueness

"A person does not possess the full range of his uniqueness after merely passing through adolescence. . . . The process of formation continues through stages of life that we are just beginning to recognize," wrote Gould (13) in his introductory remarks to an explication of adult learning. The study of how adults learn has accelerated in recent years; the results have often been unusually enlightening in comparison to what had been known. Even so, Gould cautions, "We are many years away from having the experience and the studies necessary for an in-depth understanding of the adult period comparable to our current understanding of childhood and adolescence" (p. 74).

More than chance

All people (excluding those who are extremely mentally handicapped) continue to learn throughout life. For many, learning is not a well-articulated programmatic sequence of experiences; it is characterized by an ad hoc adventitious set of random learning bits. Although one might argue that random learning is natural and should not be tampered with, potential for significant learning throughout the lifespan is too great and the process is too complex to leave it to chance. The demands of the present and the predicted future necessitate much more.

Using the discussion of the desirable characteristics of lifelong learners, we can establish more clearly the nature of learning and the potential for learning throughout the lifespan. Learning research continues to add to the volume of knowledge. What is written at any given time about learning must be critically questioned on a regular basis if we are to keep pace with the changes in people that take on new meaning almost daily.

Impact of early learning

Blakely (1) notes that recent findings have revealed that the most rapid and formative period of individual development takes place prior to school entry, that the school as one institution is probably not the most powerful of the influences, and that schooling merely as preparation, regardless of its duration, is not adequate for subsequent life stages.

Early learning

The importance of early development and learning is reinforced by the work of Bloom (2) who reports that half of a child's future height is reached by the age of two and a half years and that his I.Q. at four years is a fairly accurate indicator of his I.Q. at age 17. This information should reinforce the need for increased educational opportunities during the early childhood years.

Common beliefs questioned

In considering the impact of childhood development and learning on future development, Hunt (17) notes six common beliefs that have been questioned on the basis of recent research. Of the six, those having the most bearing on this discussion are the belief in fixed intelligence, the belief in predetermined development (genetic influences), and the belief in the insignificance of experience during the early (especially prespeech) years. Freed from such restraints, recent research has supported the dynamic and integrated relationship between early childhood experiences and future development.

Learning and stages of development

Stages in human development

The importance of the contributions to the knowledge base regarding learning made by the various theoreticians in the field of developmental psychology is recognized. The work of Erikson (7) has special significance for the study of lifelong learning due to the conviction that the promise and potential of lifelong learning will be realized maximally only when the psychosociological factors of development, which form the focus of Erikson's work, are addressed directly.

In addition, Piaget's stages of cognitive development and Havighurst's developmental tasks contribute heavily to this discussion of learning in informal structures and for particular stages of development. But if learning is truly to become a life-filling possibility, Erikson's insights must be taken into consideration and used in the development of attitudes that will foster positive dispositions toward learning at all stages of development.

Erikson (7) notes that an analysis of learning throughout the lifespan does indeed reveal some differences between the learning of youth and that of adults. His work presents human development in eight distinct but related stages. Stage one (birth through the first year) is characterized by the establishment of trust or mistrust patterns of other people. Stage two (the second and third years) is an extension of the first wherein the child begins to sense autonomy and have confidence that he has some control over his environment. Stage three (fourth and fifth years) is a crucial step in the child's ability to assume more and more initiative. He can develop good feelings as well as guilt feelings about taking initiative.

Stage four (ages 6 to 11), the preadolescent stage, is important to the development of the child's acceptance of himself and his potential. A feeling of inferiority can develop during this time. Stage five (ages 12 to 18) is commonly referred to as the period of adolescence. Developing a sense of identity and sorting out a variety of roles to establish some tentative life plans is a dominant concern of this stage.

Stage six (from the end of adolescence to early middle age) normally includes development of relationships with others, including those outside the immediate family. Collegial relationships are initiated during this time. Stage seven (middle age) finds the individual capable of extending himself to concerns beyond his own foreseeable years and being concerned about others. The opposite also can result—the individual can become absorbed in his own lifespace and not be concerned about others. The last stage (old age) is characterized by contemplation of one's life. The nature of this assessment may range from feelings of accomplishment and fullness to emptiness and despair.

Learning as a function of past, present, and future

Effective learning at any stage is facilitated by an interrelatedness of the past, present, and future dimensions of learning experiences. It is also influenced by self-perception, individual goals, cultural expectations, and demands on the time available for learning. This interrelatedness is particularly important because of the ad hoc and intermittent nature that is characteristic of much adult learning. It places an especially heavy burden of responsibility on the function of counseling at all levels and particularly for individuals not involved in formal schooling as a means of developing a tailormade program of lifelong learning that is relevant to the unique needs of an individual's learning to be.

Learning potential

Scrapping the myths

The potential for learning does not deteriorate over time. Contrary to some earlier theories, there is now growing confidence in the ability of adults to learn and a scrapping of the myth that learning is a role relevant only to childhood and youth. In 1928 Thorndike (27) stated that age, per se, should not be a barrier to learning. He also reported, however, that the ability to learn peaked at age 22 and declined at a rate of approximately 1 percent a year until age 50. Calculations showed that this decline would result in a learner only 72 percent as proficient at age 50 as at age 22. By contrast, the results of more recent research, especially that generated by longitudinal rather than horizontal studies, present a more positive view regarding the adult as a learner. Schaie and others (21), for example, used cross-sequential and time-sequential statistical analyses to separate the age and generational effects. Their results indicated that cognitive functioning is stable during most of the adult years when generational effects are controlled. Significant declines were found only after age 60. Another example is the work of Gould (13) in which he notes that "children mark the passing years by their changing bodies, adults change their minds. Passing years and passing events slowly accumulate, like a vicious wave, eventually releasing their energy and assuming new forms . . ." (p. 78).

Learning how to learn

Value in knowing how to learn

The concept of learning how to learn has become a pervasive part of current thinking regarding lifelong learning. It is recognized that the individual cannot learn in one stage of development all that will be required in subsequent stages, hence the need to develop the intellect as an instrument of learning rather than as a storehouse of knowledge.

Havighurst (14) reasoned that if the schools can provide for students the skills of being a self-initiated learner, the child can continue to learn as an adult. In well-planned programs concerned with individualized instruction, nongraded education, continuous progress, and independent learning, strong emphasis is given to the idea of self-initiation, self-direction, and self-motivation as worthwhile goals toward which to work.

The emphasis on learning how to learn does not cease with the termination of formal schooling, nor is it the sole responsibility of formal educational institutions. Indeed, preschool development is important to future potential. Learning how to learn must be emphasized at all stages of development and in all learning experiences.

The process of lifelong learning

The act of learning is a process of great complexity. The potential to learn is present in varying degrees for each individual, but it is seldom realized to its maximum because the act of learning is influenced by so many factors over which the individual has little or no control. Learning is too often viewed as an end result or product of an act or encounter between learner and object rather than as the process itself. To be sure, there are end results to the learning process. The individual comes to know or to be able to do or to feel as a result of his interaction with content from some source. This source in turn may be mediated by some agent other than the source. The entire learning act is a process that seeks to integrate learner needs with the influence of the past experiences as stored in the memory of the learner. This suggests that any effective intervention in the process must occur at various levels and continue throughout the learner's life. It also suggests that the learning process must be more carefully explicated and studied in terms of critical intervention points and strategies. Such study will require commitment and resources.

Lifelong learning as an integrative process

Facilitating the learning process has often been viewed either as the captive province of professional education in schools or as a natural phenomenon of life so complex that it defies effective intervention. Both of these perspectives are inadequate and result in a waste of resources and a diminution of the quality of life for society as well as for the individual. Lifelong learning may be pursued within an institutional setting or independently. Regardless of the setting, characteristics of the process of lifelong learning are likely to provide a more nearly adequate concept and lead to an improved quality of life and resource utilization, thereby facilitating the process.

In the following sections I discuss a number of these characteristics in random order. To attempt a prioritization is difficult, if not unwise. Further caution should be exercised in thinking about the characteristics in isolation from each other. Individually they merely focus attention upon certain aspects of the process. Taken together they describe a dynamic integrated process whose whole is greater than the sum of its parts.

Easy entry, easy exit

The lifelong learning process is *accessible.* The opportunity for engaging in the process, for entry, for continuation, or for exit from the process is made subject to human rather than institutional needs. Immediacy of opportunity to engage in learning with a minimum of bothersome constraints must be the guiding principle in making learning accessible. The tendency to build structures for the convenience of institutions rather than to facilitate learning must be resisted.

Formal and informal

The lifelong learning process is *comprehensive* in that it encompasses both formal and informal efforts. It includes all levels of learning from initial experience through refined knowledge and skill development. In the latter sense the emphasis is on optimum individual self-actualization at a level in keeping with the individual's personal goals and expectations.

Flexibility

The process is *flexible* in terms of the time of occurrence and regularity or irregularity of occurrence as the needs of the population and sufficiency of resources may dictate. It also permits flexibility of action on the part of the participants in the process.

To provide this kind of flexibility requires more planning than that associated with more conventional provisions for learning. This comparison is illustrated by likening a flexible pattern of learning to a well-planned sight-seeing trip. The better the planning for the trip, the greater the options for those who are to experience the trip. They need not be bored by having to participate in an activity that is all too familiar to them; instead, they may explore other options. The degree of flexibility is reduced commensurate to planning. This analogy breaks down in some obvious places, but it is useful in illustrating the point that *structure* or *planning with flexibility* is extremely important.

Options for learning

Wide *diversity* is also important. Diversity would be observable in the large number of optional methods or approaches to learning made available for learning a concept, an idea, a piece of information, an attitude, or a skill that the individual might desire. The individual, alone or in concert with others, could identify the best means of facilitating his own learning. In addition, a variety of delivery systems would be available as support for the process.

Continuous opportunity

The process of lifelong learning is *continuous,* not in the sense of having a responsibility or objective to achieve—which, if achieved, is immediately replaced with a new objective, thus leading to a treadmill sense of futility and endlessness. Rather, it is continuous in the sense of the opportunity being available for short- or long-term, intensive or superficial, practical or recreative involvement in a learning activity that serves to foster one's development of his self-awareness and purposive becoming. To speak of lifelong learning in these terms is difficult because of the traditional association of any organized learning with institutionalized education or formal instruction, which is normally time-specific, controlling, limited, and limiting. What is being affirmed is that the process is continuous in its flow like a mighty river with an unrestricted watershed. Some may want a little learning; others may want in-depth study. In either case the resources must be available without restrictions.

Variation in depth of learning

The process is *humane* and is characterized by the noblest actions and intent of man to develop, maintain, and improve the quality of life for all mankind. This suggests that man does have a controlling hand in the development, maintenance, and improvement of the process itself. Man's role is to affect the process in such a manner that it will improve the opportunities for others to become what they may, to be creative, to dream impossible dreams, to plug into resources outside themselves, to explore for deeper meaning. The humane process is supportive of the individual in his search for meaning and supportive of the process itself so as to affirm in its existence the centrality of individual growth or becoming from birth to death.

Man helping man

The lifelong learning process is characterized by ongoing *evaluation* based on the extent to which the characteristics are realized and by opportunities for participants to evaluate the process and their involvement with the process in terms of personal goals. As a result of the continuous evaluation and assessment of the process and the outcomes, both formative and summative, the process is continuously undergoing modifications.

Continuous evaluation

The process of *diagnosis* involves the collection and interpretation of data regarding the learner's assets, liabilities, and needs. The difference between what the learner wants or needs to do and his present state represents the prescription. The use of the term *prescription* is in no way intended to imply a restriction to narrowly defined low-level cognitive skills. Prescription can

Creative prescription in all domains

and should be as open and creative as is required to meet the learner's needs. It is sensitive to all levels of the cognitive as well as the affective domain. It recognizes the need for self-fulfillment and self-actualization.

Guidance only as needed

The evidence is quite clear that the need for guided learning diminishes as the learner matures. Thus, the lifelong learning process is characterized by an ever-developing *opportunity for self-direction.*

The emphasis of the process must be on providing a wealth of learning aids, opportunity for self-selection by the learner, and guidance only as needed rather than as a constant required ingredient. Such an emphasis is further characterized by learning that is relevant to needs because it deals with the present time and lifespace of the learner. Where it is most appropriate, this learning will be related to, and occur in, the real world as contrasted with the simulated conditions of the formal classroom.

Implications for instruction and curriculum development in the content areas

This chapter has been focused on lifelong learning in its broadest perspective–as a function of the entire lifespan, and not to be confused with formal schooling. Because formal schooling plays such an important role in the process, however, some of the implications of lifelong learning in the school setting, most specifically the secondary school, are presented here.

Schools and alternatives

The lifelong learning movement should not be confused with the recent rather popular idea that schools are no longer functional. Shane and Weaver (23) point out clearly that what is needed is not "alternatives to schools, but rather a need to foster more alternatives within a reorganized and revitalized educational community." What is needed is "a cooperative planning effort on the part of local, state, and federal agencies along with individual citizen action" in order to "move the lifelong learning concept to the forefront of educational development" (p. 4).

New roles for teachers

Enhanced roles for teachers

As with other movements (for example, individualized instruction, nongraded schools, alternative schools, and career education), enhanced teacher roles are also demanded for lifelong learning. A role refinement that has always been characteristic of the really great teachers is needed here. The teacher must become an inquirer along with the student. This is not to say that the teacher occupies the same role in cognitive development as does the student; for we assume the teacher possesses a relatively high level of knowledge of content. What is called for is a teacher who exudes a spirit of inquiry and excitement toward the subject so that the student sees it as alive and relevant to his needs.

Let students "grow the flowers"

The teacher must function as only one of many resources available to the student. On a progressive basis she or he must "wean students" from dependency and permit them to "grow the flowers," as it were, rather than hand them a cut bouquet. Functioning this way will be a more demanding role for the teacher and will require a higher level of day-to-day preparation as well as a higher level of preservice and inservice preparation.

The teacher must develop skills as a diagnostician, as an expert in motivation (not more management), and as a program developer. This role is essential to provide the variety of options and to encourage the growth in personal insight on the part of students so that they can become self-directed, goal-oriented, motivated learners.

A variety of course structures and options in course sequencing

Variety

"Preparing our students to be lifelong learners will call upon us to make further efforts to expose students to self-contained foreign-language experiences, not only to motivate them toward our school programs, as is now the case, but to try to interest them generally in languages as an area of study *sometime* in their lives" (Strasheim, 26, p. 19). Strasheim continues to call attention to a number of changes in foreign language education, which if encouraged, can add to lifelong learning opportunities.

1 Providing an infinite variety of both credit and noncredit offerings
2 Moving away from "standard sequences" and moving into a diversification of curricula
3 Considering language study as a vehicle rather than as an end in itself

4 Restructuring language experiences to fit the learner rather than expecting the school to restructure itself to meet the requirements of foreign language teachers
5 Working with individualization, small groups, simulation, and gaming
6 Employing a variety of learning modes and using a variety of materials
7 Assisting students in planning their studies accordingly.

Teacher education

The least that can be expected from programs in teacher training is to provide better models for preservice teachers. This will entail, in simple terms, adhering to many of the things described above. Students in preservice teacher education must be given opportunity to inquire, to experience a variety of learning modes and materials, and to become independent self-directed learners.

Preservice teacher education

Institutions charged with the responsibility for teacher education must find ways, as difficult as this may be, to certify only those teachers who have come to love learning, who are excited about opening doors for others to enjoy learning, and who have a high level of tolerance for the many who will experience difficulty along their learning paths. Teachers must become experts in motivation, and this begins with a motivated teacher. The twenty-first century cannot tolerate anything less than a profession of humane scholars determined to teach, not just to serve the moment but to serve a lifetime . . . to promote lifelong learners.

Selecting teachers who love learning

References, Lifelong learning

1 Blakely, R. J. In *The School and Continuing Education:Four Studies*. Paris:UNESCO, 1972.
2 Bloom, Benjamin S. *Stability and Change in Human Characteristics*. New York:Wiley, 1964.
3 *A Climate for Individuality*. Washington, D.C.: NEA Department of Rural Education, AASA, ASCD, and NAASP, 1965.
4 Coppedge, Floyd L. "Goals of Individualization." *Educational Technology* 15,viii(1975):25–28.
5 Dave, R. H. *Lifelong Education and School Curriculum*. Hamburg:UNESCO, 1973.
6 ———, and N. Stiemerling. *Lifelong Education and the School*. Hamburg:UNESCO, 1973.
7 Erikson, Erik. *Childhood and Society*. New York: Norton, 1950.
8 Everett, Samuel. *Values in Curriculum Decision Making*. Washington, D.C.:ASCD Yearbook (1961): 33–48.
9 Faure, Edgar, et al. *Learning To Be*. Switzerland: UNESCO, 1972.
10 Fraenkel, Jack R. "Value Education in the Social Studies." *Phi Delta Kappan* 50(1969):457–61.

11 Frymier, Jack. *Motivation and Learning in School*. Bloomington, Indiana: Phi Delta Kappa Educational Foundation, 1974.
12 Gage, Gene G. "The Nordic Example." *Saturday Review* 2,xxvi(1975):19.
13 Gould, Roger. "Adult Life Stages Growth Toward Self-Tolerance." *Psychology Today* 8,ix(1975): 74–78.
14 Havighurst, Robert J. "Changing Status and Roles During the Adult Life Cycle: Significance for Adult Education." In Hobert W. Burns,ed, *Sociological Background of Adult Education*, Notes and Essays No. 41. Syracuse, New York: Syracuse University, 1964.
15 Hesburgh, Theodore M., et al. *Patterns for Lifelong Learning*. San Francisco: Jossey-Bass, 1973.
16 Hillson, Maurie, and Joseph Bongo. *Continuous Progress Education*. Palo Alto, California: Science Research Associates, 1971.
17 Hunt, J. McVicker. "The Psychological Basis for Using Preschool Enrichment as an Antidote for Cultural Deprivation." *Merrill-Palmer Quarterly of Behavior and Development* 10(1964):209–48.
18 Knowles, Malcolm S. *Toward A Model of Lifelong Education*. [A working paper prepared for the Consultative Group on "Implications of the Concept of Lifelong Education for School Teaching and Curriculum" of the UNESCO Institute for Education, Hamburg, Germany, October 9–12, 1972.]
19 Lengrand, Paul. *An Introduction to Lifelong Education*. Paris: UNESCO, 1970.
20 Overly, Norman, Floyd L. Coppedge, and R. Bruce McQuigg. "Toward a Definition and Conceptualization of Lifelong Learning." *Chapter Reports* 1,i (1975):16–18. [Bloomington: Indiana University Chapter of Phi Delta Kappa.]
21 Schaie, K. W., et al. "Generational and Cohort-Specific Differences in Adult Cognitive Functioning: A Fourteen-Year Study of Independent Samples." *Developmental Psychology* 9(1973):151–66.
22 Shane, Harold. *The Educational Significance of the Future*. Bloomington, Indiana: Phi Delta Kappa, 1973.
23 ———, and Roy A. Weaver. "Education as a Lifelong Process." *Vital Issues* 24,X(1975). Washington, Connecticut: Center for Information on America.
24 Singer, Benjamin. "The Future-Focused Role Image." In Alvin Toffler,ed. *Learning For Tomorrow*. New York: Random House, 1974.
25 Smith, Vernon H. *Alternative Schools*. Lincoln, Nebraska: Professional Educators Publications, 1974.
26 Strasheim, Lorraine A. *Lifelong Language Learning*. [Paper prepared for the Southern Conference on Language Teaching, New Orleans, October 2–4, 1975.]
27 Thorndike, E. L., et al. *Adult Learning*. New York: Macmillan, 1928.
28 "Toward a Model for Lifelong Learning." [Unpublished paper prepared by the Phi Delta Kappa Commission on Curriculum Models for Lifelong Learning, Bloomington, Indiana, 1976.]
29 Trump, J. Lloyd, and William Georgiades. "Doing Better With What You Have: NASSP Model School Project." *NASSP Bulletin* 54(1970):106–33.
30 UNESCO. *The School and Continuing Education: Four Studies*. Paris: UNESCO, 1972.

3

Small-group learning

Reid E. Baker
Ohio Department of Education

Overview

The concept of grouping is not new to the foreign language teaching profession. Homogeneous grouping on the basis of students' abilities has been a long-standing practice in many language programs. Since the mid-1960s flexible or modular scheduling, team teaching, and differentiated staffing arrangements have helped to organize instruction for large groups, small groups, and independent study. But only recently has the attention of the profession begun to focus on reorganizing integral, heterogeneous classes into small groups for various kinds of learning activities.

Small-group work is most frequently associated with individualized instruction. Increasingly, however, teachers are discovering its potential for maximizing the effectiveness of instruction in the conventional classroom setting. In this chapter I explore the concept relative to its application in both individualized and conventional instruction. A rationale for small-group learning is developed. Operational procedures are examined in depth and a representative selection of small-group activities appropriate for either secondary or college-level classes is presented. The chapter concludes with a description of ways in which prospective teachers can be prepared for the task of or-

---

Reid E. Baker (A.B.D., The Ohio State University) is State Foreign Language Supervisor with the Ohio Department of Education. A graduate of Washington and Lee University (B.A). and Middlebury College (M.A. with studies in France), he has taught French, science, and mathematics in junior and senior high school, and French, applied linguistics, and foreign language methods at the college level. In addition, he has supervised student teachers and has been a language laboratory director at both secondary and college levels. He has served as consultant at ACTFL preconference workshops on Teacher Education, Career Education, and Humanizing the Foreign Language Classroom and has conducted numerous inservice workshops throughout Ohio. He has also served as president of the Columbus Area Modern Language Teachers Association and editor of *The Cardinal,* the state foreign language newsletter. Currently he is Acting Vice Chairman of the Board of Directors of the Central States Conference on the Teaching of Foreign Languages, and *ex officio* member of the Executive Board of the Ohio Modern Language Teachers Association. Other professional affiliations include ACTFL, AATF, NALLD, and NCSSFL.

ganizing small-group learning in the foreign language classroom.

Rationale: Why group?

Passive student roles

Traditionally education has tended to place students in passive roles. A French cartoon effectively illustrates the model. The teacher, Mademoiselle J'Enseigne (I Teach) is depicted as a large pitcher pouring knowledge into a set of small pitchers, her students. The obvious implication is that the teacher's function is to fill students with knowledge that they are expected to absorb passively.

Professional awareness

Despite its absurdity in the light of what educators today know about teaching and learning, the "pitcher" model persists. Generally one has only to visit his community schools to see it in operation. To be sure, we know little enough about the teaching-learning process, but we have certainly reached the stage of professional awareness where we can acknowledge that our students are quite capable of learning by themselves and from each other much (if not most) of what we want them to learn. Given the right conditions they can often learn it better. For the foreign language education profession this realization has been humbling but salutory, because it has propelled us toward a fundamental rethinking of our role as teachers. It has also led us to develop instructional strategies that more successfully exploit our students' vast potential for learning from each other. The systematic use of small groups in the foreign language classroom is such a strategy.

Homogeneous grouping

Of the various grouping procedures employed in schools today, homogeneous grouping is probably the most familiar. Characteristically, homogeneous grouping involves the scheduling of students into classes on the basis of their learning abilities. In this sense it can be considered an *administrative* (rather than *instructional*) strategy. It is intended to optimize learning conditions for the student by placing him with others of similar ability. Students can work at a rate commensurate with their capabilities. The procedure can help to overcome one of the most common problems related to heterogeneous classes–the necessity for the teacher to gear instruction to a vaguely defined middle range of student ability while the more able students become bored at the "slow" class pace and the slow learners gradually fall behind.

Weaknesses

Homogeneous class grouping, however, has several inherent weaknesses. First, it is an attempt to deal with student differences in only one dimension—academic talent—and other important learning-related factors such as interest and creativity are ignored (Clark and Ramsey, 32). While the concept is student-centered in theory, the climate of homogeneous classes tends to be highly favorable to teacher-centered and subject-centered instruction. Also, students in lower-ability classes are frequently stigmatized by their peers. In reality the appearance of homogeneity is largely illusory. All class groups are heterogeneous in one way or another or to a greater or lesser degree in any given dimension (Kennedy, 81). In any group individual differences in students' abilities, needs, interests, and motivation inevitably emerge and must be dealt with.

Attitudes toward ability grouping

In a study conducted by Papalia (109) a representative sample of foreign language teachers largely favored ability grouping. School administrators, however, tended to favor heterogeneity in the classroom citing the following reasons:

1 It is difficult to schedule foreign language classes according to abilities in the target language.
2 The solution to problems of learning is not to be found in some scheme of ability grouping; the key to what happens in any instructional group is the classroom teacher.
3 Students need opportunities to work in common purpose with a wide range of people.
4 Grouping practices that separate students on the basis of abilities as determined by I.Q. or standardized tests reduce the possibilities that students will be exposed to a broader range of ethnic and cultural differences in the classroom (p. 54).

On the basis of his findings, Papalia recommends that foreign language teachers employ small-group work in their heterogeneous classes, grouping students according to their abilities in the various language skills. His recommendation is supported by the experience of Grittner and LaLeike (61) who state that "from the standpoint of student learning there is nothing that can be done in a large group that cannot be done better in small-group or individual learning situations" (p. 2).

Once homogeneous grouping moves out of the school scheduling office and into the classroom it becomes an *instructional* strategy that the teacher can employ with considerable flexibility. Students can be grouped and regrouped according to general ability, degree of specific language-skill mastery, interest, and other variables. In Kennedy's (81) program, for example, teachers provide for subgrouping, independent study, and other individualized arrangements. Bingham's (15) homogeneously scheduled classes are grouped randomly for various kinds of oral practice activities with faster students acting as group leaders. Through differentiated assignments and learning activities Parker (112) enables students of varying ability to cover the same course content, attaining different degrees of competence. Albert (1) divided a third-year French class into three separate interest groups, each of which worked with different material throughout the year. Finstein (46) grouped college students according to their progress in reading skills; by the end of the year even the slowest group had developed skills sufficient to read French at the "self-instructional" level.

Grouping in heterogeneous classes

"The primary purpose of small-group instruction," emphasize Clark and Ramsey (32), "is to provide each individual a chance to relate his knowledge and skills to and with others in a meaningful way" (p. 3). This interaction among students in a small group is a decisive factor in both the quality and meaningfulness of their learning. Much practical learning involves a social transaction or interaction between people (Olmstead, 106). Teacher-centered or subject-centered learning is based on a fixed body of knowledge (for example, facts, concepts, principles, relationships) together with a set of learners who have not yet acquired either the knowledge itself or the skills necessary to apply it in a practical way. In this view learning is the transactional or interactive process by which learners acquire the knowledge and skills from someone (a teacher) who already possesses them. Small-group learning, however, can be regarded as a transaction between a learner and other learners, all of whom constitute a group. In this process a great deal of learning to use knowledge in a practical way occurs through interaction between learners. New information provided by the teacher is

Small-group instruction

Teaching each other

integrated with learners' past experience and knowledge and reshaped into a workable system which can then be applied on a practical basis. "Thus in small-group instruction the principal interaction is within the learning group and learning results [largely] from the exchange that occurs within the group" (p. 89).

In the small-group environment, then, students learn in one of the most effective ways possible–by teaching each other (Birkmaier, 16; Herbert, 69; Moskowitz, 105). Working together, students help each other clarify and internalize concepts and integrate new material meaningfully with that already assimilated (Clark and Ramsey, 32). In the process, "learning ability is expanded for all group members, as more competent pupils reinforce their knowledge and pupils who have had difficulties profit from working with their peers" (Ghan and Rickel, 52, p. 238). The collective results tend to be superior to what individual students could achieve singly (Carstens, 27; Grittner, 60). In foreign language classes "the apparent disadvantage of the teacher's being unable to hear each student and correct each error is more than outweighed by the benefit of involving more students in the learning activity and developing their confidence and foreign language fluency in the relaxed atmosphere of a small group" (Disick, 41, p. 418).

Sociopsychological implications

In addition to learning effectiveness, the small-group context has significant socio-psychological implications. Ciotti (30, 31) sees the small group as the most fundamental social unit and cites evidence that it has a decisive function in satisfying socio-emotional needs that are a prerequisite to task work. She notes, however, that "group processes have not been adequately examined by investigators of second language education to determine the forces and conditions capable of influencing group interaction and thereby linguistic outcomes" (30, p. 11).

Heard (68) considers the foreign language classroom a culture in itself that should permit students to exercise the roles they will assume later in life. "Producer-consumer" role exchanges between teacher and students predominate in most classrooms. What students need is more opportunities to interact meaningfully in the roles of "citizen" and "friend." Noting that "students are remarkably adept at synthesizing, creating, and developing their own unique and often very effective teaching styles," Heard recommends a number of small-group activities in which students can work together, "participating in creative learning" (p. 316).

Teacher and student roles

Boylan and Omaggio (21) also provide many ideas for small-group work which can help to expand teacher and student roles beyond the usual reciprocal information-giving, information-getting, and manipulative functions. Clark and Ramsey (32) underscore the importance of group work in relation to the learning and practice of democratic processes. Herbert (69) points out that students working in groups "can more readily learn and practice the skills of leadership, organization, [acceptable] behavior, management, communication, and cooperation" (p. 9). Thus, "the group is not of significant value to the individual if the aim is primarily the acquisition of factual information since this kind of activity can be carried on effectively enough by the student working alone. That which can be learned in a group is how to be a good group participant" (Ciotti, 30, pp. 17–18).

Individualized instruction

That students in an individualized foreign language program should have opportunities to work in groups is by now axiomatic. As Logan (96) aptly puts it:

> Man is a social animal, and if "lock-step" teaching has often gone too far by forgetting that he is . . . an individual, many individualized programs have gone too far by forgetting that he had a need to socialize and to interact. It is especially ironic to isolate him almost completely during the process of acquiring a skill for communication (p. 51).

Steiner (142) emphasizes that in a good individualized program the student does alone what he can best do alone; at other times he should be able to interact with the teacher and with other students in small groups. While some students may find independent work satisfying, individualization that provides only for interaction with a learning packet, with little or no peer-group interaction, can eventually prove deadly and stultifying (Grittner, 59). To paraphrase a familiar saying: "All individualized work and no group play makes Johnny a very bored student" (Braswell, 22, p. 106). Fortunately, only a few programs are operating on a completely independent or programmed basis; the vast majority systematically incorporate group work into the instructional process (Phillips, 113).

Self-pacing facilitated

Reinert (119, 120) feels that flexible grouping facilitates self-pacing. As students move at different rates through the program, they should be guided into various groups according to their language-skill performance and interests. Each student should be encouraged to be with *some* group at all times, though not always with the *same* group. His view is substantiated by a national survey of successful individualized programs (Sutton, 148). Respondents strongly favored flexible grouping procedures in which students may work alone or in different-sized groups, depending on the activity in which they are engaged and their interest or ability, and are allowed to move from one group to another on the basis of needs or interests. Sutton also indicates that in her own individualized high school classes students seldom work alone; they tend to form small groups regardless of whether their materials explicitly call for them to do so.

Importance of teacher's role

Gougher (56) agrees that small-group work is both a practical and an efficient way to facilitate learning at an optimum rate for the individual student. But he cautions that "the group method is not good for solving all the problems involved in foreign language study" (p. 3). He stresses the importance of the teacher's role in deciding when to work in groups and when to work on a one-to-one basis.

"Quality control"

From the standpoint of efficiency Reinert (119) and Sonnanstine (141) point out that it is virtually impossible for the teacher in an individualized program to exercise the necessary degree of "quality control" for each and every student separately. By sitting down with a group of four or five students, however, he can assess their individual mastery of a given set of materials in a matter of minutes. In so doing he is using his valuable contact time with the students in the most efficient manner possible—to do what they cannot do alone (Steiner, 143). From the feedback thus obtained he can identify potential learning difficulties as a basis for prescribing subsequent individual and group activities (Clark and Ramsey, 32).

Many ways to individualize

There are many ways to individualize instruction. Unfortunately, the concept is largely equated with a continuous-progress system in which each student moves at his own pace. Warriner (156) warns of the danger inherent in such a view:

> The majority of teachers who cannot go that far will sit back and not do anything . . . [But] if we view individualized instruction as a goal that can be sought in varying degrees, every teacher can, if he tries, take at least one or even a few steps along the way (p. 34).

Partial approaches

Freilich (50) has taken more than a few steps. In her "flexible classroom" whole-class presentations of basic content are followed up with individual, partner, and small-group work by students. Wells (159) also takes a partial approach to individualization. In her weekly schedule three days are devoted to whole-class instruction; one day is reserved for individual and small-group work focusing on oral practice and interest-centered activities. On the fifth day students work in groups at "skill-building centers," concentrating on pronunciation, comprehension, conversation, grammar, and enrichment. In both cases students proceed through the course at the same rate, but extensive provision is made for accommodating their individual abilities and interests. Both situations support the contention that through flexible grouping procedures and imaginative learning activities, "conventional" or nonself-paced instruction can be effectively individualized in the foreign language classroom.

Individualization in traditional setting

An experiment conducted by Papalia and Zampogna (110, 111) represents another important step toward individualization in a traditional setting. Forty-five third-year French students were randomly assigned to two classes. The control class was taught on a whole-class basis with instruction conducted primarily in the target language; audiolingual and cognitive code-learning procedures were combined with various culture-learning activities. The experimental class met one period per week as a whole class; the rest of the time students participated in curriculum planning, development of self-instructional materials, and a wide variety of interest-centered projects and small-group affective communication activities. At the end of the year 63 percent of the experimental class (as compared with 35 percent of the control class) enrolled for fourth-year French, expressing strong positive attitudes toward their experiences. The experimental class also registered significantly higher achievement in the four language skills as measured by the MLA Cooperative French Tests ($p < .05$). The authors conclude:

1 Teaching and learning is a process of communication among individuals in a group setting.
2 It is not necessary to have any special kind of school scheduling in order to individualize instruction. The effective teacher may individualize instruction in an inflexible lockstep setting by grouping students on the basis of ability for some activities and on the basis of interest for other activities.
3 Communication games aid in promoting a classroom climate conducive to interaction. They require active participation, present the opportunity for students to learn from each other, increase students' responsibility, and contribute to a greater achievement in the four basic skills in French (111, p. 306).

Communicative competence

Group work can also facilitate the development of communicative competence. Logan (96) refers to the irony of isolating students in a self-paced program during the process of acquiring a skill intended for communication. Birkmaier (16) expresses a similar concern in relation to conventional instruction:

> Making students sit next to each other and learn a language without allowing them to communicate with each other through it, giving them a means for interchange of opinion and information and then not providing for the use of it, is the equivalent of installing a telephone in a house and not connecting it to the exchange (p. 351).

Social context for communication

By definition, communication takes place in a group setting. Minimally, it occurs between two persons, the smallest group possible. Horne (70) argues that "since language is the process of social communication, instruction should be conducted at least in part in an atmosphere of controlled social interaction, i.e., within a small group" (p. 103). Booth (18), too, feels that the small group is important for establishing and maintaining social relations among students while they learn communication skills. She also believes that conversation in small groups can help to reduce the tension the learner experiences when trying to speak a strange language. Her view is supported by Giauque (54) and Otto (107) who point out that students are less inhibited in small-group situations than in the whole-class environment where they are frequently intimidated at the prospect of having to "perform" before a substantial number of their peers. Disick (41) notes that students experience less embarrassment and self-consciousness when corrected in small-group situations.

The literature pertaining to the development of communicative competence contains numerous references to communication activities to be performed by students in pairs or other kinds of small groups. On the basis of their extensive review of the literature Schulz and Bartz (131) recommend "as many [such] activities as our convictions and our creativity permit so that we [may] lead the student toward the attainment of [the] ability to share his experiences with others in the target language" (p. 89).

Communication activities

Small-group learning also has a considerable affective potential. In addition to maximizing opportunities for meaningful communicative interaction, Birkmaier (16) believes that it can help satisfy the student's desire to communicate and to assert himself, his wish to help others and to be helped, and his need for responsibility for his own work and for that of the group. The results of Papalia and Zampogna's (11) experiment in individualization through small-group interaction indicate that students "were challenged, cared about each other . . . and were [highly] satisfied with the work of the class" (p. 306). Larger-scale foreign language programs have been developed that extensively and systematically incorporate small-group affective communication activities (Love and Honig, 97, pp. 65–73, 215–24; Sonnanstine, 140; Stoller et al., 144; Wilson and Wattenmaker, 160; see also Chapter 7 in this volume). Evidence supports the conclusion that such activities contribute substantially to students' positive feelings about themselves, toward others, and toward language learning as a meaningful personal experience. Disick and Barbanel (43), however, point out that "as individualized instruction and techniques of affective education spread to more and more foreign language classrooms, it becomes increasingly important for teachers to understand the group processes that affect the behavior and learning of students" (p. 198). Where ability grouping is involved to any appreciable extent, teachers must guard against the negative feelings

Affective outcomes

Positive feelings

Negative feelings

that can result when "one's group is consistently identified, even though not in so many words, as the 'dumb' group" (Allen and Valette, 3, p. 24).

The small-group process: Making it work

Theoretical considerations

Groups do not develop because the teacher says, "Let's work in groups" (Papalia and Zampogna, 111). "Students cannot be set down in groups, or sent off in pairs, and told to interact in the foreign language" (Rivers, 122, p. 29). Successful small-group learning is the result of careful planning and preparation based on a knowledge of the characteristics of small groups and the processes involved in their functioning. Most authors who write about group methods assume, however, both interaction among group members in their native language and a relatively long duration of student association with the same group. For this reason the principles and procedures described are difficult to apply to the special conditions of the foreign language classroom where the primary purpose of group work is to facilitate students' acquisition of skills in a second language and where students characteristically do not remain in the same groups over long periods of time. The following discussion of theory and research is therefore highly selective. It should serve as a guide to the foreign language teacher who wishes to implement small-group work in his classes.

Planning and preparation

Ciotti (30, 31) reviewed the voluminous literature on grouping up to 1969. From her research emerges the definition of a group as "a number of persons who communicate with each other over a short span of time, and who are few enough that each person is able to communicate with all the others . . . face to face" (30, p. 13; 31, p. 79). She emphasizes, however:

Group defined

> A gathering of people does not comprise a group. Certain characteristics must be present within that gathering for it to be identified as a group. These include the elements of interaction, goals, norms, roles, and cohesiveness that develop and function according to the input characteristics of the members and of the immediate and large environments. What evolves is a group "life" that represents a distinctive set of

Group "life"

interpersonal relationships and resultant productivity (31, p. 79).

Benson (14) conceptualizes the group on a "sliding continuum scale" rather than in terms of a dichotomy between "group" and "nongroup." He identifies five elements or dimensions that are present in varying degrees at any developmental stage of "groupness." There is some overlap between his elements and those mentioned by Ciotti.

Characteristics of groups

Cohesiveness. Feelings of unity and common bonds can create powerful attractions to the group and among its members. As cohesiveness is developed through the sharing of common experiences and personal concerns, the amount of influence that group members can exert on each other increases. Psychological support for the individual to try new behaviors is enhanced.

Norms. The standards of what is right or desirable [that] are held in common by the group members become powerful influences on member attitudes and behavior in groups as they become more cohesive. Group norms may make it easier to change group attitudes than to change individual attitudes.

Models. As groups become more cohesive, the members who are attractive in some way to group members will be imitated by others in the group.

Reality testing. Groups can constitute miniature societies in which individual members can test others' reactions to their ideas and their behavior.

Productivity. In terms of group problem-solving "the whole is greater than the sum of its parts" in that the interaction of members in a group will often produce more creative solutions to problems as well as more personal accountability for action (Benson, 14, p. 3).

Group size

How small is a "small" group? Clark and Ramsey (32) feel that for instructional purposes it should be small enough to allow all students to relate meaningfully to each other but large enough to allow for diverse opinion and knowledge. Gougher (56) indicates that it may include as many as 10 to 15 students. Horne's research (70) points to a definition in terms of five to

Group size

nine members; a lesser number constitutes an "individual" instructional situation, while "mass" instruction involves 10 or more students.

Summarizing from sociological research, Ciotti (31) states that the small group may consist of from two to 20 members with two additional features: the absence of two or more stable well-defined subgroups and the presence of substantial face-to-face contact among members. The optimum size, however, appears to be between five and seven. Most people seem to prefer a group of this size because it permits both a high degree of verbal interaction and a variety of personalities and talents. Groups of less than seven are less likely to have verbal nonparticipants; thus, group size can be a more critical variable for the low participator than for the high participator. An odd number of members is more desirable than an even number for task accomplishment because no deadlock is possible; in a group of five the common three-two division results in no one's being left alone. Beyond these limits the addition of members "causes more demands on the leader, a decrease in communication time, more feeling of threat and inhibition, a more pronounced distinction between the most verbal participator and the other members, and more mechanical interaction" (p. 79).

Optimum size

Negative effects of larger groups

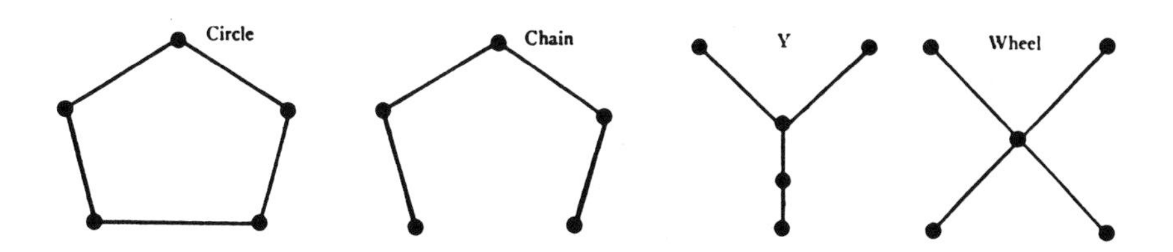

Roles within groups. From her research Ciotti also identifies four predominant patterns of communication within groups (Figure 1). In the "circle" communication is slow and uneconomical due to the absence of a leader; but the pattern is flexible, and more information is transmitted. More errors are made, but more are corrected. At the opposite end of the continuum the "wheel" has a leader in a position of influence and is thus more conducive to rapid group achievement; however, members experience less satisfaction because they are in noninfluential positions. There is also a higher tolerance of errors. In the "chain," information is transmitted back and forth be-

Patterns of communication

tween the leader and the two terminal points. The "Y" increases the flow of information to and from the leader because of the additional terminal point.

> In summary, it can be stated that from the "circle" to the "wheel" member satisfaction and interaction decrease while the leadership role of the central member and the stabilization of the paths of communication to him increase. One can conclude that for satisfying social-emotional needs the "circle" is preferable since it allows more freedom for interaction and more personal involvement. Where leadership functions are necessary for the completion of the task, one of the other networks is more appropriate (31, p. 80).

Teachers' role perceptions

Many teachers have strong reservations about breaking their classes up into groups. Strasheim (147) suggests that their apprehensions stem largely from their tendency to equate good teaching with maintenance of discipline and order in the classroom. Even when seating arrangements are "loosened up" for greater flexibility, the authority figure of the teacher dominates the classroom and the interaction taking place within it. Such interaction characteristically involves the role functions of information giving and getting (Boylan and Omaggio, 21). In a predominantly teacher-centered classroom the teacher disseminates information (content, directions, assignments, and so on) to the students who passively receive it. At a later point the teacher solicits information from the students as a measure of how well they assimilated the original information. Thus, the teacher and the students function alternately as *information-givers* and *information-getters,* with the students almost always in subservient positions. In the process the student functions primarily as a *manipulator* of language forms and cultural facts.

"Producer-consumer" exchanges

Heard (68) calls these kinds of interaction "producer-consumer" exchanges.

> Assumption of this [producer-consumer] role . . . shifts from teacher to student to teacher in a predictable pattern. The teacher structures and dispenses information and then markets it for student consumption. At some point in the instruc-

> tional time line the student is asked to reproduce what he has consumed. The pattern practice as a pedagogical device is a case in point. . . . Formal testing procedures are another example . . . (p. 315).

Producer-consumer exchanges are of course necessary in any instructional situation. But Heard feels that they predominate in the foreign language classroom. She argues in favor of the small-group context as a means of providing students opportunities to exercise the roles of "citizen" and "friend" in an atmosphere of mutual help and reciprocity.

Expanded roles

Boylan and Omaggio (21) emphasize the necessity of "expanding" students' roles beyond those of passive recipient and manipulator of language forms and content (Figure 2). By setting up such activities in the classroom and by providing a supportive nonjudgmental atmosphere in which students can express themselves without feelings of pressure or inadequacy, the teacher can expand his role beyond disseminator of information to that of facilitator of learning.

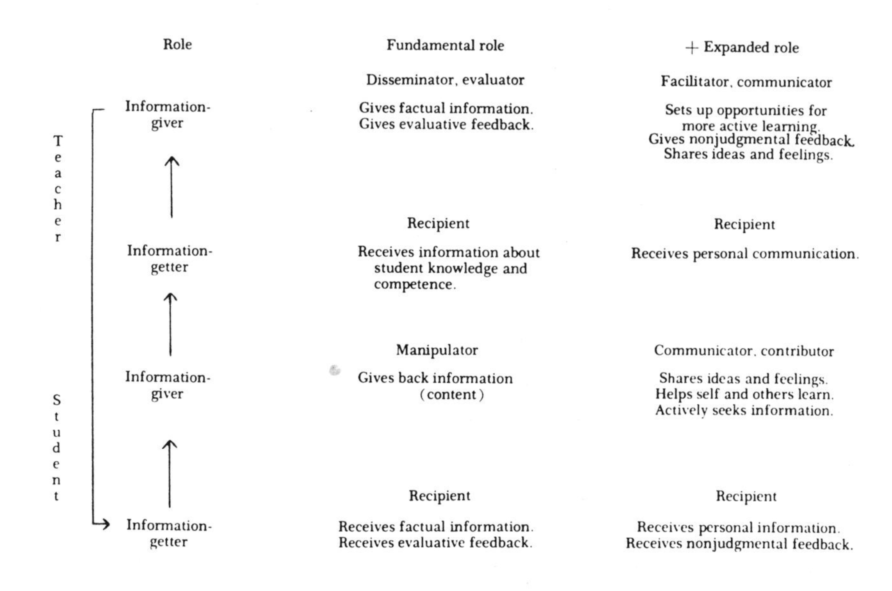

Other teacher roles

Small-group work also permits the teacher to function more effectively as a diagnostician and prescriber. By systematically observing students engaged in group activities, the teacher is able to obtain valuable feedback regarding their level of content and language-skill mastery far better than he can in the whole-class situation. At the same time he can frequently identify potential or actual learning difficulties and prescribe appropriate individual or group remedial activities. His observations can also form the basis for judging the effectiveness of whole-class presentations (Clark and Ramsey, 32). Other roles the teacher exercises in working with groups include listener, consultant, resource person, guide, discussion leader, participator, and evaluator (Arendt, Barrett, and Mackey, 7; Booth, 18).

Student-centered teachers

A study conducted by Papalia (108) suggests that many teachers are either ready to assume these various roles or are already functioning effectively in them. In responding to the Minnesota Teacher Attitude Inventory and the Teacher Description Instrument, teachers generally manifested supportive attitudes toward students, favoring students' self-motivation and open interaction in the classroom. They largely disagreed with statements to the effect that increased freedom in the classroom creates confusion and that the teacher should exercise more authority over students. "Students, in identifying and rating their teachers' classroom behaviors, confirmed that . . . teachers displayed student-centered classroom behaviors and that they actualized learning by being sensitive to the needs and abilities of students" (p. 231).

Practical approaches

Getting started

One of the first questions a classroom teacher asks in relation to grouping is "How do I start?" Wattenmaker (157) suggests that the teacher begin on a limited controlled basis with a single group of perhaps five students. Preferably, they should be students with whom he feels comfortable, perhaps chosen from a "favorite" class. While the rest of the class completes a written assignment, the teacher can conduct one or several well-structured activities with the group. As he gains confidence and experience, he can gradually move to less-structured activities, include additional groups, and eventually involve the entire class. Valette and Disick (154) recommend teaching in "the usual way" for half of the class period, then dividing the class into groups of two or three students for oral practice.

Commitment

Sonnanstine (141) believes that the teacher should make a whole-hearted commitment to group work before implementing it in the classroom. She recommends that he begin by reading everything available on the subject in an effort to learn from others' experience what can be done better in groups than in the whole-class situation and why. She also underscores the necessity for the teacher to convince students that he is vitally concerned about the quality of their learning and that he wants to use this new way to help them learn more effectively. She cautions against the teacher's becoming defensive when students react with less than 100 percent enthusiasm to activities he has developed. She feels that students' constructive criticism and suggestions can only serve to improve the quality of the activities and the materials.

Initiating group work

Arendt, Barrett, and Mackey (7) recommend a procedure for initiating group work in a program of self-paced individualized instruction:

1 Begin with the traditional class group.
2 Break the class into small groups as soon as students are observed pulling away or lagging behind.
3 Group either according to ability, achievement, interest, or how students motivate each other—how they work with each other.
4 Dissolve small groups into independent learning when small groups become unproductive, allowing students to pair themselves at any time naturally, then regrouping.
5 Bring students together often in small- and intermediate-sized groups (p. 115).

Learning styles

Hosenfeld (71) has explored students' differential learning styles and the implications these have for foreign language instruction. From the work of Hunt she identifies three distinct conceptual levels on which students characteristically operate. Conceptual level and the degree of structure in the learning environment stand in inverse relation to each other: In general the lower the student's conceptual level, the more he needs structure in his learning environment. She elaborates procedures for identifying students' conceptual levels and for structuring learning environments accordingly. Included are suggestions for how and when to move students from full-class work to small-group work, together with indications of group activities appropriate for students of different conceptual levels.

Cognitive-style mapping

Lepke (89, 90) is also concerned with differential learning styles. Her approach, based on the work of Hill and others, utilizes cognitive-style mapping procedures to derive a coded schematic representation of individual language learners' tendencies to derive meaning in certain ways. A Cognitive Preference Inventory instrument is used to identify major, minor, and negligible cognitive preferences in the areas of symbolic orientation (how the learner responds to, and learns from, symbols and sensory stimuli), cultural determinants (how he responds to, and behaves in, a given learning environment), and modalities of inference (how he applies patterns of reasoning to arrive at meanings). Organization of test data into coded categories yields a tentative profile or "map" of each student's cognitive style. The profile is then verified or adjusted on the basis of further data obtained through an interview and observations of the student in various learning situations. In relation to small-group work cognitive-style mapping can evidently help the teacher identify, for example, students who perform well with peers; those who enjoy role-playing, simulation, and games; those who are good organizers and thus effective group leaders; those who are sensitive to others' feelings and thus likely to be patient when working with slower learners; and those who need substantial amounts of authority and supervision. While Hosenfeld (71) reports that cognitive-style mapping requires difficult and expensive inservice training, Lepke (89, 90) maintains that a one-week workshop is sufficient to train teachers in the necessary procedures.

Grouping procedures

Various kinds of groupings are possible within the context of both conventional and individualized instruction. For some kinds of activities the teacher may decide to form the groups himself; in other cases students can be permitted to group themselves. Remedial work, for example, generally requires that the teacher assign students to a group. Grouping by ability also necessitates a certain amount of teacher control. Sutton (149), however, has observed that in her individualized classes students tend to group themselves with others of similar ability. She also notes that a given group usually includes one or more students of greater or lesser ability because other group members are friends. In these cases the group tends to adjust its efforts upward or downward to match the ability level of the member with the most dominant personality. Sutton believes that the teacher can capitalize on the leadership potential of this kind of student, because she has observed that others in the group will often make extraordinary learning efforts to maintain their group status. With more direct control the teacher can systematically assign the more able students to work with those of lesser ability.

Group leaders

Some degree of teacher control is also desirable in grouping students for what Rivers (122, 125) calls "skill-getting" activities (for example, dialogue practice, structure drill, directed dialogue, vocabulary practice, simple question/answer exercises). Here the teacher's primary concern should be to pair or group students who can best help each other (Sonnanstine, 141; Wise, 161). For this purpose the high-ability student is not necessarily the best group leader or helper because he is sometimes impatient with those of lesser ability. A better choice is the one who relates well to others, who is supportive and encouraging, and who can get group activities going and keep them moving efficiently. The slower student should be placed in a group with a leader who will be receptive and attentive to him and who will help to integrate him into the group.

"Skill-getting" activities

Students may also be grouped randomly for some kinds of activities. Wilson and Wattenmaker (160) and Stoller et al. (144) suggest this as one appropriate procedure for affective communication exercises because it usually assures a variety of opinions and personalities. Reinert (119), however, points out that in an individualized program groups established randomly by the teacher do not work well; students should be allowed to group themselves according to their progress. Because students at the beginning of a first year are usually not ready to assume responsibility for their own learning, he recommends a period of four to six weeks before permitting them to form groups. He also observes that "grouping according to interest instead of according to position in the text will bring together students who might otherwise have relatively little contact with one another" (p. 100). Among possible target-culture areas of interest that students might explore together in groups, he lists stamp collecting, cooking, sports, music, scientific terms in the target language, and games such as Monopoly and Scrabble.

Random grouping

Interest groups

Is there a relationship between group size and group activi-

Group size and activities

ties? If so, what kinds of activities are best adapted to groups of different size? Such questions are difficult to answer, for there is no empirical research in foreign language education pointing conclusively to an optimum group size for specific activities. Although the rapidly growing literature on small-group activities frequently mentions group size in relation to specific activities, a clear, unambiguous pattern is difficult to discern from the numerous reports. Nevertheless, most references indicate the group size of five to seven delineated by Ciotti (31, p. 79). While many activities that involve two, three, or four students are reported, there is virtually no mention of groups larger than eight.

Structured activities

Pair-grouping appears to be an appropriate context for highly structured "skill-getting" activities (Bingham, 15; Joiner, 77). It is the easiest kind of group work to organize (Freed, 48); it maximizes student participation; and the pace of interaction is rapid (Sonnanstine, 141). Baker (9), however, observes that these kinds of activities can be successfully conducted in groups as large as five if appropriate materials are provided. For more open-ended "skill-using" activities, especially those calling for spontaneity and creativity on the part of students (for example, creating dialogues, skits, and dramatic productions; summarizing reading material; preparing group oral or written compositions; exploring cultural themes), groups of four to seven seem to be the norm. This group is also widely used for free or partially controlled conversation, though a conversation group of three is sometimes preferred for maximum student participation and minimum inhibition (Bonin and Birckbichler, 17; Lamson, 88). For role-playing, simulation, and games, the size of the group depends on the number called for by the specific activity.

Open-ended activities

Conversation groups

In general, as group size increases, the pace of student-to-student interaction decreases, and group productivity in terms of the amount of material that can be effectively covered is significantly reduced. At the same time, student inhibition appears to increase as the size of the group increases. Inhibitions, frustrations, and feelings of anxiety, however, can be minimized if a warm, supportive, nonjudgmental climate is maintained (Boylan and Omaggio, 21). In such an environment affective-communication exercises that focus on the sharing of personal feelings and experiences can be conducted in groups of as many as 16 (Stoller et al., 144; Wilson and Wattenmaker, 160; Wise,

Affective exercises

161). Yet, limiting the size of the group to 10 for affective communication will afford students more opportunity to participate within the time allotted (Sonnanstine, 140, 141).

Careful planning and preparation are necessary if group work is to be effective in terms of students' learning. As a standard procedure, Freed (48) recommends that small-group activities center initially on specific tasks, such as obtaining personal information from other group members in the target language or asking simple prepared questions. The information thus obtained should then be shared with the whole class. In her experience, group work "tends to disintegrate" when these two conditions are not met. Torres (153) offers the following practical suggestions for the teacher, based on his experience in working with undergraduate classes:

Practical suggestions

1 Review and role-play each activity before having students engage in it.
2 Double-check the accuracy of any activity materials before giving them to students to work with.
3 Explain activities carefully, first in a general explanation to the entire class, then in specific explanations to each group.
4 Plan a variety of short activities so that different groups can exchange activities within the allotted time.

Baker (9) feels that activities should be well structured to maximize the possibility that they will constitute productive learning experiences:

1 Students should clearly understand the *purpose* of a group activity and how the activity ties in with what they are learning.
2 Each group should have appropriate *materials* to work with. These should contain explicit instructions for use and be organized in such a way that they can be handed to groups without lengthy complicated explanations.
3 Students should clearly understand the *outcome* or *product* of each activity. Performance objectives are especially helpful in this connection.

Ground rules

Sonnanstine (141) believes that certain ground rules are essential for effective group work. Students must accept the fact that if they are going to work in groups and if they find it enjoyable to do so, their full cooperation is necessary. For the sake of efficiency they must be willing to give the teacher their full attention at times for whole-class presentations, instructions, administrative details, and other necessary classroom procedures. They must also realize that the teacher depends on them for a smoothly functioning classroom operation and that their peers depend on them for the quality of their learning. In short, students must develop a sense of responsibility and a spirit of cooperation toward each other and toward the teacher. This is best built on mutual trust and concern. The teacher must be able to trust his students and must be deserving of their trust.

Help for the teacher

Although the foreign language teacher by himself can do much to implement small-group work in his classes, his effectiveness can be considerably extended through the use of classroom aides. Advanced students are the most readily available source of help. With proper training, they can serve both as group leaders and on a one-to-one tutorial basis with lower-level students. The mutual benefits are numerous. Logan (96) notes that student-to-student tutoring is frequently more effective than teacher-to-student teaching because the student tutor has often just learned a given skill himself and may be in a better position to see what the learner's problems are. In addition, many students who need help will seek it from another student more readily than from the teacher. The student assistant himself has repeated chances to reinforce previously learned skills under conditions more meaningful to him than those under which he originally acquired them. "The realization that another student is depending on him for assistance and, indeed, sometimes for survival in the course gives [him] the stimulus he needs to redirect his own learning efforts" (Heard, 68, p. 318).

Advanced students

Two-way motivation

Knop (84) observes that peer-teaching can have a two-way effect on motivation. Lower-level students are able to observe firsthand how well advanced students can communicate in the target language and realize that the attainment of a similar level of skill is possible for them within a reasonable length of time, rather than at some point in the distant future. At the same time the advanced students can hear the difference between their speaking ability and that of the lower-level students. This gives them a sense of accomplishment and satisfaction. Braswell (22) reports that close working relationships develop between high school student aides and the junior high school students with whom they work. The experience evidently has a substantial effect on the younger students in terms of their motivation to continue with language study, for many of them look forward to becoming aides themselves when they reach high school. According to Warriner (156), considerable enthusiasm resulted when fourth-year French students worked two periods a week throughout the year with second-year students. In Semke's (133) college-level German classes—where second-year students as part of their course work regularly conduct various skill-practice activities with small groups of first-year students—reactions are also highly positive. Peer-teaching by high school students can bring meaningful, enjoyable foreign language learning into the elementary classroom, according to Barnett (10) and Beach (12).

Qualifications

What qualifications should the student assistant possess? Cameron-Bacon (25) feels that he should be "linguistically capable," with a general comprehension of the basic rules of grammar and a desire to improve himself. He need not necessarily be the most outstanding student and need not be fluent in all four skills. But he should be able to express himself orally, especially if he is to conduct conversation sessions. Of prime importance, however, is his interest in the individual as an active learner. Archibeque (5) believes that punctuality, maturity, good rapport with younger students, and a sense of responsibility are also essential traits.

Recruiting student assistants

Generally, recruiting advanced students as classroom assistants is not difficult. Many are willing to contribute their efforts and unscheduled time on a volunteer basis, though Otto (107) cautions against overreliance on volunteers. Archibeque (5) and Grittner (58) suggest that students whose study schedules do not permit them to enroll full-time in an advanced course can be kept actively involved in the language program and maintain their language skills by serving as aides. In many school situations these students and others recruited from advanced courses can be awarded partial or even full credit for their work. Braswell (22) feels that such credit is a strong recruiting incentive. He also recommends close cooperation between the language department, the counseling staff, and the school administration.

If advanced students are to work on a one-to-one basis with lower-level students, they should receive proper training for their tutorial tasks. Materials appropriate for this purpose have been developed by Brown (23). They specify how the student tutor should prepare for and conduct his sessions, and they contain step-by-step procedures for teaching various kinds of material, for reinforcing correct responses, and for reporting the results of tutorial sessions.

Native aides

Native-speaking aides can also provide a substantial measure of assistance to the classroom teacher at both the college and the secondary school levels. Students have the benefit of extended personal contact with young people near their own age who are authentic models of the target language and representatives of the target culture (Gilman and Flippo, 55). American students often respond positively to the opportunity–and the challenge–of communicating with a native speaker in his own language; moreover, they may find it more natural to speak the target language with a native than with an American teacher (Giauque, 54). Untrained natives, however, are largely unaware of the structure of their own language and the learning problems it presents, and they are generally unable to evaluate their own culture objectively. Skill, planning, and careful supervision are required of the classroom teacher to utilize their linguistic and cultural resources to the best advantage (Cameron-Bacon, 25; Deveny and Bookout, 40; Hammelman and Nielsen, 64).

Part of the team

Classroom aides should be made to feel that they are "an integral part of a team that helps *all* students to learn" (Braswell, 22, p. 114). The responsibilities of the teacher, as team leader, include providing materials, assigning responsibilities to the assistant, and giving constructive feedback on the assistant's performance. The assistant should be included to the maximum extent possible in instructional planning, should be given opportunities to evaluate his own performance, and should be permitted to critique or contribute to any aspect of the course (Cameron-Bacon, 25; Deveny and Bookout, 40; Hammelman and Nielsen, 64). When college students are used as aides, Kline

(83) believes that they should receive financial remuneration rather than be "paid" by a course grade. He points out that grade pressure contributes to the maintenance of a traditional student-teacher relationship, whereas students who are paid a stipend feel they are justly compensated for their skills, develop a sense of professionalism, and are more openly receptive to criticism.

Representative small-group activities

Commercially available material

Teachers desiring to implement small-group work in their classes are obliged to create most of their own activities, for there is little ready-made material available on the commercial market. I reviewed teacher's manuals and teacher's editions of 17 of the most widely used French, German, and Spanish textbook series. The search revealed virtually no mention of grouping, let alone ideas or suggestions for small-group work. One notable exception was the teacher's edition of *Voix et visages de la France* (Coulombe et al., 36). The edition includes an article by Gougher (57) in which he describes procedures for moving from whole-class to small-group work. The teacher's section contains detailed directions for 13 different learning games involving small groups. Another excellent source of ideas is the recently published *Connaître et se connaître* (Jarvis et al., 73). Essentially a basic French reader focusing on topics of high interest to contemporary teenagers, the book contains an abundance of communicative activities, most of which can be readily adapted for use in small groups. A similar publication for Spanish (Boylan et al., 20) is currently in press. The following methods texts and guides contain suggestions for small-group work: Allen and Valette, 3; Disick, 42; Rivers, 121; Valette and Disick, 154. In these books the index rubrics *group* or *small-group* should be consulted.

Although there is little commercially available material on small-group learning, the professional literature of foreign language education contains a veritable wealth of ideas. The following description is necessarily selective and condensed. It will, however, convey some idea of the scope of possible activities and should serve as a reference for both college-level and secondary-school teachers.

Arendt (6) lists possible small-group activities on three levels of sophistication:

Least Sophisticated

Working together on special short assignments such as worksheets and Unipacs
Practicing and presenting dialogues
Performing pattern drills
Practicing dictations
Reading aloud and clarifying meaning
Asking and answering questions on dialogues and narrative content
Creating and performing simple recombinations of known dialogue material
Viewing visuals and listening to recorded material
Playing simple games
Recording simple dialogues
Working on remedial exercises
Making simple reports [probably in English]
Putting up bulletin boards
Preparing and presenting pantomimes
Competing with other groups in solving crossword puzzles
Competing in preparing and presenting a song

Least sophisticated

More Sophisticated

Doing group planning
Working together in a heterogeneous group on exercises in which there are minimal and maximal possibilities for study activities
Working together in a continuous progress program in which all students complete the same assignments
Writing and performing guided skits
Playing moderately sophisticated games
Choosing alternatives (various techniques and media) to solve problems
Preparing for and carrying on a discussion with a native speaker who comes to the class as a resource person
Preparing cuttings from dramatic works (pp. 109–10)

More sophisticated

At the level of greatest sophistication Baker (9) has modified Arendt's list and expanded it with specific examples:

Most Sophisticated

Working in a group in which members decide upon special assignments for each student
Preparing and producing a foreign language assembly
Planning activities for a foreign language fair or camp
Preparing and executing a tour of the school in the target language
Preparing a taped foreign language commentary to accompany an exhibit put on by another department
Publishing a student foreign language newspaper
Creating original films, radio or TV programs, puppet shows, etc.
Teaching and tutoring lower-level students
Performing individual research and combining information for a cumulative activity
Preparing and presenting a panel discussion or debate in the target language
Preparing and presenting cultural materials
Preparing a tape-slide presentation on aspects of the target culture and its people
Planning a real or simulated trip to a foreign country
Preparing and presenting an historical skit ("You Are There")
Demonstrating and describing how to do something
Writing original stories and poems
Role-playing in a variety of simulated communication situations (Arendt, 6, p. 110; Baker, 9; 62)

Most sophisticated

For structured skill-practice activities Baker (9) suggests the use of cards. These can be prepared in the following manner:

Use of cards

Use 3x5, 4x6, or 5x8 cards, depending on the type and quantity of material each card is to contain. Different kinds of activities can be color-coded (for example, blue cards for dialogue practice, orange for structure drills). If multiple packets are to be provided, material can be photocopied, mimeographed, or spirit-duplicated, then cut up and pasted on cards. Students can do this as a group activity. Each card packet should have a "header" card with appropriate identifying information (type of activity, textbook references, and so on). The header card might include directions for students, a variety of suggestions for using the cards in the packet, and performance objectives.

Dialogue practice. Use a separate card for each dialogue line. One side of the card contains the dialogue line in the target language and a sequencing number that will permit the cards to be easily arranged in the proper order. The opposite side contains either the English meaning of the dialogue line or a drawing illustrating the meaning of the line.

Structure drills. Use a separate card for each drill item. One side of the card contains the drill cue, the other side contains the correct response. Cards should be numbered for proper sequencing.

Question/Answer exercises. Use a separate card for each question. One side contains the question, the other side the answer. Several possible answers may be included for some kinds of questions. Sequencing is not necessary unless the questions follow a logical order.

Cards can be used by pairs of students or in groups of up to five. In pairs students alternate drilling each other with the cards. In groups a leader can conduct each exercise, or the cards can be distributed randomly among the group members who take turns asking questions or cuing drill items. With illustrated dialogue cards the picture is shown as a cue and students try to say the dialogue line it suggests.

Testing vocabulary

Sonnanstine (141) uses cards to test vocabulary in groups of five or six. Students are given face down sets of cards. Each card contains a contextual clue to a previously learned vocabulary item without giving the item itself. Each student turns over one of his cards and constructs a sentence containing the required vocabulary item. The procedure continues around the group until the supply of cards has been exhausted. Additional procedures for dialogue practice, structure drill, directed dialogue, vocabulary practice, question/answer exercises, and other skill-practice activities are described by Disick (42, pp. 171–73), Freilich (50), and McLennan (98).

Creating dialogues and skits

Once students have learned a dialogue, they can create their own variations of it in groups of two or three. Each group then presents its variation to the class (Knop, 85). On a more sophisticated level groups of four or five can create their own original dialogues and skits for presentation to the class (Ghan and Rickel, 52; Tiefenbrun, 152). Alternatively, the presentations might be tape-recorded or videotaped. One week is suggested as an appropriate length of time for adequate preparation, including planning the situation, writing the script, revising the script with the teacher's help, practicing and rehearsing, and presenting the finished product (Ghan and Rickel, 52).

Oral production

Group oral compositions also require cooperative effort on the part of group members. In this procedure students pool their linguistic and imaginative resources to describe what is happening in a picture (Heard, 68). Similar activities include oral resumes of reading material and oral presentations on assigned or chosen topics, both of which can lead to additional exploratory comments and questions (Quinn, 118). Students can also construct stories based on cartoons (Freilich, 49).

Hahn (63) describes a procedure that, though implemented in a FLES class, could be readily adapted for high school or college students. Students were grouped according to fluency level. Each group consisted of four members and a peer leader. Leaders practiced with tape-recorded questions and possible answers focusing on discussion of a picture or creation of a story based on pictures. Under the leader's guidance each group prepared a story, skit, or sample discussion and presented it to the entire class. Surprisingly good presentations were developed by all groups.

Writing

While such activities involve primarily oral skills, they can also be organized as writing exercises, with each group preparing a written composition in lieu of, or as a follow-up to, an oral presentation (Baker, 9). Here again the quality of the group product often exceeds that which even the best students might be able to achieve by themselves (Carstens, 27).

Listening comprehension

Kalivoda, Morain, and Elkins (80) have developed the "audio-motor unit," a listening comprehension strategy that can be easily adapted for student performance in pairs or small groups The technique requires students to respond physically to a series of oral commands organized around a central theme (for example, making a stew, going on a picnic).

An activity that combines listening comprehension with oral practice is described by Pill (115). Each group member is given a different short passage accompanied by several comprehension questions. He reads the passage aloud, reads the questions, rereads the passage, then puts the questions to the other group members. When one passage is exhausted, the process is repeated by the next reader with the next "minicomprehension." For a group of three, six questions give two per listener, nine questions give three per listener, and so on. Separate content is not necessary for each group; any number of different groups can work with the same passages and questions.

To develop listening comprehension in combination with writing skills Carstens (27) suggests giving tape-recorded passages to groups of four to seven students. Each group prepares its written consensus (not merely a transcription) of what is said on the tape. Alternative strategies for completing the exercise are provided on worksheets.

Conversation

The art of conversing freely in the target language is difficult to master, but conversation skills can be developed through small-group activities. Hanzeli and Love (65) report the results of a summer Spanish course in which groups of students were simply encouraged to talk informally among themselves in the target language during part of each class period. The instructor circulated among the groups, stimulating involvement. After 40 contact hours students were conversing freely and accurately on a number of subjects. Such felicitous outcomes, however, may not always emerge from unstructured conversational situations. Rivers (124) feels that carefully chosen topics of interest rather than the group mood are more likely to stimulate conversation. In this connection Ciotti (30) observes that group members communicate more when there is a discrepancy in group opinion. But Klin (82) maintains that controversial topics tend to inhibit rather than stimulate conversation because they place on the student the double burden of having to express a point of view in the foreign language and of marshalling supporting arguments in its favor. Gianetti (53) believes that all topics of high interest can stimulate active group conversation. He lists 110 such topics. Conner (33) suggests panel discussions involving five students–two on each side of the question and a moderator who introduces the topic and keeps the discussion going.

Rotation drill

To facilitate the transition from mechanical drill to liberated conversation Sinnema (135) suggests the use of the "rotation drill," which is a sequence of conversational questions with a variety of answers to each question provided on a guidesheet. For a group of four each question has four proposed answers. The leader asks the question and the others give the various answers in clockwise rotation around the group. The leader gives the fourth answer to his own question; the next question is asked by the student to his left, and the procedure continues until all questions on the guidesheet have been exhausted.

Structured conversation

Logan also takes a structured approach to the development of conversational skills. He has produced graduated materials centering on specific topics such as greetings, shopping, traveling, eating. These consist of "directed dialogues" that suggest in English what the student might say in the target language. Students learn the essential vocabulary and structures before gathering in conversational groups of four to six where they practice the structured conversations with guidesheets under the guidance of a teacher, native-speaking paraprofessional, or student assistant (Logan, 95; Morrey, 104).

Ciotti's procedure (30, 31), based on her extensive research on group dynamics, utilizes various networks of communication in three conversational stages: controlled, partially controlled, and noncontrolled. As the constraints of leadership are gradually withdrawn, the verbal interaction in these stages progressively assumes the characteristics of natural conversation.

Conversation and interview cards

Another systematic progressive approach to the development of conversational skills has been developed by Bonin and Birckbichler (17). Their technique utilizes conversation and interview cards containing questions of graduated difficulty. Questions are direct at the least sophisticated level, and students may simply ask them of each other in the group. At the intermediate level, indirect questions of greater length and complexity require a higher degree of language skill on the part of both questioner and answerer. At more advanced levels, the questions elicit reasons, explanations, opinions, and feelings from answerers.

Fusion of four skills

Elkins, Kalivoda, and Morain (44) have devised a strategy that fuses the four skills for communicative exchange. The procedure involves two groups of six students. The groups are then divided into subgroups of three. In each group a story is read, then retold to others who write it down. After several such exchanges within and between groups in a designated pattern, the final versions are compared with the original ones and the successes and failures of communication are discussed.

Simulation

Simulation and role-playing are excellent means of developing students' communicative competence in a group setting. As a "culminating experience," Lafayette (86) proposes that each instructional unit conclude with a simulated communication exercise that would apply the material introduced in the unit and involve students creatively in the use of the language. Runte (126) and Zajac (164) demonstrate how the classroom can be transformed into a simulated bank, restaurant, filling station, hospital, international airport, or *métro* station to provide a realistic environment for communicative exchange. Carton-Caprio (28, 29) gives detailed descriptions of shopping and restaurant simulation experiences. Piehl and Bell (114) show how students can create simulated radio programs. Wells (158) and Morgenstern (102) propose more sophisticated simulations such as mock trials, U.N. debates, and U.S. Senate committee investigations. Purcell (116) describes a course in Business Spanish in which students created a mock Spanish-speaking company.

Telephone activities

Use of the telephone is the focus of simulation exercises adapted by Baker (8) from a format created by Lichet (91). Communication tasks are graduated in difficulty and complexity; they range from simple information-seeking to giving a caller the bureaucratic runaround by referring him to a succession of other phone numbers. Hartley's (67) students use interoffice telephone lines to make mock emergency calls (fire, police, ambulance) and to converse with each other in the target language.

Role-playing

Zelson (165, 166) has developed many role-playing activities to be performed by students in pairs or small groups. The following are examples:

> Make excuses to your instructor for not having completed a long-term assignment. Try to get an extension. Your teacher is opposed to it [because] you have been known to do this on many other occasions (165, p. 28).

> [Females] A girl whom you and several of your friends despise has married a fellow whom you all really like and had thought you would like to get serious about. Gossip about her! [Any number can play.] (166, p. 35).

Dramatic productions

Dramatic productions of various kinds afford students many

opportunities to work together in groups. Morain (103) points out that a prepared dramatic script provides practice in reading and speaking, and students can get further language practice by writing their own scripts. In addition, she emphasizes that physical action accompanying verbal expression enhances acquisition of language skills. There is also a wealth of culture and vocabulary to be explored in the learning of stage directions and production techniques. On a simple level Birkmaier (16) suggests that groups take turns acting out a familiar story or a new one they have read. She points out that difficult passages can often become more comprehensible when group members assume roles and perform the actions of the characters. Students in groups can make up their own skits based on reading selections or assigned topics. The skits can then be recorded as radio or television plays (Shepherd, 134) or produced as films (Listerman, 92, 93; Meredith, 100).

Production of teaching materials

A useful group activity is the production of teaching materials. Becker and Powell (13) describe in detail how groups of students can make their own tape-slide presentations on topics such as cooking; making plans for a trip; a day in the life of a student; and going to a restaurant, the library, or the zoo. After reading a Spanish fairy tale, Carfora's (26) advanced students produced it as a puppet show and videotaped the performance. The videotape was used for teaching the story to other classes.

Newspapers and magazines

Target-language newspapers and magazines furnish a wealth of material for small-group work. De Ponte (39) displays clippings on her bulletin board that form the basis for group activities focusing on foods, current events, sports, employment, and other topics of interest. Among other suggestions for group activities using newspaper and magazine material, Jorstad (78) offers the following:

Writing want ads for items students wish to buy or sell
Selecting a room or apartment that meets specified conditions
Interviewing each other for advertised jobs
Inquiring about jobs offered, housing advertised, etc.
Spending a designated sum of money in a department store whose ads appear in the newspaper
Writing letters to the editor
Creating news broadcasts based on published stories
Preparing TV commercials based on newspaper ads

Games

Games are an ever-popular group activity. Joiner (76) describes a variety of simple guessing games that are especially appropriate at the early stages of language learning. Vocabulary practice is the focus of other games developed by Hartley (66). Cooper (35) has invented a German map game with a cultural orientation. Even the distasteful chore of language review can be made enjoyable if it is structured as a group competition, as demonstrated by Bornscheuer (19). For detailed descriptions of other group games the reader is referred to Coulombe et al. (36, pp. 44–45, 71–82), Saunders (130), and Strasheim (145, 146). Jenks (74, pp. 109–10) lists a number of companies marketing various games that can be played in small groups.

Affective techniques

With its potential for reducing inhibition and maximizing student-to-student interaction, the small group is an ideal context for learning experiences designed to help students explore their beliefs, values, interests, and concerns through the target language. Disick and Barbanel (43) have surveyed a number of these affective techniques, including values voting, rank order, exercises in life examination, incomplete sentences, reflective listening, human development program communication exercises, and interview techniques. More detailed descriptions of the activities can be found in Papalia and Zampogna (111), Stoller et al. (144), Wilson and Wattenmaker (160), Wolfe and Howe (162), and Wolfe, Howe, and Keating (163). (See also Chapter 7 of this volume.)

Culture-learning activities

Many culture-learning experiences can be effectively structured as small-group activities. Meade and Morain (99) advocate the use of the *culture cluster,* a set of interrelated culture capsules each of which introduces a different aspect of a central theme. The procedures outlined permit group role-playing and simulation in an accurate cultural context. Santoni (127, 128, 129) has developed an approach that combines authentic cultural documents (for example, interviews with representative members of major socioeconomic classes in a French village) with role-playing and videotaping. Role-playing and simulation are also suggested by Cooke (34), Disick (42, p. 214), Smithson (139), and Taylor (151) as a means of reinforcing cultural concepts and of developing positive attitudes toward the target culture. Elkins, Kalivoda, and Morain (45) show how the audiomotor unit can be adapted to small-group cultural exploration.

Publications by Walpole (155) and Scott (132) contain a number of useful ideas for small-group activities centering on concepts related to French- and Spanish-speaking cultures respectively.

Tamarkin (150) found one satisfactory solution to the perennial problem of creating cultural materials. While on a trip to Puerto Rico, she had groups of her students prepare minidramas based on their observations and experiences in the target culture.

The communications media constitute another source of material. Sonnanstine (141) cuts up magazines, newspapers, and even foreign telephone directories. She arranges the material topically, pastes it on cards, and files it for later use. The procedure is much more efficient than accumulating stacks of publications. The cards can include questions directing students' attention to significant aspects of the material. Jenks (75) suggests that student groups prepare dialogues based on articles pertaining to the target culture selected from American newspapers and magazines. He points out that foreign publications are generally too difficult for any but the most advanced students and those designed for American students often fail to provide stimulation and pleasure. Loew (94), however, finds target-language publications a suitable resource that groups of students can use in developing culture packets on topics such as automobile parts, clothing fashions, foods. In Piehl and Bell's (114) classes groups taped French shortwave broadcasts, then prepared materials comparing American commercial radio and television with the French state-controlled electronic media.

Edible culture

A unique culture-learning experience is described by Michaels (101). Her students studied the structure of a typical French city. Each of five groups then constructed a different section of a miniature town—out of cake and other edible material. When the project was completed, other classes were invited to share in eating it!

Teacher Education

If, as Rivers (123) believes, the day is at hand when language teachers "will be expected to break up the more easily controlled lecture-practice class hour to allow for a variety of groupings . . .

and differentiated learning approaches" (p. 25), teachers will have to be trained to do so. Ideally such training should begin in the preservice phase of their professional preparation. Rivers advocates a general foreign language methods course for students of all languages, followed by an *in practicum* language-specific methods course in which prospective teachers can practice, among other things, "the organization and conduct of small-group learning" (p. 29).

Methods-course exercises

Such an arrangement may not be possible for all teacher education institutions, but there is certainly much that can be done within the context of present programs and courses. Smith (136) suggests that methods students can be given descriptions of the various ability and interest levels existing in a hypothetical class and develop schedules for a class of 40 to 50 minutes, showing how students can be grouped, regrouped, and worked with as a full class. As part of a lesson-planning exercise, they can construct remedial and enrichment activities for a 10- to 15-minute grouping session at the end of a class period. Allen (2) describes a course in the teaching of intermediate foreign language in which students prepare performance objectives, learning activities, and assignments for three different ability groups; construct materials and activities for various interest groups; and develop activities appropriate for small-group and large-group instruction. Baslaw et al. (11) recommend that methods courses include instruction in the dynamics of small groups, coordination of groups within the classroom, and techniques for small-group and individual evaluation of content.

Direct experiences

Hubbard (72) advocates direct experiences for methods students with real learners in a live language class. By working informally with individuals and small groups, she argues, the prospective teacher can develop sensitivity to pupils' diverse needs, interests, and abilities. Purcell (117) uses his undergraduate Spanish classes as a methods laboratory; with materials they have prepared, methods students conduct small-group structure drill, directed dialogue, question/answer exercises, games, and task-oriented communication activities. Fryer and Dannerbeck (51) have methods students observe, prepare for, and teach small-group conversation sessions in a self-paced undergraduate program. Smith (138), too, arranges for methods students to serve as aides in individualized undergraduate

Discussion groups

classes where they conduct group conversation activities. To illustrate grouping procedures, he divides his methods classes into small discussion groups for various purposes:

1 To explore techniques for teaching language skills
2 For bit-teaching demonstrations and critiques
3 To discuss classroom observations with the teachers
4 To explore apprehensions about student teaching with student teachers
5 To discuss with high school students what good language teaching should be
6 To prepare individualized instruction units that are then taught to other groups (Smith, 137).

Moskowitz (105) believes that prospective teachers should learn how to learn on their own. She constructed a successful simulation exercise that required groups of methods students to develop solutions to the problem (realistic in relation to today's job market!) of preparing to teach a second subject in which they were not certified. At Indiana University Lafayette and Strasheim (87) also give simulation assignments that focus on tasks that beginning teachers commonly face in the field. One assignment required groups, acting as high school language departments, to develop a student-oriented rationale for foreign language study. Three students produced a comic strip featuring "Captain Fore Lang," a costumed hero charged with the task of persuading students to study a language (Burden, Summers, and Renner, 24). The humorous but effective presentation has been adapted as part of *ACTFL's Accent on Promoting Foreign Languages*.

Simulation

Microteaching offers other possibilities for group experiences in teacher education. At the University of Minnesota methods students microteach to groups of peers (Jorstad, 79). To simulate beginning classes, microlessons in one language are taught to students of other languages; advanced classes are simulated by grouping students of the same language. DeLorenzo (37, 38) suggests forming microteaching teams of four or five students, noting that a greater number significantly reduces valuable critique time. In his process each team studies videotapes of basic audiolingual teaching skills before taping individual team mem-

Microteaching

bers performances of the skills. After systematic critique and any necessary reteaching, team members prepare different segments of a lesson plan supplied by a local high school teacher. They team-teach the lesson to the teacher's class of real pupils at the school. By increasing student-to-student interaction, the procedure reportedly facilitates the peer critique process, enables the less-confident students to profit from their peers' suggestions, and helps to develop necessary receptivity to constructive criticism.

Teaching to small groups

Altman and Ramirez (4), however, felt that conventional microteaching did not provide sufficient opportunity for the prospective teacher to teach different kinds of lessons to diversified groups of learners. They found it more effective to assign intern teachers on a rotating basis to heterogeneous groups of beginning, intermediate, and advanced students, ranging in size from three to twenty. Each intern received extensive experience in instructing small groups and in tutoring individuals, together with limited experience in whole-class instruction.

Training teaching assistants

Freed (47, 48) is concerned with the often neglected training of graduate teaching assistants in charge of undergraduate language classes. As part of their methods instruction at the University of Pennsylvania, she gives teaching assistants suggestions for dividing large classes into small groups for various kinds of activities: paired oral practice and information-getting, student-prepared questions on reading material, group written compositions, and so on. She observes, however, that while teaching assistants are generally receptive to the rationale for more active student participation through group work, the pressure of having to meet departmental objectives, combined with other influences, tends to limit the extent to which they are willing or able to implement group work.

Summary

1 Small-group work is an indispensable component of a self-paced individualized instruction program. But its effectiveness is not limited to this instructional mode. To the contrary, small-group work can make possible a high degree of individualization in the conventional instructional situation. There is little that is done in the whole-class situa-

tion that cannot be done at least as well, and in many cases better, in small groups.

2 If small-group work is to be a productive learning experience for students, the teacher must plan and prepare carefully. Students need to understand why they are working in groups, what they are expected to do, and how they can go about doing it. Group work should start as early as possible in the language sequence with well-structured activities. It should continue at subsequent levels with increased flexibility, provision for creativity, and opportunities for students to make decisions regarding the kinds of activities they prefer.

3 While there is no empirical research in foreign language education to confirm the hypothesis, group size appears to be a significant factor in relation to some kinds of activities. In general, the smaller the group the greater the amount of verbal interaction and the quantity of material that can be covered effectively. Sociological research points to an optimum group size of from five to seven members. Larger groups, especially those engaged in task accomplishment, may become unproductive.

4 Various kinds of help are available to the teacher who wants to implement group work in his classes. Group leaders can be selected from within the class itself. Native paraprofessionals can also serve as aides. When they work as classroom assistants, advanced students seem to have a strong motivating effect on lower-level students and in turn are often motivated to greater learning efforts.

5 As textbook publishers gradually move toward the development of more flexible materials, they would do well to consider the inclusion of procedures and suggestions designed to help teachers adapt the materials for small-group work.

6 Ideally, the place for teachers to acquire the basics of small-group learning is in their preservice preparation. Teacher education programs can offer various kinds of group-related training, ranging from simple lesson planning to actual experiences in working in and with groups. The most valuable contribution a teacher education program can make, however, may well be a fundamental reorientation of the prospective teacher's role perception

from that of dominant authority figure to that of helper, from that of information-giver and getter to that of facilitator of learning. With this kind of reorientation, small-group learning is much more likely to become an option the teacher can freely and deliberately choose.

/

References, Small-group learning

1 Albert, Renaud. Personal Communication, 1976. [Letter.]

2 Allen, Edward D. "A Course in the Teaching of Intermediate Foreign Language." *Modern Language Journal* 56(1972):414–17.

3 ——— and Rebecca M. Valette. *Modern Language Classroom Techniques.* New York:Harcourt Brace Jovanovich, 1972.

4 Altman, Howard B., and Arnulfo G. Ramirez. "Beyond Micro-Teaching:Some First Steps in Individualizing Preservice Training for Foreign Language Teachers." *Modern Language Journal* 55(1971):276–80.

5 Archibeque, Joe D. "Utilizing the Advanced Spanish Student As a Classroom Tutor." *Hispania* 53(1970):70–72.

6 Arendt, Jermaine D. "The Function and Techniques of Group Work in an Individualized Program," 105–13 in Howard B. Altman and Robert L. Politzer,eds., *Individualizing Foreign Language Instruction.* Proceedings of the Stanford Conference. Rowley, Massachusetts:Newbury House, 1971.

7 ——— Martin T. Barrett, and Lola A. Mackey. "Reports and Recommendations:Committee on Group Work in an Individualized Foreign Language Program," 114–16 in Howard B. Altman and Robert L. Politzer,eds., *Individualizing Foreign Language Instruction.* Proceedings of the Stanford Conference. Rowley, Massachusetts: Newbury House, 1971.

8 Baker, Reid E. *Developing Communication Skills Via Telephone Simulation.* [Paper presented at the Central States Conference on the Teaching of Foreign Languages, Detroit, April 1976.]

9 ——— *Ideas for Small-Group Activities in the Foreign Language Classroom.* [Unpublished Workshop Materials.] [Mimeo.]

10 Barnett, Harriett. "Peer Teaching." *Hispania* 52 (1973):635–38.

11 Baslaw, Annette S., Joan S. Freilich, William E. DeLorenzo, Thomas H. Geno, Charles R. Hancock, and Robert R. Sherburne. "Training for Student-Centered Language Programs," 15–72 in Warren C. Born,ed., *Toward Student-Centered Foreign-Language Programs.* Reports of the Working Committees, Northeast Conference on the Teaching of Foreign Languages. Montpelier, Vermont:The Conference, 1974.

12 Beach, Jo Love. "Are Your Advanced Students Bored?" *Accent on ACTFL* 4,ii(1973):5.

13 Becker, James E., and Patricia B. Powell. "Students Can Prepare Their Own Slide Show." *Accent on ACTFL* 5,ii(1975):18–19.

14 Benson, Arland N. *Personalized Education Using Group Methods.* St. Paul:Minnesota Department of Education, 1974. [EDRS: ED 109 521.]

15 Bingham, Vernon A. Personal Communication, 1976. [Letter.]

16 Birkmaier, Emma M. "The Meaning of Creativity in Foreign Language Teaching." *Modern Language Journal* 55(1971):345–53.

17 Bonin, Thérèse M., and Diane W. Birckbichler. "Real Communication Through Interview and Conversation Cards." *Modern Language Journal* 59(1975):22–25.

18 Booth, Venita. *Guidelines for Implementing Individualized Instruction in Foreign Languages.* Corpus Christi, Texas:Corpus Christi Independent School District, 1973. [EDRS: ED 081 258.]

19 Bornscheuer, Joan H. "Review Can Be Fun." *Accent on ACTFL* 5,ii(1975):9–10.

20 Boylan, Patricia, Marty Knorre, John A. Lett, Jr., Aristobulo Pardo, and William Ratliff. *Cara a cara:A Basic Reader for Communication in Spanish.* New York:Holt, Rinehart & Winston, in press.

21 ——— and Alice Omaggio, *Person-Centered Education:Expanded Roles for Foreign Language Classes.* [Detroit:Advancement Press, forthcoming.]

22 Braswell, David M. "Individualizing a Junior High School Foreign Language Program," 103–15 in Howard B. Altman,ed., *Individualizing the Foreign Language Classroom:Perspectives for Teachers.* Rowley, Massachusetts: Newbury House, 1972.

23 Brown, Loree. "Study Materials for Tutors," 34–40 in *Guidelines for Individualization of Foreign Language Instruction.* Salt Lake City: Utah State Board of Education, 1972.

24 Burden, Debra S., Elizabeth G. Summers, and Terri L. Renner. "The Continuing Story of Captain Fore Lang." *Accent on ACTFL* 5,i(1975): 9–11.

25 Cameron-Bacon, Susan M. "Using the Student

Assistant in Individualized Foreign-Language Instruction." *Foreign Language Annals* 7(1974): 353–56.

26 Carfora, Juanita. "Video-Taping Class Shows Builds Library of Aids." *Accent on ACTFL* 4,iii (1974):4.

27 Carstens, Paul. "Small-Group Listening-Transcription: Path to a New Dimension in Foreign Language Learning?" *American Foreign Language Teacher* 3,iii(1973):32–33.

28 Carton-Caprio, Dana. "Enlivening the Adult Education Foreign Language Conversation Course." *Modern Language Journal* 58(1974):343–45.

29 ——— "Learning By Doing: A Practical Foreign Language Classroom Experience." *Modern Language Journal* 59(1975):97–100.

30 Ciotti, Marianne C. *A Conceptual Framework for Small-Group Instruction in French.* Columbus: The Ohio State University, 1969. [Doctoral Dissertation.]

31 ——— "A Conceptual Framework for Small-Group Instruction in High School." *Foreign Language Annals* 3(1969):75–89.

32 Clark, Bill M., and Marl E. Ramsey. *Why Small-Group Instruction?* Des Moines, Iowa: Polk County Board of Education, 1970. [EDRS: ED 083 234.]

33 Conner, Maurice W. "Eliciting Oral Expression in the German Class." *Accent on ACTFL* 5,ii (1975):17.

34 Cooke, Madeline A. "Suggestions for Developing More Positive Attitudes Toward Native Speakers of Spanish," 118–36 in H. Ned Seelye,ed., *Perspectives for Teachers of Latin American Culture.* Springfield, Illinois: Office of the Superintendent of Public Instruction, 1970.

35 Cooper, Thomas. "A German Map Game." *American Foreign Language Teacher* 4,iv(1974):3–5, 33.

36 Coulombe, Roger, Jean-Claude Barré, Cynthia Fostle, Norman Poulin, and Sandra Savignon. *Voix et visages de la France, Level I.* Teacher's Edition. Chicago: Rand McNally, 1974.

37 DeLorenzo, William E. "Microteaching as a Transitional Technique to Student Teaching." *Foreign Language Annals* 8(1975):239–45.

38 ——— "Rationale, Description, and Feasibility of a Partially Programmed Foreign Language Methods Course." *Foreign Language Annals* 7 (1973):224–30.

39 De Ponte, Janina. "Reinforcing the Use of Periodicals With the Bulletin Board." *Accent on ACTFL* 5,i(1975):19–20.

40 Deveny, John J.,Jr., and Jonathan C. Bookout. "The Intensive Language Course: Toward a Successful Approach." *Foreign Language Annals* 9 (1976):58–63.

41 Disick, Renée S. "Developing Positive Attitudes in Intermediate Foreign Language Classes." *Modern Language Journal* 56(1972):417–20.

42 ——— *Individualizing Language Instruction.* New York: Harcourt Brace Jovanovich, 1975.

43 ——— and Laura Barbanel. "Affective Education and Foreign Language Learning," 185–222 in Gilbert A. Jarvis,ed., *The Challenge of Communication.* ACTFL Review of Foreign Language Education, Volume 6. Skokie, Illinois: National Textbook Company, 1974.

44 Elkins, Robert J., Theodore B. Kalivoda, and Genelle Morain. "Fusion of the Four Skills: A Technique for Facilitating Communicative Exchange." *Modern Language Journal* 56(1972): 426–29.

45 ——— "Teaching Culture through the Audio-Motor Unit." *Foreign Language Annals* 6(1972): 61–67.

46 Finstein, Milton W. "French for Reading Knowledge—An Option." *French Review* 45(1972): 838–41.

47 Freed, Barbara F. "Why Train Teaching Assistants?—Foreign Language and Communication at the College Level." *ADFL Bulletin* 7,ii(1975): 9–14.

48 ——— Personal Communication, 1976. [Telephone.]

49 Freilich, Joan S. "Imagination—Let's Tap It." *Accent on ACTFL* 4,ii(1973):26,38.

50 ——— "Toward Individualization: The Flexible Classroom." *Foreign Language Annals* 7(1974): 358–61.

51 Fryer, T. Bruce, and Francis J. Dannerbeck. "An Undergraduate Experience in Individualization of Foreign Language Instruction." *Foreign Language Annals* 7(1973):119–20.

52 Ghan, Zoe Ann, and Kathryn Rickel. "The Liberated Dialogue, or 'Let the Kids Make Up Their Own Dialogues.'" *Foreign Language Annals* 3 (1969):237–46.

53 Gianetti, George. "Variety in the Advanced Spanish Class: Emphasis on Art, Music and Drama," 100–09 in Frank M. Grittner,ed., *Careers, Communication and Culture in Foreign Language Teaching.* Skokie, Illinois: National Textbook Company, 1974.

54 Giauque, Gerald S. "Using Native Speakers as Teaching Assistants." *Foreign Language Annals* 8(1975):128–32.

55 Gilman, Robert A., and Hyde Flippo. "Aides Set-Up Pays Dividends." *Accent on ACTFL* 4,ii (1973):6–7.

56 Gougher, Ronald L. "Defining Individualized Instruction of Foreign Languages," 1–5 in Ronald L. Gougher,ed., *Individualization of Instruction in Foreign Languages: A Practical Guide.* Philadelphia: Center for Curriculum Development, 1972.

57 ——— "Individualized Instruction: Solutions for Management," 21–26 in Roger Coulombe et al., *Voix et visages de la France, Level I.* Teacher's Edition. Chicago: Rand McNally, 1974.

58 Grittner, Frank M. "Maintaining Foreign Language Skills for the Advanced-Course Drop-Out." *Foreign Language Annals* 2(1968):205–11.

59 ——— "The Teacher As Co-Learner: Interest-Centered Materials," 11–29 in Frank M. Grittner, ed., *Student Motivation and the Foreign Lan-*

guage Teacher. Skokie, Illinois: National Textbook Company, 1974.

60 ——— *Teaching Foreign Languages*. New York: Harper & Row, 1969.

61 ——— and Fred H. LaLeike. *Individualized Foreign Language Instruction*. Skokie, Illinois: National Textbook Company, 1973.

62 *Guidelines for Individualization of Foreign Language Instruction*. Salt Lake City: Utah State Board of Education, 1972.

63 Hahn, Sally G. "Discussion Groups in the Foreign Language Elementary Classroom." *French Review* 42(1968):294–97.

64 Hammelman, William M. R., and Melvin L. Nielsen. "The Native Paraprofessional: Identifying His Role in the Foreign Language Program. *Foreign Language Annals* 7(1974):346–52.

65 Hanzeli, Victor E., and F. William D. Love. "From Individualized Instruction to Individualized Learning." *Foreign Language Annals* 5 (1972):321–30.

66 Hartley, Peggy J. "Varied Activities Brighten Task." *Accent on ACTFL* 4,ii(1973):19,39.

67 ——— "Dialing Data Diversifies Speaking Situations." *Accent on ACTFL* 4,iv(1974):17–18.

68 Heard, Lorraine E. "Foreign Language and the Group Context: Expanding Student Roles." *Foreign Language Annals* 5(1972):313–20.

69 Herbert, Charles H.,project director. *We Learn Together: A Small Group Process Manual for Secondary Teachers*. San Barnardino, California: San Bernardino County Schools, 1972.

70 Horne, Kibbey M. "Optimum Class Size for Intensive Language Instruction." *Modern Language Journal* 54(1970):189–95.

71 Hosenfeld, Carol. "The New Student Role: Individual Differences and Implications for Instruction," 129–67 in Gilbert A. Jarvis,ed., *Perspective: A New Freedom*. ACTFL Review of Foreign Language Education, Volume 7. Skokie, Illinois: National Textbook Company, 1975.

72 Hubbard, Louise J. "Aptitude, Attitude, and Sensitivity." *Foreign Language Annals* 8(1975): 33–37.

73 Jarvis, Gilbert A., Thérèse M. Bonin, Donald E. Corbin, and Diane W. Birckbichler. *Connaître et se connaître: A Basic Reader*. New York, Holt, Rinehart & Winston, 1976.

74 Jenks, Frederick L. "Foreign Language Materials: A Status Report and Trends Analysis," 93–128 in Gilbert A. Jarvis,ed., *Perspective: A New Freedom*. ACTFL Review of Foreign Language Education, Volume 7. Skokie, Illinois: National Textbook Company, 1975.

75 ——— "Teaching Culture Through the Use of Newspapers." *American Foreign Language Teacher* 2,iv(1972):29–40.

76 Joiner, Elizabeth G. "Keep Them Guessing." *American Foreign Language Teacher* 4,ii(1974): 16–18.

77 ——— "Tailoring Language Instruction to Student Needs," 151–84 in Gilbert A. Jarvis,ed., *The Challenge of Communication*. ACTFL Review of Foreign Language Education, Volume 6. Skokie, Illinois: National Textbook Company, 1974.

78 Jorstad, Helen L. "Newspapers and Magazines in the Second Language Classroom," 91–103 in Robert C. Lafayette,ed., *The Culture Revolution in Foreign Language Teaching*. Skokie, Illinois: National Textbook Company, 1975.

79 ——— "Training Prospective Foreign Language Teachers at the University of Minnesota." *Foreign Language Annals* 6(1973):521–23.

80 Kalivoda, Theodore B., Genelle Morain, and Robert J. Elkins. "The Audio-Motor Unit: A Listening Comprehension Strategy That Works." *Foreign Language Annals* 4(1971):392–400.

81 Kennedy, Dora F. "Innovative Programs Revisited: Oxon Hill." *Foreign Language Annals* 8 (1975):209–10.

82 Klin, George. "Content and Methods in Conversation Courses." *French Review* 43(1970):641–47.

83 Kline, Michael B. "Individualizing French Through the Credit/No Credit, Open-Ended Approach." *Foreign Language Annals* 9(1976): 22–27.

84 Knop, Constance K. "Gaining Better Student Support for the Foreign Language Program," 95–106 in Frank M. Grittner,ed., *Student Motivation and the Foreign Language Teacher*. Skokie, Illinois: National Textbook Company, 1974.

85 ——— "Toward Free Conversation." *American Foreign Language Teacher* 2,iv(1972):5–9.

86 Lafayette, Robert C. "The Case for Student Creativity." *American Foreign Language Teacher* 4, iii(1974):14–17,36.

87 ——— Personal Communication, 1976. [Telephone.]

88 Lamson, Howard. "Intensive Language and Cultural Immersion: A Cooperative Method." *Foreign Language Annals* 7(1974):668–73.

89 Lepke, Helen S. *An Exploratory Study of Cognitive Style As an Aspect of Prediction of Achievement in Individualized and Conventional Instruction in Beginning German*. Akron, Ohio: The University of Akron, 1975. [Doctoral Dissertation.]

90 ——— *What's Your Style?—Learning Style That Is!* [Paper presented at the Annual Conference of the Ohio Modern Language Teachers Association, Columbus, March 1976.]

91 Lichet, Raymond. "Jeux du téléphone." *Le Français dans le Monde* 30(January–February 1965): 32–36.

92 Listerman, Randall W. " 'Das Experiment' Stirs Campus-Wide Interest." *Accent on ACTFL* 4,iv (1974):7.

93 ——— "Innovative Involvement with Foreign Languages." *Foreign Language Annals* 7(1973): 243–47.

94 Loew, Helene. "FL Magazine Plus Planning Equal Up-To-Date Culture Units." *Accent on ACTFL* 3,iv(1973):6–8.

95 Logan, Gerald E. *German Conversational Practice.* Teacher's Guide. Rowley, Massachusetts: Newbury House, 1974. [See also parallel publications for French and Spanish.]

96 ——— *Individualized Foreign Language Learning:An Organic Process.* Rowley, Massachusetts: Newbury House, 1971.

97 Love, F. William D., and Lucille J. Honig. *Options and Perspectives:A Sourcebook of Innovative Foreign Language Programs in Action, K-12.* New York:Modern Language Association of America, 1973.

98 McLennan, Robert L. "Making Existing Materials Work in an Individualized Foreign Language Program," 145–58 in Howard B. Altman,ed., *Individualizing the Foreign Language Classroom:Perspectives for Teachers.* Rowley, Massachusetts:Newbury House, 1972.

99 Meade, Betsy, and Genelle Morain. "The Culture Cluster." *Foreign Language Annals* 6(1973): 331–38.

100 Meredith, Dennis. "Film Festival Works Wonders." *Accent on ACTFL* 3,ii(1972):33.

101 Michaels, Judith M. "Advanced Students 'Eat Up' Their Own French City." *Accent on ACTFL* 4,v (1974):24–25.

102 Morgenstern, Douglas. "Eight Activities for the Conversation Class." *Modern Language Journal* 60(1976):35–38.

103 Morain, Genelle. "Humanism in the Classroom: A Dramatic Proposal," 1–11 in Frank M. Grittner,ed., *Careers, Communication and Culture in Foreign Language Teaching.* Skokie, Illinois: National Textbook Company, 1974.

104 Morrey, Robert A. "Individualization of Foreign Language Instruction Through Differentiated Staffing." *Modern Language Journal* 56(1972): 483–88.

105 Moskowitz, Gertrude. "For Methods Instructors: A Less Visible, Less Verbal Approach." *Foreign Language Annals* 5(1972):232–36.

106 Olmstead, Joseph A. *Small-Group Instruction: Theory and Practice.* Alexandria, Virginia:Human Resource Research Organization, 1974. [EDRS: ED 094 137.]

107 Otto, Frank. "Individualizing Instruction through Team Teaching." *Hispania* 51(1968):473–75.

108 Papalia, Anthony. "An Assessment of Attitudes and Behaviors of Foreign Language Teachers." *Foreign Language Annals* 7(1973):231–36.

109 ——— "Attitudes of Students, Teachers, and Administrators Toward Ability Grouping for Individualizing Instruction." *Foreign Language Annals* 9(1975):54–55.

110 ——— and Joseph Zampogna. "An Experimental Study of Teachers' Behaviors and Their Effects on FL Attrition." *Modern Language Journal* 56(1972):421–24.

111 ——— and Joseph Zampogna. "An Experiment in Individualized Instruction through Small Group Interaction." *Foreign Language Annals* 5(1972):302–06.

112 Parker, Douglas C. "Implementing Achievement Groups for Better Modern Language Learning." *French Review* 45(1971):343–52.

113 Phillips, June K. "Individualization and Personalization," 219–61 in Gilbert A. Jarvis,ed., *Responding to New Realities.* ACTFL Review of Foreign Language Education, Volume 5. Skokie, Illinois:National Textbook Company, 1974.

114 Piehl, Helen, and Ann Bell. " 'Oh Say Can You See'—Hear, Taste, and Even Dance in Your Foreign Language Classroom?" 88–113 in Charles Jay and Pat Castle,eds., *French Language Education:The Teaching of Culture in the Classroom.* Springfield, Illinois:Office of the Superintendent of Public Instruction, 1971.

115 Pill, Geoffrey. "Mini-Comprehensions Lead to Oral Practice." *Accent on ACTFL* 4,i(1973):27.

116 Purcell, John M. "Simulation and Success in Business Spanish." *Accent on ACTFL* 5,i(1975): 4–5.

117 ——— Personal Communication, 1976. [Letter.]

118 Quinn, David J. "Individualized Learning in Three-Quarters Time." *French Review* 47(1974): 594–602.

119 Reinert, Harry. "Beginners Are Individuals Too!" 89–101 in Howard B. Altman,ed., *Individualizing the Foreign Language Classroom:Perspectives for Teachers.* Rowley, Massachusetts:Newbury House, 1972.

120 ——— "Practical Guide to Individualization." *Modern Language Journal* 55(1971):156–63.

121 Rivers, Wilga M. *A Practical Guide to the Teaching of French.* New York:Oxford University Press, 1975. [See also parallel publications for German and Spanish by Rivers et al.]

122 ——— *Speaking in Many Tongues:Essays in Foreign Language Teaching.* Rowley, Massachusetts: Newbury House, 1972.

123 ——— "Students, Teachers, and the Future." *Foreign Language Annals* 8(1975):22–32.

124 ——— *Teaching Foreign Language Skills.* Chicago:University of Chicago Press, 1968.

125 ——— "Techniques for Developing Proficiency in the Spoken Language in an Individualized Foreign Language Program," 165–69 in Howard B. Altman and Robert L. Politzer,eds., *Individualizing Foreign Language Instruction.* Proceedings of the Stanford Conference. Rowley, Massachusetts:Newbury House, 1971.

126 Runte, Roseann. "Students Can Create Cultural Mini-Dramas From Class Materials." *Accent on ACTFL* 4,ii(1973):37–38.

127 Santoni, Georges V. "Using Videotape in the Advanced Conversation Class." *Foreign Language Annals* 8(1975):233–38.

128 ——— "An Integrated Approach, Through Linguistic and Cross-Cultural Exercises, to Advanced Conversation." *Foreign Language Annals* 7(1974):425–34.

129 ——— "Langue et culture et contraste." *French Review* 49(1976):355–65.

130 Saunders, Helen V.,ed., *Fun and Games With*

Foreign Languages. Charleston:West Virginia State Department of Education, 1974. [EDRS: ED 096 857.]
131 Schulz, Renate A., and Walter H. Bartz. "Free to Communicate," 47–92 in Gilbert A. Jarvis,ed., *Perspective:A New Freedom*. ACTFL Review of Foreign Language Education, Volume 7. Skokie, Illinois:National Textbook Company, 1975.
132 Scott, Joseph Reid. *Understanding Spanish-Speaking Cultures*. Hayward, California:Alameda County School Department, 1972.
133 Semke, Harriet D. "Peer-Teaching Helps!" *Foreign Language Annals* 8(1975):123–27.
134 Shepherd, W. Everitt. "An Experiment in Individualized Advanced French." *Foreign Language Annals* 3(1970):394–99.
135 Sinnema, John R. "Rotation Drills in Teaching Conversation." *Modern Language Journal* 55 (1971):269–71.
136 Smith, Alfred N. "How to Train Prospective Foreign Language Teachers in the Use of Individualized Instruction." *Foreign Language Annals* 6(1972):220–24.
137 ——— *Individualization and the Foreign Language Methods Class*. [Paper presented at the ACTFL Annual Meeting, Boston, November 1973.] [EDRS: ED 094 555.]
138 ——— Personal Communication, 1976. [Letter.]
139 Smithson, Rulon N. "French Culture and Civilization for American High School Students," 80–87 in Charles Jay and Pat Castle,eds., *French Language Education:The Teaching of Culture in the Classroom*. Springfield, Illinois:Office of the Superintendent of Public Instruction, 1971.
140 Sonnanstine, Irene. *Personalized Designs in Practical Small-Group Instruction*. [Paper presented at the Central States Conference on the Teaching of Foreign Languages, Detroit, April 1976.]
141 ——— Personal Communication, 1976. [Interview.]
142 Steiner, Florence. "Individualized Instruction." *Modern Language Journal* 55(1971):361–74.
143 ——— "Performance Objectives in the Teaching of Foreign Languages." *Foreign Language Annals* 3(1970):579–91.
144 Stoller, Phyllis Hersh, Joanne Tuskes Lock, Virginia Wilson, and Beverly Wattenmaker. *Real Communication in French*. Upper Jay, New York:Adirondack Mountain Humanistic Education Center, 1974.
145 Strasheim, Lorraine A.,ed., *The Dialog* 9,iii (1975).
146 ——— *The Dialog* 10,i(1975).
147 ——— "The Foreign Language Student As a Social Creature:The Use of Groups in the Foreign Language Classroom." *The WAFLT* [Wisconsin Association of Foreign Language Teachers] *Bulletin* (Fall 1972):3–15.
148 Sutton, Donna E. "Problems of Individualized Instruction—How Some Successful Programs Deal With Them," 86–118 in Ronald L. Gougher, ed., *Individualization of Instruction in Foreign Languages:A Practical Guide*. Philadelphia:Center for Curriculum Development, 1972.
149 ——— Personal Communication, 1976. [Letter.]
150 Tamarkin, Toby. "Mini-Dramas Created on Location Can Stimulate Cultural Awareness." *Accent on ACTFL* 4,v(1974):12–13.
151 Taylor, James S. "Direct Classroom Teaching of Cultural Concepts," 42–50 in H. Ned Seelye,ed., *Perspectives for Teachers of Latin American Culture*. Springfield, Illinois:Office of the Superintendent of Public Instruction, 1970.
152 Tiefenbrun, Susan Wanda. "The Use of Planned Dramatic Scenes With the Audio-Lingual Method." *French Review* 45(1972):855–59.
153 Torres, Angel. *Small-Group Activities for Spanish Classes*. [Paper prepared for a methods course, Cleveland State University, Cleveland, Ohio, 1975.]
154 Valette, Rebecca M., and Renée S. Disick. *Modern Language Performance Objectives and Individualization*. New York:Harcourt Brace Jovanovich, 1972.
155 Walpole, Earl L. *Cultural Understanding:French, Level I*. Hayward, California:Alameda County School Department, 1971.
156 Warriner, Helen P. "The Teacher As Quality Control:Program Options," 30–44 in Frank M. Grittner,ed., *Student Motivation and the Foreign Language Teacher*. Skokie, Illinois:National Textbook Company, 1974.
157 Wattenmaker, Beverly. Personal Communication, 1976. [Interview.]
158 Wells, David J. "Role-Playing in the Foreign Language Class." *French Review* 48(1975):760–62.
159 Wells, Gloria T. "How About a Compromise Toward Individualization?" *Accent on ACTFL* 4,iii (1974):24–25.
160 Wilson, Virginia, and Beverly Wattenmaker. *Real Communication in Spanish*. Upper Jay, New York:Adirondack Mountain Humanistic Education Center, 1973.
161 Wise, Gail B. Personal Communication, 1976. [Interview.]
162 Wolfe, David E., and Leland W. Howe. "Personalizing Foreign Language Instruction." *Foreign Language Annals* 7(1973):81–94.
163 ——— and Marianne Keating. "Clarifying Values Through Foreign Language Study." *Hispania* 56(1973):404–06.
164 Zajac, Kathleen M. "It's a Bank, It's a Restaurant, It's a . . . Classroom!" *Accent on ACTFL* 4,ii (1973):13–14.
165 Zelson, Sidney N. J. "A Relevant Curriculum: Linguistic Competence Plus Communicative Competence Equal Proficiency," 18–32 in Renate A. Schulz,ed., *Teaching for Communication in the Foreign Language Classroom*. Skokie, Illinois:National Textbook Company, 1976.
166 ——— "Skill-Using Activities in the Foreign Language Classroom." *American Foreign Language Teacher* 4,iii(1974):33–35.

4

The Minicourse: A viable curricular alternative

Robert C. Lafayette
Indiana University

Introduction

Diversity

Diversification, pluralism, alternatives, options, individual differences are all key words that aptly describe the current major thrust in American education. During the first half of the 1970s virtually all aspects of schooling have been influenced in one way or another by the forces of diversity. There now exist more than 1,000 public alternative schools; grading systems are no longer uniform; alternative paths leading to the completion of high school graduation requirements are becoming a reality; the two-semester scholastic year is no longer sacred; most subject-matter areas are increasing curricular options; and the need to meet individual student differences is paramount. Postman and Weingartner (94) appropriately reinforce this claim when they say: "If the school reform movement has learned anything over the past two decades, it is that within any given school population there is enough diversity in learning styles to make diversity in learning programs a necessity" (p. 51).

NASSP recommendations

The National Commission on the Reform of Secondary Education urges the recognition of a wide variety of available alternatives, directly reflecting this emphasis in at least 10 of its 32 recommendations (Brown, 9). In its recent statement on secondary education the National Association of Secondary School

---

Robert C. Lafayette (Ph.D., The Ohio State University) is Associate Professor of Education at Indiana University where he is Director of the Foreign Language Education Program. He has taught French on the secondary and college levels and has conducted numerous summer workshops in Wisconsin and Indiana. His publications have appeared in the *American Foreign Language Teacher, Modern Language Journal, NAASP Curriculum Report,* and *Student Motivation and the Foreign Language Teacher.* He has edited *The Culture Revolution in Foreign Language Teaching* and has served as editor of the *WAFLT Bulletin* and co-editor of *Accent on ACTFL.* He is currently serving as Chairman of the Board of Directors of the Central States Conference on the Teaching of Foreign Languages. His professional affiliations include ACTFL, AATF, AATSP, ATE, IFLTA, and NASSP.

Principals recommends a quarter or semester elective system to enhance the choices available to students (85). Among the options available it suggests interdisciplinary courses and alternative programs. Within the realm of organizing for instruction it recommends the continuation of recent reforms that have made valuable contributions to secondary education. Included are:

> A new flexibility and attention to individualization has entered the secondary schools.
> Students have become more involved with the learning process.
> Teachers have broadened their repertoires of instruction.
> Learning has moved away from the single textbook to a multitude of resources (p. 30).

In the domain of curriculum theory Doyle (22) describes the transition from the social benefits of schooling to the personal benefits of schooling. The social-benefit theory, upon which the traditional American commitment to educational opportunity was based, stressed the contributions of schooling to the overall betterment of society. The personal-benefit theory emphasizes the importance of the individual and charges the school with the need to establish a differentiated program designed to foster individual interests and maximize individual potential. Although born in the days of progressivism, the personal-benefit theory has had little impact on actual school policy or progress. Doyle claims, however:

Personal-benefit theory

> During the present decade . . . the personal-benefit theory has moved to be the center of educational discourse and is advocated strongly as the only adequate basis for defining America's commitment to educational opportunity (p. 255).

Shane and Shane (104) state that we are in the process of moving from mass teaching to personalized teaching, from single learnings to multiple learnings. Finally, the student himself sees the need for diversity. A research project conducted for the National Institute of Education by the American Institutes for Research revealed several shortcomings in the nation's high schools as identified by a national cross-sectional sample of 30

School shortcomings

year olds, who have been periodically questioned since 1960 when they were 15 years old (26). The analysis of the 1,000 in-depth interviews with these former students pointed to seven areas of concern:

1 Grossly inadequate vocational guidance
2 Too many harmful teachers
3 Lack of individualized instruction
4 Inadequate curriculum
5 Lack of personal support
6 Too few alternative ways to learn
7 Ineffective education for citizenship in a democratic society (p. 484).

Alternative school movement

Certainly the most significant and widespread response to the call for diversity has been the currently blossoming alternative school movement. Fantini has said: "The development of public schools of choice is the only major movement in American education today" (Smith, Burke, and Barr, p. 41). According to Postman and Weingartner (94), an alternative school is "one whose conventions are entirely different from those we associate with most public schools . . . What makes it an 'alternative' is that it offers an arrangement for learning that is in sharp contrast to what is offered in the 'regular' school" (p. 129). Smith, Burke, and Barr (106) identify several types of optional alternative public schools including open schools, schools-without-walls, learning centers, continuation schools, multicultural schools, free schools, schools-within-a-school, complexes of alternative schools, and cooperative alternative schools. There are also bilingual alternative schools such as those found in Cincinnati where the public school system offers 14 different types of alternative schools ranging from The School for Creative and Performing Arts to separate bilingual alternative elementary schools in French, German, and Spanish (3).

Types of alternative schools

Alternative schools have had a significant impact on the curriculum. They have involved a greater number of people in the curriculum development process (students, teachers, administrators, parents, and other community members); they have

Curricular impact

expanded the curriculum beyond the confines of the traditional classroom by providing a variety of places and materials not common to the formal classroom environment; they have permitted learning tasks to determine time usage rather than time determining learning tasks; they have encouraged a variety of learning and teaching styles; and finally, Smith, Burke, and Barr (106) claim that "the significance of alternative school curriculum is based not upon the acquisition of new learning or new information, but rather the attachment of new meanings to information that is already known as readily available" (p. 22).

Alternatives within traditional schools

Although the alternative school movement represents the most significant step to diversify American education, there have been related alternative developments within the confines of the traditional school at all levels of instruction. Paramount among these have been the efforts to diversify the curriculum by increasing the number of available options. At times this has been accomplished by dividing the scholastic year into shorter segments such as quarters or quinmesters, and at other times by instituting minicourse or phase-elective programs.

Increased options

According to Smith (105), minicourses date back at least to 1958. He speculates, in fact, that minicourses or phase-electives in English may have been the forerunner of alternative schools. From English by choice to schools of choice was a logical step for the many English teachers who have dominated the move to alternative schools.

In addition to the pacesetting work of English teachers, there have been similar movements in the social studies, the sciences, business education, and foreign languages. In social studies Risinger (96) claims that the minicourse concept both encompasses and transcends two other recent trends, the emphasis on individualized learning packets and the impact of simulation games and role-playing. He tells of rising overall enrollments, higher grades, and improved student and faculty attitudes toward their classes. He concludes by describing five different programs in Indiana and New York that offer between 45 and 66 short-term social studies courses. In science Beers (5) describes the success of activity-centered minicourses with disadvantaged students in an isolated California desert community high school.

> I am convinced after six years of teaching short secondary courses in science and one year teaching mathematics minicourses that the use of minicourses can make it possible to achieve equality of educational opportunities, and can do so at a much lower cost than by our present antiquated system (p. 26).

Bryant (11) recounts how biology modules at Huguenot High School in Richmond, Virginia, were implemented because too many students had been turned off by biology. She claims that the opportunity to elect the six-week modules has been a success with students, teachers, counselors, administrators, and parents. A desirable by-product has been the disappearance of discipline problems. Malsbary (72) lists 10 recent developments in the area of business education. Among them is the increased number of minicourses offered within the business curriculum, especially within service courses such as money management, insurance, contracts, and investments—all of which appeal to both business and nonbusiness students. Finally, the trend toward diversification in the foreign language curriculum is clearly reflected in chapter titles of past ACTFL Reviews of Foreign Language Education: "Free to Explore: Curricular Developments" (Fryer, 33); "Free to Reach Out" (Warner, 112); "The Changing Curricula" (Papalia and Zampogna, 91); "Many Learners, Many Goals, Many Curricula" (Mullen, 84); "Curricula for New Goals" (Lipton, 64).

Foreign language

Be they the 12 minischools of Manhattan's Haaren High School (Karlin, 56, pp. 212–14), one of which is the English as a Second Language Minischool; or a one-teacher foreign language minicourse program in a small rural community, diversity in its many forms is here to stay. Bruce Howell, superintendent of schools in Tulsa, Oklahoma, describes clearly the prospects:

> As for me, I see unity through diversity. A diversity in educational design that will permit parents moving from Houston, New York, or Los Angeles to find a curriculum program and

> an organizational pattern amenable to their thinking. . . . Flexibility and diversity are difficult to manage but, to me, the alternative to diversity is educationally untenable. The alternative is standardization and conformity. It is untenable because now in education we speak of uniqueness, of individuality. This mandates alternatives (Smith, Burke, and Barr, 106, p. 42).

Not everyone agrees, however. McDanield (70) states:

Warning

> The idea currently popular in education [sometimes manifested in minicourses] that diversity alone can reform the curriculum is similar to the idea of auto makers that a diversity of models solves the problem of good transportation; it equates relevance with immediacy rather than with ideas and gives us an "overchoice" of "nonchoices" (p. 109).

Grittner (36) also reminds us that history has questioned the wisdom of separating the curriculum into cognitive and affective components for the purposes of individualization. He further warns of an inherent danger in the present-day minicourse movement, where courses are sometimes called good because of high enrollment rather than intellectual integrity and where the bad courses would in reality drive out the good.

Although there may exist inherent dangers in the minicourse movement, it is a viable means to curricular change. The change to a minicourse curriculum is an example of what Postman and Weingartner (94) refer to as "convention modification." In fact, some of the characteristics of minicourses are reflected in their definition of a good school.

A good school

> A school is good . . .
>
> when its daily time sequences are not arbitrary but are related to what the students are doing
>
> when it allows students, at least to some extent, to organize their own time
>
> when it does not require all students to engage in the same activities, but gives them considerable latitude in choosing from among the options
>
> when students are offered the widest possible range of subjects from which to choose

when it is so organized that it can capitalize on what its teachers do best and know most about

when students are not objects to which things happen, but are encouraged to be active shapers of their own school experiences

when it offers a variety of alternative programs to the many publics that comprise a community (pp. 30–43).

Definition of terms

The current emphasis on alternatives within the curriculum has manifested itself in a variety of elective programs that are sometimes labeled in different ways. For the most part the specific components of these programs have been called *minicourses* or *phase-electives*. Other terms have included *self-contained courses, nonsequential courses,* and *terminal courses*. Self-contained courses and nonsequential courses refer basically to the same phenomenon: courses with no prerequisites but with stated terminal objectives. For purposes of clarification and because foreign language teachers identify with the notion of sequence, courses in this category will be referred to as nonsequential courses. According to Rivers (97), terminal courses should be designed so that the student who completes the course takes away with him a full and enriching experience. In her words, terminal courses are in essence "not pre-anything" (p. 116). This does not imply that students enrolled in such courses may not continue the study of a second language. In fact, many of these courses do indeed create sufficient interest and enthusiasm among students to persuade them to pursue further their study.

Different labels

Terminal course

It seems beneficial, however, to expand Rivers' definition of a terminal course to include courses that are still not "pre-anything," but may be "post-something." A terminal course may not always be nonsequential in that it might be predicated upon some established language competency. For example, a course entitled Business Spanish, open to students with a knowledge of basic Spanish vocabulary and syntax, might be terminal in that it does not specifically prepare for another course in the sequence, but it could not be said to be nonsequential because it does have a prerequisite.

Thus, there are two types of terminal courses: those that are also nonsequential and those that are built upon a certain basic knowledge of the language. Most prominent among the first type are exploratory courses whose basic aims, according to Fearing and Grittner (28), are

1 To provide students with a satisfying introductory foreign language experience
2 To provide motivation for further language study
3 To inspire appreciation for other cultures
4 To increase self-awareness through an awareness of cultural differences
5 To provide a basis for selection or nonselection of further language study
6 To provide an introduction to language
7 To improve first language skills
8 To develop limited skills in the language presented.

Exploratory courses have gained increasing interest and stature among the profession. Morrow (82), for example, describes a basically language-oriented exploratory course; Bourque and Chehy (8) provide interesting details about one that is culture-oriented; Keller and Ferguson (58) explore the benefits of a college-level exploratory course; the exploratory course offered in the Prince George's County Public Schools (31) definitely reflects a career orientation.

Other examples of this first type of terminal course could include the five-week (two hours per week) minicourses entitled Survival French at the College of San Mateo, California (Cordes, 16) and the French, German, Spanish for Travelers nonsequential semester courses offered in the public schools of Prince George's County, Maryland (32, 34).

The second type of terminal course differs from the first in that it is based upon a prerequisite of defined language skills. Thus, it cannot be considered nonsequential. A common example would be the genre-type or author-based literature course offered at most universities. These courses typically have as a prerequisite the completion of one or more survey of literature courses, but they are terminal in that they are not usually designed to prepare the student for any other specific course. Another example is secondary school minicourses that have as a prerequisite the completion of two years of basic language instruction.

According to Postman and Weingartner (94), minicourses are simply courses that are shorter than the usual semester-long ones. This is true in most situations, but in cases such as described by Carter (13) at Dalhousie University, minicourses are as long as one semester. This stems from the fact that this institution operates on the basis of full-year instead of semester courses. In the broadest sense, then, minicourses are courses that are shorter than the established length of the normal academic unit, be that a quarter, a semester, or a full year.

Minicourse

Phase-electives are minicourses that have been developed for various levels of difficulty (Hillocks, 45). For example, Bloomington (Indiana) High School North (6) offers 45 nine-week phase-electives in its junior and senior English program. The five different phases are described as follows in the school's course description booklet:

Phase-elective

> *Phase 1:* Includes courses designed for students who may have reading or learning problems and for those who have, to date, shown little or no interest in English studies. In the selection of materials and in the planning of activities, care has been given to (1) increasing interest through greater enjoyment and greater relevance and (2) developing basic skills. Much student involvement is strongly recommended.
>
> *Phase 2:* Courses are designed to increase motivation and competence in reading, language usage, and composition. A course bearing this phase designation does not include books of known difficulty or great length but stresses interpretation and transfer of understandings in works at a comparatively easy reading level.
>
> *Phase 3:* Courses require a higher level of reading competence than do Phases 1 and 2 as well as a willingness to extend this and other language skills. The application of basic principles in literature, language, and composition makes a Phase 3 course a more structured approach to learning.
>
> *Phase 4:* Includes courses that require students to work at a more sophisticated level and to demonstrate a higher degree

> of motivation. Course materials and activities demand a high reading level, a grasp of language structure, and a degree of proficiency in writing. This level, as well as Phase 5, is highly recommended for those planning to enroll in college.
>
> *Phase 5:* Designates courses containing a design that presupposes students with highly developed skills and understanding as well as maturity in thought and purpose. Both Phases 4 and 5 focus on depth and quality rather than on breadth and quantity of work (pp. 4–5).

In addition to being shorter than the standard academic unit, the minicourse may also assume one or more of the other above characteristics. It may be terminal and nonsequential, such as Survival French at the College of San Mateo, California; it may be terminal like the Level IV and V courses offered at Ridgefield (Connecticut) High School where most students must complete three years of German study prior to electing minicourses (Moore, 78); it may be phased as described in the Bloomington (Indiana) High School North program (6). Finally, some school districts such as Dade County, Florida, have formalized the minicourse into an existing standard-length academic unit called the quinmester. In those cases many minicourses become sequential in nature because they constitute part of the normally sequenced instruction in basic language skills.

Formalized minicourse

English elective programs

Historically, the trend to diversify the secondary school curriculum via short-term electives has its beginnings in English elective programs. These programs have much in common with foreign language programs; some of them were established almost a decade before their foreign language counterparts. Much of the information included herein has been extrapolated from three major publications on the topic by Hillocks (44, 45, 46).

Both Hillocks (44) and Smith (105) trace the beginnings of elective English programs back to the late 1950s. The movement was slow to develop, however. Not until the late 1960s did various types of elective programs begin to proliferate. The often-cited program at Trenton High School in Michigan began full implementation in the fall of 1967.

Of the 76 program descriptions collected by Hillocks (44), 33 described elective programs in grades 10 through 12 and 18 in grades 11 and 12. The remaining programs offered electives at various other combinations of grade levels. Semester-length courses were offered in 50 programs, while the remainder offered courses of four, six, nine, ten, or twelve weeks in length. A more-or-less formal method of phasing was used in 21 of the programs.

Predominance of literature

A tabulation of the 1,900 courses listed in the program guides of 70 individual high schools revealed that 61 percent fell into the literature category, while less than 20 percent dealt explicitly with composition, and only 3 percent had to do with language as language (grammar, linguistics, general language study). Among the literary offerings there was a trend away from duplicating college-type courses toward offering courses with a thematic focus. This trend did not prevent the offering of approximately 700 literature courses falling in the college-type category, however. These figures partially support the criticism of LaRocque (61) who maintains that elective English programs do not necessarily meet individual needs because these needs are rarely assessed. Hillocks (44) also admits a lack of attention to needs assessment and recommends that more serious consideration be given to developing a rationale for the courses offered in elective programs.

Program accomplishments

In his extensive evaluation of the Trenton (Michigan) High School program, Hillocks (47) confirms the informal results of many programs that show that students in English elective programs have more positive attitudes toward their English courses than do their counterparts in traditional programs. Hillocks also found that the elective program produced no significant change on test scores of reading and writing even though the program had undergone a radical change away from the reading and writing experiences usually found in traditional programs.

Although Hillocks (44) points to deficiencies in rationale, needs assessment, evaluation, and other aspects of English elective programs, he firmly believes that they "represent the first massive shattering of the structures that shackled curricula in English" (p. 123). He summarizes their accomplishments:

Elective programs have demonstrated that there is no need

for all students to study the same material at the same time or in the same way. They have shown that there is no need to group students according to arbitrary chronological divisions or in mandatory ability tracks. They have demonstrated that allowing the student a greater role in planning his own education does not trail disaster in its wake. They have developed a great variety of approaches to English, and many of the specific course designs are superior to anything in traditional programs. They have brought a more concrete awareness of student attitudes toward what they are supposed to be learning in English, an awareness that has been long in coming.

New professionalism

But perhaps most important of all, they have engendered a new sense of professionalism among teachers. . . . With the disappearance of the traditional patterns, teachers have begun to take an active role in the planning of curricula for their own students. They are no longer content to be controlled by an outmoded curriculum (pp. 122–23).

Foreign language minicourses: Historical perspective

First FL programs

The first foreign language minicourse programs were born 3,000 miles apart in the fall of 1969. In Morgan Hill, California, Logan began his individualized German minicourse program, and in Ridgefield, Connecticut, Moore inaugurated a level IV–V series of German minicourses. That same fall, ACTFL, NASSP, and the Indiana Language Program cosponsored a secondary school conference at which Hoye (48) and Ryberg (100) presented the beginnings of an excellent program of parallel minicourses designed to fit a modular schedule at Marshall-University High School in Minneapolis. Due to a series of unfortunate circumstances, the latter program was never fully implemented. Many refreshing ideas can be gained however, from the still available detailed program description (Strasheim, 108). During the next few years one or more new minicourse programs were introduced yearly. In 1970, Commack (New York) High School added minicourses to its total immersion program. This was followed in 1971 by programs in Bloomington, Indiana, Dade County, Florida, and Jefferson County, Kentucky. The numbers increased gradually from year to year until the fall of 1975 when the author was able to identify from only scattered reports at least

30 minicourse programs. There is no doubt that many more actually exist and others are in the planning stages.

Limited literature

The existing literature in the concept of minicourses in foreign language teaching is indeed limited. Four programs (Commack, New York; Dade County, Florida; Morgan Hill, California; Ridgefield, Connecticut) are described by Love and Honig (68). Logan (66) gives a complete account of the Morgan Hill program. The Marshall-University High School program has been described by Ryberg (100, 101). Fearing and Arendt (27) suggest numerous ideas for short-term courses and present a useful interest questionnaire. Lafayette (60) offers suggestions for minicourse implementation, and the 1974 Northeast Conference Report includes a substantial section on minicourses (Born, 7). Several past contributors to the ACTFL *Review of Foreign Language Education* (Fryer, 33; Joiner, 53; Lipton, 64; Mullen, 84; Papalia and Zampogna, 91; Phillips, 93) also treat minicourses, but in most cases, these discussions are brief. Loew (65) represents the most recent mention of minicourses in her New York state update of Love and Honig (68).

Results of questionnaire

Questionnaire response

To obtain an overall view of minicourse programs throughout the country, I sent a letter to state foreign language supervisors, state newsletter editors, and selected individuals asking them to identify programs that might fall within the minicourse category. Scattered responses enabled the identification of approximately 70 possible minicourse programs. A somewhat detailed questionnaire was then sent to these program directors. Thirty-two responses were received, 25 of which described minicourse programs. Among these programs, 7 were designed for post-secondary school programs, 14 for high school, two for middle school/junior high school, and one for elementary school. It should be noted that these figures do not properly reflect the actual number of existing programs because of the constraints in gathering unpublished information and that information used here to create a general overview of minicourse programs is limited to the programs already described in the professional literature and to the questionnaire responses from those individuals who found time to reply.

The lack of formal foreign language instruction in elementary schools has prompted sporadic *ad hoc* programs. Hancock (40) reports a once-a-week 10-week Spanish minicourse at Maywood Elementary School in Albany. The program is the only one in a foreign language among six minicourses offered as electives to interested fourth-grade students. It focuses on basic language instruction using limited vocabulary and includes discussions about Spanish-speaking peoples. Similar *ad hoc* programs have been used as laboratory experiences for future teachers. Rodewald and Evans (98) describe German and French programs in Mount Pleasant, Michigan, and Ashley (4) reports a long-standing French program in Franklin, Indiana. The St. Paul Public Schools offer FLES minicourses at their magnet learning centers established as part of the city's desegregation effort (Jorstad, 55).

FLES minicourses

At the middle school/junior high school level, all minicourses examined fell into various types of exploratory programs.

The minicourse phenomenon is undoubtedly most prevalent in high school programs. Salient characteristics of these programs (based on detailed information from 18 different programs) are described below. Among the 18 schools, 17 offered minicourses in French, 7 in German, 5 in Latin, and 16 in Spanish. The two large county districts responding, Dade County, Florida, and Jefferson County, Kentucky, also offered programs in Hebrew, Italian (Dade only), and Russian.

Where minicourses fit in the high school foreign language curriculum

Programs at advanced levels

The great majority of the programs examined limit their minicourse sequences to one or more of the advanced levels of instruction (III, IV, V). This is true of all schools that operate on a semester basis except the Morgan Hill, California, program, which consists totally of minicourses (Logan, 67), and the Ridgefield, Connecticut, program, where there are a large number of minicourses available for use in conjunction with the elementary and intermediate courses of study (Moore, 77). The only other programs that offer minicourses at levels lower than advanced exist in those school systems such as Dade County, Florida (Alonso, 1), and Jefferson County, Kentucky, where the minicourse pattern has been formalized by adopting full-year quinmester or quarter plans (Ensminger, 25). Offering minicourses at lower levels of instruction is not pedagogically unsound, though it is doubtful that many teachers will bear the burden of transforming their entire curriculum to a minicourse program unless they are forced to do so by a system-wide adoption of a full-year quarter, quinmester, or 45–15 plan. Furthermore, curricular change in modern-day foreign language teaching is probably most easily accomplished at the advanced levels of instruction, thus making the promotion of change more attractive at that point. Lafayette (60) offers four considerations to support his recommendation that minicourse alternatives are most attractive after Level II:

1 In Levels I and II, students gain a basic vocabulary, a command of basic grammatical structures, and familiarity with some simple culture concepts; and they have had opportunity to apply these to listening, speaking, reading, and writing. This should provide a dependable preparation for the pursuit of different avenues in the foreign language field.

Basic skills

2 It is at the end of Level II that the greatest degree of dropout occurs; only about one third of Level II students enroll in Level III. Many discontinue their study of foreign language at this point because they think they have satisfied "college entrance requirements," but others drop out because Level III is heavily literature-oriented in most cases and not to their liking. Diversification is much needed at this juncture, and minicourses offer a means of providing it.

Combat dropout

3 Most academic fields now offer elective courses on a semester or even shorter basis. So long as these short-course opportunities are not available in the language field, numbers of students will decide to develop their programs by combining a number of semester courses and thereby rule out year-long foreign language courses.

Competitive offerings

4 In many small high schools, and some larger ones too, insufficient enrollments result in dropping Levels III and IV courses or in combining the two. A group of minicourses could mean a more attractive curriculum for those two years than a combination of the usual upper-level courses,

Solution to combined levels

> and they can mean the existence of opportunities for advanced study where none existed before (p. 2).

Length of minicourses

Length based on calendar

The length of high school minicourses ranges from one to 18 weeks, the latter being the exception. There are two basic criteria used in determining course length. In more than half of the schools responding, the minicourse length is based on a unit of time such as a grading period, a quarter, or a quinmester. In each of these cases all minicourses in a particular school are of the same length, and they range from nine to 12 weeks long. The other criterion used to determine length appears to be the needs of the course itself, though in many cases it seems to be little more than a teacher's desire to spend four weeks on one topic and three on another. A program based on this criterion usually offers courses of varied length. The courses in these programs are shorter, ranging from one to four weeks in length. The student then takes as many as needed to complete a semester's work. In Waukesha, Wisconsin, for example, the fall semester complement of minicourses includes one four-week, three three-week, and three two-week courses (Elifson, 24).

Length based on course needs

On the surface the programs with shorter minicourses appear to be more flexible, but in all but one situation this is not the case because there are only as many minicourses as are needed to fill the semester timespan. Thus, the student is actually enrolling in a set of minicourses for a semester's credit. In the area of program change, however, schools with the shorter courses can more easily replace or alter a component than those where the courses are at least nine weeks long.

How minicourses are scheduled

The information gathered revealed several scheduling patterns, most of which seemed to suggest that the scheduling of minicourses need not be a complex task. The illustrations included below provide the reader with several different designs, but they include only the minicourse portion of the program. They do not reflect the fact that in some cases the minicourse program is offered in addition to parallel traditional advanced-level courses and in others it replaces them.

Quarter plans

Plan A. No options (Brooke High School, Wellsburg, West Virginia) (Hartline, 43)

1st Quarter	2nd Quarter	3rd Quarter	4th Quarter
Course 1	Course 2	Course 3	Course 4

Plan B. Options—Same period (Half Hollow Hills High School, Dix Hills, New York) (Lyons, 69)

Same Period	1st Quarter	2nd Quarter	3rd Quarter	4th Quarter
Teacher A	Course 1	Course 3	Course 5	Course 7
Teacher B	Course 2	Course 4	Course 6	Course 8

Plan C. Options—Different periods (Ridgefield High School, Ridgefield, Connecticut) (Moore, 78)

Same Teacher	1st Quarter	2nd Quarter	3rd Quarter	4th Quarter
German IV Period A	Course 1	Course 2	Course 4	Course 6
German V Period B	Course 1	Course 3	Course 5	Course 6

Two-year cycle

Plan D. No options—Two-year cycle (Ada High School, Ada, Ohio) (Minto, 73; Neiswander, 87)

Same Teacher	1st Quarter	2nd Quarter	3rd Quarter	4th Quarter
Year 1	Course 1	Course 2	Course 3	Course 4
Year 2	Course 5	Course 6	Course 7	Course 8

Minicourses plus tradition

Plan E. Combination required work and minicourse options (English Program, Columbus East High School, Columbus, Indiana (17, 18, 19)

	1st Quarter	2nd Quarter	3rd Quarter	4th Quarter
Sophomore English	Required units for all students			3 minicourses
Junior English	Required units		3 minicourses per quarter	
Senior English	Required units	Student selects three 3-week minicourses per quarter		

The selection of any one plan is naturally dependent upon specific school needs. Plan D, for example, is especially designed for the small high school where low enrollment often mandates combining Levels III and IV. The two-year cycle permits two years of advanced study without having to repeat content. Plans A, B, and C reflect not so much student enrollment as they do the availability of staff. Plan E presents an interesting model to the teacher who might want to combine a traditional approach with a minicourse option during the same academic year. He might use the whole-class instructional mode for the work required of all students and an individualized mode for the minicourse segment in order to offer a variety of courses.

Semester Plans. Most of the schools using a semester plan do not maintain a standard minicourse length. Usually the semester consists of several one to four-week courses adding up to a total of 18 weeks. In the programs where the minicourses are primarily teacher-directed, the student enrolls for a semester of an already identified and sequenced set of courses.

	3 Weeks	2 Weeks	4 Weeks	2 Weeks	4 Weeks	3 Weeks
Teacher	Course 1	Course 2	Course 3	Course 4	Course 5	Course 6

Although this plan can be expanded to resemble the models under the quarter plan, no schools offer such an expanded version. The only semester-based programs that offer a choice of courses within the semester are those where some form of individualization constitutes the mode of instruction. Both the Morgan Hill, California (Logan, 66), and the Bloomington, Indiana (Morrow, 83; Thrasher, 110), programs permit students to design their own individual plan of study selecting from a wide array of available minicourses. A model of the Bloomington program is outlined later in this chapter.

Modular-Plans. Schools on modular schedules may elect to define course length by the number of modules per week or cycle instead of the number of weeks. This means that students are enrolled in parallel rather than sequenced minicourses. The original Marshall-University High School, Minneapolis (Ryberg, 100) plan was based on such a proposal but, unfortunately, it was never fully implemented. A student in a modular-based plan (15-minute time unit) would select minicourses that total a minimum of 16 modules of class time per week.

Parallel minicourses

Semester	
Course 1	8 modules per week
Course 2	6 modules per week
Course 3	6 modules per week
Course 4	4 modules per week
Course 5	4 modules per week
Course 6	2 modules per week
Course 7	2 modules per week

The content of minicourses

Expanded content

Probably the most significant change brought about by minicourses has been the move to broaden content at the advanced levels of foreign language instruction. The accusation that minicourses (or a similar system of electives) represent nothing more than "the same old baloney sliced differently" (LaConte, 59, p. 107) is far from the truth in many of the programs examined. On the contrary, there are some who would say that programs are too far away from the college-oriented content of traditional advanced-level programs.

If one of the primary reasons for adopting the minicourse format is to alleviate attrition and attract a broader range of students to foreign language instruction, the expansion and diversification of content is a necessary element. College-oriented programs cannot expect to enroll noncollege-bound students, no matter how the academic year is partitioned. Unlike English elective programs that can logically maintain traditional content because their students are usually required to enroll, for foreign language programs to adopt the minicourse format would seem fruitless if there were no intention to enlarge content.

Table 1 represents the distribution by content and language of 318 identifiable minicourses. For an additional 20 or more courses either the language or the content was not specified, making classification impossible. Almost all courses represented here fall into the advanced-level category. The 60 or more minicourses or units available in each language for enrichment at all levels of French, German, and Spanish instruction at Ridgefield (Connecticut) High School (Moore, 79, 80, 81) are not included in this table because of their unique natures and because their inclusion would distort data that are already

TABLE 1

Number and percent of minicourses by content and language

	French		German		Latin		Spanish		Total	
	N	%	N	%	N	%	N	%	N	%
Language	33	29	19	32	3	10	25	21	80	25
Culture c	44	39	10	17	4	14	33	28	91	29
Culture C	20	18	11	19	5	17	17	15	53	17
Literature	11	10	16	27	17	59	26	22	70	22
Other	5	4	3	5	0	0	16	14	24	7
Total courses	113		59		29		117		318	
Total different courses	43		26		12		39			
Number of programs	17		7		5		16			

difficult to interpret. Also excluded from this count are all sequential beginning and intermediate basic language minicourses because most of them exist only by virtue of system-wide short-term calendar plans. The category labelled Language Courses includes all those focusing on grammar or any of the four skills as well as nonsequential Foreign Language for Travel courses. The Culture c category is comprised of the "everyday" culture courses and the numerous possible subdivisions dealing with subjects such as food, sports, teenagers. In Culture C one finds the various formal culture topics such as history, geography, and fine arts. Literature courses include many simply entitled Literature and others with more specific genre, century, or author designations. Many of the courses overlap and could easily have been placed in different categories. The decision to categorize in this particular way was primarily arbitrary. For example, courses entitled Reading were placed in the language category, but depending on specific content, they could as easily have been classified under literature.

Language

Among the language courses, more than half deal specifically with conversation. Another 25 percent are devoted to grammar review; and the remainder are divided among listening comprehension, reading, and writing. This is not surprising because in many cases listening comprehension is probably subsumed under conversation; reading is included under literature; and writing often falls into the same category as grammar. Some programs do not offer any language courses because they treat grammar and skills in all minicourses regardless of the specific content.

Culture

The Culture c category represents the greatest degree of diversity and digression from traditional course content. The most prevalent minicourse in this category offers units on foods and cooking; general "everyday" culture courses are next in popularity. Among other Culture c minicourses, one finds titles such as Fashion, Brown Power, Popular Songs, Something for the Boys–Cars, and Teenagers. Music and fine arts constitute half of the Culture C courses, and the other half consists almost totally of historical topics.

Literature

Probably the most misleading figures in Table 1 appear in the Literature category, which consists primarily of courses simply called Literature and others identified by century. The only genre course that appears in all three major languages is drama. These figures present interpretation problems because 15 of the 26 Spanish literature courses and 14 of the 17 offered in Latin come from two programs–Dade County and Jefferson County. The large number of literary offerings in these two programs not only inflates the figures in the literature category but distorts the other data as well.

The Other category includes mainly independent study and "fun-and-games" courses. Courses with a career-orientation focus are also included in this category, but these were limited primarily to Spanish and especially to the Dade County program which offers several business education courses in Spanish.

Differences among languages

One might expect Latin to present a somewhat different image than do the modern languages in Table 1; it is perhaps surprising that almost 60 percent of German minicourses fall in the language and literature categories and both French and Spanish have only about 40 percent of their courses in the same two categories. Moreover, German has more C than c courses; French and Spanish maintain an almost two-to-one ratio in favor of c courses. Are student needs that different from one language to another? Do German teachers see a greater need for language and literature offerings? Have French and Spanish teachers emphasized culture too much? Although there are as yet no conclusive answers to these questions, they do warrant some reflection.

Although there are visible differences from language to language, the presence of minicourses has altered significantly the content of instruction in all languages especially at the advanced level. The diversity of all types of cultural offerings has increased greatly, as has the specificity of language and literary options. Indirectly the implementation of minicourses also has prompted a much needed clarification of goals throughout the curriculum.

Criteria for minicourse content

Preference polls

Lafayette (60) suggests the need to examine three specific criteria in establishing course content–student interests and needs, teacher qualifications, and availability of materials. Data gathered from questionnaire responses indicate that a preponderance of program directors use various polling devices to determine course offerings. Students are usually presented with a list of options and asked to rank them in order of preference. This, however, constitutes only partial student input because the original selection is highly teacher-dominated and is often based on a subjective assessment of interests, needs, qualifications, and materials.

Primary mode of instruction in minicourse programs

Eclectic instructional approaches

The information gathered suggests that there is no primary mode of instruction. All but three of the 16 high school respondents indicate more than one of four choices: whole-class, small-group, individualized instruction via LAPs, and independent study. Small-group instruction is indicated most frequently, followed very closely by identical counts for the other three modes of instruction. This information in no way shows the use and importance of any one mode in relation to others within specific programs; it does, however, indicate that minicourses are adaptable to varied instructional approaches and that teachers are taking advantage of that fact. It seems plausible that the use of varied instructional modes in these schools is directly related to the implementation of minicourse programs.

How minicourse programs are evaluated

Evaluation

Almost all evaluation of minicourse programs is limited to student opinion surveys, subjective teacher evaluation, and examination of student enrollment figures. No formal attempt to measure cognitive and affective gains is reported for any program, although Pearl (92) does state that SAT scores of students enrolled in minicourses have increased noticeably. Minicourse programs can be criticized for their lack of attention to evaluation. However, the student opinion surveys used to evaluate at least seven of the programs probably represent a greater effort at program evaluation than is normally found in traditional programs. In addition, an increase in student enrollment is not necessarily an indication of student cognitive or affective gain. Nevertheless, increases such as those reported in almost all programs at the advanced levels are particularly noteworthy in a subject area that suffered significant losses during the past five years. The program in Waukesha, Wisconsin, for example, witnessed a 33 percent increase in advanced level enrollments after initiating its minicourse program. Logan (67), Pearl (92), and Seagrave (102) report a doubling of enrollment. Snyder High School in Fort Wayne (Vizino and Rodriguez, 111), a 10-to-12 school with an enrollment of 1,600 students, reports an increase in foreign language enrollment from 650 to 800 for 1976–77. Vizino and Rodriguez attribute this increase and the almost total disappearance of attrition after Level II to the planned implementation of a three-"track" advanced-level program for 1976–77 – "traditional," conversational, and minicourse.

Enrollment gains

Results from student opinion surveys indicate highly positive attitudes among students enrolled in minicourse programs. In addition, subjective teacher evaluations reflect a high level of morale among teachers. There is no doubt that the evaluation of such programs needs to be strengthened; however, the positive results already obtained through these devices should not be totally disregarded.*

Positive attitudes

In-depth examination of one program

The information gathered from questionnaires sent to minicourse program directors is valuable because it indicates the

*In reporting the results of the questionnaire, it has been impossible to cite all responding programs. In addition to the several schools already mentioned, the following persons contributed significantly to the data used throughout the chapter: Clapper, 15; Grant, 35; Hansel, 41; Moore, 76; Nease, 86; Nichols, 88. This chapter also makes no mention of existing minicourse programs at the college level. Interested individuals should consult the following sources and persons: Buck, 12; Carter, 13; Cordes, 16; Ebling, 23; Heesen, 42; Keller, 57; Keller and Ferguson, 58; Moffett, 75; Seaman, 103; Stewart, 107; Tamarkin, 109; Wilkins, 113; Woloshin, 114.

vast array of options within the minicourse concept. For a more detailed examination of one specific program the author has selected the Spanish program at Bloomington (Indiana) High School South because it has been in operation since 1971; it includes by design the three major modes of instruction (whole-class, small-group, and individualized); and it is structured with a maximum of flexibility.

Bloomington High School South

Bloomington (Indiana) High School South, which has a total enrollment of approximately 1,500 students, is one of two high schools serving the Monroe County Community School Corporation. The school includes grades 9 to 12 and offers five levels of French and Spanish and three levels of German. The staff includes one French, one German, and two Spanish teachers. Until recently all language courses were traditional in character except for the advanced levels (III to V) of Spanish, which operated on a minicourse format. Beginning in the fall of 1975, a minicourse program for the advanced levels of French was also initiated. Because the French program is still in beginning stages, discussion here is limited to the Spanish program.

Like most other programs of this type, it was developed to provide students with a larger and broader selection of offerings at the advanced levels. This would attract and meet the needs of a larger number of students who had little or no intention of continuing their language study in college. Since its inception the number of students enrolled has grown considerably even though the total school population has dropped by more than 500 due to school corporation redistricting. During the past three years enrollment in the minicourse program (Levels III to V) has been between 80 and 100 students, thus permitting four separate sections paired back-to-back two periods of the day.

Student input

Students have been involved from the beginning in the development and evaluation of the program. In the spring of 1971 they submitted ideas for courses of two, four, five, and six weeks duration. Since that time they have participated in yearly evaluations and have been instrumental in influencing many of the content and format changes that the program has undergone during its first five years.

Series format

Initially the program consisted of 14 minicourses of varying length combined into eight semester series, each offering four or five different courses. Two sample series follow:

Series A: Conversation and Grammar Review (6 weeks)
Revolutionaries (5 weeks)
Trips (3 weeks)
Contemporary Life (4 weeks)
Series B: Conversation and Grammar Review (4 weeks)
Writing, Presenting Dramas (4 weeks)
Brown Power, Spanish-Speaking Americans (5 weeks)
Reading (5 weeks)

Under this design every series began with either a four- or six-week Conversation and Grammar Review course. Third-year students were required to select a six-week series, and fourth- and fifth-year students could elect either option. Most students selected the longer one. During the review course students paced themselves individually through a series of individualized grammar packets. In the other minicourses students usually worked in small groups of three or four. They received a set of guidelines on what they had to do and what they were expected to know by the end of the course. In most courses students determined the manner of evaluation, but no matter how long the course, they had to be evaluated in some form or another every week.

Program changes

The program became more flexible with time. The notion of series was abandoned and students were permitted to design their own personal series with teacher consultation. Time also gradually did away with the predetermined length of each minicourse. The guidelines (*Hay que hacer* sheet) for each course are now designed to include what a student must complete in one week's time in each of the 22 available minicourse topics. The student, in consultation with the teacher, determines how many weeks he will spend studying each topic. In addition to making the minicourses themselves more flexible, the staff also added more structure to the total program by instituting two-week teacher-taught minicourses offered periodically throughout each semester. In 1975-76 the program assumed the following design:

IVR = Individualized Review of Verb Tenses
SSMC = Student-Selected Minicourses
TTMC = Teacher-Taught Minicourses

First	4 Weeks	4 Weeks	2 Weeks	4 Weeks	2 Weeks	2 Weeks
Semester	IVR	SSMC	TTMC	SSMC	TTMC	SSMC

Second	4 Weeks	2 Weeks	4 Weeks	2 Weeks	4 Weeks	2 Weeks	2 Weeks
Semester	SSMC	TTMC	SSMC	TTMC	SSMC	TTMC	SSMC

As the program is presently structured, the three basic modes of instruction–whole-class, small-group, and individualized–are intentionally incorporated. Students begin the academic year with a self-paced review of verb tenses. Using a sequenced series of individualized learning packets covering the formation and usage of regular and irregular verbs in 10 different tenses, the students complete as many packets as possible in the allocated four weeks. Each packet includes an information sheet telling the student what he must know. When he is ready, he takes a diagnostic pretest. If he shows 90 percent accuracy, he then moves on to the next learning packet in the sequence. If he does not achieve the 90 percent level, he works on the weak areas identified by the pretest–listening comprehension, speaking, reading, or writing–until he feels ready to take the mastery test. He is issued a grade commensurate with his level of achievement on the test; should he prefer a higher grade, he is permitted to retake the same test. The number of packets completed during these initial four weeks determines the group in which the student will be placed for the teacher-taught minicourses (TTMC) during the remainder of the year. Students completing fewer than seven packets are placed in one group and those completing seven or more in another.

Verb review

Teacher-taught minicourses

During the first TTMC, which occurs after four weeks of student-selected minicourses (SSMC), the two teachers focus on additional grammar. In the "slower" group, the teacher pays attention to those tenses not reviewed by the students during the initial four-week period. In every case this includes the subjunctive mood. The "faster" group also studies grammar during its first TTMC, but pays attention to some of its more complex features. The content of the other TTMCs offered periodically throughout the year is primarily determined by the teacher and

Student-selected minicourses

might include additional grammar or a concentration on one of the four skills or culture. In most instances the content reflects student needs identified during the preceding four-week SSMC. Morrow (83) indicates that one of the rationales for incorporating TTMCs is an intent to meet the remedial needs of students. Many students in the SSMCs were making the same basic errors, and the staff decided that correcting these basic mistakes in a whole-class atmosphere would be most efficient. In addition, the fact that students worked almost exclusively in small groups or independently during the SSMCs led to a lack of class identity. The introduction of periodic TTMCs served to reinstate this identity. Finally, Morrow points out that as an individual, she too needs a change of pace. Like most teachers, she wants to get up in front of a class and teach once in a while.

Flexibility

The student-selected minicourses (SSMC) constitute the largest and most important segment of the program. They are interesting not only because of their high degree of flexibility, but also because of their built-in opportunity for small-group work. During the 1975–76 school year students were able to select from the following list of minicourses:

1 Animals of Latin America
2 Arts and Crafts in the Spanish-Speaking World
3 Art (famous artists–Mexican muralists)
4 Brown Power: Spanish-Speaking Americans
5 Searching for Spanish Pirate Fleet Treasure
6 Songs
7 Cooking (limited to 2 weeks)
8 Listening Comprehension
9 Having Fun in Spanish (limited to 2 weeks)
10 Dramas
11 Pre-Columbian Indians
12 Reading (literary and nonliterary)
13 Contemporary Mexico
14 Multimedia
15 Music
16 A Period of History
17 Individual Project
18 Revolutionaries from Different Centuries and Countries

19 Daily Situations
20 Interviewing Native Speakers
21 Trips
22 Contemporary Life

Each of these courses does not represent a finite set of objectives and learning activities on a specific topic. Rather, each represents a framework within which the student identifies (with the help of the teacher) specific objectives, learning activities, and mode of evaluation. Each course is accompanied by a *Hay que hacer* sheet that identifies the type and amount of work needed to complete one week's work. Such a design permits students to spend from one to four consecutive weeks on any one topic. It also means that students can repeat minicourses during the following semester or year, provided that the subject lends itself to additional study and the students identify different objectives and activities.

Weekly evaluation

No matter how the students design their course sequence, they must undergo some form of weekly evaluation. Most courses require that students make up lists of new vocabulary words, submit them to the teacher, and take a quiz based on the lists. Every week they either turn in a project or make an appointment (*cita*) with the teacher for a final minicourse oral evaluation or a weekly progress report in the case of longer courses. Students are given grades not only on the content of their presentations but also on grammatical and phonological accuracy. In addition, they must submit a bibliography of sources used in their learning activities.

Use of small groups

One of the most interesting aspects of the SSMCs is the use of small groups as the mode of instruction. At the beginning of the first block of time devoted to SSMCs students identify a maximum of three other individuals with whom they would like to work during the first semester's SSMCs. No restrictions are placed on the composition of the groups; consequently, some constitute homogeneous groupings of more advanced students, and others are composed of individuals at varying levels of ability and length of foreign language study. Students not wishing to work with a group do have the option to complete the minicourses independently. In cooperation with the two staff members, these groups or individuals then plan their selection of minicourses for the semester. The group always works together on the same minicourse topic, but individuals within the group may have different objectives and activities to complete. For example, the group may have selected the minicourse, Reading, for a period of two weeks, but the selections to be read may vary both in kind and level of difficulty for each individual in the group.

Advantages of small groups

The staff maintains that allowing students in Levels III to V to work together in small groups offers several advantages:

1 Because Spanish is the mandated vehicle of communication in these classes, lower-level students can benefit from the more advanced students' facility with the language, which in turn sharpens the incentive of the former.
2 The plan allows for good students at all levels to work together if they so desire and less able ones to do the same if they wish to avoid the competition often inherent in the traditional class.
3 When the teacher is not available, better students at all levels are called upon for help by their peers.
4 Scheduling difficulties are reduced because two time slots are available to all advanced-level Spanish students (74).

Hay que hacer

To better understand the flexibility of these minicourses, *Hay que hacer* sheets for three different topics are included below. They do not follow the formal pattern of learning activity packets as set forth by Rosenthal (99) and others in the professional literature. A careful inspection does reveal, however, that they do indeed include all the components needed for student completion of the required task. Objectives, for example, are often subsumed in the learning activities or in the directions for evaluation.

Hay Que Hacer Bloomington High School South

Brown power

Brown Power: Spanish-Speaking Americans

1 Read *at least one* book or pamphlet in Spanish. The remainder may be in English. Make sure to keep a detailed bibliography as you read, including page numbers.

2 Keep a vocabulary list of 10 words per week to be turned in to the teacher. Tests may be at the end of each week or at the end of the minicourse, as you wish.

3 From each of the lists below, choose one topic of particular interest to you. These should then be researched more in depth. You should spend approximately one week developing each topic. Remember to keep a detailed bibliography.

I–Problems	II–Contributions
Health	Arts (artesania)
Education	Music
Housing	Missions
Employment (general)	Architecture
Migrant workers and labor/management conflict	Food

4 Evaluation

a Define the term *Spanish-speaking American.*

b In either written or oral form, be able to discuss the following:

1 The origins and current location of major Spanish-speaking American groups–indicate population statistics if possible.

2 Assimilation problems–their causes and effects–in relation to #3, I. You may include additional problems. Remember that one of these problems will have to be discussed more thoroughly.

3 Contributions of Spanish speakers to past or contemporary American life. Again, remember one of these contributions will have to be discussed more thoroughly.

c Give your personal opinion on one of the following (in English):

1 Do you believe that Spanish-speaking Americans have more problems assimilating into the Northamerican culture than other ethnic groups (Italians, Germans, etc.)?

2 An Indiana Senate investigating committee made the following proposal to better migrant worker conditions in Versailles, Indiana. Workers were to receive

15¢ less per basket of fruit picked. This money saved would then be applied toward better living conditions. The workers turned down the proposal. The committee interpreted this to mean that the migrant had no interest in better living conditions. React to this.

3 Given the problems of Spanish-speaking Americans, to what extent should state or federal government agencies be involved in their resolution. Do you have any personal responsibility?

d Vocabulary test—10 words per week—use half the list in sentence form.

Hay Que Hacer Bloomington High School South

Interviewing Native Speakers

Native speakers

1 Contact a visitor from a Spanish-speaking country before the minicourse begins or as soon as possible. A list of foreign students at Indiana University may be obtained from your teacher. Try to find nonstudents and people of various ages to interview also.
2 Research the visitor's country and make a list of questions that cover a wide range of topics. Submit the list for comment and correction. A minimum of 10 questions per person is required. Ask questions that will elicit more than a one-word answer, about subjects in which you are interested.
3 Keep a vocabulary list of new and important words (minimum of 20 words). Give a copy to your teacher. You will be tested on this vocabulary.
4 Before your actual interview: Listen to interview tapes from other groups or listen and make notes with the *Circling the Globe* record series. Check Holt, Rinehart & Winston filmstrip series concerning the country of your visitor.
5 Make a tape recording of the interview. This will be evaluated.
6 Compose a short oral or written report containing:
   a Newly learned information
   b Your own reaction to the visitor
   c Major benefit obtained from the course

7 Evaluation:
  a Vocabulary test
  b Tape recording
  c Final report

Hay Que Hacer Bloomington High School South

Listening Comprehension

Listening comprehension

There are four series of listening tapes: A, B, C, and D. Series A is the Berlitz series, and the easiest. Series B includes tapes from ALM I & II, the *Segundo libro,* and *Nuestro mundo.* Series C is *Tal como es.* Series D, the most difficult, is from *Circling the Globe.*

1 Get the vocabulary list for the unit from the teacher. Review the list; learn new words *before* doing any listening. Practice saying words aloud. Take test before listening to tape.
2 Listen to tape (for Series A, watch filmstrip at same time). Listen a maximum of two times. Once begun, *do not stop tape* to relisten to any section. (Remember, the idea is to strengthen your listening abilities, not to test the strength and quality of the tape.)
3 Immediately take the pretest (provide your own paper for this). If you have 90 percent or better on the pretest, proceed to next packet.
4 Optional but recommended: With a teacher or on tape, give as many statements as possible in Spanish about the content of the dialogue.
5 If you have less than 90 percent correct on the pretest:
  a Restudy vocabulary. Write one sentence with each new vocabulary word.
  b Relisten to tape.
  c Give oral summary of tape (*not* optional in this section).
  d Take mastery test.

The minicourse program at Bloomington High School South has been evaluated annually since its inception in 1971 via a variety of instruments, all designed by the local staff. The results of these evaluations have been directly responsible for many changes. Individual courses have been added or deleted;

specific content has been changed or increased; learning activity guidelines have been clarified; and the design of the program itself has undergone significant alteration.

Program evaluation

Results from a questionnaire administered to students in the spring of 1976 indicated overwhelmingly positive feelings about the program. Asked if they preferred taking advanced Spanish through a minicourse program rather than through a traditional one (students have been exposed to traditional programs in Levels I and II), 32 percent strongly agreed, 56 percent agreed, and only a total of 11 percent either disagreed (10 percent) or strongly disagreed (1 percent). The program demonstrated its power to combat the dropout problem when 55 percent of the students either strongly agreed or agreed with the statement that they continued the study of Spanish after Level II because of the minicourse program. The most revealing and implication-laden evidence found in the data was the fact that 94 percent (46 percent strongly agree, 48 percent agree) of the students agreed that they enjoyed the small-group approach used in the program. This evidence is in direct contrast to that gathered by Brown (10) in a recently completed study. Using a semantic differential, Brown studied the attitudes of administrators, parents, students, and teachers toward 12 specifically defined characteristics of individualized instruction including small-group work. He found that both administrators and parents ranked small-group instruction almost at the very top of the list, and students and teachers placed it almost at the very bottom. Brown explains this finding by saying that his personal observations of small-group instruction in the participating schools revealed serious misuse of the concept, thus causing both students and teachers to harbor negative feelings toward it. He concludes that the greatest need of teachers involved in individualized programs is high quality inservice training in the use of small-group instruction.

Effect on language skills

Like all other minicourse programs examined in the professional literature or the questionnaire responses, Bloomington High School South has not formally evaluated the effect of its program on the four specific language skills. Both staff members agree that the students are definitely more comfortable and daring in their everyday oral use of the language, but they also conclude that the students do not pronounce the language as well and have more difficulty within the realm of grammar. This impression was corroborated by the results of the 1976 questionnaire. Asked to react to the statement, "since beginning minicourses my grammatical skills in Spanish have improved," 6 percent responded, a great deal; 31 percent, much; 56 percent, some; and 6 percent, none at all. When queried about improvement in their ability to speak Spanish, the response was 15 percent, a great deal; 31 percent, much; 46 percent, some; and 8 percent, none at all. The latter is somewhat difficult to interpret because one does not know whether the students interpreted *speak* to mean ability to communicate or ability to construct orally and pronounce properly correct grammatical utterances. In addition to annual evaluations, the staff has also closely followed the results of college-bound students on Spanish placement tests, especially those administered by Indiana University. In general, results have shown that students have been performing at approximately the same level or slightly higher than that of students who had taken these tests prior to the inception of the minicourse program.

Unbiased comments

The comments of unbiased undergraduate foreign language majors concerning the minicourse program are interesting. Having observed the program as part of their teacher training at Indiana University, they made the following remarks:

> In talking to the students, I discovered an overwhelming positive response to the minicourse program. They pointed out that it is much more interesting than the traditional classroom (Machia, 71).
>
> I was very impressed by the minicourse format. The students were well organized and knew exactly what they were supposed to do. This format created a relaxed classroom atmosphere (Johnson, 52).
>
> Ruth and I wandered around the room filled with a steady hum of voices. Several largish round tables were occupied by groups looking up words or composing compositions together. An occasional loner was reading a Spanish masterpiece or a Mexican newspaper and taking notes. None of the students was too shy to speak to us or was disturbed by our presence. What amazed me more than anything was that they

understood me and always made a valiant effort to reply in full, correct sentences. When someone would stop for a word, his friend would jump in with help (Relkin, 95).

Among the student comments written on the latest evaluation, several indicated room for improvement in specific courses. Some students wanted the removal of the easy courses, but most interesting of all, when asked which minicourses they wanted eliminated, the one mentioned most often was the teacher-taught segment.

All things considered, the minicourse program at Bloomington High School seems to provide opportunities not found in a traditional program. It is best summed up in the words of one student who wrote: "I really like the change of the minicourse-type class during the school day. It adds variety; therefore, it isn't such a boring daily schedule." That this statement reflects influence of the program not only on this student's study of Spanish, but more importantly, on his/her entire education as well is significant.

Variety

Guidelines to implementing a minicourse program

Rationale

Any significant curricular change must be based on a sound rationale. Teachers must be able to justify program changes not only to administrators, parents, and students, but to themselves as well. In building a program rationale care must be taken not to base a program on a series of unexamined assumptions. The validity of assumptions upon which minicourse programs are based should be continually examined and evaluated. Below, the reader will find a set of statements from which he may select those most appropriate to build a rationale for his own unique situation. Minicourses provide an opportunity:

1 For competing with other elective programs
2 To serve a larger clientele
3 To better meet the needs and interests of individual students
4 To involve students in curriculum development
5 For teachers to make use of their specialized talents
6 For goal clarification

7 For limited curricular and instructional change
8 For student choice
9 For remedial as well as enrichment offerings
10 For partial curricular additions, deletions, and modifications
11 For breadth and/or depth of language, literature, and culture offerings

Although a teacher is capable of building a sound rationale for a minicourse program in his school, he is not necessarily ready to implement such a change. He may first want to seek answers to several important questions suggested by Jenkinson (50).

1 *How large must a school be to offer a minicourse program?* Programs exist in schools ranging in size from 400 to 4,000 students. In some small schools minicourses are responsible for maintaining advanced-level programs.
2 *How much time is required to plan a minicourse program?* Most schools have spent one year in designing the program and preparing instructional materials.
3 *Can a partial program of minicourses be successfully implemented?* An important advantage of minicourses is their flexibility. Teachers may wish to refer to the Columbus (Indiana) East High School (17, 18, 19) design which maintains at least part of the traditional sequence at every level of instruction.
4 *What is the cost of a minicourse program?* When asked that very question, almost all program directors mentioned no increase in actual monetary expenditures. However, they did affirm a substantial increase in teacher preparation time.

Student involvement

A well-conceived minicourse program will involve students in the planning, implementing, and evaluating stages. Phillips (93) claims that "the minicourse most fully involves the students in curricular planning" (p. 235). Folta (29) recommends seven different ways to involve students in curriculum planning: as motivators for curriculum change; as respondents to questionnaires; as evaluators of total program design; as evaluators of single courses; as course designers; as team writers of course descriptions; as reviewers of textbooks and materials.

Planning the program

In listing the steps to planning a minicourse program we assume that all disinterested members of the foreign language faculty will at least permit those interested to proceed without interference. If not, perhaps a curricular change should not be contemplated.

Step 1 Assessing student interest. Step 1 consists of determining what the students think of the proposed curricular change and identifying specific areas of student interest, not only within the boundaries of language learning but also in their daily lives. An excellent example of a student questionnaire designed to meet the latter objective is found in the appendix of *The Extended Foreign Language Sequence with Emphasis on New Courses for Levels IV and V* (Fearing and Arendt, 27).

Step 2 Assessing student needs. The area most neglected by teachers contemplating curricular change is probably assessing student needs; yet it could very well mean the difference between program integrity and improbity. If minicourses are to follow basic language instruction, student proficiency should be evaluated in each of the four skills to determine specific student needs. This may be accomplished via standardized or teacher-made tests or through the use of learning activity packages that include pretests. Teachers must realize that student interests do not always coincide with student need, and determining both is the teacher's responsibility.

Step 3 Seeking administrative support. Armed with the results of the first two procedures along with a solid rationale, the staff should seek support from both administrators and counselors. Possible scheduling difficulties must be discussed with both, and the possibility of partial credit must be explored. Teachers might also wish to enhance positive administrative reaction by seeking parental support.

Step 4 Proposing curricular selections. In addition to data identifying student interests and needs, the faculty must now consider staff adequacy and qualifications as well as availability of materials to establish possible curricular offerings. At this point the staff must weigh the differences between interests and needs and then reconcile the proposed offerings with the overall goals of the foreign language program.

Step 5 Identifying specific minicourses. Students are now polled to determine the courses to be offered. Based on the decisions made in Step 4, the polling instrument may be totally open or it may force the selection of courses within identified categories such as language, literature, and culture.

Step 6 Planning for course development. Besides examining the specific suggestions recommended below, teachers should consider attending one of the numerous workshops offered by universities and professional organizations throughout the country and abroad. A listing of these appears annually in the April issues of both *Foreign Language Annals* and *The Modern Language Journal.*

Searching for appropriate materials

Among the many minicourse programs examined for this chapter, virtually all respondents indicated that the materials used were primarily homemade. This has probably constituted the most serious constraint in the growth of minicourse programs. Language teachers often burdened with numerous preparations have simply found it impossible to devote the time necessary for the development of totally new courses. The recent review by Jenks (51), however, predicts that help is on the way. Relating materials to recent foreign language trends, he says about the deviation from the full-semester course structure:

Help on the way

> The bulk of supplementary materials reviewed and the infrastructure of many recent textbooks indicate that the topical articulated short course or "stretched" unit has gained respectability. Further manipulation of the time-length schedules should continue if today's materials are any barometer for tomorrow's classroom organization (p. 123).

Jenks further claims that "possibly the most pervasive new development in language textbooks is their flexibility and adaptability for individualizing instruction" (p. 101). He then lists several recent specific texts. Such a development is important to the growth of minicourses because many are at least partially predicated on that mode of instruction. Jenks also suggests a plethora of cultural sources already prepared as minicourses or easily adaptable to the format. No teacher actually contemplating curricular development of any kind should proceed without first reading this useful chapter.

Other absolutely indispensable resources to existing materials include the three guides prepared by Moore: "Interdisciplinary German-Language Cultural Units" (80), "French Culture from A to V (Actualités to Vins)" (79), and "Spanish Culture from A to V (Actualidades to Venezuela)" (81). Each of these items identifies specific resource materials and numerous suggested activities for many different cultural topics.

Teacher-made materials

Although teacher-made materials rarely reflect the standards of professional publishers, many merit serious consideration for use in minicourse programs. Every year since 1972 the University of Minnesota has published a list of Foreign Language Curriculum Units (30) prepared by the participants in their annual summer workshop abroad. Photocopies of these units, many of which are adaptable for local use, are available from the University of Minnesota. Indiana University, through its Coordinator for School Foreign Languages, also offers materials prepared by summer workshop participants (62). Grittner (37) describes the "borrow and copy" approach used by his office in Wisconsin to share teacher-prepared materials. After selecting from lists of *French, German, Latin or Spanish "Borrow and Copy" Unipacs,* teachers receive an original from Grittner, copy the parts they need, and return it promptly. The approach has worked well. Grittner cautions that these units be so designed to supplant rather than merely supplement existing texts. As an example, he cites the learning packet on Nicaragua, Wisconsin's "sister state," prepared by Ozete (90). Finally, teachers preparing minicourses are advised to examine the large number of Dade County quinmester courses in French, German, Hebrew, Italian, Latin, Russian, and Spanish—all available through ERIC.

Developing individual courses

The particular format used by each individual teacher for developing courses will depend largely on a combination of interrelated factors: mode of instruction, individual teacher preference, student need, and nature of available materials. The suggestions that follow merely represent a general format that can be adapted to specific local needs.

1 Identify course topic.
2 Identify general ideas to be developed within the scope of the topic. Before delineating specific student objectives, the teacher should list in general terms the possible outcomes of each course.
3 Identify specific student objectives using terminology easily understood by students. Performance terminology should be used wherever applicable. However, there is no reason for teachers to refrain from using nonbehavioral terms if all parties agree on the meaning of these terms.
4 Make a list of available materials.
5 Identify possible learning activities. This involves correlating materials with the desired mode of instruction. At this point teachers might also wish to distinguish between required and optional learning activities.
6 Prepare instruments needed to evaluate course objectives. Depending on the nature of the course, this might include the preparation of pretests, selftests, and posttests.
7 Prepare a brief course description for use by administrators, students, parents, counselors, and colleagues.
8 Prepare a short evaluation form to gather student reaction to the course.

Individuals wishing to consult more detailed guidelines for course preparation should refer to Gunderson (39) who suggests a somewhat different format and includes the specific details of both a language- and a culture-oriented minicourse. In the publication *Extended Foreign Language Sequence with Emphasis on New Courses for Levels IV and V*, Fearing and Arendt (27) present yet another model for course development.

Evaluating the program

Improved evaluation needed

The data collected indicate increased attention to evaluation among minicourse programs. Although this represents an improvement over the evaluation of traditional programs, it is far from the systematic evaluation procedures needed to demonstrate the value of minicourse programs, especially because the latter constitute curricular change, which demands a greater degree of substantiation. Hillocks (44) recommends eight different procedures for evaluating English elective programs. These are adapted below to fit the particular needs of foreign language minicourse programs.

1 Review broad educational goals in terms of the program rationale and evaluate specific course objectives in terms of the broad purposes. Does the rationale withstand careful scrutiny? Do the specific course objectives reflect the wider purposes of the program? Are the specific course objectives clear enough to permit meaningful evaluation?
2 Evaluate individual courses in terms of student objectives. Have the students learned to do things they could not do before taking the course?
3 Invite local colleagues and nearby interested university personnel to visit the program. Does the class exhibit characteristics appropriate to the program rational and course objectives? If communication is a primary goal, are the dynamics of classroom interaction suitable?
4 Conduct a faculty review of the total program on a regular basis. Ask administrators and other interested parties to join the review. Do the course offerings really satisfy the needs and abilities of all students enrolled?
5 Use a well-constructed questionnaire, the items of which reflect the basic purposes of the program, to ascertain student attitudes. Use the same questionnaire every year to monitor negative and positive changes. Such an instrument is best developed by a student-faculty committee.
6 Use attitude surveys in each course consisting of restricted and free-response items related to the particular nature of the course. Do students believe that they have learned something? What revisions do they suggest?
7 Administer language tests at the beginning and end of the year to monitor progress in the four skills. In preparing these tests, teachers should distinguish between testing for linguistic and communicative competence.
8 Use the results of all these to examine the validity of the total program and individual course offerings. Which

> courses and program features should remain intact and which ones should be revised or eliminated? What additions should be made to the program? What areas warrant further study (pp. 102–03)?

Jorstad (54) offers additional specific information on program evaluation, while Jenkinson (50) suggests several kinds of questions that might be answered through evaluation.

Summary

1. The 1970s have witnessed significant diversification in all phases of American education best exemplified by the rapid growth of alternative schools.
2. Short-term electives have been introduced into the high school curriculum in business education, English, foreign languages, science, and social studies in an attempt to expand student options.
3. A minicourse is a course shorter than the standard academic unit. It may be phased, sequential, nonsequential, terminal.
4. Born in the mid-1960s, English elective programs have shattered the traditional structure of the English secondary curriculum and have engendered a new sense of professionalism among English teachers.
5. The majority of foreign language minicourses are offered at advanced levels of instruction and they vary in length from one to 12 weeks.
6. Minicourses have significantly broadened content at the advanced levels of foreign language instruction. The greatest impact has been in the area of "everyday" culture.
7. Minicourse programs tend to use a combination of instructional modes with a marked increase in the use of small-group instruction.
8. Although program evaluation needs to be strengthened, present procedures indicate highly positive attitudes among students and teachers. Minicourse programs also show significant enrollment gains.

9 The profession is witnessing a dramatic increase in the availability of materials suitable for short-term courses.
10 The viability of minicourse programs rests on the presentation of a sound rationale, the implementation of a plan for program and course development that includes student input, and the establishment of systematic evaluation procedures.

Conclusion

The growth of a curriculum in American education based on the personal-benefit theory has been examined in this chapter. We have seen its manifestations in the alternative school movement and in the development of elective programs throughout the secondary-school curriculum. Within the area of foreign language teaching, we have focused on the minicourse, a limited yet potentially influential outgrowth of the diversified curriculum. We have witnessed variety even within the boundaries of this limited concept, and more importantly, we have observed success.

All of this does not imply that we have found "yet another cure." Rather, it simply signifies the acquisition of one additional resource to help serve the needs of all our clients. Chastain (14) sees the minicourse as only one of 10 significant developments in modern foreign language teaching. Lippmann (63) claims that "the words that should best describe a successful foreign language department of the future are service and diversity" (p. 66). Minicourses might help us achieve that success, but only if accompanied by our deep personal commitment to the needs and interests of our students. In the words of Beatrice and Ronald Gross:

> We cannot sink back into an ideology, a style, an approach, a technique. To teach truly means that every day, every minute we must be ready to engage directly that specific situation before us, bringing to bear upon it everything we have learned and been. Of course, we will always fall short of this ideal of aliveness and conscientiousness, but it must remain our ideal (38, p. 11).

References, The Minicourse: A viable curricular alternative

1 Alonso, Elizabeth B. Dade County Schools, 1444 Biscayne Boulevard, Suite 215, Miami, Florida 33132. [Questionnaire.]

2 ——— and Mirta R. Vega. "Quinmester Courses: What Are They," *American Foreign Language Teacher* 2,iv(1972):12–13.

3 *Alternative Schools '75.* The Superintendent's Annual Report, Cincinnati Public Schools, Cincinnati, Ohio. [A Special Supplement of *The Cincinnati Post,* 24 March 1975.]

4 Ashley, Gardner P. Personal Communication, 1976.

5 Beers, Ransom B. "The Use of Activity-Centered Minicourses to Solve Difficult Educational Problems," *The Science Teacher* 40,vi(1973):26–29.

6 *Bloomington (Indiana) High School North: Course Descriptions.* Bloomington, Indiana: Bloomington High School North, 1976. [Mimeo.]

7 Born, Warren C.,ed., *Toward Student-Centered Foreign Language Programs.* Reports of the Working Committees of the Northeast Conference on the Teaching of Foreign Languages. Montpelier, Vermont:Capital City Press, 1974.

8 Bourque, Jane, and Linda Chehy. "Exploratory Language and Culture:A Unique Program," *Foreign Language Annals* 9,i(1976):10–16.

9 Brown, B. Frank. *The Reform of Secondary Education:A Report to the Public and the Profession.* New York:McGraw-Hill, 1973.

10 Brown, Timothy F. *The Identification of the Key Components of a Totally Individualized High School Curriculum as Delineated by Educational Writers and The Perception of These by Students, Teachers, Parents, and Administrators in Selected, Individualized High Schools.* Bloomington:Indiana University, 1976. [Doctoral dissertation.]

11 Bryant, Anne. "Biology Broken Into Modules," *The Science Teacher* 41,i(1974):39–40.

12 Buck, Kathryn. "Report on the 1974–75 Survey of Non-Traditional Curricula." *Bulletin of the Association of Departments of Foreign Languages* 7,i(1975):12–16.

13 Carter, Thomas P. "Diversification through Minicourses," *The Canadian Modern Language Review* 31,v(1975):428–31.

14 Chastain, Kenneth. *Developing Second-Language Skills:Theory to Practice, Second Edition.* Chicago:Rand McNally, 1976.

15 Clapper, William O. Roanoke County Public Schools, 526 College Avenue, Salem, Virginia 24153. [Questionnaire.]

16 Cordes, Henry M. "Keeping the Door to the Future Open through Imaginative Course Development," 209–13 in Wilga M. Rivers, Louise H. Allen, Sandra Savignon, and Richard T. Scanlan, eds., *Changing Patterns in Foreign Language Programs:Report of the Illinois Conference on Foreign Languages in Junior and Community Colleges, 1972.* Rowley, Massachusetts:Newbury House, 1972.

17 *Descriptions of Junior English Minicourses, 1976.* Columbus, Indiana:Columbus East High School, 1976. [Mimeo.]

18 *Descriptions of Senior English Minicourses, 1975-76.* Columbus, Indiana:Columbus East High School, 1975. [Mimeo.]

19 *Descriptions of Sophomore English Minicourses, 1975.* Columbus, Indiana:Columbus East High School, 1975. [Mimeo.]

20 DiStefano, Philip P. *A Comparison of Student Attitudes Toward Traditional and Diversified Elective English Offerings.* Columbus:The Ohio State University, 1974. [Doctoral dissertation.]

21 ——— "The Elective Curriculum:A Breakthrough for Urban Students?" *English Education* 7,ii(1976):99–103.

22 Doyle, Walter. "Educational Opportunity—A National Commitment," *Educational Leadership* 33, iv(1976):252:56.

23 Ebling, Benjamin. Western Michigan University, Kalamazoo, Michigan 49002. [Questionnaire.]

24 Elifson, Lucy. Waukesha High School, 401 North Grand Avenue, Waukesha, Wisconsin. [Questionnaire.]

25 Ensminger, Donald C. Jefferson County Schools, 10675 River City Mall, Louisville, Kentucky 40202. [Questionnaire.]

26 "Ex-Students Pinpoint Wrongs in Nation's High Schools," *Phi Delta Kappan* 57,vii(1976):484–85.

27 Fearing, Percy, and Jermaine D. Arendt. *The Extended Foreign Language Sequence:With Emphasis on New Courses for Levels IV and V.* St. Paul, Minnesota:State Department of Education, 1971. [EDRS: ED 047 586.]

28 ———, and Frank M. Grittner. *Exploratory Foreign Language Problems in the Middle School.* A Curriculum Report produced by participants in the ACTFL Pre-Conference Workshop. Denver, Colorado:1974. [EDRS: ED 104 174.]

29 Folta, Bernarr. "Seven Ways to Involve Students in Curriculum Planning," *English Journal* 63,iv (1974):42–45.

30 *Foreign Language Curriculum Units.* Foreign Language Curriculum Materials Center, University of Minnesota, 224 Peik Hall, Minneapolis, Minnesota 55455.

31 *Foreign Language Exploratory:Resource Guide and Handbook.* Upper Marlboro, Maryland: Prince George's County Public Schools, 1975.

32 *French for Travelers—Spanish for Travelers: Nonsequential Semester Courses in the Foreign Language Area Guidelines and Handbook.* Upper Marlboro, Maryland:Prince George's County Board of Education, 1973. [EDRS: ED 074 800.]

33 Fryer, T. Bruce. "Free to Explore:Curricular Developments," 9–46 in Gilbert A. Jarvis,ed., *Per-*

spective:A New Freedom, ACTFL Review of Foreign Language Education, Volume 7. Skokie, Illinois:National Textbook Company, 1975.

34 *German for Travelers:Guidelines and Handbook.* Upper Marlboro, Maryland:Prince George's County Public Schools, 1975.

35 Grant, Kay. Sycamore High School, 7400 Cornell Road, Cincinnati, Ohio. [Questionnaire.]

36 Grittner, Frank M. "Individualized Instruction: An Historical Perspective," *Modern Language Journal* 59(1975):323–33.

37 ——— Personal Communication, 1976.

38 Gross, Beatrice, and Ronald Gross. *Will it Grow in a Classroom?* New York:Delacorte, 1974.

39 Gunderson, Barbara L. "Creating Elective French Courses," 44–47 in Lorraine A. Strasheim,ed., *Foreign Language in a New Apprenticeship for Living.* Bloomington:Indiana Language Program, Indiana University, 1971.

40 Hancock, Charles R. SUNY Albany, Maywood Elementary School, Central Avenue, Albany, New York 12222. [Questionnaire.]

41 Hansel, Nancy. Whittier Middle School, 2000 West Brooks, Norman, Oklahoma 73069. [Questionnaire.]

42 Hartline, James D. Brooke High School, Box 610, R.R. 1, Wellsburg, West Virginia. [Questionnaire.]

43 Heesen, Philip T. Millersville State College, Millersville, Pennsylvania 17551. [Questionnaire.]

44 Hillocks, George, Jr. *Alternatives in English:A Critical Appraisal of Elective Programs.* Urbana, Illinois:ERIC Clearinghouse on Reading and Communication Skills, 1972.

45 ——— "Speaking of Choices" *Curriculum Report* 2,iv(1973):1–12.

46 ——— "Making the Choices" *Curriculum Report* 2,v(1973):1–8.

47 ——— *An Evaluation of Project APEX:A Nongraded Phase-Elective English Program.* Trenton, Michigan:Trenton Public Schools, 1971.

48 Hoye, Almon G. "Flexibility—From Folly to Promise," 29–33 in Lorraine A. Strasheim,ed., *Foreign Language in a New Apprenticeship for Living.* Bloomington:Indiana Language Program, Indiana University, 1971.

49 *Initiation Series.* Corson Associates. Box 4388, Alexandria, Virginia 22303.

50 Jenkinson, Edward, comp. and ed., *Some Questions and Answers about Planning Phase-Elective Programs in English.* Terre Haute:Indiana Council of Teachers of English, 1972.

51 Jenks, Frederick L. "Foreign Language Materials:A Status Report and Trends Analysis," 93–128 in Gilbert A. Jarvis,ed., *Perspective:A New Freedom,* ACTFL Review of Foreign Language Education, Volume 7. Skokie, Illinois:National Textbook Company, 1975.

52 Johnson, Ann. *Diary of Classroom Observations.* Bloomington:Indiana University, 1975.

53 Joiner, Elizabeth G. "Tailoring Language Instruction to Student Needs," 151–84 in Gilbert A. Jarvis,ed., *The Challenge of Communication,* ACTFL Review of Foreign Language Education, Volume 6. Skokie, Illinois:National Textbook Company, 1974.

54 Jorstad, Helen L. "Testing as Communication," 223–73 in Gilbert A. Jarvis,ed., *The Challenge of Communication,* ACTFL Review of Foreign Language Education, Volume 6. Skokie, Illinois: National Textbook Company, 1974.

55 ——— Personal Communication, 1976.

56 Karlin, Muriel Schoenbrun. *Administrator's Guide to a Practical Career Education Program.* West Nyack, New York:Parker, 1974.

57 Keller, Howard H. Murray State University, Murray, Kentucky 42071. [Questionnaire.]

58 ——— and John W. Ferguson. "A Cultural Introduction to Foreign Languages," *Foreign Language Annals* 9(1976):50–55.

59 LaConte, Ronald T. "Electives, Objectives and Distorted Perspectives," *NASSP Bulletin* 58, ccclxxxiii(September 1974):104–09.

60 Lafayette, Robert C. "A Foreign Language Option:The Minicourse." *Curriculum Report* 3,i (1973):1–12.

61 LaRocque, Geraldine E. "Is the Elective Program Another Case of Professional Doublespeak?" *English Education* 7,ii(1976):104–09.

62 *Learning Activities Packets.* Coordinator for School Foreign Languages, Memorial East M21, Indiana University, Bloomington, Indiana 47401.

63 Lippmann, Jane N. "Rationale for Language Study," 37–69 in Gilbert A. Jarvis,ed., *The Challenge of Communication,* ACTFL Review of Foreign Language Education, Volume 6. Skokie, Illinois:National Textbook Company, 1974.

64 Lipton, Gladys. "Curricula for New Goals," 187–218 in Dale L. Lange and Charles J. James,eds., *Foreign Language Education:A Reappraisal.* ACTFL Review of Foreign Language Education, Volume 4. Skokie, Illinois:National Textbook Company, 1972.

65 Loew, Helene Z. "Options and Perspectives Updated:An Overview of Some Foreign Language Offerings in New York State," *Foreign Language Annals* 9(1976):66–70.

66 Logan, Gerald E. *Individualized Foreign Language Learning:An Organic Process.* Rowley, Massachusetts:Newbury House, 1973.

67 ———Kleine Schule/Live Oak High, Box 927, Morgan Hill, California 95037. [Questionnaire Response.]

68 Love, F. William D., and Lucille J. Honig. *Options and Perspectives:A Sourcebook of Innovative Foreign Language Programs in Action, K-12.* New York:Modern Language Association, 1973.

69 Lyons, Kathleen. Half Hollow Hills High School East, 50 Vanderbilt Parkway, Dix Hills, New York 11746.

70 McDanield, Michael A. "Tomorrow's Curriculum Today," 103–31 in Alvin Toffler,ed., *Learning for Tomorrow.* New York:Vintage, 1974.

71 Machia, Gloria. *Diary of Classroom Observations.* Indiana University 1975. [Unpublished.]
72 Malsbary, Dean R. "Curriculum Up-Date: Business Education," *NASSP Bulletin* 59(1975):95–100.
73 Minto, Karen L. Ada High School, Grand & Turner Avenues, Ada, Ohio 45810. [Questionnaire.]
74 *Minicourses for Advanced Spanish.* Bloomington, Indiana: Bloomington High School South, 1974. [Mimeo.]
75 Moffett, Oren E. Weber State College, Ogden, Utah 84408. [Questionnaire.]
76 Moore, Elmer C. Assistant Superintendent for Instruction, Franklin County Board of Education, 916 East Main Street, Frankfort, Kentucky 40601. [Questionnaire.]
77 Moore, Merriam M. Ridgefield High School, 700 North Salem Road, Ridgefield, Connecticut 06877. [Questionnaire.]
78 ——— *Minicourse Curriculum for German IV and German V.* Ridgefield, Connecticut, Ridgefield High School, 1971. [EDRS: ED 050 633.]
79 ——— *French Culture from A to V (Actualités to Vins):63 French-Language Interdisciplinary Cultural Units.* Ridgefield, Connecticut: Ridgefield High School, 1975. [Mimeo.]
80 ——— "Interdisciplinary German-Language Cultural Units," *Die Unterrichtspraxis* 7,i(1974): 197–98.
81 ——— *Spanish Culture from A to V (Actualidades to Venezuela):73 Spanish-Language Interdisciplinary Cultural Units,* Ridgefield, Connecticut: Ridgefield High School, 1976.
82 Morrow, Judith C. "Exploratory Courses for the Middle and Junior High School," 119–43 in Frank M. Grittner,ed., *Student Motivation and the Foreign Language Teacher.* Skokie, Illinois: National Textbook Company, 1974.
83 ——— Bloomington High School South, 1965 South Walnut, Bloomington, Indiana 47401. [Questionnaire and interview.]
84 Mullen, Wahneta M. "Many Learners, Many Goals, Many Curricula," 37–71 in Gilbert A. Jarvis,ed., *Responding to New Realities,* ACTFL Review of Foreign Language Education, Volume 5. Skokie, Illinois: National Textbook Company, 1974.
85 National Association of Secondary School Principals. *This We Believe:Secondary Schools in a Changing Society.* [A Statement on Secondary Education Prepared by the Task Force on Secondary Schools.] Reston, Virginia: NASSP, 1975.
86 Nease, Janice A. Sissonville High School. 6301 Sissonville Drive, Charleston, West Virginia 25312. [Questionnaire.]
87 Neiswander, Soni. Ada High School, Grand & Turner Avenues, Ada, Ohio. [Questionnaire.]
88 Nichols, Pamela T. Thomas McKean High School. 301 McKennans Church Road, Wilmington, Delaware 19808. [Questionnaire.]
89 Nushy, John M. *A Comparative Analysis and Evaluation of Student Achievement and Attitude in a Secondary Elective and Conventional English Program.* Los Angeles: University of Southern California, 1974. [Doctoral dissertation.]
90 Ozete, Oscar. *Nicaragua:A Look Across Cultures.* Madison: Wisconsin Department of Public Instruction, 1975.
91 Papalia, Anthony, and Joseph Zampogna. "The Changing Curricula," 299–328 in Gilbert A. Jarvis,ed., *The Challenge of Communication,* ACTFL Review of Foreign Language Education, Volume 6. Skokie, Illinois: National Textbook Company, 1974.
92 Pearl, Lauren F. Oxon Hill Senior High, 6701 Leyte Drive, Oxon Hill, Indiana. [Questionnaire.]
93 Phillips, June K. "Individualization and Personalization," 219–61 in Gilbert A. Jarvis,ed., *Responding to New Realities,* ACTFL Review of Foreign Language Education, Volume 5. Skokie, Illinois: National Textbook Company, 1974.
94 Postman, Neil, and Charles Weingartner. *The School Book.* New York: Delacorte, 1973.
95 Relkin, Jackie. *Diary of Classroom Observations.* Bloomington, Indiana: Indiana University, 1975. [Unpublished.]
96 Risinger, C. Frederick. "Minicourses and Phase Electives: Panacea or Poppycock?" *News and Notes on the Social Sciences* (Spring 1974):3–5.
97 Rivers, Wilga M. *Speaking in Many Tongues: Essays in Foreign Language Teaching.* Rowley, Massachusetts: Newbury House, 1972.
98 Rodewald, Janet R., and Charlotte B. Evans. "Teacher Training: Dollars and Sense," *Die Unterrichtspraxis* 5,i(1972):10–12.
99 Rosenthal, Bianca. "Developing a Foreign Language Learning Activity Package." *Modern Language Journal* 57(1973):195–99.
100 Ryberg, Donald C. "Flexibility at Work: Marshall-University High School's Foreign Language Program," 34–38 in Lorraine A. Strasheim,ed., *Foreign Language in a New Apprenticeship for Living.* Bloomington: Indiana Language Program, Indiana University, 1971.
101 ——— and Marcia Hallock. "Development of Minicourses at Marshall-University High School: Individualization and Interest" 119–29 in Ronald L. Gougher,ed., *Individualization of Instruction in Foreign Languages:A Practical Guide.* Philadelphia: Center for Curriculum Development, 1972.
102 Seagrave, Maryalice D. North Tonawanda Senior High School, 405 Meadow Drive, North Tonawanda, New York. [Questionnaire.]
103 Seaman, David. Davis and Elkins College, Elkins, West Virginia. [Questionnaire.]
104 Shane, Harold G., and June Grant Shane. "Educating the Youngest for Tomorrow," 181–96 in Alvin Toffler,ed., *Learning for Tomorrow.* New York: Vintage, 1974.
105 Smith, Vernon. *Beyond Phase Electives:English Programs in Optional Public Schools.* Bloomington: Indiana University, 1975. Mimeo.]

106 ——— Daniel J. Burke, and Robert D. Barr. *Optional Alternative Public Schools.* Bloomington, Indiana: Phi Delta Kappa, 1974.
107 Stewart, H. E. Clemson University, Clemson, South Carolina 29631. [Questionnaire.]
108 Strasheim, Lorraine A.,ed., *Foreign Language in a New Apprenticeship for Living.* Bloomington: Indiana Language Program, 1971.
109 Tamarkin, Toby. Manchester Community College, P.O. Box 1046 Manchester, Connecticut 06040. [Questionnaire.]
110 Thrasher, Edith. Bloomington High School South, 1965 South Walnut, Bloomington, Indiana 47401. [Questionnaire.]
111 Vizino, Harold and Sofía Rodriguez. Personal Communication, 1976.
112 Warner, Pearl M. "Free to Reach Out," 259–84 in Gilbert A. Jarvis,ed., *Perspective: A New Freedom,* ACTFL Review of Foreign Language Education, Volume 7. Skokie, Illinois: National Textbook Company, 1975.
113 Wilkins, Wynona H. University of North Dakota, Department of Languages, Box 8198 Grand Forks, North Dakota 58202. [Questionnaire.]
114 Woloshin, David J. University of Arizona, Tucson, Arizona. [Questionnaire.]

5

The student view: Attitudes toward foreign language learning

John L. Walker
University of Texas of the Permian Basin

Introduction

The barbers' problem

When the craze for long hair swept through the ranks of the young men of this nation a few years ago, parents, educators, and law enforcement personnel tried their best to eradicate it—without avail. As proved time and again, young people will choose music, clothes, and mannerisms that are quite different from those considered "normal" or desirable by adults, mainly because the young people want to be themselves. Actually, the very clamor by adults against long hair may have convinced young people that they had a good thing going. Thus, the fashion caught on and caused a sizeable proportion of the population of this country some frustration. Some barbers refused to admit that the trend was anything more than a passing emotional reaction born of a sense of rebellion. They tried to gain adherents to their short-hair crusade by predicting dire consequences for the nation's barbers if such a trend persisted. But the long hair stayed, and a number of the protesting barbers made their own dire predictions come true by failing to adjust to change and consequently going out of business. Other barbers recognized that the trend might continue. They resigned themselves to a belt-tightening existence, confining themselves mainly to cutting the hair of those diminishing few who had not yet been struck by the new fever. They accepted the trend, but chose to live outside it.

John L. Walker (Ph.D., University of California at Los Angeles) is Assistant Professor of Spanish and Assistant to the President at the University of Texas of the Permian Basin in Odessa, Texas. He previously was Assistant Professor of Spanish and Portuguese at the University of Texas at El Paso. Among his publications are articles in *Hispania*, the *Latin American Literary Review* and *Foreign Language Annals*. He is currently active in the development of both administrative and language instruction programs for Texas' first upper-level and graduate university.

A third group of barbers recognized that long hair was an established fact. These enterprising and optimistic businessmen started looking for ways to benefit both young people and themselves. They decided that they could emphasize well-groomed rather than unkempt long hair as a way to capitalize on the trend. Styling shops began to open; new and fashionable hair arrangements were created; and well-styled long hair became an important part of male grooming. Subsidiary industries boomed; men's hair spray, electric hair dryers, and other products sold briskly. The barbers even found that they could charge more for their specialized styling services.

A solution

The implications to language teachers are clear. Certain aspects of student relations must be recognized. One of these is students' desire for a greater voice in their educational programs. This desire is not, however, the fanatical impulse of the 1960s when students pitted a little theory and a lack of experience against the permissive attitude of adults, thereby succeeding in their efforts to take over established organizations and to channel them toward vague ideals of operation. In the 1970s adults and young people have realized that both idealism and practicality have their place in helping civilization grow. The students of the 1970s therefore seem to be more practical in their outlook. They want to have a say in their own educations in accordance with what they view as the pragmatic needs of their lives and the lives of those around them. Of course, the changed economic picture has had its part to play; students of the 1960s had a free and easy lifestyle that permitted them to exploit their theoretical political views. Students of the 1970s see that people can be out of work through forces that are not easily explained or understood. Today's students face a real set of economic problems, problems that have replaced the vague spectres of war, deprivation of rights, and political unrighteousness that troubled students of the last decade. These factors combine to produce a student who is aware of his strength, of his own needs, and of the necessity for a practical education in the world of the late 1970s. This student has greater freedom of choice than in past years, and he often has questions about the use of what he is learning, questions that are making educators sit back and reevaluate their own cherished attitudes and beliefs.

The 1970s student

Economy's role

The educator's choice

We educators can choose not to admit the presence of these new factors, but if we do, we hazard the probability of having the students pass us by and leave us behind. We may find ourselves out of business and of no value to anyone, or we can accept the idea that many students wish greater opportunities to participate in the determination of educational policy. Like the enterprising barbers, we can recognize the firm existence of this trend and seize upon it as a chance for greater accomplishment in the teaching of foreign languages and help ourselves to rewarding futures as well.

Student participation

To accomplish this goal we must consider the question of student participation in the establishment of language pedagogy, the evaluation and revision of teaching methodologies, and the type of graduate desired. We must gauge the scope of student input, assess the value of such data, and discover what students want in their language studies today and what they see as their needs for tomorrow. This does not necessarily mean that we allow students to dictate what we do, the way every lesson should be taught, or exactly what every standard must be; for they themselves will admit that they do not have the experience in language study to do this. It does mean, however, that we should recognize that many of today's students will follow their own impulses and will want the freedom to do so. Thus, it behooves us as language educators to ascertain what today's students want in language study and, based on our own experience and our understanding of their needs, to create the best possible language learning program. The combination of our expertise and their expressed needs should result in an increasing number of young people with skills in communicating, sensitivity to other people's needs and viewpoints, and the perspective of one's own place in the world—insights that language study can give.

Current trends

Statistics from the nation's elementary schools, high schools, and colleges show that language study has been down at all levels for several years. FLES programs have been disappearing, in part because of economic pressures for cutbacks without counterbalancing pressures for retention from students and parents. In the early 1970s high school language requirements were modified in many places, and over 40 percent of all colleges and universities abolished or reduced their language requirements (Lippmann, 27). The emphasis of the 1950s on reading and grammatical review as one of the unexplained requirements of one's basic education fell to the rebellious and questioning spirit of the 1960s where the emphasis was on instant competency. Because this was an unrealistic goal, interest in languages waned (Levy, 26), and the downward trend continued through the first years of the 1970s. In addition, dissatisfaction was expressed by students (and parents) about the language requirement. Vague claims about increased communicative ability did not seem satisfactory. Consequently, an emphasis on finding a practical reason for their study has occurred. Stress is on practical usage of language in one's work, in communication with speakers of other languages here in this country, and in travel.

Practical education

In the student view a new emphasis is placed on practical education to deal with practical problems. Vocational community colleges are the fastest growing educational institutions, and having an education is coming to mean having a marketable skill. Because higher education is no longer the privilege of the elite, it must have a strong role in helping a student cope with today's economy as well as giving him a deeper understanding of the society in which he must function.

Language study seems to be benefiting from this trend. In the early years of this decade college language enrollment dropped 28 percent in French, 24 percent in German, 12 percent in Russian, 5 percent in Spanish, and 3 percent in Italian. The biggest losses in Spanish and Italian were between 1970 and 1972; in the past few years enrollment in these languages has gone up slightly. The decline in French also shows some signs of leveling off. Unfortunately, enrollment in German seems to continue to drop. However, the signs of recovery are present. Perhaps students are realizing that language study teaches communication in an abstract sense, promotes understanding of other people, gives us an impartial look at ourselves from the outside, and can help people succeed in their chosen professions as a result of this increase in sensitivity. Or students may be realizing that knowledge of a particular language is of great practical use in daily communication with foreign language speakers (for example, Spanish in the Southwest.) In this age of increased student self-determination and awareness, some of this upturn is probably due to the fact that educators are now more frequently listening to their students, and the students are offered courses that they themselves see as important to their specific plans and goals.

This aspect of listening to the students is an important development. Language teachers have tended to set the same goals for all students; these goals have dealt mainly with literary analysis or some other skill that teachers thought students needed, rather than with practical skills of speaking and listening and up-to-date cultural insights that students need for today's world (Levy, 26; Lippmann, 27). Reinert (38), for example, points out that a corporation could go bankrupt if it failed to investigate the marketability of a product before pushing it on an uninterested public. Yet foreign language teachers have not only ignored the marketable aspects of their product but have also failed to convince the students of the value of the product, depending instead for enrollments on a captive audience.

Marketability

Marketability, then, can be used in two senses: Language study must be something appealing enough to the student that he will buy it and insist that it be made available, and language study must be something he can market as part of the skills package of his total education. Because the student is deciding for himself more and more these days what he will do in school and in life, he is logically the one to tell us what he needs. The role of the teacher, then, if not to anticipate these desires, is at least to use the skill and experience he or she possesses to respond to the request of the student. Because each student is an individual with his or her own goals, abilities, and preferences, these requests will be varied and must be answered on an individual basis whenever possible. Some offerings must be geared to career goals directly involving the foreign language, career goals with marginal use of language, travel, intellectual curiosity, or to the fundamental desire to have a complete well-rounded education.

Input methods

Three ways to gather such student input include asking him for his evaluation of the programs he is in now, listening to his requests and suggestions for programs, and observing his actual enrollment in and completion of the courses open to him. Obviously, this last approach is the most direct way to gather information, yet it is incomplete. To gain an understanding of what is necessary for a foreign language program in a particular school, for example, looking at the numbers of students attending courses is not sufficient. Students must be asked exactly what they like or dislike about the courses. We must go to students who have dropped courses and find out why and go to the students who are not taking languages at all to find out what they think is lacking in the program. This involves a certain amount of risk for the teacher or administrator, of course, because the student's candid opinion may be disconcerting. However, a candid assessment could also be constructive.

Students rate professors?

Not too long ago the idea of having a student rate his professor was almost insulting, and as late as 1969 in a carefully prepared book on effective language teaching for secondary schools the subject of student ratings was not mentioned (Smith and Leaman, 45). Undoubtedly many educators still feel that allowing a student to criticize what goes on in the classroom is demeaning. But Bailey (4) points out that an aspect of individualized instruction is evaluation of the program and the attitudes of participating students, and she gives examples of how this was done in her own individualized course in French. Grittner (15) states that teachers who maintain excessive standards of their own choosing may have no foreign language program in which to apply these standards, and he insists that the students plan their programs. Setting minimum standards for them is not so useful as encouraging them to want to achieve their own maximum ability. In schools all over the country more and more teachers are turning to their students for feedback and reaction to their programs. Enrollment statistics are still the most common index, of course, and course evaluation seems to be in second place. Few schools seem to be using questionnaires in ascertaining from their students exactly what they would want if given a choice in the matter.

In the area of instructional evaluation in a 1970 poll taken by *Nation's Schools*, one question was: Should students participate in evaluation of teachers and administrators (Halbert, 17)? Approximately 40.5 percent of the school personnel polled said yes; another 42.5 percent said no; and others were not sure. Only 5 percent indicated that they already were using such evaluations. Not only is the split in opinion of interest, but the low rate of implementation even among those supposedly in favor makes one wonder a little about education's interest in evaluating itself. Another poll was taken of a different sampling and the split was about 50/50 with little difference in response between elementary and secondary school personnel. Reluctance on the part of teachers and administrators to obtain feedback from their students can be seen. On one moderate-sized campus in the West, a campaign was carried on to establish student course evaluations. Special instruments were created and made available. The department chairman overtly backed the process and urged the language instructors in his department to participate. Yet, some professors refused to sign up for the materials, and others signed as a matter of politics and then somehow never got around to administering the evaluations. We scarcely need to add that this school has a language requirement and thus does not need to be in the business of actively attracting students.

Why the reluctance?

Why this reluctance? Probably one answer is fear that the teacher's or administrator's performance might be classified as inferior. Another might be a reaction against the student take-overs of the 1960s and a desire to keep the old ways of letting the instructor do the teaching and the learners do the learning. Or it could easily be the often expressed but still meritorious opinion that a learner is not always the best decision-maker about the methods, materials, and philosophy of the teaching of a subject. This opinion can apply both to the evaluation survey and to the general opinion survey. The student is considered unable to judge the teaching process until he understands the complexities of it and has some experience in its application. But student participation in evaluation of the educational process and student participation in politics are established facts in the 1970s. Indeed, as long ago as the Middle Ages students set up their own committees to report on professors who failed to present required material in the specified time (Love, 28).

Reporters vs. judges

As to the objection that he cannot know what he wants until he knows what exists and has value, Menges (33) points out that students are really reporters and not judges in their evaluations and surveys. They can report on their feelings concerning language study, on what they observe the teacher do, on their reactions to the materials and methods used, and on what they see to be useful in the curriculum (or in a hypothetical curriculum). Although they may not be qualified to judge the skills of the teacher, they can report the effect these skills (or the lack of them) have on them as learners. They cannot always judge the actual value of language innovations that they propose, but they can indicate what would be interesting and useful to them within the framework of their own goals as opposed to the goals of the teacher. The process might be compared to our having videotape of ourselves as we teach in the classroom: We are amazed at what such an objective device shows, and we gain new insights into how others see us as revealed by this impartial report.

Data quality

One possible objection to collecting student opinions concerns the validity of the data. Here, too, there is a wide variety of opinion. Sheehan (43), for example, feels that the validity of student ratings has not been substantiated; he feels that they sometimes convey misinformation. Some of the factors that he insists have been shown to reduce validity are age, grade-point average, class size, subject matter, sex of the student and of the instructor, and whether the class is required or elective. Young people are sometimes fad-prone, emotional, and given to romanticizing situations or rejecting them in favor of immediate concerns such as dates or car repairs. Against this background, Sheehan's comments seem plausible.

Yet, Menges (33) points out the lack of a significant relationship between student ratings and the following variables: year in school; grade-point average; expected grade in the course; number of previous courses on the subject; age, sex, and marital status of the student. The only relationship he noted in the 1,200 schools he studied is a slight tendency for students expecting a high grade to give higher ratings. Instructor variables, such as age or sex, seem little related to the ratings. Menges did identify a clear relationship between class size and ratings in some studies, but this is not a variable that can be assigned to the student as an individual.

Motivation

Another positive reason for assessing student opinion is its relationship to motivation. Gardner and Lambert (13) have found that personal desire to learn is very often the key to success. Personal pride and identification with the program as a personal creation can unite the student and his language study.

Johnson (21) has shown that even fourth graders reveal the effect of attitude on their reading. In a classroom experiment 12 interest subsections were identified for the students. Then their variety of interests were correlated with their class attitudes. Those with a positive attitude toward their instructional climate showed little variation in their interests, whereas those with a negative attitude showed a tendency to wander, with varying degrees of inattention related to the 12 interest areas.

Doyle (12) sums up the positive and negative aspects of student evaluations. He affirms that, typically, evaluations by responsible students responding to rating scales properly constructed achieve high reliability. He specifies that anything less than proper preparation invalidates much of the result. Material must be gathered carefully, reported appropriately, and interpreted judiciously. He points out that such reliability can be achieved because there are measurement specialists on large campuses, and permission to use existing forms is easily obtained.

Are evaluations reliable?

Such comments, however, should not discourage the instructor from seeking to determine what his students might like to do in language study or what might induce other students to come into the language program. Most of the above comments apply only to course and instructor evaluation. But even informal discussions in the student union or school cafeteria can be fruitful, if the instructor is willing to reach out to the students for information. Variables may color the comments received in such situations, but some information is better than none at all and can guide the instructor as to where to look or how to proceed toward the more precise evaluation he seeks.

Discussing informally with foreign language students, for example, why they are studying the subject is a good introduction to their thinking processes. Marlin (30) reports the following comments from high school students:

What students say

> I think foreign languages are worthwhile if the student wishes to use the language in his career later on.
>
> Studying and working with a foreign language provides good discipline for the mind.

It presents cultural studies which may someday be the key to world understanding.

There are signs and signals that are universal in any language, and when one is unable to communicate through the language, the awareness of these universal signs is intensified. When one knows the spoken language in the country, obviously communication is easier, but the added advantage gives you an even broader understanding of the people and their culture.

It helps knowing about a language when you apply for a good job.

After college, there are many jobs in which a foreign language would be required or helpful.

Certainly the need for people to communicate is great, and the ability to communicate well is the ability to succeed in today's world.

Once I graduate I may never speak more than three words of Spanish, but through the Spanish language I believe that I've become more familiar with the English language.

Many jobs involve speaking a foreign language, and it is becoming vital to learn a foreign language.

I want to go to college, and language studies, especially three or four years, look good on an application.

Cultures different from our own help broaden knowledge of the outside world.

I think that a foreign language can be beneficial in almost any field you go into.

I think I started a foreign language because it was different from other classes.

To explore the Spanish language is to open up the doors of the narrow-minded American society and walk into a new world with new cultures and new ideas.

Certainly the primary impact of such conversations is the great diversity among our students and the need to satisfy a great variety of plans and goals.

Generally the variables affecting the outcome of such simple surveys and conversations are usually those connected with the teacher and the philosophies and methods applied in the classroom. Sole (46) took a survey of lower-division students in the University of Texas at Austin Department of Spanish and Portuguese. He noted that the difference between skilled and unskilled teachers did not seem to show up in areas such as a student's enjoyment of the course, criticism of the intellectual content, or the value of Spanish in rounding out a student. But the skillfulness of the teacher was significantly related to the value of the course in increasing the student's knowledge, role of language, interest in travel, and desire to study Spanish past the level of the language requirement. Students can also tell us what they are planning to do with their language education, and the Austin students were brutally frank in this. There were 700 of them, taught mostly by teaching assistants. Only 12 percent took Spanish as an elective, and only 8 percent were majors or minors. The rest (80 percent) took Spanish because of the language requirement. Half of these students said they would not be taking Spanish if it were not a requirement, and another 13 percent were not sure they would—that is, more than half the sample easily might not be enrolled in foreign language if they had a choice. In this survey, 49 percent indicated they definitely would not take Spanish beyond the language requirement, and 22 percent were undecided about it—a total of almost three quarters of the sample students. Only 6 percent of the students in the survey took Spanish because it fits into their goals or programs or interest, an example of the isolation of Spanish from other programs.

UT Austin Survey

Two thirds of the students polled want to use Spanish reasonably well. We should note the stress on the word *use*—reading skill comes in a poor third. The students are stressing the fact that they want a living language that they can utilize in their plans, not just a course of study that someone thinks is good for them. They cite the benefits they want from Spanish: 33 percent mention travel, 28 percent mention jobs. Only a slight 6 percent cite literature as a long-range benefit. Language instructors may decry the way education is perceived by these students but we must recognize the trends and try to take them into consideration. The student emphasis in the 1970s is on the

Use stressed

practical use of a language. It becomes a tool to help students benefit in other fields, rather than being an end in itself. The "I-took-two-years-of language-and-I-still-can't-say-anything" complaint, familiar to student opinion researchers over the past few years, is not going to be the refrain of the student of today if there is anything he can do about it. In the Austin survey the higher the students rated their courses in teaching them to speak the language, the higher they also rated them in teaching culture, stimulating desire to travel, and making the student more likely to take more Spanish.

Scarcity of information

One very disturbing fact about the published survey of the University of Texas Spanish students has nothing to do with the survey itself: It is one of very few surveys published for all to know what students are saying. A search of most publications concerned with the pedagogy of language instruction reveals few surveys of the evaluation type. There are occasional comments on higher enrollments obtained by this or that innovation, but few surveys, and almost no open opinion surveys of the type in which students tell what they would like to do in language study. This is disturbing; for it means that there is little information available to the language teacher to use in determining basic directions in which programs should be moving. Such information is being collected, but it often exists in a particular teacher's files. The problem is that it is not disseminated to others. A teacher may be reluctant to survey his own students for fear this would be too limited a sampling, or it might not be technically the best method to use, or it might be interpreted as a sign of weakness on the part of the teacher. But samples of student opinions (even if the sampling procedures are not technically perfect) can at least give some indications of what students think.

In an effort to determine whether new information was in existence, personal letters requesting any available information were sent to chairmen of language departments of community colleges, colleges, and universities all over the country as part of the preparation of this chapter. Those who replied were most gracious, and some good information was gleaned. But the rate of return was appallingly low. Perhaps 10 percent, to be generous, of these personal letters, even of those to acquaintances, were ever acknowledged. Some of the materials sent were unusable and amazingly superficial. Perhaps those who did not reply had nothing to offer or had sampled student opinion and preferred not to reveal results.

To determine whether the surveying of attitudes is more common in high schools, and in a further effort to collect grassroot student survey information, a smaller group of letters was sent to selected high school teachers in various parts of the country. We offered printed credit for the information, so others would know of the good work they were doing and to allay fears that another person might take the credit for their innovations. Only one of these letters was acknowledged.

What can be said about such a devastating apathy, especially when it means language teachers are out of work because of decreasing enrollments? All that can be done here is to report what few things have been found concerning student opinions in hope that this will stimulate a desire on the part of the nation's teachers and school administrators to plan to evaluate course curricula.

Career objectives

Students seem to be saying generally the same things whenever they are given a chance. In a survey of career perceptions of foreign language majors in four states, Allawala (3) found that 80 percent of the students surveyed said that a career objective was an important factor in electing a foreign language major. Only a few years ago girls who wanted a college education but did not plan a career often chose a foreign language major. Now the emerging role of women in the world of industry and the professions must be taken into account. Allawala found also that the potential market of foreign language majors was 78 percent female. Most students surveyed said they preferred teaching or government jobs, but these fields are already well supplied, and graduating majors are going to have to look to business for a career. It is a little difficult to see how a knowledge of *Don Quixote*—however useful it may be to the overall education of the individual (indeed, scholars in many languages would agree it is vital)—can be of much use in business except through its psychological insights. This is not to say that such masterpieces should be eliminated entirely from study; but business or scientific language study should also be available for the major who needs this type of practical skill when he gets out into the world. Twenty percent of the students are interested in scientific and technical writing. Tamarkin (49) says that she has found a much smaller attrition level in her career language courses than in the traditional program.

Active use

Rivers (40) found that students in required courses want more listening and speaking practice and they want to read newspapers and magazines to keep up on current events and cultural insights in the foreign country. Such materials could easily be incorporated into all stages of learning the language.

Reinert (38) found that high school students in the West want more speaking practice and some short-term courses for specific or practical goals.

Reinert also calls attention to the great diversity of student opinions on various subjects. For instance, about one quarter of the students said they work best under teacher-imposed deadlines; other students preferred to set their own deadlines or commented that a teacher's deadline had no effect on them. These opinions reflect the fact that self-paced instruction may not be for everyone (and experience has shown that students tend to meet imposed deadlines but put off their own). In one school a great number of students said they wanted foreign languages for travel; in another school almost no one did. This shows that an entire school can have a character of its own—all of which must be taken into consideration in setting up language programs. Indeed, the young people themselves indicated this in Reinert's survey by generally agreeing that they need greater opportunities for different rates of progress. Apparently students are recognizing themselves as individuals and want their language instruction geared to them. In discussing how and why she set up a self-paced individualized learning system, Harper (18) noted that students requested language courses based on their degree requirements, travel plans, job opportunities, professional possibilities, interests, and backgrounds. All this led to the decision to offer modern European languages in an individualized system so that each student could have the greatest chance of satisfying his or her specific needs within a general language curriculum. Lippmann (27) has warned that students may object to foreign language classes because they often lack flexibility. Individualized or self-paced instruction may not be suitable for a particular school, but language educators today must be willing to adopt methods that are most

Individual advancement

suitable for the students of today, even if those methods involve extra work.

Innovative programs and student attitudes

Two schools in Colorado can serve as examples of restructuring, and their success stories can serve as inspiration for others who are hesitant to make too many changes in time-honored disciplines. The Department of Spanish and Portuguese at the University of Colorado at Boulder adopted individualization in 1972 utilizing teacher presentation as one method, teacher-student interaction as another, and independent study as the third—each used according to a special overall format. Independent study was used because of the belief that the most intense learning takes place when the student makes the decision to study. The results of this program were rather startling. A comparison of summer enrollments for lower-division Spanish between the pre-1972 and post-1972 figures showed that enrollment actually doubled upon implementation of the individualized program, in spite of the fact that total university enrollment dropped 10 percent. Furthermore, the teaching assistants who had taught both the pre- and post-1972 methods said that student achievement in the four skills, especially speaking and writing, was noticeably higher with the individualized program.

An interesting experiment

The value of scrambling

Despite this positive response to this particular effort to present what students say they actually want, the objection could be raised that such programs are just fads and that students may want something entirely different tomorrow. Educators could spend all their time struggling to come up with the materials necessary to satisfy student whims. An answer to this objection might be that a program of education that is not a continual effort to try to do better can easily become dormant or stagnant. Education must remain as alive and vital as the youth it serves, and it can if it keeps adding meaning, usefulness, and enrichment to the lives of its constituents.

Another experiment

At the University of Colorado in Colorado Springs, McKay (32) cites great growth in the language department just three years after both entrance and graduation requirements and placement tests were abolished and the Spanish major was recreated. Programs were completely revamped to suit the particular needs of the institution's own undergraduate students. New courses were developed for interdepartmental use (for example, bilingual courses comparing authors of specific works in English and Spanish). This type of interdisciplinary program can help cut down on the typical isolation of Spanish from other subject areas. Specific courses dealing with regional language areas (such as Mexico and the Southwest) were created for relevancy. Basic literature survey courses were eliminated and replaced by minicourses dealing with specific authors' literary works, or movements, thus giving students specific highlights with which to identify and leaving the less vital areas of literary history to be filled in during graduate study. A critic could say that giving the students what they want in this fashion causes them to miss seeing the overall development of literature, with the web of influences and modulations that give even the lesser-known works scholarly importance. If we give our youth some exposure to literature and if we do it right, we will whet their appetites for more. It cannot be denied that at Colorado Springs students are now present in class in greater numbers. Enrollments nearly doubled after the first year of the new system; three years after implementation they had nearly tripled.

Some innovative ideas

As part of the Colorado Springs program McKay also describes culture courses; a speaker's bureau whose members address local community organizations about foreign languages, culture, and other topics; publication of the work of students involved in creative writing in target languages; foreign language poetry and essay contests in which prizes are awarded; and an annual Hispanic week. All of these are vital, up-to-date ways for students (and teaching staff) to accomplish their purposes through language study. Creative writing, for example, is popular today on many college campuses, and organizations with their own publication media are formed to help the works of members to reach the reading public. How natural to do this for foreign language students as well! Expanding this natural, creative, and possibly, career-oriented skill to language study courses enhances both the skill and the language art.

Student improvement

Bailey (4) noticed some other interesting things about students in her individualized French classes. They earned much higher grade-point averages, almost all A's and B's, as opposed to the typical spread of grades from A to F earned by students in regular classes. This should not be interpreted as part of the problem with grade inflation, which is receiving so much publicity these days. It is due to the fact that the student can repeat any particular module of such a program until able to pass the final exam with a high score because there is no need to keep up with other students. She noted further that students were spending fewer hours per week in class activities in the individualized program, partly because they were involved in task-oriented activities rather than the clock-watching practices of the regular classes.

Even more interesting in relation to student feedback is that class evaluations (by means of the university's teaching evaluation questionnaire) were uniformly much more positive. The 15-item feedback questionnaires were more variable for regular class students. This interesting effect could be due to the greater achievements of the individualized students or to the fact that these students were really evaluating their own program, one that they had been helping to create. Possibly they were showing that they appreciated the opportunity to proceed along the lines that they themselves would choose. The main point is that the student who is positive about his program is going to get more out of it and will encourage others to take and enjoy it. This student will also have better memories of it when as a taxpayer he will help decide what programs should be supported. Bailey also reports a 50 percent increase in the number of students who go on to study more French from the ranks of the individualized program, a sign that these positive feelings can have an immediate beneficial effect on a foreign language program.

Student self-concept

As another example of positive student attitude, Hoeh and Spuck (19) tell of a short-term but intensive travel/study abroad for some high school French students. They report great gains in the listening and reading skills of these students and improved student self-concept: The attitude toward the real self closely approached that of the ideal self, as determined by pre- and posttesting. This is encouraging, though not all teachers and students can afford this kind of learning experience. If, however, this kind of satisfaction and self-fulfillment could be transmitted to other prospective language students, it could result in a gratifying growth in language study in the United States.

Students in other parts of the country are also expressing what they like in language programs. Love and Honig (28), for example, mention a program in Topeka in which students can sample classes of five different languages to see which one they might wish to take. Each class lasts six weeks, thus affording plenty of opportunity to give a good overall view of each or even a firm mastery of a small segment. Obviously for such a program to succeed there must be some instant outcomes. There is, as can be expected, great growth in the Topeka school language program.

The Topeka language sample

Biehn (7) reports on a public school FLES program in grades 3 through 6 in which high school students act as tutors to run the language program for the elementary school children. The high schoolers have been responsible as well as enthusiastic, and the elementary children have been eager to work with them. The tutors have been amused at how proud the elementary students have been to be able to take home real homework. Semke (42) discusses a college-level German program in which second-year students serve as leaders in small-group peer-teaching sections of a first-year class. At the end of the year the first-year students voted 26 to 1 to keep the program, and typical comments from the second-year students centered around the fact that they learned more than the beginners did (which all language teachers know) and that they felt they were helping others in a positive way.

High school tutors

A similar approach was used in Portuguese classes at a component of the University of Texas system. The second-year students were delighted to be able to use their new language skills as a medium of communication with others and to help others attain the same level of awareness. These second-year students also eagerly went to the local high schools, going from class to class presenting short programs of Brazilian songs and talks in Portuguese (translated by others in the group, as at a meeting of politicians) about the benefits to the students if they took Portuguese when they enrolled at the University.

The Portuguese program that inspired this interest at the University was inaugurated in spite of the reluctance of several administrators who had never seen it done successfully at that school. The professor secured a room and an hour on his own persuasion, however, and then sallied forth to shake hands with students all over the campus and invite them to join the new

Portuguese campaigners

class, pointing out that if they wanted to deal in South American affairs they ought to know both Spanish and Portuguese. The students responded to this practical approach: On the first day of class there was standing room only, and the new program was well on its way.

In another survey (Walker, 52), from a geographical area in which a foreign language is spoken by much of the population, students showed their concern for the practical. They were accustomed to practical language use by their very surroundings, which makes them an extremely good source of information on how to set up a more practical curriculum. The comments came in open essays on what they would like to see in the university language program. They expressed a desire for a speaking knowledge, for fewer principles taught, and for more time spent in learning well the things that were most important so that a certain mastery could be obtained. The view seems to be that if the student spends a lot of time learning *about how to speak* in every conceivable situation with the correct grammar for that situation, he will never have time to learn anything well enough *to use* in even general situations. The desire for real use and communication even led students to request not to be marked down for each and every error, because this sidetracks them from real communication and destroys their confidence. Of course, a teacher with very high standards of perfection would regard this as laziness, but such a teacher may not have many students on which to impose those standards. In fact, in the survey the most complimentary descriptions given preferred professors were "inspiring" and "enthusiastic," for these professors helped the student to do his individual best by communicating and interacting with him, leading him to accomplish his individual goals. As Lippmann (27) pointed out early in this decade, students do not respect the idea of learning by discipline and pain; they prefer to regard life and learning as pleasure. Sabine (41) presents a great many specific comments of high school students about their teachers and emphasizes that a principal student concern is how such teachers care for and understand their students, listening to them and getting them to think for themselves, but at the same time insuring that they work hard enough in their classes that they have a sense of accomplishment at the end of the course of study.

What students say they want

The survey also indicated some of the practical things desired

Practical elements

in the language classes of these particular students (Walker, 52). These include means of infusing modern culture into language learning. Students want to learn of current customs, manners, traditions, art, money, hand gestures, and slang; and they would like to learn these by utilizing movies, slides, records, tapes, guest speakers, newspapers, magazines, stories, games, and even comic books and advertisements. In addition to these cultural aspects, their practical desires include walking trips around campus or town, learning how to comment on the daily things they see; telephone practice; panels, debates, seminars, and "rap" sessions; creative writing opportunities; language tables or even language dormitories; interaction with students in advanced classes; and other such meaningful experiences that will take language out of the museum as an interesting object to study and give it to the student who wants to use it as a communicative instrument in accord with his own plans and goals.

Career orientation

Tamarkin's (49) career Spanish program stresses aural-oral ability, task assignment, and group efforts to help students communicate well in their chosen professions. Although foreign language can be used as a medium for teaching about communication in the abstract to the personal benefit of every student, we must also remember that there are still needs for business and government people and journalists who can not only speak the languages of other countries but also the foreign tongues preferred by people living within the borders of the United States. Courses in medical or business or other terminologies, even scientific or musical, can lead to communication in a person's own chosen field. Police, social workers, local or worldwide businessmen are examples.

At lower levels of language learning perhaps some of the elements of Bailey's (4) successful program could be implemented: choice of tracks to fit a student's particular future plans, use of various media, use of students as tutors and as proctors for the individual exams, multiple testing and remediation opportunities, immediate feedback on work, and as much self-pacing as possible. In her program the library staff records all inquiries, complaints, and criticisms of the materials during daily interaction with the students, and changes are made quickly based on this evidence.

Harper's (18) behavioral learning program at Tarrant County Junior College, consisting mainly of individualized self-paced learning, makes use of constant student feedback for improvement. Possibly because of this sensitivity to student opinion, her program has shown a 60 percent increase in enrollment, while campus enrollment has gone up only 10 percent.

Another success story

Summary

Today's student is practical and accustomed to having a voice in his future. There is evidence that if language teachers seek the opinions of students concerning what should be included in foreign language programs offered them in the nation's schools, the resulting programs will better satisfy the student's real need and will earn his support because of the increased importance of his own activity and input. More efforts must be made to this end and must be published for the benefit of all.

References, The student view: Attitudes toward foreign language learning

1 Aiken, L. R.,Jr. "Procedures and Problems in Designing a College Course Evaluation Questionnaire." *College and University* 50(1975):247–53.

2 Alden, D. W. "Status of French." *The French Review* 48(1974):7–10.

3 Allawala, Aslam U, et al. *Survey of Foreign Language Majors.* Irving, Texas: Dallas University International Institute, 1973. [EDRS: ED 096 837.]

4 Bailey, Leona G. Florida State University, Tallahassee. Personal communication, 1976. [Letter.]

5 Barsalon, J. M., et al. "Student Evaluation of Staff in Secondary Schools." *NASSP Bulletin* 58(1974): 10–14.

6 Bickness, Gunther. "Study Abroad. Part I: A Comparative Test of Attitudes and Opinions." *Foreign Language Annals* 7(1974):325–36.

7 Biehn, Aubrey. "Peer Teaching in the Valley of the Genessee." *Hispania* 58(1975):929–31.

8 Brown, Charles T. "Communication and the Foreign Language Teacher," 5–35 in Gilbert A. Jarvis, ed., *The Challenge of Communication.* ACTFL Review of Foreign Language Education, Volume 6. Skokie, Illinois: National Textbook Company, 1974.

9 Cadenhead, Kenneth, and Peggy Dodd. *Assessing Student Attitudes and Behaviors in an Open Teacher Education Learning Environment.* Auburn, Alabama: Auburn University School of Education, 1973. [EDRS: ED 096 246.]

10 Callas, Howard. "A Survey of Student Attitude at the University of Texas at Austin." *Bulletin of the Association of Departments of Foreign Language* 6,i(1974):52–56.

11. Dalton, Starrett L. *Evaluating Foreign Language Placement: An Alternative Approach.* Bloomington: Indiana University, 1974. [EDRS: ED 096 330.]

12 Doyle, Kenneth O.,Jr. *Student Evaluation of Instruction.* Lexington, Massachusetts: Heath, 1975.

13 Gardner, Robert C., and Wallace E. Lambert. *Attitudes and Motivation in Second Language Learning.* Rowley, Massachusetts: Newbury House, 1972.

14 Grittner, F. M. "Foreign Language Education: a Kaleidoscopic Perspective; A Report on the Central States Conference, April 18–20, 1974." *Modern Language Journal* 57(1974):255–60.

15 ——— *Student Motivation, Foreign Language Bandwagons and Instructional Realities.* [Paper presented at the Utah Foreign Language Association Spring Conference, April 1974.] [EDRS: ED 095 722.]

16 Gronen, C. J. Eastern Washington State College, Cheney, Washington. Personal Communication, 1976. [Letter.]

17 Halbert, Susan J. "Student Evaluation of Teachers and Administrators." *Oregon School Study Council Bulletin* 18,viii(1975). [EDRS: ED 106 927.]

18 Harper, Jane. "A Behavioral Learning System in Foreign Languages at Tarrant County Junior College." *Foreign Language Annals* 8(1975):327–34.

19 Hoeh, James A., and Dennis W. Spuck. "Effects of a Three-Phase Acculturation Process on Language

Skill Development and Social and Personal Attitudes of High School French Students." *Foreign Language Annals* 8(1975):221–26.
20 Jackson, M. H. "Foreign Language: Yesterday, Today and Tomorrow." *Today's Education* 63(1974): 68–71.
21 Johnson, Joseph C., et al. *An Analysis of Certain Interactions Obtaining among Intermediate Grade Students with Respect to Specified Psychological Constructs and Reading Comprehension Response.* [Paper presented at the annual meeting of the Educational Research Association, Chicago, April 1974.] [EDRS: ED 101 300.]
22 Kelly, Sam B. "Effective College Teaching." *Teacher Education Forum Series* 18,ii(1974). [Bloomington: Indiana University.]
23 Kiernan, I. "Student Evaluations Reevaluated." *Community and Junior College Journal* 45(1975): 25–27.
24 Kougioulis, Karen. "What Can We Do? A Student's Viewpoint." [Paper presented at the 25th annual conference of the PNCFL, Spokane, Washington, 1974.] [EDRS: ED 102 852.]
25 Kult, L. E. "Using Teacher Evaluations of Students." *The Clearing House* 49(1975):11–13.
26 Levy, Stephen L. "The Realities Facing the Profession," 9–34 in Gilbert A. Jarvis,ed., *Responding to New Realities.* ACTFL Review of Foreign Language Education, Volume 5. Skokie, Illinois: National Textbook Company, 1973.
27 Lippmann, Jane N. "Rationale for Language Study," 37–69 in Gilbert A. Jarvis,ed., *The Challenge of Communication.* ACTFL Review of Foreign Language Education, Volume 6. Skokie, Illinois: National Textbook Company, 1974.
28 Love, F. William D., and Lucille J. Honig. *Options and Perspectives.* New York: Modern Language Association, 1973.
29 "Language Enrollments." *MLA Newsletter* 7,iii (1975):3.
30 Marlin, Martha D. Carroll High School, Dayton, Ohio. Personal Communication, 1976. [Letter.]
31 Mauldin, Larry J. *Assessment of the Impact of Individualized Instruction on Students—Technical Report.* Patchogue, New York: Suffolk County Board of Cooperative Educational Seminars, 1974.
32 McKay, Douglas R. *Some Revitalizing Effects of the Undergraduate Literature Mini-Course.* [Paper presented at the AATSP National Conference, Chicago, December, 1975.]
33 Menges, Robert J. "The New Reporters: Students Rate Instruction," 59–77 in Robert C. Pace,ed., *Evaluating Learning and Teaching.* San Francisco: Jossey-Bass, 1973.
34 Monsees, Anita. "Public Awareness: How Associations and Institutions Use Public Relations Skills," 71-89 in Gilbert A. Jarvis,ed., *The Challenge of Communication.* ATCFL Review of Foreign Language Education, Volume 6. Skokie, Illinois: National Textbook Company, 1974.
35 Mullen, Wahneta M. "Many Learners, Many Goals, Many Curricula," 37–71 in Gilbert A. Jarvis,ed., *Responding to New Realities.* ACTFL Review of Foreign Language Education, Volume 5. Skokie, Illinois: National Textbook Company, 1973.
36 Papalia, Anthony. "An Assessment of Attitudes and Behaviors of Foreign Language Teachers." *Foreign Language Annals* 7(1973):231–36.
37 Reinert, Harry. *Foreign Language Student Opinion Survey: Questionnaire and Survey.* Lynnwood, Washington: Edwards School District, May 1971. [EDRS: ED 094 549.]
38 ——— *Use of Student Opinions as a Basis for Curriculum Planning.* [Paper presented at the 25th annual meeting of the PNCFL, Spokane, Washington, 1974.] [EDRS: ED 102 838.]
39 Rivers, Wilga M. *Speaking in Many Tongues: Essays in Foreign Language Teaching.* Rowley, Massachusetts: Newbury House, 1972.
40 ——— "The Non-Major: Tailoring the Course to the Individual—Not the Image," in K. Jankowski, ed., *Language and International Studies.* Monograph Series 26. Washington, D.C.: Georgetown University Press, 1973.
41 Sabine, Gordon. *How Students Rate Their Schools and Teachers.* Washington, D.C.: National Association of Secondary School Principals, 1971.
42 Semke, Harriet D. "Peer Teaching Helps!" *Foreign Language Annals* 8(1975):123–27.
43 Sheehan, Daniel. "On the Invalidity of Student Ratings for Administrative Personnel Decisions." *The Journal of Higher Education* 46(1975):687–700.
44 Shuy, Roger, and Ralph W. Fasold,eds., *Language Attitudes: Current Trends and Prospects.* Washington, D.C.: Georgetown University Press, 1973.
45 Smith, George E., and M. Phillip Leaman,eds., *Effective Foreign Language Instruction in the Secondary School.* Englewood Cliffs, New Jersey: Prentice-Hall, 1969.
46 Sole, Carlos. *Summary of Results of Student Evaluation Survey.* Austin: University of Texas Department of Spanish and Portuguese, 1973. [EDRS: ED 107 125.]
47 Stansfield, Charles W. "An Individualized First-Year Spanish Program at the University of Colorado." *ADFL Bulletin* 6,ii(1974):36–40.
48 Strevers, Peter. *The Training of Language Teachers: A Look at the Future.* Honolulu: University of Hawaii, 1974.
49 Tamarkin, Toby. Manchester Community College, Manchester, Connecticut. Personal Communication, 1976. [Letter.]
50 Tobias, Sigmund, and Robert E. Hanlon. *Attitudes toward Instructors, Social Desireability, & Behavioral Intentions.* New York: City University of New York, 1974.
51 Walker, B. D. "Anticipated Grade and Student Rating of Teacher." *Improving College and University Teaching* 22(1974):220–21.
52 Walker, John L. "Opinions of University Students about Language Teaching." *Foreign Language Annals* 7(1973):102–05.

6

Coping with the real problems in the secondary schools

Introduction

R. Marshall Brannon
David E. Cox
Virginia State Department of Education

Predicament of teacher

Foreign language teachers are probably better prepared today than at any other time in history, and most are desirous of doing a good job. Yet they are often faced with problems over which they have little control. Teachers who teach four or five classes per day, monitor a study hall, and spend a portion of their lunch period on cafeteria duty have little time for research to seek solutions to these problems. As a result, the problems are often ignored to the detriment of the foreign language program.

Purpose of chapter

The purpose of this chapter is to delineate a number of real problems confronting the teacher in the classroom and to offer strategies (not necessarily solutions) for coping with them. The

---

R. Marshall Brannon (M.A., Appalachian State University) is Assistant Supervisor of Foreign Languages for the Virginia State Department of Education. His B.A. is from the University of Virginia, and he has attended NDEA Institutes in the United States and France. He has taught French at the secondary level, served as coordinator of foreign languages for a local school district, and has taught foreign language methodology courses in the Evening School at Virginia Commonwealth University. His professional affiliations include ACTFL, AATF, NCSSFL, and FLAVA. He has given presentations at the 1975 North Carolina State Foreign Language Conference, the 1974 AATF Convention, and he has moderated a panel at the 1975 ACTFL Convention. In addition, he served as one of the Local Arrangements Chairpersons for the 1975 ACTFL Convention and is currently in charge of the national distribution of foreign language promotional bumper stickers sponsored by the Foreign Language Awareness Campaign Committee of NCSSFL.

David E. Cox (M.A., Appalachian State University) has been Assistant Supervisor of Foreign Languages with the Virginia State Department of Education since 1970. He received his B.A. degree from Roanoke College and has participated in two NDEA Institutes. He has taught foreign languages at both the elementary and secondary levels. His professional affiliations include ACTFL, AATF, NCSSFL, FLAVA, and Phi Delta Kappa. He has appeared as a program participant at the 1975 Central States Conference on the Teaching of Foreign Languages and the 1975 ACTFL Convention. He has also served as Secretary-Treasurer of NCSSFL.

problems were selected on the basis of experiences encountered by the authors in their work as state supervisors and as a result of letters of inquiry to classroom teachers and local and state foreign language supervisors. The strategies presented are based on field observations by the authors, feedback from the teachers and supervisors, and a review of the literature. In determining which strategies to present we have tried to keep in mind the possible diversity of situations encountered by the reading audience—the Latin teacher who happens to be the only foreign language teacher in a small rural junior high school and who also teaches a class of English and another of history as well as the teacher of Italian in a multi-teacher language department of a large metropolitan high school.

Definitions

Problem, as used in this chapter, refers to a difficult situation that may face a foreign language teacher. It may be related either to classroom instruction or to the total program. A *strategy* is a plan for coping with or possibly solving a problem.

Problems treated

No degree of priority is attached to the following problems discussed in this chapter:

Maintaining enrollments in advanced classes
Teaching combined classes: strategies and options
Selecting a junior high/middle school exploratory offering
Coordinating the foreign language sequence
Lack of support for the foreign language program
Teaching the handicapped student
Teaching the culturally disadvantaged student
Accommodating the needs of the occasional student of limited English-speaking ability
Lack of opportunities for professional growth

Although the focus of this chapter is on problems encountered by foreign language teachers in the secondary schools, the information presented will be helpful as well to colleagues who teach at the college and university levels, because they work with former students of secondary programs. It is particularly recommended for teacher candidates in foreign language education programs who, undoubtedly, will encounter some of the same problems in their future teaching experiences.

Maintaining enrollments in advanced classes

Attrition has always been a problem in secondary school foreign language programs. In spite of many teachers' insistence that a sequence of at least three or more years is necessary to attain proficiency in the four skills, students continue to drop out after one or two years. National statistics show that 90 percent of the students who begin foreign language study in the ninth grade drop out before their fourth year of study (Torres et al, 79). Lafayette (39) points out that less than 25 percent of the students who begin foreign languages ever continue beyond the second year. Budget-conscious administrators complain that the overall teacher-student ratio is lower in the foreign language department than in other curriculum areas because of low enrollments in advanced classes. Fourth- and fifth-year courses are often eliminated when the enrollments are not sufficient (as determined by the school administration). The problem is evident. If we advocate long sequences in our programs, we must do something to maintain student enrollments in the upper-level courses.

Attrition statistics

Problems caused by attrition

A number of studies have been conducted to determine what initially attracts students to foreign language classes and why they do not wish to continue. Reinert (64) conducted a survey of 1,000 junior and senior high school students and concluded that the main reason they chose to study a foreign language was to satisfy college entrance requirements, and that of the second-year students who chose not to continue, approximately 70 percent indicated that they were dropping because the requirements had been completed. In a survey of more than 4,000 seniors in 32 different schools located throughout Virginia, Warriner (80) also found that college entrance requirements ranked first in the reasons given, but running a close second was the student's own interest. The primary factor cited as causing them to drop foreign language study when they could have continued was a decline in interest, though completion of college entrance requirements ranked high as well. College entrance requirements have been significant in attracting students to foreign language classes. Warriner's conclusions, however, give us reason for concern. Why do students say that the second most important factor in electing a foreign language

Loss of interest

was their own interest and then later that the primary reason for dropping or failing is the loss of interest (p. 7)?

Oppenheimer (56) believes that students lose interest in foreign languages because they are disappointed in the degree of proficiency achieved after a few years of study. Smith (75) agrees that students become impatient but adds that many students cannot take the pressure from too much emphasis on grades. Papalia's (59) study of attrition indicated that the majority of the students in the study discontinued foreign languages after the second level, and the second most commonly given reason was *fear* that the third year would be too difficult.

Certainly a number of other factors contribute to the attrition problem. Nielsen (54) believes that scheduling is a major cause of attrition because advanced classes are often scheduled in direct competition with required courses, college-preparation courses, or popular electives. Jones (38) says that many foreign language teachers in Norfolk, Virginia, feel that expanding the options in high school electives has a detrimental effect on the foreign language program. It is difficult to compete with appealing courses like Witchcraft, Yoga, or Marriage and Family Living. Saunders (68) also mentions scheduling as a problem in view of what she calls the growing number of "part-time students" who, for one reason or another, are permitted to leave school each day after they have remained a certain number of hours.

Relevancy of the curriculum

Jackson (35) would take issue with any one of the foregoing reasons given for the attrition problem. She states firmly that "if foreign language courses are relevant, students will enroll in them" (p. 71). Pomeroy (62) believes that our best salesmen are our students and that the student's decision about remaining in the language program depends on his perceptions of the language-learning experience.

What can be done?

Need for increasing beginning enrollments

If we expect to have good enrollments in advanced foreign language classes, we must recruit more students at the beginning levels. Whenever a program is geared only to the college-bound, it automatically excludes a large percentage of potential students. As foreign language entrance requirements in colleges and universities are reduced, enrollments in secondary school programs designed mainly for college-bound students can be expected to diminish. If teachers really believe in the value of foreign languages in the curriculum, the doors should be opened to any interested student. Instead of "screening" students from our classes, we should be recruiting them through activities like festivals, assembly programs, active foreign language clubs, and student-to-student recruitment. Unless we make our progress more visible to the students and let them know that *all* are welcome, they cannot be expected to flock to our classes.

Recruiting students

Historically, because most foreign language programs have been aimed primarily at preparing students for college entrance, the advice given to students has often been to plan their programs to terminate their high school foreign language study during their senior year. This advice was based on the assumptions that the students would be required to study a foreign language in college, and they could continue the same language. In view of the scheduling conflicts already noted, the increased number of course offerings in the curriculum, and other factors that affect students' choices of subjects during their junior and senior years and, in addition, considering the fact that many colleges have abolished or reduced either entrance or degree requirements, perhaps the advice to students today should be to enroll in foreign language classes as early as possible when their schedules are less complicated and their choice of electives is more limited. One might still advise students who intend to continue the same foreign language in college to consider terminating their study during their senior year. Building up the base of the foreign language program should result in higher enrollments at the upper levels.

Assuming that the students respond favorably to the recruitment techniques, their experiences should be enjoyable and maximum opportunities for success should be afforded them. Smith (75) emphasizes that nothing fosters high motivation and positive attitudes as does success.

Success factor

The principles and techniques involved in the more formal approaches to individualization have implications for every foreign language teacher who is concerned about helping a greater number of students attain success. Among the more notable principles are the following:

Individualizing

1 Course content should be based on both long-term and short-term realistic measurable objectives to which both the teacher and the student are committed. Covering a certain number of pages or chapters in a textbook within a given amount of time is *not* a good objective.
2 There is nothing sacred about the traditional layout of the classroom.
3 Teaching strategies must vary in accordance with the objectives. Large-group instruction, for example, may be good for giving facts or explanations to students, but oral skills are sometimes developed more efficiently when students practice in small groups. There is more opportunity for each student to speak, and the setting is more realistic.
4 The teacher is not the sole individual from whom the students may learn. The wise teacher will make use of peer teaching whenever feasible and will profit from the aid of student assistants from advanced classes.
5 Students should be tested only on what they are taught. To put on tests items that have received little emphasis in class is invalid. The use of criterion-referenced tests is recommended.

Teacher self-evaluation

Each teacher must constantly reevaluate his own teaching practices. Questions that should be considered might include:

1 What percentage of my students are failing or are achieving below their capabilities? What can I do about those who are?
2 How much do I know about each individual student, his academic strengths and weaknesses, previous experiences, cultural background, and chief interests outside my class?
3 Are my expectations realistic for all the students in my classes?
4 How can I use the resources available to me to help each student achieve in accordance with his own abilities?
5 What additional resources do I need to provide even greater opportunities for all students?
6 Do I evaluate each student fairly and individually? Do I have difficult achievement standards for individuals with different abilities or past achievements?

7 Is every student in my classes assured of my interest in him?
8 Do students enjoy my classes and do they experience a feeling of success?

A careful and honest appraisal by each teacher of his own attitudes and teaching practices and a real desire to strengthen existing weaknesses should make foreign language learning an enjoyable and successful experience for a larger segment of the total school population.

Intermediate level

Disick (12) says that the intermediate-level class is the most crucial period in the foreign language sequence because the novelty of first-year language study has worn off but the students are not yet able to communicate easily and effectively in the target language. Many become impatient or bored and decide not to continue. She recommends that extra efforts be made at this level to provide sufficient opportunities for self-expression by having the students use the language in meaningful situations—in short, to *personalize* the instruction. Most students enjoy talking, but many of our foreign language textbooks give them little to talk about that is relevant to them. Jarvis (36) proposes that students be encouraged to talk more about themselves, their desires and true feelings, their relationships to other people, and their values. He believes that the foreign language class has greater potential than any other area of the curriculum for achieving humanistic goals that focus upon discovering one's identity, because we are not bound to teach a specific area of knowledge or information. Yet, many teachers continue to teach only the dialogue lines and practice the pattern drills in the text. Their students fail to see the relevance of the language and tend to look upon it as something found only in a textbook.

Personalization of content

Diversity in advanced levels

The trend in advanced-level classes is toward greatly increased diversity and choice in both content and materials. Minicourses are being used extensively to increase enrollments, particularly after the first two years of foreign language study, when effective motivation is necessary and perhaps most difficult.

Minicourses

Cooperation and planning play an important part in the successful implementation of a minicourse program. Students cooperate with their teachers in choosing the topics, and teachers cooperate with each other in the planning, developing, and execution of the various courses. The following is a partial listing of minicourses described by Papalia (58) that have been developed and have been or are being taught in French, Spanish, and German classes at Half Hollow Hills High School in Dix Hills, New York. All are advanced-level courses.

French

Advanced Conversation
French for Travelers
Creative Writing
Current Events in France
French Movies and Theater
Advanced Reading
Everyday Life in France
French Folklore and Mythology
Human Dynamics in French
French Drama Workshop

German

German for Travelers
Advanced Conversation and Comprehension
Scientific German (reading)
The Culinary Arts of the German–Speaking Countries
German Ecology
Fun and Games in German
German Art, Architecture, and Music
U.S. Relations with Germany: Economics and Politics
Current German Politics

Spanish

Spanish for Travelers
Commercial Spanish
Everyday Life in Latin America
The Great Spanish Philosophers
The Faces of Spain: Geography and People
Modern Spanish Literature
The Indians of Latin America
Current Events in the Spanish-Speaking World

Student-developed minicourses

Sellman (72) has her students develop their own minicourses, which are later taught to other students. A partial listing of the most successful follows:

La Presse française
La Française aujourd'hui
Le Cinéma français
La Musique classique
Les Français au travail
La Musique moderne

Baker (2) attributes high enrollments in her French IV classes to the use of several activity-oriented units inserted into the course periodically throughout the year. The activities are numerous. For example, in a unit titled French Artistic Expression from Prehistoric to Modern Times, the students participate in art sessions in which they imitate the style of their favorite painters, make a verbal portrait of a scene, and paint a mural. They also take field trips to local art museums as well as to the National Gallery of Art and The Phillips Gallery in Washington, D.C. In the unit entitled *Les Sports et l'aventure,* the students discuss in French the value of sports, French sports heroes, the right of women to participate in so-called "men's sports," and the overemphasis on sports. They also design and write in French a sports page for the newspaper.

Activity-oriented units

Because minicourses satisfy student interests and can be implemented within a regular school program and ordinarily require no special facilities beyond those already existing in most secondary schools, they are becoming increasingly more attractive as alternatives to the conventional upper-level foreign language curriculum.

Other options are also available. Deutch (10) advocates a job-oriented course for the noncollege-bound student who has had two years of French. These students would be placed in part-time jobs (either after school or on weekends) that would require them to use French. Possibilities for employment might include food markets, beauty parlors, and restaurants whose clientele is French-speaking. Work with travel agencies, sales and service of foreign cars, and babysitting for French-speaking families are other possibilities. Course content would prepare the students for on-the-job work experience through the use of dramatic playlets to create the illusion of a real situation. While Deutch's proposal may appear a bit unrealistic, especially to teachers in an area in which the target language is not spoken extensively, Freilich (23) reports on "internships" for advanced students that have included activities such as teaching in a local elementary FLES program and serving as interpreters in community organizations and hospitals.

Job-oriented courses

Foreign language internships

Teachers who are contemplating revisions in the curriculum aimed at attracting more students into advanced levels should remember that a successful strategy in one school may not be successful in another. Perhaps the best way to ascertain what changes, if any, the students would like to see made is to ask them, either informally or through the use of a survey questionnaire. Garrett (28) reports that every student who drops out of a foreign language class at T. C. Williams High School in Alexandria, Virginia, is asked to check from a list of 27 possible reasons all those that influenced him in any way to drop the course. The reasons range from "I had to do too much homework" to "It was too easy." The student is also invited to give any other reasons that might be applicable but are not suggested on the checklist. This information is then used by the teachers in making curriculum-related decisions.

Student opinions

Obviously, there are no magic formulas for maintaining enrollments in advanced classes. The key, however, appears to be diversification and student involvement. As Lafayette (39) points out, programs should be tailored to fit students instead of seeking students to fit an already-established program.

Teaching combined classes: Strategies and options

A real problem for a substantial number of secondary school foreign language teachers is that of teaching two or more courses during the same period each day. This problem sometimes occurs in spite of the teachers' best efforts in implementing strategies aimed at maintaining sufficient enrollments in the advanced levels to justify separate classes. In fact, it is sometimes a direct result of having too many students in one level and a lack of staff to cover the number of instructional periods needed. For example, from an administrative point of view, the solution to an overcrowded Level-III class might be to divide it into two groups, one of which would be assigned to a Level-IV class. More often, however, the situation is a result of insufficient enrollments to justify separate classes, because administrators usually look closely at the total teacher/student ratio when making teacher assignments. The problem is particularly acute in small rural schools with low student populations. There are still high schools in this country with total enrollments of fewer than 200 students in grades 9 through 12. For example, Emmons (14), who teaches Spanish at Keokee Combined School in the sparsely populated Virginia mountains,

Reasons for combining classes

reports that to offer three levels of Spanish he has been required to teach as many as three levels during the same class period.

The teaching of combined classes places an extra burden on teachers who are often already overworked. The frustrations encountered by both the teachers and students can be overwhelming if care is not exercised in the planning of the courses and if all parties involved do not approach the situation cooperatively. In the following paragraphs the strategies for coping with this problem are based on information supplied by classroom teachers who have had experience in teaching combined classes.

Cooperative planning

Independent study

When a few students wish to take an advanced course, a teacher who is willing might agree to teach them on an independent basis. Such an arrangement usually requires that the teacher and student formulate objectives for the course and outline activities that lead to the attainment of the objectives. The student may be assigned to a foreign language section on a regular basis or he may work totally on his own, reporting to the teacher at regular intervals for a "progress check" or for individual help. The logistics should be decided mutually by the teacher, the student, and the administration, and the degree of success would depend on the maturity of the student(s) involved. If the student completes the required work and achieves the stated objectives, he should receive credit as he would if the course were available as a separate class.

Split-period approach

One approach employed by some teachers is to seat the two levels in separate sections of the room; the teacher works with one class during the first half of the period while the students in the other group do written work or silent reading. Then the procedure is reversed during the last half of the period. Occasionally the two groups may be brought together for a cultural presentation or for working on a special project such as making *piñatas* in Spanish classes.

Dividing the class

Modified split-period approach

The split-period approach may be modified in several ways.

Schell (70) suggests that the time spent by the teacher with the two groups be alternated, depending on what is being taught. Instead of dividing his time equally during each class period, the teacher may work two days with one level and three days with the other, reversing the procedure during alternate weeks. Each class may be assigned meaningful long-range projects on which they work while the teacher is meeting with the other class, and both groups are brought together at regular intervals to share the results. Enwall (15) encourages as much variety in class scheduling as possible by:

Strategies for variation

1 Allowing each level to work separately during portions or all of some class periods
2 Having the higher-level group make occasional presentations to the lower-level or assist the lower-level students on a one-to-one basis
3 Leading both classes in the same activity but requiring different levels of response
4 Encouraging both groups to work together in a new activity from time to time

Interaction between the two classes should be beneficial to both.

Individualized approach

When a teacher is faced with three or more classes in the same classroom, the situation can be unwieldy. Some form of individualization seems to be the most viable alternative. Feagin (17) offers the following suggestions for establishing a program of this nature:

1 Develop performance objectives for each level. Get student input so that these objectives are centered around their needs and interests.
2 Use minidramas and audio-motor units for interaction and to encourage class unity.
3 Set up "centers" in the classroom so that all students can work independently. Centers could be set up, for example, for the following topics:

Art	Literature
Music	Grammar

Current Events	Creative Writing
Conversation	Games
Listening	

4 Use strategies such as peer teaching, small-group discussions, and one-to-one pairing to assure optimum learning in the time allowed.

This arrangement does not necessarily imply a self-pacing program whereby each student moves through the materials at his own rate and according to his individual ability. It merely provides a manageable framework for three different groups, each at a different proficiency level, to function efficiently in the same classroom.

Structure and content

Rotating levels

Varying sequence

Advanced Latin classes are frequently offered on a rotating basis in a two-year sequence. Thus, Cicero might be offered to both the Latin III and Latin IV students with credit awarded simply for Latin III or Latin IV, depending on the number of years (levels) of previous study. The following year Vergil might be offered to the same group in a similar manner. The sequence is unimportant from a scheduling standpoint. In modern language classes in which the degree of difficulty is usually related to sequence, the solution is not so manageable. In instances in which alternatives to the sequential program are being sought, however, the principle of rotating levels has possibilities.

Special-interest courses

Varied objectives

In the high-level classes (fourth, fifth, and sixth year), one may wish to consider offering a special-interest class to all levels at the same time. Although the content is basically the same in this type of course, the objectives and expectations of student participation and performance vary according to each level.

Love and Honig (46, pp. 285–87) list a one-semester course, French Drama, for students in French V, VI, and VII at Walt Whitman High School in Baltimore, Maryland. Meeting for two hours each day, all three classes work together in producing and presenting one long play. (Several shorter ones are presented by each level separately.) The students make their own costumes and props, as well as direct, edit, and act. At the end of the semester, the full-length play is presented to all of the French classes in the school auditorium.

Student-aide programs

Foreign language educators have long recognized the value of peer teaching for both the learner and the student who serves as teacher. One excellent possibility for offering advanced foreign language instruction, without even scheduling a separate class period, is the implementation of a student-aide program. Although initially a great deal of work and planning must go into establishing a program, the dividends can be most rewarding.

Responsibilities of aides

Guidera and Floyd (31) have developed and implemented a successful student-aide program involving third- and fourth-year Spanish students at Conway Senior High School in Horry County, South Carolina. At the beginning of the year each aide is assigned certain first- and second-year students with whom he is to work daily in an individualized program. He is given a handbook that lists his privileges and responsibilities, the subject matter with which he must be familiar, and specific strategies for helping lower-level students. Additional responsibilities include the development of materials, such as taping audio programs and creating learning centers. Each aide receives a grade for the course as he would for any other, and one-half unit of credit is awarded per semester. Evaluation is made by the teacher, by the students with whom he has worked during the semester, and by the aide himself. When the aide has participated in the program for two semesters, he is awarded a certificate of merit.

Thoughtful organization and structure are vital if an aide program is to be successful. It must also have the support of the administration because credit is awarded.

Selecting a junior high/middle school exploratory offering

Foreign language exploratory courses appear to be cyclic; they seem to come and go. For the most part, they disappeared during the 1960s, having yielded to the FLES movement. During the early 1970s, however, with the fading of the FLES programs, they soon reappeared. The decision to initiate one of the exploratory options at the junior high school level, as opposed to the lowering of the regular sequential program to the seventh or eighth grade, has been and seemingly will continue to be a matter of debate.

Ahrens, Ruffin, and Wilson (1) list as one of the purposes of the junior high school curriculum providing ". . . those broad exploratory experiences which are necessary in the educational development of early adolescents" (p. 31). Among the values derived from such experiences are:

Values of exploratory experiences

1 The development of present and future social and recreational skills and interests
2 The introduction to new experiences that broaden students' intellectual horizons
3 The development of new and useful skills
4 The assistance they lend in helping students make vocational plans
5 Their contribution in assisting students to make wise choices in future educational experiences (p. 31).

From within the profession Strasheim (77) notes the need for ". . . an exploratory foreign language experience with heavy emphasis on the listening and speaking skills and centered about societal universals—family, daily routines, customs, the behavior of the people, with provision for deliberate cross-cultural studies" (p. 22). Pei (60), recognizing the need for a language exploratory program in junior high schools, comments:

> I would strongly urge for all of them, without exception, a general language survey course of one semester or one year, prior to the actual selection of a specific language, to familiarize the students with the language situation throughout the world, the chief languages spoken, their location, the extent of their speaking populations and economic potentialities . . . (pp. 74–75).

Definition

Enwall et al. (16) define an exploratory course as "a course designed to allow students to explore some area of foreign language study for the purpose of acquainting them with the phenomenon of language itself, of determining their interest and potential in future foreign language study, or of meeting some special student need" (p. 1). According to Grittner (30), the purpose of the exploratory program is to provide a language learning experience for all students, which is worthwhile for its own sake, and to provide a basis for each student to decide whether he wishes to pursue additional study of a foreign language.

Classification

Content in exploratory options may be divided into two categories: courses that provide samplings or small doses of certain languages and cultures and that are usually patterned, to some extent, after those language offerings available in the regular sequential language program; and courses devoted to no specific foreign language but that concentrate on developing the broader concepts one encounters in studying the nature of language. Courses within either category may be taught as elective or required offerings, from six weeks to a year in duration. There are also those within the profession who consider the regular Level-I sequence, or a part thereof, a bona fide exploratory option (Fearing and Grittner, 18).

The language-sampling course

The most popular of the exploratory course possibilities is the language-sampling offering which has been termed "The Language Potpourri Course" by Fearing and Grittner (18) and referred to as "The Trial Language Study Course" by Enwall et al. (16).

Content of language-sampling course

Content usually includes the learning of basic vocabulary, sentence structure, and cultural associations (Love and Honig, 46) as well as the more common expressions, in the foreign language, such as, "How are you?" "My name is __________," "How is the weather today?" "Open your book," and so forth (Grittner, 30).

Limitations

This type of exploratory course is subject to certain limitations:

1 Unless instructional material is sufficiently different from that of the regular Level-I course offering, problems due to duplication of content are likely to occur when the student who elects to continue the language begins the first year of regular study.

2 In order not to give an unfair advantage to certain language offerings in the sequential program, measures must be taken to insure that all languages taught at the senior high school are represented in the exploratory program.
3 If one teacher is responsible for teaching two or more languages within the exploratory program, instruction may be affected by personal biases and varying language competencies. If each language is taught by a different person, personality may be a determining factor in the student's decision of which course to pursue at a later time.

Fearing and Grittner (18) report that some teachers feel that where a large number of language samplings were included in the exploratory program, students would tend to become confused by what may have been only superficial exposure. Grittner (30) mentions resistance on the part of parents, administrators, and senior high school teachers to a noncontinuous program. Where several teachers staff the exploratory program, Enwall et al. (16) emphasize the importance of maintaining consistency in content and instructional approach.

The general language course

Because of the stated limitations of the conventional or language-sampling category of exploratory offerings, the Virginia State Department of Education, in conjunction with four local school divisions, embarked on the development of an exploratory option that fits within the "nature of language" or "general language" framework. Entitled Introduction to Foreign Languages, the one- or two-semester offering includes units on: the nature of language, man's basic communication needs, the sounds of language, the signs of language, the structure of language, and nonverbal language. Native "informants" are frequently invited to visit the classes where they introduce students to the languages and cultures of their respective countries. No effort is made to teach foreign languages in the conventional sense. To broaden the students' linguistic perspective, emphasis is given to exposing them to the less common languages. The course also includes an instructional component on learning a foreign language. Moreover, there has been discussion concerning the adaptation of this course for senior high students.

Language-based humanities course

Limitations of general course

The greatest difficulty with a course of this nature is securing the services of a teacher who has had adequate preparation to teach all facets of the offering (Enwall et al., 16, Fearing and Grittner, 18). Duda (13), in selecting instructional personnel for one of the Virginia school districts in which the course was taught, established the following criteria: The teacher must be a person who has a foreign language background or has had extensive experience in a foreign country, can handle the extra work and research that would be necessary, and is flexible and has good rapport with students.

With regard to such courses within the general language framework, Fearing and Grittner (18) report that teachers voiced concern "that students will equate the study of language with that of philology, anthropology, and so on, thereby failing to realize that a great deal of skill development is also involved in the proper learning of a second language" (p. 6). Enwall et al. (16) state that this type of course may more properly suit students at the senior high school level.

The regular Level-I course

Those who favor this exploratory approach are of the opinion "that the best way to explore a language is to begin the serious study of it and that to begin a language sequence does not obviate the exploratory value to be derived from such a beginning" (Fearing and Grittner, 18, p. 3). Students who find that they do not wish to continue the study of the foreign language are, however, usually "locked in" for at least a semester and at times the entire year. In some schools, moreover, only the academically-talented students are permitted to enroll, a practice that appears to be contrary to the junior high school philosophy of maintaining a curriculum of an exploratory design for all students.

Limitations of Level I

The responsibility of selecting and implementing one of the exploratory possibilities is not an easy task. It appears that there are many within our profession who are opposed to implementing an exploratory option that replaces an established, well-articulated sequential program (Enwall et al., 16; Fearing and Grittner, 18). Each exploratory variation has its strengths and weaknesses as well as a following within the profession who maintain strong feelings either for or against it.

Where there is interest in implementing an exploratory course, the following guidelines are offered:

Guidelines for implementing an exploratory course

1 Research and literature. Communicate with appropriate personnel whose programs appear best suited to your school's needs. Both Enwall et al. (16) and Fearing and Grittner (18) provide descriptions of exploratory options, the latter including a listing of contact persons who are familiar with courses initiated in their respective locales. Fryer (24, pp. 27–31), Love and Honig (46, pp. 49–55), and Morrow (52) provide descriptions of specific exploratory offerings. Grittner (30) discusses exploratory programs for grades 5 to 8.
2 Reexamine the school's philosophy to ensure that the specific exploratory possibilities in which you are interested are compatible with the school's stated purposes.
3 Arrange for inservice activities for the teachers who will be responsible for the exploratory course as well as for those responsible for the regular sequential offerings. Not only is it essential to involve both groups for the betterment of articulation, but the success of the new offering will depend on the complete cooperation and endorsement of all the teachers.
4 Select personnel who have demonstrated the ability to work effectively and successfully with adolescents.
5 Strive to maintain consistency in both content and instructional practices in those programs involving more than one teacher.
6 If the language-sampling exploratory option is selected, ensure that all languages taught in the regular program are equally represented.
7 Design a course that will be an enjoyable and meaningful learning experience in itself.

Among the recommendations, in the form of "do's and don'ts," offered by participants attending the 1974 ACTFL Pre-Conference Workshop are:

Do's and Don'ts

Do

1 Set up small-scale pilot programs . . . before committing the entire district to the concept

2 Involve parents and other community members in the program and make the purposes of the course known
3 Encourage cultural and interdisciplinary experiences . . .

Don't

1 Exclude students on the basis of criteria such as low English grades, low I.Q., or lack of intention to follow the college preparatory track
2 Overload students with homework and busy work
3 Leave the students at the end of the exploratory program with the impression that the course is nothing but fun and games
4 Neglect the evaluation of the exploratory programs (Fearing and Grittner, 18, pp. 10–11).

Coordinating the foreign language sequence

Need for coordination

No greater limitation can be placed on a foreign language program than that resulting from a lack of coordination. It not only confines growth but in certain situations weakens the program to the point that its courses are comprised of a series of unrelated isolated classes.

There is no national curriculum and in most instances there are no state curricula. Where no local curriculum exists, teachers often alter, according to instructional needs, the amount of content presented in a semester or year. When staffing is increased, however, so is the difficulty in maintaining instructional consistency in the language sequences. The need for an organized and properly coordinated program of studies soon becomes apparent.

We make no attempt to set forth a procedure for developing a fully comprehensive curriculum guide; however, regardless of the size of the foreign language department, the time and effort to delineate certain statements and guidelines and initiate communicative practices would be well spent. If adhered to, they would bring about the development of a more cohesive, articulated foreign language program.

Philosophy and objectives

Establishing a framework

If there is to be coordination within a program, teachers must agree on certain principles which collectively establish the framework for developing a comprehensive philosophy. Objectives that lead to the implementation of the philosophy are no less important.

Some questions teachers may raise in developing their philosophy and objectives include:

1 What are the basic principles governing the inclusion of foreign languages in the school's curriculum?
2 Who should study a foreign language?
3 Which foreign language learning skills are to be stressed?
4 Is the teaching of culture to be an integral part of the program?
5 What types of language programs (sequential, exploratory, conversational) are to be offered?

Minimal course objectives

Consistency in content

To develop consistency in content from one level of instruction to the next, throughout the sequence minimal course (semester or year) objectives should be established for each level of each language. Rather than setting a certain number of pages or units of a textbook, such objectives are designed to set forth basic content items that will have been mastered by *all* students at the end of a given period of time. These are *minimal* objectives that in no way limit the teacher from covering additional material as time permits. In formulating the objectives one may wish to consult past tests and exams as well as, of course, the basal textbook.

All teachers who teach the same language must cooperate if the endeavor is to succeed. Revision is necessary if there is a change in the school's or department's philosophy or if a new textbook series is adopted. Coordination of content is no less important in courses based on teacher-prepared materials or excerpts from a variety of sources.

Instruction

Consistency in instruction

Teachers should utilize instructional approaches that are consistent in developing the desired degree of proficiency in the skills emphasized. The intent is not to make all teachers teach alike, but to attain a degree of compatibility that will reduce the amount of time necessary for a student to become acclimated to another teacher's approach to instruction and evaluation.

Coordination

The difficulties of maintaining coordination and consistency within the foreign language program are greatly reduced when specialist supervision is available. The degree to which the foreign language supervisor is successful in carrying out his responsibilities hinges on the establishment of communication with teachers and among the teachers themselves. Districtwide meetings provide an opportunity for teachers to discuss interests and problems of mutual concern; it is difficult, if not impossible, however, to request such a meeting each time a need arises. In Roanoke County, Virginia, Clapper (5), together with the local teachers, has established the Roanoke County Foreign Language Council which consists of one teacher-representative, elected by departmental personnel, from each school. The Council, which meets monthly, functions separately from the department chairpersons and is responsible for countywide program policy, curriculum matters, and information dissemination. While the foreign language supervisor works with department chairpersons where individual problems exist, the Council is concerned with problems affecting the total foreign language program and has developed over the past two years a philosophy of foreign language education and guidelines for Levels I and II in French, Latin, and Spanish. In Norfolk, Virginia, similar meetings are conducted each month; a copy of the minutes is sent to each teacher in the district (Jones, 38).

Specialist supervision

Specialist supervision is the exception to the rule; for in the large majority of school districts supervision of the foreign language program falls under the auspices of a general supervisor. In spite of his intentions, the generalist is at a disadvantage. Usually his time is divided among several disciplines of which he may have expertise in only one, and rarely is he a former foreign language teacher. Nevertheless, he can:

Generalist supervision

1 Provide moral support for language teachers
2 Provide opportunities for teachers to meet together to work out their own problems
3 Secure consultants and supervisors who are specialists in

teaching foreign language to supplement his more general assistance

4 Coordinate such housekeeping details as the ordering of materials and supplies and assuring adequate teaching facilities
5 Assist with decisions relevant to the role of foreign languages as a part of the school curriculum
6 Assist in analyzing the successes and shortcomings of the foreign language program (21, pp. 86–87).

Teacher initiative

Where there is no specialist supervisor and in some cases where only generalist supervision is available, the initiative for providing leadership must come from among the teachers, each of whom must work more closely with school administrators. Initially divisionwide meetings may have to be conducted on personal time. After progress has been made and results are apparent, the administration may be convinced of the importance of granting professional time for improving articulation of the foreign language program.

> Language learning is a continuous process which can be likened to a pyramid. Each level is built upon those beneath it; none can be skipped if a higher one is to be reached. The responsibility of the teacher is to supply a given step at a given time. Failure to do this results in retarding, or preventing, the construction of the pyramid. Each teacher functions not alone but as a member of the team operating in each student's language-learning career (p. 86).

A document, however modest it may be, which states a philosophy, includes objectives, and delineates certain articulatory procedures is necessary to provide a sense of coordinated direction for the program. One of its greatest values, however, may be the resulting feeling of worthwhile accomplishment on the part of each teacher who participated in the development of the project.

Lack of support for the foreign language program

> We were caught in the risky game of marketing products to ourselves. We did not keep in mind that the successful for-

> eign language program is not necessarily the result of a new approach, a new text, a new set of educational terms, but the establishment of positive relationships between the department and the inner (intra-school) and outer communities (Lavergneau, 40, p. 111).

This point is well taken, for in the face of declining enrollments, reduced language requirements, and tightened budgets, we as a profession, can no longer sit back and engage in what one might term "communicative inbreeding." To establish and maintain open lines of communication that place the foreign language profession in direct contact with key personnel within the local schools and within the community has become more important.

Communicating outside the profession

The purpose of this section is to provide suggestions for establishing communication and improving relationships with community patrons, school administrators, and guidance counselors. Without their support, today's foreign language programs face a somewhat uncertain tomorrow.

The community

The language festival

The foreign language festival or fair is rapidly becoming one of the most popular means of exhibiting the program to the community. Such an event provides an excellent opportunity to explain the purposes and goals of foreign language study as well as an occasion for students to demonstrate, before parents and friends, their linguistic talents. South Carolina's annual Foreign Language Day attracts students from throughout the state. In addition to art exhibits, a parade of "greats," and costume fashion shows, there is competition in architectural modeling, creative stitchery, gourmet cooking, extemporaneous oration, foreign language scrapbooks, drama, and dance. Students are also encouraged to set up booths where food and other commodities are sold (Enwall, 15).

Meyer (50) provides a detailed blueprint for organizing and carrying out a language festival from the preplanning stages to postevaluative activities. She emphasizes that the key to success is student involvement in all aspects of the function.

Community involvement

Miller (51) makes the following recommendations for involving members of the community in the festival:

1 Invite local dignitaries such as superintendents, mayors, American Legion and Veterans of Foreign Wars officials to ride in parades and serve as judges.
2 Ask local merchants to display foreign language exhibits in their shop windows.
3 Issue special invitations to speakers of other languages to be present and to participate in the festivities.
4 Begin the festival with a parade that will pass through the downtown area.
5 Request local companies with international connections to have floats in the parade and to sponsor booths.
6 Involve local religious leaders, some of whom may be willing to offer the invocation in a foreign language.
7 Have the mayor officially proclaim Foreign Language Week and Foreign Language Day.

In North Carolina organizers can contact the Special Forces Teams at Fort Bragg. With sufficient advance notice they will take part in parades and opening ceremonies as well as make parachute jumps. Members of the Special Forces are not only trained in the martial skills but must also attain fluency in at least one foreign language (Miller, 51).

Coverage in the printed media

Garfinkel (27) reports that, based on a survey (1972–73) of articles appearing in *The New York Times, The Christian Science Monitor* and those listed in *The Readers' Guide to Periodical Literature,* nationally distributed magazines and newspapers generally portray foreign language study in a favorable light. To increase coverage in the media, he suggests that the profession at the local and national levels report every accomplishment on a regular and thorough basis. Furthermore, we must communicate the values of foreign language learnings, as well as our concerns, to letters-to-the-editor columns and to individuals who help form public opinion. In the final analysis, "coverage will be afforded our profession in amounts that are proportionate to our efforts to generate it" (p. 111).

Language bank

In Richmond, Virginia, Beck (3) has organized a language bank of 80 individuals representing 40 different languages. The roster, with addresses and telephone numbers, is sent to each police station, major hotel, hospital, nursing home, airport, charity organization, and all Red Cross offices in the community.

Because of our commitment to the humanities, Preller (63) emphasizes the necessity to become active in art leagues, symphonic societies, library boards, civic theater groups, and literary groups.

Crane (9) suggests that teachers maintain contact with the community by involving parents in foreign language booster clubs, having students present language programs to Parent Teacher Associations, and involving themselves in community projects. Jones (37) encourages communication with civic groups and recommends participation of foreign language clubs in international friendship organizations such as the Partners for the Americas. In a Franklin, Virginia, high school, an Amity Aide gave 42 talks to various church and civic groups and was featured on a local radio show (Blaine, 4). Miller (51) suggests that foreign language clubs purchase advertising space in local newspapers for the purpose of expounding the value of language study. In Orange, Virginia, the senior high school cooperates with the local Junior Women's Club in organizing, as one of the club's international activities, an international banquet (Fitzhugh, 20). Teachers are advised to make reports or presentations relevant to the foreign language program in person at local school board meetings (Loew, 44). She also encourages the practice of inviting school board members to visit and observe foreign language classes.

Civic opportunities

School board meetings

One should use the foreign language curriculum as a vehicle to the community (Loew, 45). When it will not have a negative effect on enrollments in the existing foreign language program, one may wish to initiate additional courses representing the languages of community ethnic groups, either with a conversational orientation or as an addition to the regular sequential program. In certain situations offering the less commonly taught languages on an independent study basis might be more feasible. Loew also recommends representation from the community on curriculum committees; for the administration is far more likely to approve proposals developed jointly by parents, students, and teachers than those prepared exclusively within the foreign language department.

In spite of the activities suggested, which should lead to greater community involvement, the profession's most valuable and most accessible link to the community is the foreign language student. We should not take this lightly; for the impression that the teacher makes on the student is taken home daily where, quite likely, it affects dinner table conversation and evening activities.

The student

Administrators

Many of the ideas presented for improving communication with the community are just as applicable to administrators. Gage (25), however, offers specific guidelines for promoting positive relationships with administrative personnel:

Communicating with administrators

1 *Have a good exciting program.* What interests administrators most are the positive day-to-day learning activities within the classroom that involve and stimulate students.
2 *Invite administrators to classes.* Always maintain an open-door attitude toward administrators; when a particularly interesting activity is to take place, inform them of it and, if necessary, go get them.
3 *Be ready to listen.* Administrators frequently view the foreign language program from a different vantage point. If they offer suggestions or recommendations, always consider their comments with an open mind.
4 *Know your subject area.* Administrators probably know less about foreign languages than any other discipline. They consider you an expert. Keep them informed about the values of foreign language study.
5 *Give them credit when credit is due.* If you have been granted specific requests or have received unsolicited support from your administrators, acknowledge such help and thank them.
6 *Be supportive of the total school program.* Remember that foreign languages are but one of many subject areas. Do not expect support for your program on a nonreciprocal basis.
7 *Include administrators in pictures you take of activities.* Whenever the school newspaper or local media come to take pictures, always request that the administrators be on hand and included in the photographs.
8 *Be practical and realistic.* Many administrators have become alienated by foreign language teachers who have

lured students into their programs without distinguishing between minimal proficiency and fluency. Do not promise more than can be delivered.

9 *Promote your area.* Expect equal but not special treatment from administrators. They expect you to sell the foreign language program.

10 *Always use tact.* A lack of diplomacy in dealing with administrators can lead to the eradication of administrative support for the foreign language program.

Crane (9) suggests that foreign language teachers not only keep administrative personnel informed by forwarding pertinent information to them but that they also assist with tasks and activities that are not necessarily foreign language related.

Guidance counselors

Communicating with counselors

Paine (57), who reprimands foreign language teachers for excluding students, parents, and counselors from their discussions about the rationale for language study, maintains that counselors would not hesitate to direct students to foreign language classes if they knew that the classes were fresh, appealing, and relevant. Because of their interest in *all* students, they are particularly concerned about the elitist approach, which still has the support of some within the foreign language profession.

Loew (43) offers the following guidelines as ways in which the foreign language teacher can improve relations with guidance personnel:

1 Offer your services to explain the language program to the entire guidance staff early in the year and again at scheduling time.
2 Invite guidance personnel to language department meetings.
3 Suggest that a member of the guidance staff be assigned to each department as a liaison person.
4 Offer to place all transfer students by interviewing each one individually.
5 Insist that no student be dropped from or transferred to another language course without being thoroughly interviewed by his teacher and the chairman.

6 Insist on being included in parent interviews where language is a major topic to help support the counselor as well as the program or teachers involved.
7 Assist guidance counselors with the choices of colleges for your junior or senior students.
8 Assume the advisorship for summer study, travel, exchange, and work programs for students.
9 Assist guidance counselors in evaluating and assigning credits from summer study programs, other school districts, and foreign schools.
10 Help keep the students' guidance files current.
11 Contact the guidance counselor early in the year about difficulties rather than waiting until they become too hard to resolve.
12 Emphasize career possibilities for students of foreign languages.
13 Meet all deadlines for turning in enrollment data, recommendation applications, and so forth.
14 Verbalize and write out your praise for guidance counselors when deserved.

Influence of the counselor

Within the school there is no other single group of individuals who, potentially, can exert more influence on students than the guidance counselors. We, as foreign language teachers, must seek and maintain cooperation with them in every respect.

Teaching the handicapped student

Traditionally the foreign language teacher has not often had to deal with special problems of students with severe physical, mental, or emotional handicaps, because they have either been placed in special schools or have been assigned to separate classes in the regular school. Because counselors, administrators, and teachers realized that the presence of these students in foreign language classes would pose certain unusual problems, they have been generally advised not to take foreign languages. Russo (66) points out, however, that recent court decisions mandate equal educational opportunities for handicapped children, and some state courts have required that these students be placed in regular public schools instead of special schools. The prevailing philosophy among school psychologists and special education experts today appears to be one of "mainstreaming" these students into as many regular classes as possible in an effort to improve their self-images. Of the seven million youngsters in the United States who suffer some form of physical or mental handicap (Russo, 66, p. 26), some will probably wish to enroll in foreign language classes.

"Mainstreaming" handicapped students

In this section suggestions are offered that should prove to be helpful to the teacher who has had no previous training for coping with these special problems. The discussion is limited to three categories: the hearing impaired, the visually impaired, and the speech impaired.

Categories discussed

The hearing impaired

Hearing-impaired children suffer hearing loss that significantly restricts participation in the normal classroom program and necessitates modifications in the instruction. The foreign language teacher has probably not been confronted with a deaf student because, as Diamant (11) points out, foreign languages had not been taught even in schools for the deaf, except at the college level, prior to 1972. According to Clarke (6), an authority in the field of special education, the child who functions in other classes with the use of a hearing aid should not encounter any special problems in a foreign language class.

Definition of hearing impaired

There are students, however, who do not hear well but who have adapted themselves to their environment without realizing it. These students' hearing problems sometimes go unnoticed until they are confronted with unfamiliar sounds, and the foreign language teacher may be the one to detect them. The teacher who suspects that one of his students has a hearing impairment should first check the child's permanent record to see if there are notations related to the suspected problem and, if so, what has been done about it. If this search yields no clues, he should mention it to the child, although care should be taken to avoid embarrassing the student. Preferably, the conversation would take place in private, perhaps after class, and the teacher might say simply, "I'm not sure that you are hearing me well. I noticed today that when I told the class to open their books, you did not respond." The problem may be inattention and not related to a hearing difficulty, but if it continues to persist, the

Detecting hearing impairments

parents should be contacted and permission to consult a hearing specialist should be secured. Many school divisions employ full-time specialists for the hearing impaired, but if one is not available, a speech pathologist or even a public health nurse would probably be able to administer an audiometric test in order to ascertain the severity of any defect. Referral then might be made to an ear specialist.

Pettyjohn (61) offers suggestions for the individual teacher to determine certain auditory problems that may cause difficulty in learning a foreign language; the strategies implemented will depend on the nature of the problem. To determine whether the student is "tone deaf," the teacher may simply talk to the child, varying the tones of his voice on different occasions to discover which tones the student hears. To find out if a student has difficulty with auditory discrimination, meanings may be assigned to several different unfamiliar phonemic words and the student required to relate the meanings when the words are called at random. (Most language aptitude tests contain auditory discrimination sections.) The student who has difficulty in hearing phonemic differences will need special help from the teacher and extra listening practice, especially with phonemes in the foreign language that do not exist or are not often used in his native language. To determine the degree of auditory memory of a given student, a simple test may be used whereby he is asked to repeat numbers at one-second intervals. The teacher begins with three digits such as 6, 5, 8 and asks the student to repeat them. He would gradually increase the number of digits to a maximum of six for a seventh grader and seven or eight for a tenth grader. Subsequently, the student might be asked to repeat three or four of the numbers backwards. If the student is not able to perform satisfactorily on this test, he probably has a problem remembering sounds and will, more than likely, experience difficulty in remembering dialogue lines and pattern drills. Again, he will need individual help from the teacher.

Determining tone deafness

Auditory memory

After the student's specific auditory problems have been determined, the teacher will have to develop strategies for assisting the student. He will need to make tapes available for extra listening practice, preferably on a take-home basis. Words containing sounds that are difficult for the student can be drilled on an individual basis. The difference between success and failure for these students may depend on the teacher's ability to determine what the problems are.

Clarke (6) offers several general suggestions:

1 Always call the student's name before directing a question to him.
2 Seat him close to the teacher.
3 When addressing the entire class, try to remember his presence in the room. For example, do not write on the board and talk at the same time.
4 Make the environment as comfortable as possible so that the student will not mind asking for repetition of what he has not heard clearly.
5 Offer him extra help on an individual basis.
6 In initiating oral responses from the student, rely less on auditory cues and more on visual aids such as pictures, drawings, and filmstrips.
7 Depending on the degree of severity of the problem, do not expect the student's performance to be as good as that of his peers who do not have similar problems.

The visually handicapped

Range of visual acuity

Visual acuity may range from the partially sighted child (20/70 vision or less in the better eye with the best correction) to one who is totally blind. Most of Clarke's (6) general suggestions for teaching the hearing impaired may also be applied to the partially sighted. However, the student who is totally blind will need some additional considerations. Certainly, the textbook used by the other members of the class will be of no value to a blind student. Most states have a commission for the blind that will transcribe texts into braille. (A telephone survey of three prominent foreign language textbook companies revealed that texts are not available in braille from the publishers.) Nalls (53), who teaches a blind student in one of her Spanish classes at Byrd Middle School in Henrico County, Virginia, states that teacher-made worksheets, puzzles, and other supplementary materials can be transcribed by a person trained in braille. Moreover, written work done by the student in braille can also be transcribed for the teacher. Harrison (33), who has a blind student in his Spanish III class, reports that his student types most of her written assignments.

Teaching the blind

The cassette tape recorder can be particularly useful in working with a blind student. The teacher can record objectives, activities, reading selections, and tests on a tape for the student to use either in class or at home.

Use of tape recorder

Both Harrison (33) and Nalls (53) strongly recommend asking other students in the class to assist the blind student in certain activities. Some of the ways in which students can assist are:

Peer assistance

1 During the visual introduction of new vocabulary to the class, the blind child can be given a list of vocabulary items written in braille in English and the target language, and another student can whisper a description of the visual. Whenever feasible, the blind student can be given the actual objects (pen, pencil, book, paper, articles of clothing, fruits, and other portable items), and the student assistant can manipulate the objects to provide practice in identifying them in the target language by the blind student.
2 Another student can read assigned selections to the handicapped student.
3 In certain manipulative activities, such as the use of the audio-flashcard machine or verb charts, the blind student can work with a classmate who explains all visual matter.

Although a blind student can be expected to participate in most of the normal classroom activities, alternatives are sometimes necessary. For example, Nalls reports that when her students were assigned a project of constructing written advertisements in the target language, her blind student was allowed to make an original tape of a radio commercial in Spanish.

Alternatives a must

The visually impaired or even the totally blind can certainly be successful in a conventional foreign language class. According to Nalls, the main consideration for the teacher in working with students with severe visual handicaps is to compensate for the lack of vision by placing more emphasis on the listening and speaking skills.

The speech impaired

Persons who are speech impaired have an abnormality of speech that calls adverse attention to itself or interferes with

Definition of speech impaired

communication. Because much emphasis is placed on the speaking skill in most modern foreign language classes, one might expect a child with a speech handicap to experience a great deal of difficulty. This is not necessarily true. Pettyjohn (61) points out that "the single most important factor in determining whether or not the student succeeds is motivation. The greatest joy that a student with this particular handicap may experience can be accomplishing something that is difficult. He will more than likely compensate for his weakness if he is motivated." Clarke (6) agrees that children with *certain* speech problems can succeed as well as any other student.

Motivation factor

Articulation and stuttering are the main speech problems encountered in secondary schools. Articulation problems are usually manifested either in the omission of certain sounds or in the substitution of one sound for another. For example, some children substitute *w* for the *r* sound (*w*un for *r*un, *w*ight for *r*ight) or *d* for *th* (*d*is for *th*is, *d*ese for *th*ese). If a student has a problem in articulating a particular sound in English, he will probably have difficulty with that sound if it occurs in the foreign language. The teacher will have to work with the student individually with the aid of visuals, tapes, and other supplementary materials in order to "un-teach" the incorrect sounds in favor of the correct ones. If the child is already receiving help from a speech pathologist, the foreign language teacher should work closely with this expert in providing the proper guidance for the student. Teaching target language sounds that do not exist in English should pose no more problems for these students than they do for the nonhandicapped because they have not been learned incorrectly.

Articulatory problems

Speech experts do not agree on what causes stuttering, though many believe that it is a neurological problem (Clarke 6). Stuttering is difficult to overcome without the aid of expert assistance, and the foreign language teacher who is confronted with the problem should exercise caution in prescribing activities designed to help the student. A speech pathologist or a psychologist should be consulted for advice on how to work with the particular student.

The stuttering child

Clarke offers several general suggestions that may be helpful because they deal mainly with interaction in the classroom and not specific therapeutic devices:

1 The stuttering child should be encouraged to speak the target language in class, but he should *not* be put "on the spot." He should never be asked to stand in the front of the room to recite dialogues or other material unless he volunteers.
2 Care should be taken to avoid embarrassment to the child because of his manner of expressing himself.
3 The teacher should remember to accentuate the positive. A brief compliment related to the child's manner of dress, accomplishments outside of school, or performance on a particular classroom-related assignment or activity can do wonders for the child's self-concept and may result in better classroom performance.

A student with a serious speech, visual, or hearing handicap should be made aware of the demands of language learning. The handicap should not, however, be a basis to deny him the opportunity to learn a foreign language. Instead, provisions should be made for individual differences in learning and for evaluating achievement accordingly.

Teaching the culturally disadvantaged student

In 1970 John Lawson (41), a school superintendent, challenged the foreign language profession to enroll 75 to 100 percent of all secondary students in a foreign language by 1980. Soon after Lawson's seemingly unrealistic challenge, Sandstrom and Pimsleur (67) and their colleagues on Working Committee III of the 1970 Northeast Conference proposed that *all* students, not only the intellectually elite, be encouraged to study foreign languages in our schools. If the profession truly believes that the study of a foreign language offers advantages, both practical and humanistic, that cannot be gained from participation in any other subject area of the curriculum, it must consider that the student who does not go to college may never again have the opportunity to be exposed to this dimension of human behavior. Is it not a responsibility of the schools to make all students aware of the advantages of studying other languages and a responsibility of language teachers to seek effective methods of instruction that make second language learning possible for all students who desire it?

All students included

All is an encompassing word. No one is excluded, not even the low-ability student, the low achiever in other subject areas, nor the culturally disadvantaged. Lawson specifically mentions that the study of foreign languages by disadvantaged students can have positive results by improving self-concepts and attitudes toward their schools, as well as in benefiting their English speech habits. According to Clift (7), the major reason an increasing number of black students fall below their grade level in performance is that *substandard performance is expected of them*. He says that the schools are doing a grave injustice to these students while making an honest effort to help them. If accomplishments are to be made, teachers must think positively; instead of grouping all minority children and poor children together and calling them "disadvantaged" and then setting up easy subjects for them, we must start by accepting each individual child for what he is when he comes to us. We must assume that his *potential* for learning is, on the average, as good as that of any other student, and then we must work to help that child develop his own potential to the maximum.

Values derived

Few specifics can be found in the professional literature. Either little has actually been done in this area or what has been accomplished has not been communicated to the profession. Judging from personal observations, we believe that opportunities to study foreign languages *are* now being extended to a more diverse group of students than previously and that indeed many culturally disadvantaged students are attracted to our programs. Some are succeeding; others are not. Teachers who have never had the experience of teaching these children too often become frustrated and give up. To hear teachers say, "Those students really have no business in French in the first place," or "I tried to work with them, but they can't even speak English correctly; how can I be expected to teach them Spanish?" is common. These teachers need practical help—the sooner the better.

Definition of Disadvantaged

The culturally disadvantaged child has not had the opportunities for learning and the kinds of cultural experiences that the majority of children in the same age group have had. Many are members of ethnic minority groups, but as Skinner (74) points out, there are Caucasians living in the Appalachian region who are, in their own way, just as "disadvantaged" as minority-group children who live in the ghettos of our large cities. The culturally disadvantaged child may be as intelligent as any other, provided we define intelligence as *potential* for learning.

Intelligence

Love (47) has identified six general characteristics of the culturally disadvantaged child; although certainly not all deprived children fit into each category, most are characterized by:

Characteristics

1 Poor self-concepts, even inferiority complexes
2 Lack of motivation to succeed in life
3 Lack of concentration on most school tasks
4 Difficulty in abstract reasoning
5 A need for immediate rewards
6 A need for involvement in action-oriented activities.

Hallahan (32) adds that disadvantaged children usually possess very short attention spans, are highly distractible, and often act impulsively.

If one of the objectives of encouraging culturally disadvantaged children to enroll in foreign language classes is to improve their self-concepts, the class should provide each student as many opportunities as possible to achieve success. The classroom atmosphere should be as informal as facilities will permit. Converse (8) states that in her inner city high school French class grades are earned through active participation and good attendance. If a formal test is given, it always tests material that every student has had ample opportunity to master. The students should be told exactly what is expected of them, and they should be tested on exactly what they have been told. Normand (55) says that his students in a ghetto school will prepare for a quiz if the content is specific and if the quiz will count for them if they succeed but not against them if they fail.

Need for success

The teacher should get to know his students as well and as rapidly as possible. A feeling of personal interest in them as individuals is necessary, and praise should be given every time it is merited. Materials to which they can relate should be used. For example, visuals should depict members of minority groups, as well as the middle-class Puerto Rican, German, or Frenchman. The teacher must remember that one objective should be to expand the students' cultural horizons—to help them to see and understand some of the characteristics, mores, and lifestyles of other cultures. In addition to the use of films, filmstrips, slides, records, and other realia, these students should be involved in firsthand cultural experiences such as field trips to museums or foreign restaurants or visits to the classroom by native speakers.

Emphasis on usage

Because abstract reasoning is difficult for many of these students, emphasis should be on language usage and not grammar *per se*. An inductive approach should be followed in most cases. In teaching the reading skill, they should not be expected to "read between the lines." Instead, they should be taught to look for main ideas first and then for details. If, however, there are students in the class for whom abstract reasoning poses no problem, they should certainly be challenged.

Varied experiences

If disadvantaged students are characterized by a lack of concentration on school tasks and short attention spans, variety should be the password in the activities of any class period. Many experiences of varied difficulty should provide each student with an opportunity to achieve success. Converse (8) describes a number of activities that emphasize communication, such as games, minidramas, rolling dice to learn numbers, and discussions in which the students are encouraged to communicate their own thoughts by any means necessary—touch, jump, scream, point, or cry—as long as they communicate. All of these require a great deal of movement and interaction. Verbalization and communication may be especially important to them, because some may not have been allowed to verbalize their own language at home.

Normand (55) successfully uses what he calls an "all-skills approach" in which the four skills are integrated from the very first class. One skill follows the other in rapid succession. The written skills are used immediately to reinforce what the students have just learned orally. Most of the written work takes place in class under supervision, because the students cannot be relied on to do homework assignments.

Teaching foreign languages to culturally disadvantaged children is a real problem faced by teachers throughout the country. The problem exists because we have ignored these students for too long, and now that they are responding to our invitation to "try a language course," we are not prepared to deal with them and *their* problems. They can be successful if the proper conditions for learning exist. But the profession desperately needs more firsthand information from experienced teachers, research, and a better means of sharing what we do know. Foreign language education departments must prepare teacher candidates for the possibility of employment in a large inner-city school or in a poverty-stricken rural area. In the meantime, teachers must be resourceful. The recent focus on individualized learning has made us more aware of individual differences in ability, interest, learning style, and rate of learning. But the disadvantaged student brings with him another difference, that of his experiential background, which is likely to be as foreign to the teacher as the foreign language is to the student.

Accommodating the needs of the occasional student of limited English-speaking ability

Approximately 5,000,000 children in today's schools require assistance in learning English. Languages from virtually all over the world are represented (Levenson, 42). Even in the most isolated areas of the country, we find nonnative Americans whose ability to communicate in English may vary from limited to nonexistent. With the publicity accompanying the recent influx of Indochinese refugees, local school districts have become more conscious of their responsibility to provide assistance to meet the needs of these students.

In areas that have bilingual/bicultural or organized ESOL (English to Speakers of Other Languages) programs, the impact from an instructional point of view has been considerably less than in small rural school districts that had no need to implement similar programs. In this case, however, accommodating the student of limited English-speaking ability may be a confusing and frustrating experience for both student and teacher.

A confusing experience

Selection of the teacher

The most important decision the administration is to make in providing ESOL instruction is selecting the teacher. Although the foreign language teacher appears to be the most likely candidate for the position because of his background and training

The teacher: key to success

in other languages and cultures, priority must be given to any person who exhibits qualities of empathy and understanding.

> The teacher who analyzes her feelings about not being able to communicate with this child will recognize them as but a fraction of the strangeness, isolation and frustration that the child is feeling. The first step in teaching the non-English speaker is to understand and emphathize with him.
>
> If a native-born child arriving at a new school is apprehensive, the foreign-born is more so. He is not familiar with the regimen of an American school, the games, the customs; and he most certainly does not know the language. He is not stupid, nor is he deaf. He has brought with him concepts of another language and a wide range of experiences to talk about, but in this new situation he is unable to communicate his needs. Clearly, this child deserves special attention from the moment he arrives at school (Thiele, 78, p. 1).

The selection of the *right* teacher will greatly enhance the development of a positive self-image and a sense of security within the student.

Orientation

The first few days

During the first few days the student should be given a tour of the school facilities. Assigning a "buddy" to accompany him through the day's activities may be advisable. One should attempt to secure the services, if available, of a local resident who is familiar with the new student's language or who shares the same language background. (This community volunteer may later agree to assist as an instructional aide.) Location of restrooms and water fountains, lunchroom procedures, and the transportation system (if the student rides a bus) must be shown or explained to him on the first day. Even if no translating assistance is available, much can be accomplished through nonverbal communication.

Some orientation should be provided for all school personnel, from school administrators to bus drivers. If nothing else, they should at least be informed of the student's presence. They should be made aware of basic cultural differences which, if misunderstood, could lead to embarrassing situations. This is particularly significant in instances in which the student represents a nonwestern culture.

Instruction

Generally, in the absence of a qualified ESOL teacher, a modern foreign language teacher is selected to provide instruction because of his pedagogical background. This does not preclude teachers in other disciplines from teaching English to the students of limited English-speaking ability; however, they should be familiar or willing to acquire familiarity with instructional approaches and techniques. The frequency of ESOL instruction may vary, depending on the availability of the teacher and the degree to which the student is handicapped. In the Arlington County, Virginia, Public Schools, one to three class periods of ESOL instruction are recommended per day, the least proficient students receiving the maximum amount of instruction possible (Shiels-Djouadi, 73).

Instructional approaches

The works of both Finocchiaro (19) and Saville-Troike (69) can serve well as basic methodology references; the latter includes chapters on survival skills for the teacher with no special training in the teaching of English as a second language. Robson and Sutherland (65) have compiled a comprehensive annotated bibliography including sections on instruction, testing, culture, and reference materials, which is applicable to ESOL instruction in general. Marckwardt (48) has prepared a selected list of instructional materials. A similar listing which is devoted exclusively to audiovisual aids is also available (71). In Maryland the Montgomery County Public School System has established instructional objectives and a content outline for beginning and intermediate ESOL classes. Following an audiolingual approach, beginning instruction centers around a variety of topics including classroom and school procedures, food, social formulas, numbers and measurements, health and safety, weather, shopping, family and occupations, home and community, recreation, and transportation (Frank et al., 22).

Content-area instruction

Content-area teachers, sensitive to the particular needs of the student of limited English-speaking proficiency, should be encouraged to work as closely as time and other responsibilities permit. Providing in advance summaries or resumes of content to be covered in each class is helpful; caution must be exercised, however, in the selection of vocabulary items. Specific problems or difficulties encountered in the content-area classes should be reported to the ESOL teacher who should keep the content-area staff apprised of the student's progress. Such communication between teaching personnel is vital to success.

Course of study

A copy of a student's transcript will provide insight into his past academic achievement and courses of study completed. If no record of past study is available and translating services are unobtainable, one must gather as much information as possible from initial interviews with the student and through subsequent ESOL instruction. However, one should not overlook the possibility of a student's already existent ability to communicate in a second more commonly taught language.

Placement

Students of limited English speaking ability should generally be placed in courses where knowledge of English is less a determining factor to success. Such courses might include art, music, physical education, math, and industrial arts. Offerings in health, social studies, regular English, and science, where a broad knowledge of vocabulary is necessary, may pose insurmountable problems. Regardless of placement, the student should be enrolled in classes with students of his own age. Consideration may also be given to enrolling the student in a beginning foreign language offering, provided that the instructional approach is of a multisensory nature with minimal dependency on a knowledge of English, and the foreign language is of the same language family as the student's native language.

Should the student's native language be one that is taught within the school's foreign language program, he may be placed in an advanced level offering pursuing, basically, the normal course of study, or his services may be utilized as an instructional aide or resource person at any level of instruction.

The placement of the student in a particular course should not necessarily be considered permanent; there should be a degree of flexibility in scheduling, permitting him to be placed in a learning environment where he is most likely to succeed.

Credit

Credit for ESOL instruction will be governed by state or local regulations. It may conceivably be awarded in lieu of a regular English requirement or as a foreign language elective. The student is working under extenuating and frequently demanding circumstances in his pursuit of an education. Where ample progress is demonstrated, credit is due, whether on the basis of achieving certain objectives or classroom hours of instruction.

Lack of opportunities for professional growth

The teacher is the key to what goes on in the classroom. No matter how much technology invades the classroom in the form of equipment and materials, the teacher will always play the principal role in designing instruction. His job is becoming increasingly challenging as a result of many new demands and problems. If he is to meet these challenges with any degree of success, he must not rely solely on his preservice training but must continue to grow professionally by taking advantage of every opportunity to learn. Today's foreign language teacher cannot become complacent in his attitudes or stagnant in his teaching. Included among the opportunities available for improving the professional qualifications of teachers are inservice activities designed to familiarize them with current trends and practices and to maintain or improve language skills.

Constraints

Teachers, however, are not superhuman. They are constrained in their efforts to improve themselves professionally by obstacles such as lack of time due to schedules overloaded with clerical, curricular, and extracurricular responsibilities; lack of funds, both professional and personal; and sometimes lack of support for professional improvement from the administration. Some teachers are isolated geographically and, because of their locations, find it difficult to share ideas with colleagues or to maintain their language skills. Merely stating that teachers should take advantage of opportunities for professional growth is not enough, because those opportunities do not always exist. The teacher who is genuinely interested is still occasionally stymied by a lack of opportunities for professional growth.

Inservice programs

Divisionwide meetings

Most school divisions provide some type of inservice programs. These programs are not, however, always suited to the needs of foreign language teachers. They should request that the administration schedule specific time slots for them to meet together to share ideas and discuss strategies for dealing with common problems, and they should ask that practical workshops dealing with specific problems they face be conducted by outstanding well-informed teachers from within the school system or by speakers and leaders brought in from other areas. Because the administration may not be familiar with their specific needs, the teachers should be willing to share in the responsibility for developing their own inservice programs.

School departmental meetings

One type of inservice activity that should be implemented in each school is the regular departmental meeting. The members of the foreign language staff should meet together to discuss problems within the school. Topics for discussion and study might include achievement goals for each level of instruction, testing and evaluation, appropriate use of supplementary aids, or ways of raising the visibility of the foreign language program within the school. They may wish to develop a departmental handbook that could be made available to administrators, guidance counselors, other members of the faculty, and interested parents.

Topics for discussion

Professional meetings

Attending foreign language conferences, workshops, and professional meetings at the regional, state, and national levels helps to keep the teacher informed about developments within his teaching field and in contact with colleagues. In large schools or school divisions administrators can hardly be expected to provide financial support and released time for all teachers who wish to attend a specific meeting. A plan should be established, however, to assure that the school division is represented at such meetings and that the highlights of the meeting are communicated to all teachers in the system.

Organizations

One professional obligation of every teacher is participation in professional organizations. Each teacher should belong to his foreign language organization (AAT group for modern languages and the American Classical League for the classics) and to the American Council on the Teaching of Foreign Languages (ACTFL), which is the only national organization of teachers of all languages dedicated to bringing about unity in the profession and to providing direction for the future. In addition, there are many active state organizations that need teacher support.

Professional literature

To keep abreast of what is going on in the profession, the teacher should survey the literature. In addition to the regular publications of the professional organizations, there are several other outstanding ones to be considered. Among them are The ACTFL Foreign Language Education Series, The Modern Language Journal, and the various Reports of annual regional language conferences from throughout the country (Northeast, Southern, Central States, Pacific Northwest, and so on). Teachers may wish to purchase some of these documents for their own personal libraries. Familiarity with available materials by the members of a department may result in a sharing arrangement whereby teachers purchase different publications or subscribe to separate journals and then make them available to each other. Library subscriptions are also suggested. Many teachers are not aware that school divisions are required by accreditation agencies to maintain professional libraries and that in most cases the media specialist will order books or subscribe to journals for departments that request them.

Sharing professional publications

The geographically isolated teacher

Gage (26) reports that there are three counties in Oklahoma in which there are *no* foreign language teachers and several others in which there are only one or two. For persons who seldom have an opportunity to share ideas with colleagues, Crane (9) offers the following suggestions:

Professional sharing

1 Share ideas with teachers in related subject areas—for example, discuss cultural concepts with social studies teachers and music and art of the countries whose language you are teaching with the teachers in those departments.
2 Find other staff members who have studied a foreign language and organize "get-togethers."
3 Share ideas by tape with colleagues in other localities.
4 Invite a foreign language teacher from a nearby college to visit your classes.
5 Contact the office of the state supervisor of foreign languages for assistance on specific problems.

Teacher observation

One excellent inservice opportunity that is often overlooked is that of visiting and observing competent language teachers. The isolated teacher can profit especially from the experience of visiting another teacher in a different school system to observe instructional techniques and exchange ideas. Where available, videotapes may be utilized in a similar fashion.

Maintaining language skills

Reasons for loss of fluency

Most foreign language teachers are not privileged to visit regularly the countries in which the languages they teach are spoken. Consequently, they lose some fluency, especially when their teaching assignments are concentrated in lower-level classes. The teacher must seek opportunities in which he may practice the target language in real situations outside the classroom. Such opportunities often are difficult to find.

Recommendations of Nebraska Study

Based on his study at the University of Nebraska of teachers who had successfully maintained their proficiency in the four language skills, Hughes (34) made several recommendations that are summarized as follows:

1 The foreign language teacher should seek opportunities to speak and hear the target language by practicing with other teachers in the school, foreign exchange students, and native speakers in the community.
2 He should make periodic recordings on a tape recorder to analyze his own pronunciation and intonation.
3 He should view as many foreign language films as opportunities permit.
4 He should regularly carry on correspondence in the target language with friends both here and abroad.

Other suggestions that should be considered are listening to shortwave radio broadcasts in the target language, reading foreign newspapers and magazines, and writing letters to persons who live in the target culture.

If today's foreign language teacher is to meet the many challenges that confront him, he must be both competent and knowledgeable in his field. He must continue to grow professionally by participating in effective inservice activities and by maintaining his proficiency in the use of the target language.

Conclusion

Interrelationship of problems

Many of the problems that confront secondary school foreign language teachers are interrelated and remedies suggested in this chapter for some have implications for others. Due to the degree of overlap, drawing any specific conclusions is difficult.

Some of the problems discussed here are recurring ones that escape solution, while others are unique occurrences but no less important when they do arise. In most cases the strategies offered have been based on real experiences of classroom teachers who have had to work out their own solutions. The reader should choose among the options offered, modifying and adapting suggested remedies to fit his own situation.

Advice to the reader

For the authors, one of the outcomes of this endeavor has been the revelation that many teachers are of the opinion that their contributions would be insignificant or of little value to anyone else. Nothing could be further from the truth; for it is they who, in the final analysis, face the problems in the classroom every day. We must find ways to bring about a greater degree of sharing on the part of those who represent the "heart" of the profession—the classroom teacher.

References, Coping with the real problems in the secondary schools

1 Ahrens, Maurice, Durell Ruffin, and Raymond Wilson,eds., *The Junior High School Program.* Atlanta:The Southern Association of Colleges and Schools, 1964.

2 Baker, Carolyn. Personal Communication, 1976. [Mimeo.]

3 Beck, William J. "Have You Thought of Establishing a Foreign Language Bank?" *Accent on ACTFL* 5,iii(1975):14–15.

4 Blaine, John A. "Señor Pepe Worth Preparation for Nine-Week Fiesta." *Virginia Journal of Education* 69,vii(1976):15–16.

5 Clapper, William O. Personal Communication, 1976. [Letter.]

6 Clarke, Lucille J. Personal Communication, 1976. [Interview.]

7 Clift, Virgil A. "Further Considerations in the Education of the Disadvantaged." *The Educational Forum* 34,ii(1972):223–28.

8 Converse, Genelle. "Stimulating Interest in French in a Center City School." *Accent on ACTFL* 5,iv (1975):16–18.

9 Crane, Joanna B. Personal Communication, 1976. [Letter.]

10 Deutch, Rachel F. "A Lure for the Reluctant Learner." *The French Review* 45(1972):635–41.

11 Diamant, Jay. "Teaching Spanish to Deaf Children." *American Foreign Language Teacher* 3,ii (1972):13.

12 Disick, Renée S. "Developing Positive Attitudes in Intermediate Foreign Language Classes." *The Modern Language Journal* 56(1972):417–20.

13 Duda, Brenda C. Personal Communication, 1976. [Letter.]

14 Emmons, Frederick E. Personal Communication, 1976. [Letter.]

15 Enwall, Beverly. Personal Communication, 1976. [Letter.]

16 ——— Percy Fearing, T. D. Jackson, and Mary Beth Williams. *Exploratory Foreign Language Programs.* [A working draft of a Position Paper prepared for the annual meeting of the National Council of State Supervisors of Foreign Languages, ACTFL Convention, Washington, D.C., November 1975.] [Mimeo.]

17 Feagin, Caro. Personal Communication, 1976. [Letter.]

18 Fearing, Percy, and Frank M. Grittner,eds., *Ex-*

ploratory Foreign Language Programs in the Middle School. [A Curriculum Report produced by participants in the ACTFL Pre-Conference Workshop for Foreign Language Consultants and Supervisors in Denver, Colorado, November 1974.]

19 Finocchiaro, Mary. *English as a Second Language: From Theory to Practice.* New York:Regents, 1974.

20 Fitzhugh, Evelyn. Personal Communication, 1976. [Letter.]

21 *Foreign Languages and Foreign Language Learning in Virginia Schools.* Richmond, Virginia:State Department of Education, Foreign Language Service, October 1969.

22 Frank, Gloria, et al. *Instructional Objectives and Content Outline, English for Speakers of Other Languages(ESOL).* Bulletin No. 275. Rockville, Maryland:Montgomery County Public Schools, 1974. [EDRS: ED 112 686.]

23 Freilich, Joan S. "What the . . . is Going On in High Schools?" *The French Review* 49(1975):5–10.

24 Fryer, T. Bruce. "Free to Explore:Curricular Developments," 9–46 in Gilbert A. Jarvis,ed., *Perspective:A New Freedom.* ACTFL Review of Foreign Language Education, Volume 7. Skokie, Illinois:National Textbook Company, 1975.

25 Gage, Alfred. *Outreach to Administrators.* Oklahoma City, Oklahoma:State Department of Education. [Mimeo.] [No date.]

26 ——— Personal Communication, 1976. [Letter.]

27 Garfinkel, Alan. "The Public Image of Foreign Language Instruction." *The Modern Language Journal* 58(1974):109–12.

28 Garrett, Mary Neale. Personal Communication, 1976. [Letter.]

29 Glaude, Paul M. "Adding Another Foreign Language to the Secondary School Program." *The Modern Language Journal* 54(1970):245–47.

30 Grittner, Frank M. "Foreign Languages and the Changing Curriculum." *Bulletin of the National Association of Secondary School Principals* 58, ccclxxxiv(1974):71–78.

31 Guidera, Bonner, and Alice Floyd. *A Successful Student Aide Program From the Foreign Language Department of Conway Senior High School.* [Mimeo.] [No date.]

32 Hallahan, Daniel P. "Cognitive Styles—Preschool Implications for the Disadvantaged." *Journal of Learning Disabilities* 3,i(1970):5–9.

33 Harrison, John T.,Jr. Personal Communication, 1976. [Letter.]

34 Hughes, George. "Maintaining the Teacher's F. L. Skills—A Nagging Problem." *American Foreign Language Teacher* 2,iii(1972):15–17.

35 Jackson, Mary H. "Foreign Languages—Yesterday, Today, and Tomorrow." *Today's Education* 63,iv(1974):68–71.

36 Jarvis, Gilbert A. *What Really Comes from Studying a Foreign Language.* [Paper presented at the Virginia State Foreign Language Conference, Roanoke, Virginia, October 1974.]

37 Jones, Gaston R. *Changing Community Attitudes: Public Relations and Publicity for Foreign Language Teachers,* 1975. [EDRS: ED 112 677.]

38 Jones, George W.,Jr. Personal Communication, 1976. [Letter.]

39 Lafayette, Robert C. "Diversification:The Key to Student-Centered Programs." *The Modern Language Journal* 56(1972):349–54.

40 Lavergneau, René L. "Careers, Community and Public Awareness," 108–53 in Warren C. Born,ed., *Toward Student-Centered Foreign-Language Programs.* [Reports of the Working Committees of the Northeast Conference on the Teaching of Foreign Languages] New York:Modern Language Association Materials Center, 1974.

41 Lawson, John H. "Should Foreign Language be Eliminated from the Curriculum?" 3–7 in James W. Dodge,ed., *The Case for Foreign Language Study:A Collection of Readings.* New York:Modern Language Association Materials Center, 1971.

42 Levenson, Dorothy. "Many Languages Are Spoken Here." *Teacher* 93,ii(1975):68–70.

43 Loew, Helene Z. "Guidance à Go-Go. . . ." *New York State Association of Foreign Language Teachers Bulletin* 24,iii(1973):19–20.

44 ——— *How to Influence the School District and the Board of Education.* [Paper presented at the International Conference, Rochester, New York, March 1973.] [Mimeo.]

45 ——— *The Use of Community Resources in a Foreign Language Program.* Albany, New York:State Education Department, Bureau of Foreign Language Education. [Mimeo.] [No date.]

46 Love, F. William D., and Lucille J. Honig. *Options and Perspectives:A Sourcebook of Innovative Foreign Language Programs in Action, K-12.* New York:The Modern Language Association of America, 1973.

47 Love, Theresa. Personal Communication, 1970. [Class lectures.]

48 Marckwardt, Maybelle D. "A Selected List of Instructional Materials for English as a Second Language:Secondary Level." *CAL-ERIC/CLL Series on Languages and Linguistics,* No. 20. Arlington, Virginia:ERIC Clearinghouse on Languages and Linguistics, Center for Applied Linguistics, May 1975. [EDRS: ED 105 754.]

49 Masciantonio, Rudolph. "Latin for the Disadvantaged." *Changing Education* 3,iv(1969):44–45. [EDRS: ED 038 882.]

50 Meyer, Gertrud. "Making the Foreign Language Program Visible to the Public:The Language Festival," 45–65 in Frank M. Grittner,ed., *Student Motivation and the Foreign Language Teacher.* Skokie, Illinois:National Textbook Company, 1974.

51 Miller, Virgil. *Promotional Ideas for Increasing Foreign Language Enrollment in North Carolina.* Raleigh, North Carolina:Department of Public Instruction, Division of Languages. [Mimeo.] [No date.]

52 Morrow, Judith C. "Exploratory Courses for the Middle and Junior High School," 119–43 in Frank

M. Grittner,ed., *Student Motivation and the Foreign Language Teacher.* Skokie, Illinois: National Textbook Company, 1974.

53 Nalls, Faye. Personal Communication, 1976. [Letter.]

54 Nielsen, Mel. Personal Communication, 1976. [Letter.]

55 Normand, Krueger G. "Inner-Big-City Classroom Plan Integrates 4 Skills Immediately." *Accent on ACTFL* 4,iii(1974):6–9.

56 Oppenheimer, Max, Jr. "Foreign Language Study —Neglected Dimensions." *The Educational Forum* 37(1973):279–85.

57 Paine, Louise. "The Foreign Language Teacher and Guidance Counselor." Shubael T. Beasley,ed., "The Counselor and the FL Teacher are on the Same Side." *Foreign Language Beacon* 11,i(1975): 7,17.

58 Papalia, Anthony. "Implementing Student-Centered Foreign Language Programs," in Warren C. Born,ed., *Toward Student-Centered Foreign-Language Programs.* [Reports of the Working Committees of the Northeast Conference on the Teaching of Foreign Languages] New York: Modern Language Association Materials Center, 1974.

59 ——— "A Study of Attrition in Foreign Language Enrollments in Four Suburban Public Schools." *Foreign Language Annals* 4(1970):62–67.

60 Pei, Mario. *How to Learn Languages and What Languages to Learn.* New York: Harper & Row, 1973.

61 Pettyjohn, Jack H. Personal Communication, 1976. [Interview.]

62 Pomeroy, Marion. "Selling Foreign Language Instruction." *Utah Foreign Language Speaker* (August–September, 1975): 17–20.

63 Preller, Arno G. "Are You Gaining Visibility?" *Accent on ACTFL* 5,ii(1975):6–7.

64 Reinert, Harry. "Student Attitudes Toward Foreign Language—No Sale!" *The Modern Language Journal* 54(1970):107–12.

65 Robson, Barbara, and Kenton Sutherland. *A Selected Annotated Bibliography for Teaching English to Speakers of Vietnamese.* Arlington, Virginia: Center for Applied Linguistics, 1975.

66 Russo, James R. "Mainstreaming Handicapped Students: Are Your Facilities Suitable?" *American School & University* 47(1974):25–33.

67 Sandstrom, Eleanor L., and Paul Pimsleur. "Foreign Languages for All Students?" in Joseph A. Tursi,ed., *Foreign Languages and the 'New' Student.* [Reports of the Working Committees of the Northeast Conference on the Teaching of Foreign Languages] New York: Modern Language Association Materials Center, 1970.

68 Saunders, Helen. Personal Communication, 1976. [Letter.]

69 Saville-Troike, Muriel. *Foundations of Teaching English as a Second Language.* Englewood Cliffs, New Jersey: Prentice-Hall, 1976.

70 Schell, Marjory D. Personal Communication, 1976. [Letter.]

71 *Selected List of Instructional Materials for English as a Second Language: Audio-Visual Aids.* Arlington, Virginia: Center for Applied Linguistics, April 1974. [EDRS: ED 090 797.]

72 Sellman, Ethel. Personal Communication, 1976. [Letter.]

73 Shiels-Djouadi, Marie. Personal Communication, 1976. [Interview.]

74 Skinner, Vincent P. "The Literacy Problem in Appalachia." *Southern Education Report* 3(1967): 18–19.

75 Smith, Alfred N. "The Importance of Attitude in Foreign Language Learning." *The Modern Language Journal* 55(1971):82–88.

76 Sowell, Rayford M. Personal Communication, 1976. [Interview.]

77 Strasheim, Lorraine A. "Foreign Language: Part of a New Apprenticeship for Living," 18–25 in Lorraine Strasheim,ed., *Foreign Language in a New Apprenticeship for Living.* Bloomington: Indiana Language Program, 1971.

78 Thiele, Margaret. *Initial Guidelines for Teaching English to Speakers of Other Languages.* Virginia Beach, Virginia: Virginia Beach Public Schools, August 1975. [Mimeo.]

79 Torres, Eduardo E., et al. *Foreign Language Dropouts: Problems and Solutions.* Sacramento, California: State Department of Education, 1970. [EDRS: ED 043 262.]

80 Warriner, Helen P. "Student Attitudes Toward Foreign Language Study—Results of a Survey." *Public Education in Virginia* 8,i(1972):4–7.

81 Williams, Percy V. "Education of Disadvantaged Young: Teachers vs. Administrators." *The Educational Forum* 34,ii(1970):229–34.

7

Humanistic education: A mosaic just begun

Beverly Galyean
Confluent Education Development and Research Center

Introduction

Humanistic education is an incomplete body of knowledge, emerging from the frontiers of humanistic psychology and sociology, the underpinnings of idealism, progressivism, existentialism, and interest in human potential. Since 1973 its appearance in language education has proliferated under the multi-headings of "personal," "affective," "confluent," "facilitative," "psychological," and "humanistic."

Surveying the mosaic

In this chapter I 1) survey the mosaic of humanistic education by viewing its component branches as organized bodies of knowledge each influencing language education in its own way, 2) explore the viability of humanistic methods as affecting both personal-social development and language achievement, 3) consider some cautionary measures, and 4) suggest areas for research and development.

Several strategies are presented to illustrate practical applications of humanistic theory in language classes. Readers are reminded that these have been designed and implemented by teachers familiar with humanistic practices. Teachers are en-

---

Beverly Galyean (Ph.D. Candidate, University of California at Santa Barbara) is the Language Education Coordinator of the Confluent Education Development and Research Center in Santa Barbara. She has taught French, Latin, and ESL as well as courses in Confluent Methods of Language Teaching. She has established a network of confluent training programs for language teachers and is currently researching the effects of confluent teaching on the achievement, self-identity, interpersonal relations, and attitudes of language students. Her publications include *Human Teaching in the Language Class:A Confluent Approach, Art and Fantasy:A Gestalt Approach to Counselling and Language Development,* and *Language from Within:A Handbook of Strategies for Personal Growth in the Language Class.* Her articles have appeared in *The Live Classroom, Confluent Education Journal,* and *CATESOL Occasional Papers.* She has done workshops for various language associations. Professional memberships include ACTFL, CEDARC, CFLTA, and Association for Humanistic Psychology.

couraged to seek experience in the theory and practice of the various systems *before* electing to use the strategies on a regular basis.

Presenting the strategies

A variety of methods and strategies is observable in humanistic language classes; these cluster, however, around four cornerstone goals:

1 Use of student output as the basis for language practice. This personal content may be either cognitive (ideas, thoughts, theories) or affective (feelings, interests, values, concerns, images).
2 High levels of student interaction and conversation.
3 The exploration of feelings and the sharing of personal affective content.
4 Awareness of "here and now" events both within an individual and within the class.

Goals of humanistic language teaching

The axiomatic goal for humanistic language teaching is to *enable students to use self-reflective language as the basis for target language practice.* Implicit in this goal is the dual assumption that the use of self-reflective language will enhance language learning and at the same time benefit the student in his or her search for self-fulfillment. This latter assumption is the source of some consternation about the appropriateness of using personal strategies for teaching language. A look at the foundations of humanistic education will clarify the perimeters within which humanistic theories and practices developed and illustrate under what conditions humanistic pedagogy has evolved.

The foundations

Self-reflective language

The search for personal values systems (Maslow, 107; Severin, 155), self-actualizing behaviors (Aspy, 5; Maslow, 108; Rogers, 145), meaningful relationships (Buhler, 25), the skills of productive decision-making (Patterson, 129), a knowledge of personal potential (Perls, 130), a clear understanding of one's fantasy life (Assagioli, 7), and a grasp of intrapsychic processes (Progoff, 135) are the fundamental goals of Humanistic Psychology.

Humanistic psychiatrists and psychologists such as Alschuler (1), Glasser (65), Jourard (88), Maslow (109), May (112), and Rogers (141) suggest that educational systems employ psychological strategies for maintaining healthy personal and interpersonal growth. Education is an experience in living. Feelings of inadequacy, hatred, a desire for power; feelings of love, fear, dread are all an open part of the curriculum as worthy of exploration as history or mathematics. In fact, this openness to feelings enables students to learn content more readily (Rogers, 141). Maslow (109) adds that the schools should help students to look within themselves to discover their own truths.

Humanistic psychology is addressed to the questions "Who is a person? What can he or she become?" (Jourard, 88), whereas humanistic sociologists treat the question "Where does a person belong" (Lynd, 104, p. 55)? Heath (76) indicates that young people are seeking refuge from feelings of alienation, boredom, and purposelessness (p. 3). Etzioni (44) views people as searching for authentic and nourishing relationships (p. 88).

Social growth and personal growth

Bugenthal (24) and Chaudhuri (114) claim that social growth is contingent upon personal growth. "However ideally we may change the structure of society, as long as the inner man does not change, we will not solve our basic problems" (p. 36). Freire (51) adds that the process of creating wholesome societies is a praxis of action-reflection upon what one does to oneself and to others. Thus, a syngergistic relationship exists between persons and societies. Personal actualization and societal actualization take place at the same time (Richards and Richards, 139).

Goals of humanistic sociology

Fostering traits of love and concern among individuals (Fromm, 54), espousing the reality that persons grow profoundly in interactions with others (Staude, 165), and encouraging free expression and utilization of feelings (Rogers, 141, p. 288) assure the development of a society that fosters maximal conditions for healthy human growth (Gouldner, 69, p. 175). Educators are asked to be mindful of these conditions when designing curriculum. Some questions and matrices for consideration in language classes are: What word describes how you are feeling today? Name three important persons in your life. What word describes how you want others to see you? When do you feel lonely? Where do you go to be alone? When

Language strategies

are you bored? List five good qualities about yourself. Brag about yourself.

The tenets of humanistic education are also rooted in idealism, progressivism, and existentialism. Persons are viewed as essentially benevolent (Kneller, 92); this essential goodness, however, is nurtured in a society where people treat each other as ends rather than as means.

Progressivists uphold the premise of change rather than permanency as the *sine qua non* state of human life. Dewey (37) claims that because education's primary task is to prepare individuals to cope with change, students must be helped to see themselves as the primary agents of learning. The role of the teacher is that of "cartographer" (Bridges, 17), following the natural instincts of the learner (Brown, Phillips, and Shapiro, 22).

Existentialism

The existentialist educator, grounded in the premise that "the real is what we experience at a given moment" (Sartre, 148), focuses on "here and now" events as the basis for lesson presentations (Bridges, 17) and encourages students to seek out their own truths rather than ingesting those of others (Van Cleave, 172). Only "extrinsic" language (Korzybski, 96), or those words perceived as meaningful by the learner (Frankl, 50), have any bearing on personal growth. These are worthy of exploration in language classes (Korzybski, 96). Teachers use questions emerging from the immediacy of classroom moods and events: What's the most positive thing you can say about our class today? Who looks tired? Excited? Energetic? What's our class mood? What's your mood?

Language strategies

Interest in the development of human potential (Givens, 64), responding to the questions, Who am I? and Where am I going? (Severin, 155, p. 1), and probing the multidimensional possibilities of human life (Roberts, 140, p. 231) are crucial to all branches of humanistic education. Despite differences in methods and strategies, each branch egresses from the basic

Learning and self realization

Self-knowledge is affected by learning to decode inner voices, premise that all learning must be related to one's drive for self-realization. What a person is, he must become (Maslow, 108). personal imagery, and feelings and by cultivating one's spiritual powers (Castaneda, 27; Dass, 36; Yogi, 185). People have grown into a new awareness of human powers, of what better worlds

Skills of self-awareness

they can create (Bailey, 9; Friedenberg, 53). "Education should, then, concern itself with the realization of higher values" (Bailey, 9, p. 116) and teach students the skills of self-awareness as well as fostering in them a healthy receptivity to other dimensions and possible ways of being. Psychological Education seeds the curriculum with strategies intended to achieve these goals.

Psychological education

The basic theory of psychological education states that the mentally healthy person is one who functions as a whole person, is in command of all his or her faculties, feels good about the self, relates well to others, loves freely and without demand for love in return, and has a sense of power and control over his or her life. This person accepts responsibility for personal choices and seeks alternatives to habitual behavior patterns (Alschuler, 1; Evans, 45; Maslow, 108; May, 111; Progoff, 135; Rogers, 142).

Alschuler (2) mentions four goals emerging from this theory:

Goals of psychological education

1 Development of the unique fantasy life of each person
2 Nonverbal expressions
3 Recognition of emotional responses to the world
4 Living fully in the "here and now" experience of life (pp. 24–26).

Optimal environment for growth

Achievement of each goal is contingent upon an environment that nurtures openness to self and others (Rogers and Stevens, 145). Simpson and Hastings (162) describe an optimal environment for healthy psychological growth:

1 Trust and security. Individuals grow more effectively in an environment that is consistent and nonthreatening.
2 Acceptance and support. Each person has an unconditioned positive regard for the others. Signs of such acceptance are attentive listening and demands for clarification.
3 Honesty, openness, and authenticity. Each person shares self openly and with integrity, keeping in mind the feelings of others.

4 Understanding and empathy. Each person makes a decided effort to understand the others' feelings and opinions.
5 Warmth, affection, and love. One does not hold back sincerely felt feelings of warmth and recognition.
6 Respect and esteem. Individuals are given the space to grow in their own unique way and time.
7 Freedom. No one is coerced or manipulated into doing what he or she does not wish to do. This freedom is nurtured within the limits of recognizing the needs of others as well as of oneself.
8 Models for growth. Because personal growth is the conscious goal of psychological education, teachers are encouraged to work continually toward expanding their own self-awareness, so as to model this for students (p. 5).

"Lifelong processes" for growth

Psychological strategies are intended to provide individuals with lifelong processes for personal growth (Alschuler, 3). The choice of strategy will vary with the cognitive and affective objectives of the lesson and with teacher preference and preparation in the use of psychological modes for teaching.

In one hypothetical lesson, for example, the teacher begins with a values exercise suggested by Wolfe and Howe (182), embellishes it with guided imagery suggested by Stevens (166), and concludes it with a discussion of feelings arising from the "here and now" events of the classroom (Brown, 21; Castillo, 28; Lederman, 97).

Language lesson

T: List several things you like to do. Place a "$" by those which cost you money; a "P" by those you prefer to do with others; an "A" by those you want to do alone. Then indicate your five favorite activities. (Pause) What have you learned or relearned in doing this exercise?

The use of guided imagery enables students to recreate the events in an existential manner.

T: Close your eyes and concentrate on the one activity you would most like to do throughout your entire life. (Pause) What are you doing? Are you alone or with others? What word or words describe how you are feeling while doing this activity? (Pause) When you are ready, write about your experience. I am (activity). ________ is/are with me. I am feeling ________.

The teacher presents a matrix equal to student proficiency.

This next activity should be used only when a sufficient level of trust and comfort has been established in the class.

T: Let's look at some of our feeling responses at school. List your favorite activities at school. Then list your favorite activities in our class. At school I like to ______ and I feel ______. In this class I like to ______ and I feel ______. Some of you may wish to add what you don't like to do.

S1: At school I like to see many people. I feel friendly.
S2: In this class I like to hear tapes. I feel good. I don't like to talk in front of the class. I feel nervous.

Timmerman and Ballard (170, p. 64) offer these strategies clustered around the theme of self-concept:

"Self-concept" strategies

When I like myself I ______; when I don't like myself I ______; I could be more patient about my ______; I get my idea of who I am from ______.

Moral education

Moral education and behavior

Psychological education focuses on the internal awareness of individuals. Moral education extends this consciousness to include an understanding of what behaviors are affected by these intrapersonal processes. The aim of moral education, according to Kohlberg (94) is "the stimulation of the 'natural' development of the child's own moral judgment and of those capacities allowing him to use his judgment to control behavior" (p. 169). In taking this stand, Kohlberg (95) warns against any system that imposes its values upon a child or attempts to manipulate him or her into accepting a certain body of knowledge as absolute dogma. This idea is further developed by Gauthier (62), who strongly emphasizes that "the role of the schools is to enable the child to reflect on personal values underlying decision-making and to understand the consequence of these actions" (p. 141).

Gustafson (74) and Narveson (124) emphasize the importance of encouraging students to look within themselves for answers and to analyze their own values. "We want to avoid teaching children a set of ready-made answers to moral problems" (Gustafson, 74, p. 23). Baier (8) adds that education should help children clarify self-expectations—that is, "what one requires of oneself" (p. 100).

Stages of moral development

Kohlberg (94) observes that changes in moral understanding and reasoning evolve within six stages:

1 Student determines goodness or badness of acts in terms of reward or punishment.
2 What is right is determined by what is best for oneself. Me! My rights! My wants! form the criterion for goodness or badness.
3 Student acts to please others, to win approval.
4 Orientation to doing "right duty" and preserving tradition.
5 Conformity to rules.
6 Student explores alternative behaviors and chooses according to his or her own conscience (pp. 70–71).

Different conceptual levels

Joyce and Weil (89) describe how each stage of growth demands a different teaching response. For example, a student in Stage 6 would be more ready for self-reflection and interpersonal dialogue than a student in Stages 1 or 2. A student in Stage 4 would need more highly structured teaching methods than a student in Stage 6. Teachers should know the conceptual stages of their students before deciding on a particular method. Because humanistic teaching values personal response and interaction, one can see where students in the first stages of development might find the freedom and responsibility of some humanistic methods a source of anxiety and a block to learning. Rogers (141) and Brown (21) mention that not all students are ready for affective and interactive teaching. Because perceptual levels differ, some students work best under the highly disciplined conditions of frequent repetition, structured drills, written exercises, and individualized packets; other students learn more quickly through open statements, creative imagery, imaginary dialogues, and free composition (Wass, et al., 173). Human teaching calls for both.

Readiness

Valuable aids for recognizing values

Valuable aids for recognizing values and belief systems underlining moral behavior include: *Values and Teaching,* by

Raths, Harmin, and Simon (137), the fifth chapter of which emphasizes clarifying responses a teacher could use when confronted with students' belief systems. *Values Clarification* by Simon, Howe, and Kirschenbaum (159) provides a number of techniques for clarification of beliefs and values, in particular: "Rank Order," "Values Grid," "Values Focus," "Taking a Stand," "Alligator River," and "Fallout Shelter."

In *Psychosynthesis* Assagioli (7) offers a series of biographical questionnaires. In *Human Teaching for Human Learning* Brown (21) presents several helpful exercises: "You've Got It I Want It," "Trust Walk," "Animal Fantasy."

In *Born to Win* James and Jongeward (83) include six chapters of strategies related to recognition and analysis of life scripts; parental, social, and cultural influences; various ego states affecting behavior; and sexual identity.

Meanings behind choices

Samples and Wohlford (147) describe ways of deliberating meanings behind choices through art and reflective questions. They present numerous statements: The reasons you save money are ______. How often you should make love is ______. The kind of car you should buy is ______. People need education to ______. I can show fear when ______.

Gestalt vocabulary

Chapter 21 of *The Live Classroom* (Galyean, 57) includes a Gestalt vocabulary that aids teachers in asking students clarifying questions: What are you doing? What's happening within you? How are you feeling? What do you want to do? What happens when you do that? The chapter includes a transcript of a French class where a teacher used the Gestalt vocabulary as part of a lesson to help a student explicate her own learning problems.

Verbs for moral development

Certain verbs are directed at moral development. We see them frequently cited in humanistic and affective language books: I believe ______; I prefer ______; I want ______; I hope for ______; I work toward ______; I fear ______; I need ______; I dream about ______; I uphold ______; I am certain ______.

The verbs *should* or *ought to, expect,* and *demand* all flow from personal beliefs about oneself and one's interaction with others.

Sentence completions: A good student should ______; A good teacher should ______; A good parent should ______; A good leader should ______. *Listings:* List five things you feel you "ought to do." Next to each one indicate who is the source of the "ought." Cite five demands you place on yourself. When you have done this, indicate five demands you make on others.

Prioritizing concerns

In some cases students are provided with situations in which they have to *prioritize* concerns.

List 10 traits you most admire in others. Suppose now you are planning to live with someone. What traits would you want him or her to have? Rank them in order of their importance to you. Which trait do you want for yourself? What traits do others most admire in you? What traits do you most admire in yourself? Imagine you have only 10 words in your vocabulary. Try communicating with someone in the class using only these words. What are the five most important words in your life right now?

Knowledge of basic needs and a means for fulfilling them, recognition of personal needs and values that influence various decisions, ownership of behavior, and awareness of social and personal expectations are endemic to moral development. Values education provides the framework for a working knowledge of how moral themes serve as guidelines for what a person chooses as good and desirable. A consideration of how these themes affect the creation of future worlds is the concern of futuristic education.

Futuristic education

Futuristics is a relatively new field contiguous to humanistic education. Based on the theories of futurists and anthropologists such as Huxley (81), LeGuin (98), Slater (163), and Toffler (171), futuristic educators urge people to consider present philosophies and practices as responsible for creating future societies. No one will live all his life in the world into which he was born, and no one will die in the world in which he worked in his maturity. Huxley (81), Leonard (99), and Toffler (171) see the person of the future belonging to many communities, having many jobs, engaging many loves, and dabbling in multiworlds of information. The only stable feature will be a person's

Person of the future

clear knowledge of his or her inner resources and the ability to actualize latent potential through creative decisions (Toffler, 171, p. 17). This will be accomplished in collaboration with other accepting human beings. Group discussion models for classroom use (Glasser, 65; Gordon, 68; Palomares, 127; Schmuck and Schmuck, 151) provide preparatory treatment for such future conditions.

Toffler (171), focusing on the characteristics of a society emerging from technological advancement, suggests topics of concern that educators should present to students: genetic control, endless leisure, planetary travel, ocean farming, space colonies, extraterrestrial life, artificial life, robots, and computerized government. Battung (11) suggests strategies for use in language classes.

Language strategies

T: Write down the first word that comes to your mind in response to these images: genetic control, endless leisure. What year do you think of as the future? When will this planet be visited by life from outer space? When will the United States end? When will all wars end?

Living with constant change

Futurists claim that education should prepare individuals to live with constant change and to process enormous amounts of rapidly developing bodies of information. Lipton (102), in discussing new goals for language teaching, encourages preparing students for living in the future. This can be done through introducing novel situations into the classroom. Students stretch their imaginations to embrace the possible realities of future societies.

Introducing novel situations

T: You are living in a society where all work is done by machines. You have only free time. What are you doing?

T: You are about to die from an incurable disease. The doctors believe a cure will be found in a few years. If they freeze your body before you die there is a good chance that they can revive you when the cure is found. You will then live a normal life. What do you do (Battung, 11)?

Information on Futuristics is available by writing to Futures Information Interchange, School of Education, University of Massachusetts, Amherst, Massachusetts 01002.

Values education

Raths, Harmin, Simon, and Kirschenbaum are most frequently associated with values education (see Raths, Harmin, and Simon, 137; Simon, Howe, and Kirschenbaum, 159; Simon and Kirschenbaum, 160). Their theories and strategies are derived from the assumption that persons have experiences from which they learn to grow. Out of these experiences come certain general guides to behavior. These guides tend to give direction to life and may be called *values*.

Values for direction

Raths, Harmin, and Simon (137) indicate that schools should provide students with lifelong processes for recognizing prized beliefs, selecting subsequent goals, and identifying the means for achieving them.

Lifelong processes

According to Merleau-Ponty (115), values are the "aims of life." They underlie all behavior. One understands behavior by analyzing the content of values or by reflecting upon consciously set goals.

Gilchrist and Roberts (63) understand values as "existing in a person's yearning and efforts to improve himself" (p. 13). Their observations that "the principles of freedom and respect for personal worth are universal values" and that "the values of health, education, peace, and security are of universal human concern" (p. 14) have broad implications for teaching culture. For example, in language classes students are asked to examine the target culture by "standing in the shoes of the other" (Simon and Carnes, 157, p. 146). The students are then asked to express what insights were gained by exchanging places. Several values exercises lend themselves to such personal identifications.

Values and teaching culture

Choosing among alternatives

T: You are a student in France during the year of student revolts. You are nearing graduation. Your best friend is taking part in the student protests. The administration has threatened to dismiss any student associated with the protests. Do you a) march in the streets in full view of observers; b) distribute pamphlets to interested bystanders, but not join the march; c) join in round table student discussions on the matter; d) volunteer for a committee to speak with administrators; e) do nothing?

Students then contrast American and French culture through *open questions* and *sentence completions.*

T: You are asked to participate in a student protest here at school. What do you do?

T: Complete these statements as if you were a native French student. The most important aspect of my education is ______. The best thing about school right now is ______. If I could change one thing about school I would ______.

T: Now respond to these same statements as an American student.

Simon, Hawley, and Britton (158) suggest the following ranking exercise for recognizing preferred personality traits. This, too, lends itself to multicultural study.

T: Rank the following traits according to their importance to you when you: a) choose a friend; b) think about the ideal teacher; c) create the perfect "you."

____adventuresome	____considerate	____intellectual
____ambitious	____courageous	____loving
____broadminded	____forgiving	____responsive
____cheerful	____honest	____sexually attractive

Practicing the subjunctive

Students might practice subjunctive forms by stating: "I want that he/she be ______."

T: As a French person would you rank these any differently?

Sometimes values processes are used to set the tone for person-centered learning. At the beginning of the year students are asked: What do you want from this class? What do you want from me, your teacher? What do you want from yourself? What help might you need from your teacher? From others?

Evaluation

At other times value questions are used for evaluation purposes. What do you like most about this class? Like least? What would you like to change? When do you feel successful in the class? Some teachers isolate the sentences for drills on the subjunctive and conditional.

Comprehensive lists of values strategies are found in Simon, Howe, and Kirschenbaum (159). Adaptations and new developments in values curricula are available through the Adirondack Mountain Humanistic Education Center, Springfield Road, Upper Jay, New York 12987, and the Philadelphia Center for Humanistic Education, 8504 Germantown Avenue, Philadelphia, Pennsylvania 19118.

Information on values education

For more extensive discriptions of the various strategies as adapted to language practice, readers are referred to Christensen (30), Disick and Barbanel (39), Galyean (60), Morel (118, 119), Nebraska Department of Education (125), Stoller et al. (168), Weisberg (178), Wilson and Wattenmaker (180).

Another aspect of Values Education is directed at teacher awareness. Overly (126) describes how frequently covert value systems of teachers affect student performance. Teachers with high expectations for students elicit corresponding high achievement; low expectations often lead to lower results. Aspy (5) and Combs et al. (35) claim that teachers who overstress cognitive learning may be restraining the creative energies of students who need freedom to explore their own learning patterns. However, teachers who allow too much freedom may be frustrating students who need well-defined structure (Bridges, 18). The key lies in an awareness of one's teaching values and style as it affects student performance (Combs, et al. 35). Glatthorn (66) suggests providing alternatives wherever possible.

Teacher awareness

Although Kirschenbaum and Simon (91) claim that students are no longer interested in "accepting truths from the past as norms for behavior, and wish to discover their own" (p. 21), Lyon (105) claims that dealing with student concerns should take place only in a trusting environment where each student feels free to participate or not in self-disclosing activities.

Need for a trusting environment

Rubin (146) states that to understand the formation of values and belief systems, one must explore the substratum of affect, need awareness, intrapsychic processes, and transpersonal experiences. These are treated in affective, process, transpersonal, and confluent education.

Affective education

The term *affective* refers to the broad base of feelings, emotions, interests, concerns, desires, personal imagery, and values (Morton, 120). These "affective loadings" make cognitive learning meaningful, according to Borton (14), Borton and Newberg (16), Brown (22), Ediger (42), Greenberg (71), Simpson (161), and Weinstein and Fantini (176). From this assumption they derive the following goals for students:

Affective learning goals

1 Growth in self-identity and worth
2 Acquiring skills of positive relations
3 Recognition of personal values as reflected in choices
4 Acceptance of responsibility for attitudes and behaviors
5 Achieving congruence between feelings and actions
6 Openly defining values systems
7 Owning power to change personal attitudes and behaviors
8 Developing realistic expectations of selves
9 Expressing feelings as the means of self-knowledge

Curriculum of concern

Weinstein and Fantini (177) have developed a "curriculum of concern" that allows student concerns to be the focus of all teaching. Teachers begin by encouraging their students to indicate basic concerns. Problems related to these concerns are then identified, and curriculum is organized around the problem themes. Cognitive content serves as the vehicle for discussion and possible resolution of these concerns.

Basing their ideas on the theories of Maslow and Rogers, Weinstein and Fantini reduce basic human concerns to three: self-knowledge, affiliation with others, and power over one's life.

Imaginative processes

Jones (87) views affective education as developing the natural imaginative processes of students. Christensen (29) illustrates the use of imagery, fantasy, and humor in language classes. "Suppose you are overweight and you must diet. Name five things you won't eat for awhile" (p. 214). Additional activities are described elsewhere (Christensen, 30, 31).

Erickson's chart of human development serves as a resource for much affective curriculum development. According to Erickson, adolescents are primarily concerned with justice and revolution (Evans, 45). A teacher subscribing to Erickson's method would structure lessons around these emotive themes. The theme of justice is treated in the following example:

T: List five times in your life when you were treated justly. Then list five when you were treated unjustly. Next to each situation indicate the initials of the person responsible for treating you in such a manner. Then tell them how you feel toward them.

Lesson on "justice"

S: *Justly*
I was cheating. (Mr. S.) "Mr. S. is fair!"
Unjustly
I stayed for detention because X threw a paper. (S.M.) "S. M. is unfair!"

T: List three persons whom you consider to be fair. When were you fair to someone?

Bessell and Palomares (12), Glasser (65), Gordon (68), Luft (103), Patterson (129), and Schmuck and Schmuck (151) view affective education in terms of group experiences. A group is considered to be a "minimodel" of life. How one relates in a group setting corresponds to how one relates in real life. The purpose of the group is to provide support feedback for each person as he or she discusses items of personal significance. Pfeiffer and Jones (134) provide hundreds of human relations exercises for use in groups.

Group as "minimodel" of life

A proliferation of affective techniques is now available for classroom use.

Body awareness

Meditation techniques, breathing exercises, yoga, body "journeys" are introduced as a means of relaxation. Some schools are experimenting with alpha waves and meditative rest periods as aids to student concentration and learning. Weinstein's "geography of the self" lesson is adaptable for language classes (Lyon, 105).

Body awareness

T: Imagine your body is a country. You live in this country. Where do you live? Where are the forests? The trees? The rivers? Where in your body do you study? Play? Work? What parts are you most familiar with? Are there any parts you are not allowed to visit?

"Geography of the self"

Another exercise adapted from Perls' work with Gestalt calls for a dialogue between an individual and parts of his or her body (Fagan and Shepherd, 47, p. 96).

Dialogue with parts of the body

T: What is your hand doing?
S: My hand is shaking.
T: Give your hand a voice. What does it say?
S: (Speaking as the hand) I am scared because I am talking in front of many people.
T: Ask your hand what it would like to do.
S: What would you like to do right now?
(Speaking as hand) I would like to hide in your pocket.

Galyean (57) provides examples of how a French teacher adapted Gestalt exercises in her classes.

Free association

T: What do you think of when you hear the word *flabby*? *Sexy*? What images do you associate with *power*?

Use of music, art, dramatics

Rhyne uses art media as the means for self-reflection (Fagan and Shepherd, 46). Students form groups and work on "collage" drawings. They then discuss their particular roles in the group. Questions such as "Were you an initiator or a follower?" "How did you feel when someone colored over your design?" engage the students in reflection upon their roles in groups.

Songs such as "Have You Never Been Mellow?" "Feelings," and "You Are So Beautiful" provide potential affective content. For example, the teacher plays the record "You Are So Beautiful" and asks the students whom they think of upon hearing the record.

T: Who comes to your mind? Who tells you you are beautiful? To whom do you say this?

Classroom dramatics activities are used for language practice. Students are asked to form small groups and act out a particular "feeling" word. Other students try to guess the word or phrase.

Use of metaphor

Individuals are asked to assume the identity of things such as colors, animals, flowers, furniture, numbers, or other persons (Lyon, 105).

T: What color are you? What food are you here at school? at home? What furniture are you at dances? at the beach? What famous person are you?

Nonverbal expressions

Body language often replaces verbal modes of communication.

T: Imagine you are these words. Let your body show how you are feeling.

disgust	suspicion
anger	love
surprise	joy

Students then discuss their experience in the target language.

Sensory awareness

To develop sensory awareness Lewis and Streitfield (101) suggest selecting an inanimate object such as a rock or a flower and concentrating fully on its properties.

T: Here is a flower. Examine it carefully. Smell, touch, feel, taste it. Let your imagination carry you away!
S1: I feel velvet. I feel cool liquid. I feel softness.
S2: I see a round leaf. I see yellow. I see a sun.

"Here and now" content

This technique involves using whatever momentary events seem charged with energy for learning. A teacher observes, for example, that the students are excited about an after-school game. He or she uses this content as the basis for language practice.

T: You are at the game this afternoon. Which statement shows how you are feeling? a) We are the best! b) They are a better team! c) The game will be close! d) We haven't got a chance! e) Winning is everything!

Lesson objectives develop in three ways among affective educators. The first group, typified by Borton and Newberg (16) and Weinstein and Fantini (177), would examine student concerns, especially those of identity, connectedness, and power. Curriculum is then structured to facilitate resolution of these concerns. The second group, typified by Brown (21) and Simon, Howe, and Kirschenbaum (159), begins with established curriculum, and appropriate affective strategies are selected to teach given lessons. A third group deals directly with affect emerging from individual dialogue in interaction. Based on the work of Bessell and Palomares (12), and Glasser (65), and Gordon (68), they use the feelings generated within group interaction as the mode for teaching communication skills (Castillo, 28; Lederman, 97).

Three approaches to affective teaching

Although language educators such as Christensen (29), Disick (38), Grittner (73), Hancock (75), McCoy (113), Savignon (149), Stevick (167), and Wolfe and Smith (183) advocate using affective strategies, cautionary measures must be considered. Disick and Barbanel (39) indicate that affective strategies are not substitutes for psychotherapy. Brown (21) advises teachers to be aware of their motivations in using them. Teachers should experience them on a personal basis *before* using them with students. A complete list of affective education centers and publications may be obtained by writing to The Philadelphia Public Schools Affective Education Project, 21st Street, S. of the Parkway, Philadelphia, Pennsylvania 19103.

Some cautionary measures

Information on affective education

Process education

"Content learning, by itself, says nothing. It is only when content is internalized, digested, transformed, and returned in renewed form that it ever achieves any meaning" (Schroder, Karlins, and Phares, 152, p. 26). Process education is concerned with content knowledge ordered and systematized according to an individual's need to make sense of it and with the ability of a student to change in whatever direction he or she determines (Borton and Newberg, 16). To do this students must be aware of what information they are taking in, recognize habitual behavior responses, focus on their real needs, and modify behavior accordingly (Borton, 15). Combs et al. (35) state that the problem of learning involves taking in new information and discovering personal relevance in the information. The latter process takes place within an individual and presupposes an operational knowledge of oneself (Ramsey, 136). Ramsey adds that learning is a personal matter involving emotions and a sense of survival for the individual. A person can shape decisions only to the degree he or she consciously recognizes basic needs that tend to influence attitudes, behaviors, and actions (Jacks, 82). Thus, process educators are more interested in the student's ability to indicate stages of awareness than in the content itself.

Borton (15) presents a three-tiered model corresponding to three essential considerations: *What am I taking in?* (content stimuli); *So what does this mean to me?* (recalling the need for survival); *Now what will I do with this knowledge?* (future action).

Three-tiered process model

The model involves three stages of processing. In the first stage, *sensing*, individuals reflect on what information is being accepted. In the second stage, *transforming*, awareness shifts to feelings, imagery, values, and behavior patterns motivating the learner toward certain actions. In the final stage, *acting*, learners act and examine both personal and social consequences. We see the complete model operative in a language class.

Sensing

The stimulus for a lesson in sensing is a *guided fantasy* presented in the target language.

Language lesson

T: Close your eyes and imagine you are standing in front of a large body of water. Go to this water, examine it carefully, and describe it in detail. Talk directly to it! "Water, you are deep and mysterious." (Pause) Then describe yourself in the same manner. "Water, you are deep and mysterious and I am deep and mysterious." (Pause) Slowly come back to us in the room and write a description of what happened. Use the model: You are ______ and I am ______.

Transforming

Students reflect on the relationships between their imagery and themselves by working with Gestalt Projection Exercises.

T: In what ways are you and water the same?
S1: My water is cold and smooth. Many beautiful plants and fish live in my water.
T: Restate what you've said in "I" phrases.
S1: I am cold and smooth and I have many beautiful plants and fish in my water.
T: When are you cold and smooth in real life?
S1: When I don't know people. I'm shy and sometimes I am afraid to meet new people. I become tense.
S2: I think you are quiet, but not cold.
T: You say you have beautiful plants and fish. Who are they?
S1: I think my fish are my dreams. They're colorful and happy, but they come and go very fast. I don't know about the plants.

Acting

The teacher asks the students to indicate both helpful and hindering behaviors discovered as a result of the imagery. They then reflect on desired changes.

T: Choose one trait or behavior revealed in your imagery and consider when it is helpful or not so helpful to you.
S1: My water has huge waves and I have huge waves. Because they are big, you notice them and you notice me. I like you to notice me. But when the waves are too big, they scare you and you run away. I don't want you to run from me!

Lengthy training programs

Teachers involved in designing process-oriented curriculum ordinarily participate in lengthy training programs such as those sponsored by the Humanistic Education Department of the University of Massachusetts, the University of Florida, and the Philadelphia Affective Education Project.

Weinstein (175) has developed a similar model which he calls "Self-science" or "The Trumpet." He attempts to dispel the myth that personalities, behaviors, and self-concepts are immutable. "Many of us operate as if the ideas we have about ourselves and others are established truth, absolute maxims by which we live our lives" (p. 374). He contends that individuals can effect positive changes within themselves.

A student is guided through the model by the carefully selected questions of the teacher. Language teachers, though not groomed in the model itself, can use some of the questions for basic language drills. The following lesson is adapted and synthesized from the works of Bonin and Birckbichler (13), Morel (119), Wilson and Wattenmaker (180), and Wolfe and Howe (182).

1 *Confrontation.* Students are presented with an event that evokes a strong personal response. The response is examined for value content, behavior patterns, and possible alternatives and consequences.

T: Imagine that I tell you that you must write a 500-word composition on "What I do for Fun!" that is due tomorrow. What do you do?

2 *Response.* S: I panic because I want to do other things tonight.

3/4 *Patterns* and *Owning.* The teacher asks the students to examine and to own habitual response patterns.

T: When at other times do you panic?
S: I panic when I take a test, when I must talk in front of the group, and when I must write long compositions.

5 *Consequences.* T: What happens to you when you behave this way?
S: When I panic I become tense, and it's hard to think clearly.

6 *Alternatives.* T: What else might you do besides panic?
S: I could prepare well so I don't forget. I could practice with another person before class. I could take a tranquilizer.

7 *Evaluation.* Students consider which behavior seems most appropriate for remedying the situation.
T: Repeat each of your alternatives and see which one seems to be most possible for you.

S: I could prepare well so I don't forget. I could practice with someone before class. I could take tranquilizers.

8 *Choosing.* T: What do you choose?
S: I choose to practice before class.

Only advanced students would work through the entire model in one period. In lower-level classes, any one item could be used. For example, "When I panic I (*don't think clearly; shake,* and so on). Raths, Harmin, and Simon (137) have developed a seven-stage model for recognizing and commanding the flow of attitudes and beliefs as they affect choices. They claim that a knowledge of this model should provide individuals with life-long skills for recognizing personal value systems. Strategies for this lesson are adapted from Simon, Howe, and Kirschenbaum (159):

Ideas for lower-level classes

Seven-staged process model

Language lesson

1 *Choose freely.* T: List five important decisions you've recently made. Indicate if they were made by you (M), influenced by someone else (O), or forced upon you (F).

2 *Choose from alternatives.* T: It's a warm and sunny Saturday morning. The day is yours. Do you a) Stay in bed? b) Clean the house? c) Do homework? d) Go with friends?

3 *Choose after considering consequences of each action.*
T: Indicate after each possibility what would happen if you made that choice. (Word according to student proficiency.)
S: If I stayed in bed, *I would be bored.* If I cleaned the house, *I would be tired but happy.*

4 *Cherish the choice.* S: I am glad that I cleaned the house.

The final three stages are:

5 *Affirm it publicly.*
6 *Act upon the choice.*
7 *Show a consistent pattern of action.*

Perls' (131; Perls, Hefferline, and Goodman, 132) model demonstrates the process of recognizing nascent feelings that affect attitudes and behaviors and are responsible for shaping attitudes toward learning or nonlearning.

Perls' model

His theory is based on the observation that the human organism is constantly striving to nurture itself by expressing its internal needs through mental imagery and somatic reactions. He terms these organismic upheavals "gestalts." Brown (21), extending Perls' work into educational systems (confluent education), suggests that teachers aid students with their "gestalts" by encouraging them to express feelings, especially those most closely associated with the class or subject.

T: How do you feel when you speak Spanish? English?
S: When I speak Spanish, I feel tense, and sometimes romantic. When I speak English, I feel confident.

Simpson (160), mentions that exercises such as these help students to surface potentially negative attitudes. Perls, Hefferline, and Goodman (132) add that once such attitudes are no longer covert, they may be readily transformed into positive learning energy.

Transpersonal education

Transpersonal education is based on the assumption that "within each person is an endowment of wisdom, intuition, and a sense of purpose, which can become a source of guidance in everyday life" (Miller, 116, p. 123). It is rooted in the theory and practices of transpersonal psychology, the techniques of which enable individuals 1) to transcend ordinary states of awareness in order to achieve higher levels linked with universal consciousness (Sutich, 169), 2) to liberate themselves from socially imposed limitations of human potential (Moustakas, 122), and 3) to stimulate the psyche to give rise to its own self-healing material: feelings, images, voices and archetypes (Progoff, 135).

Higher states of consciousness

In contrast to humanistic psychology, which emphasizes *the experiencing individual* (Goble, 67), transpersonal psychology focuses on the *essence of what is being experienced.* Jung explains that humans are multidimensional, and a thorough knowledge of self necessitates a receptivity to infinite modes of being (Progoff, 135). Assagioli (7), Maslow (109), Jung (Progoff, 135), and Watts (174) claim that the presence of transpersonal imagery is the most profound validation of self.

Transpersonal imagery as validation of self

Heider (77) lists the basic assumptions: Spirit and matter are one (Watts, 174; Yogi, 185); inherent within everyone are continuous drives toward ultimate states of being (Sutich, 169); the realization of ultimate states depends on direct practices suited to each individual (Assagioli, 7).

Spiritual practices form the techniques of transpersonal psychology and are adapted for classroom use. They are meditation, yoga, guided imagery, "psychosynthesis," body and sense awareness, intensive journal writing, and gestalt.

Moustakas and Perry (123) recommend that schools allow such practices to become a regular part of the curriculum. Maslow (109) mentions that the schools can help students recognize their deepest potentials by providing the space and time for meditative practices and awareness exercises. In doing this, students attain more realistic attitudes about their own potentials (Jersild, 85) and recognize the various levels of their own inner resources (Gardner, 61; Leonard, 100). Perls (131) adds that these practices enable persons to gain more control over their lives.

Not a new form of education

Clark (32) and Heider (77) clarify that transpersonal education does not substitute new forms of education for existing forms. Rather, it expands the repertoire to include the skills of recognizing transpersonal experiences; and it enables one to achieve a balance between cognitive-rational and emotional-intuitive processes, to understand intrapsychic imagery, and to master techniques for self-awareness at the deepest levels.

Necessity for personal commitment

Assagioli (7), Brown (21), Leonard (100), Moustakas (122), and Schulz (154) advocate using the techniques in conjunction with curricular practices. They caution, however, that only teachers who are personally committed to spiritual practices in their own lives should use them with students. Student interest must also be considered. *Art and Fantasy* (Galyean, 56) and *Human Teaching in the Language Class* (Galyean, 58) contain several transpersonal strategies adapted for language lessons. Stevens (166) presents strategies for guided imagery.

The confluent education program at the University of California, Santa Barbara was founded on the theory and practices of transpersonal education and conducts research into the application of transpersonal techniques to educative processes.

Information on transpersonal education

Three California-based centers conduct research in related areas: Association for Transpersonal Psychology, Box 3049, Stanford 94305, Esalen Institute, Big Sur 93920, and Psychosynthesis Institute, 576 Everett Street, Palo Alto 94301.

Confluent education

Merging traditional and nontraditional goals

The purpose of confluent education is to integrate the goals of traditional teaching, such as cognitive subject mastery, with the nontraditional goals of self-awareness and acceptance, positive interpersonal relations, responsible nonmanipulative behavior, and the means for ongoing personality integration (Brown, Phillips, and Shapiro, 22).

Yeomans (184) presents confluent education as an ecological system, responding to various needs arising from the "whole" development of the human organism. He describes fully functioning individuals as those who recognize survival needs in three areas of concern: intrapersonal, interpersonal, and extrapersonal. *Intrapersonal* includes the domain of the psyche, subconscious processes, and the basic needs system. Feelings, emotions, personal imagery, dreams, life scripts, and intuition characterize this domain. *Interpersonal* refers to energies transacted when individuals meet with one another. *Extrapersonal* refers to a person's relationship to extrinsic materials such as subject matter and factual information.

Intrapersonal, interpersonal, extrapersonal

In confluent teaching, objectives are explicitly stated for each of the domains: affective, interactive, and cognitive. Students are provided the occasion to self-reflect and to learn about their intrapsychic processes while working with the established curriculum, which acts as a catalyst for evoking affective content and personal responses. This learning is effected in both personal meditative work as well as in dialogue or group interaction. Evaluation is considered for all three areas. Brown (21) comments, however, that measurement of the affective and interactive domains must be considered differently from cognitive measures and that these should lean toward the direction of

Learning about intrapsychic processes

Measurement of affective and interactive domains

"formative, linear, and holistic" evaluations more conducive to the fluidity of affective and interactive learning processes.

The confluent teaching model is based on the three types of existential worlds described by Lewis and Streitfield (101): the world of objects, of persons, and "our personally intruded-upon world" (p. 60).

Yeomans (184) contends that a symbiotic relationship exists among all three. If one has a poor self-image, for example, he has difficulty in relating well with others and mastering subject matter. If one is deficient in cognitive mastery, especially in communication skills, one does not have a strong self-concept. Teachers are urged to design objectives and activities in all three domains.

Strategies from the other branches of humanistic education, especially transpersonal and affective, are used to deepen personal-social awareness within and among both students and teachers in confluent classes. Gestalt exercises, psychosynthesis, synectics, encounter, human-relations work, group processes, intensive journal writing, values clarification, meditation, and self-science exercises form the heart of confluent methodology (Brown, Yeomans, and Grizzard, 23).

Confluent teaching strategies

Hillman (78) describes nine behaviors associated with confluent learning. In confluent awareness training, teachers engage in intensive personal work to achieve these behaviors within themselves before working with students.

1 Responsibility: the ability to respond to any situation by owning one's feelings and thoughts about the event
2 Convergency: developing congruence between external events and one's experience of the event
3 Divergency: relating the teaching experience to authentic situations in the world
4 Validation: seeking the opinions and ideas of others in order to formulate, express, and validate one's own view
5 Connectedness: positive relations with others
6 Identity: achieving a sense of self-worth and esteem
7 Power: gaining control over what is happening or could happen in one's life
8 Context: evaluating anything in terms of what is going on at the moment as opposed to imagining what is happening

9 Gestalt: making what is implicit in a situation explicit; finishing a situation so that it becomes whole

Recognizing potential affective content

Awareness training also enables teachers to recognize potential affective content "loadings" in themselves, in students, in class proceedings, and in the curriculum (Hillman, 79), and to use it for presenting cognitive material. Galyean (60) mentions teaching to naturally energizing "meaning nodes"—needs, concerns, feelings, interests, wants, moods, and using them as the basis for language practice.

Brown (21) mentions that intensive training is not necessary for using all of the strategies but that teachers should be aware of their purposes and motivations for using them.

"Language from within" exercises

The *Language from Within* program suggests the following exercises as reflective of confluent language teaching (Galyean, 60).

T: List what special gifts you have as a person. What is unique about you? (Some teachers prepare guided lists from which the students select responses.)
T: Work in groups of four and share your responses. Use the model: I am ______; I do ______.
S1: I am humorous. I laugh a lot.
S2: I am intelligent. I get good grades.

Teachers structure the drill matrices according to the proficiency level of their students.

T: Let's offer each other our unique gifts. Here's a model. "I am *open*. I offer you my *openness*."
S1: I am *humorous*. I offer you my *humor*.
S2: I am *intelligent*. I offer you my *intelligence*.

Frequently, exact translations of words are not possible, and teachers must provide students with equivalent target language expressions.

"Here and now" language lesson

"Here and now" events form the bulk of much confluent curricula (Galyean, 60). In this example the rainy weather provides the occasion for structured conversation practice. Dialogue is in the target language. Teachers assist students with difficult constructions.

T: It's raining and I am feeling kind of tired and tranquil. I'd like to be in front of a warm fireplace talking with some good friends. What about you?
S1: Me too! I'd like to read a good book.
S2: When it rains, I like to dream. It's hard to study today.
T: Close your eyes and listen to the rain. Go away to some place where you'd like to be. When you arrive there, take some time to enjoy your place. Notice if you are alone or with others. (Pause)
T: (Structuring an oral drill) Where did you go?
S1: I went to the mountains.
S2: I went to my friend's house.
T: What one word best describes this place?
S1: Peace!
S2: Friendship.
T: Imagine your favorite place has a voice and is telling you what it does for you. What does it say?
S1: I am your mountain. I offer you peace.
S2: I am your friend's house. I offer you friendship.

Gestalt projection exercises

Giving a voice to inanimate objects is an example of Gestalt Projection Exercises where individuals learn about themselves from the traits they project to other persons or things. Individuals perceive other persons and things as they perceive themselves (Perls, 131). "I am a book. I am open and I have much useful information. I help you learn many things."

Literary themes

Literary themes are approached through understanding how corresponding themes operate in one's own life. Affective loadings merge the world of the "book character" with the individual's own world of experience.

The techniques of *guided imagery, Gestalt Projection* and a *Gestalt vocabulary* allowing for in-depth exploration of feelings are used in the following lesson on *l'Etranger* (Galyean, 59). This type of experience would be considered by teachers with comprehensive confluent training. The setting is an advanced French class.

Language lesson

T: Before we read *l'Etranger*, let's consider some of Camus' basic themes, namely personal responses to death and loss. Choose someone to work with. Imagine your partner has just lost a close relative and you are responsible for informing him or her by letter. What do you say? (Pause) Exchange letters with your partner and read what you have each said. (Pause) Now close your eyes for a moment. You have just received a letter informing you of the death of an important person in your life. What does it say? How do you feel? (Pause) When you are ready, write about your experience. If you want, we'll share responses.

S1: I am in my house. The telegram says Dad died of a heart attack. I am shocked, numb, hurt. I can't talk.

S2: My sister was hit by a car. She's only eight! I feel panicky.

Students then read the opening chapter where the central person, Meursault, receives a telegram stating his mother's demise. His feelings of annoyance and detachment are contrasted with the students' feelings of pain and involvement with death. Three objectives have been accomplished: *clarification of one's own experience and attitude toward death; awareness of others' experiences; contrastive understanding of Meursault's character and values*—that is, personal (affective), interpersonal (interactive), extrapersonal (cognitive). Brown (22) admits that confluent teaching strategies are powerfully evocative tools and that teachers wishing to incorporate them into existing curriculum should do so prudently, thoughtfully, and with consideration for student uniqueness (p. 10). A comprehensive list of confluent strategies and activities for language lessons may be found in *Language from Within* (Galyean, 60).

Powerfully evocative tools

A list of confluent materials, publications, and workshops is available through the Confluent Education Development and Research Center, Box 30128, Santa Barbara, California 93105.

Information on confluent education

Why humanistic education?

Because it emphasizes student-centered personal learning and student-teacher interaction, humanistic education meets several student and teacher needs. We observe that students have a desperate need for social interaction and for discovering relevance in relationships and events (Grittner, 73; Stanford and Roark, 164). Therefore, education should allow students to talk

Meeting student and teacher needs

about themselves (Broudy, 19) and their personal experiences (Papalia and Zampogna, 128; Savignon, 150; and Schulz and Bartz, 153) and to communicate real information (Morain, 117), thereby confirming their own being (Jourard, 88). Brown (20) indicates "that poor students have never learned to comment on their own experiences–especially their feelings" (p. 7).

Alleviating anxiety

Simpson (161) observes that affective programs tend to alleviate the anxiety caused by unnatural learning structures. Dodge (40) claims that "language study is often foreign to the student and is the source of tension in foreign language classes (p. 14). This may be due to the absence of familiar cues that Jarvis has pointed out (Fryer, 55).

Use of humanistic teaching methods in language classes seems to create atmospheres of relaxation, openness, and of warmth (Christensen, 29; Galyean, 57; Moskowitz, 121; Wilson and Wattenmaker, 180).

Knowing students on a personal basis

Humanistic structures afford teachers the opportunity to know their students on a personal basis (Grittner, 73), to learn about their "survival situations" (Macnamara, 106), and to share their dreams (Brown, 20). High levels of student interaction among themselves and with the teacher make the disclosure of meaningful content possible (Aspy and Roebuck, 6; Combs, 34).

Developing communicative competence

Research from communicative competence and psycholinguistics points to the effectiveness of humanistic strategies for developing oral competence. Schulz and Bartz (153) cite several studies. Joiner (86) observes that little learning takes place during rote drills divorced from meaningful communication settings. Competence is greatly enhanced within meaningful situational contexts. Joiner (86), McCoy (113), and Savignon (149) advocate using humanistic strategies to develop communicative competence.

Cautionary measures

Cautionary measures

Enthusiasm for humanistic methods is tempered by several cautionary measures. Not all students are ready for the freedom and personal disclosure invited by humanistic teaching (Bridges 18; Rogers, 141). Bridges clearly states that to work with students "where they are" is more human than to expect freedom of expression and self-disclosure that they cannot handle. He cautions against turning a class into a group experience when students are not prepared for such interaction. Fox and Vere de Vault (49) advocate going slowly when introducing experiential practices and watching for student resistance or discomfort. Reinert (138) reminds teachers to assess student needs and interests to guard against "imposing just another new method" (Gilchrist and Roberts, 63, p. 2) or against "bandwagonism" (Grittner, 72). Alternatives should be provided for students who do not wish to participate in self-disclosing activities.

Need for a sound theoretical basis

Lyon (105) and McCoy (113) mention the need for establishing a sound theoretical basis for humanistic practices. The premises of humanistic language teaching are based on research from psychology, counseling, and psycholinguistics. While waiting for humanistic education research to reach maturity, Dyer (41) claims that teachers should work toward stating well-defined objectives and execute systematic planning to incorporate the strategies into regular classes. Wass, et al. (173) remind teachers that by creating well-ordered lessons, they guard against the "loose-endedness" and unclear norms frequently issuing from open-ended responses and process learning. Gow (70) adds that teaching for affective goals does not excuse teachers from providing students with clear insights into what they are learning. *Connaître et se connaître* (Jarvis, et al., 84), *Explorando* (Christensen, 30), *Language from Within* (Galyean, 60), and *Vistas Hispanicas* (Christensen and Wolfe, 31) contain lessons and objectives illustrative of well-ordered presentations of the various strategies that can be called humanistic.

Humanistic teaching without humanistic techniques

Teaching humanistically does not necessarily imply teaching with humanistic techniques. Bridges (17) contends that authentic human teaching emerges from the student's invested interest in and engagement with a particular situation, not from "the teacher's or student's desire to do something 'groovy.'" When meaningful learning is taking place, techniques are not necessary. Patterson (129) disavows the use of techniques because they spoil the natural flow of interests. Brown (21) and Hillman (79) agree that the apex of humanistic teaching is the ability to recognize affective content present within the teacher, the student, and the lesson and to use it as an organic basis for learning.

Facilitative teaching

Facilitative teaching is another way to approach humanistic education. Carkhuff and Berenson (26) and Moskowitz (121) in dicate that the two behaviors most greatly affecting student achievement are *an acceptance of feelings* (empathy) and *praise*. Also maximal to learning achievement are *prizing a student's personal interests* (Rogers, 143), *creating emotionally close bonds* between students and teachers (Stanford and Roark, 164), *providing emotionally supportive environments* to dispel the "future shock" of learning a second language (Grittner, 73), and *teacher self-disclosure* (Jourard, 88). Aspy (5) cites research indicating that facilitative behaviors effect significant positive changes in academic achievement of students, and Moskowitz (121) reports favorable changes in the attitudes of students toward the language.

Not all results positive

Not all results are positive, however, and they warrant consideration. Moskowitz (121) reports that attitudes of student teachers trained in interaction analysis (facilitative teaching) became less favorable toward their master teachers who had not received the training. Brown, Phillips and Shapiro (22) describe a significant decrease in "connectedness" (positive relatedness) to others during a Confluent Education Elementary Teacher Training Program. Interviews revealed that the behaviors of these teacher trainees had changed in the direction of informality and orientation to the "now," and they resented these conditions not being present in the overall school environment. We are left with the question: Does humanistic training effect such differences in operational values that individuals accustomed to humanistic practices find themselves less willing to work with colleagues not engaged in the same methods? And will the same hold true for students?

Teacher-awareness training

Teacher-awareness training is a key factor in preparing persons for humanistic teaching. Combs et al. (35), in their research on outstanding teachers, indicate that these teachers have an excellent grasp of subject matter, a clear perception of themselves and their students, and a knowledge of appropriate methods. Combs (33) adds that a keen awareness of student "personal meanings" is central to excellent teaching.

Learning to use feelings as a guide

Accurate perceptions of others are contingent upon accurate perceptions of oneself (Combs, 34). Rogers and Stevens (145) indicate that teachers must be open to experiences within themselves and learn to use their own feelings, interests, and intuitions as the guide for deciding beneficial responses to students.

Lyon (105) claims that such sensitive behaviors are learned through group interaction and feedback and that experiential methods must be learned in an experiential manner. One of the dangers inherent in humanistic education is the possibility of untrained persons using the strategies carelessly with their students—using the techniques to meet their own "ego needs" (Brown, 21).

Problem of untrained persons

Teachers are neither psychiatrists nor psychologists, but many of their functions are psychological (Ekstein, 43). Jersild (85, p. 135) claims that "because teachers are in a position to have profound psychological influence on students, for better or for worse," awareness training is necessary to clarify psychological functions and to maximize beneficial results for students —that is growth in self-identity and acceptance. Brown (21) distinguishes between "therapy" and affective teaching engaged by humanistic educators for growth purposes:

Therapy and affective teaching

> In therapy emphasis is on pathological feelings about oneself; whereas in affective teaching, emphasis is on how one responds emotionally to the universe being encountered at a given moment, and on what personal insights can be gained from the encounter (pp. 248–49).

Cultivation of flexible teaching behaviors

A benefit of humanistic education is the cultivation of flexible teaching behaviors. Fantini and Weinstein (48), Hosenfeld (80), and Joyce and Weil (89) cite differences among student perceptual systems. Individual students—and teachers—differ in their needs for high or low structure. Fantini and Weinstein (48) suggest a three-tier model for teacher education. Some teachers are excellent skills teachers; others show expertise in working with group dynamics and interpersonal relations; others have a natural bent for counseling and easily create atmospheres conducive to self-awareness and exploration. All three are necessary for excellent teaching, and teacher education programs should provide learning experiences in each of the areas. He adds that the ideal teacher is one who merges all three talents within him or herself.

Resources

Resource centers and materials have been cited for each branch; a comprehensive list of humanistic colleges and universities, growth centers, and bibliographic references is available at low cost through the Association for Humanistic Psychology, 325 Ninth Street, San Francisco, California 94103.

Workshops

Humanistic education language workshops are offered by the Adirondack Mountain Humanistic Education Center, the Confluent Education Development and Research Center, and the Philadelphia Center for Humanistic Education.

Conclusion

Humanistic education, basing much of its theory on data provided by subjective experiences, is an attempt to create new perceptual systems for understanding human beings and to make these processes available in educational settings. Although each branch claims a particular thrust responsive to specific life questions, the boundaries between them are fluid; the lines of communication are open. Curricular developments within one branch usually reflect the theories and strategies initiated within the others.

We are suggesting that language expand its realm to include humanistic practices, to use personal content as the basis for language learning, and to view personal language as the means for self-learning. We agree with Koestenbaum (93) that "language teachers are in a good position to help students find a home within themselves." Our recommendations are not made, however, without caution.

Advocates of humanistic education assume that persons working to seed education systems with humanistic practices are doing so in response to their own consciousness of the inexhaustible dimensions of human potential and their desire to bring the skills of self-realization into the classroom. These persons are neither clever technicians, "armed with a bag of tricks for Monday morning," nor therapists. They are educators willfully preparing a new educational mosaic from traditionally sound methods and materials, synergistic insights received in dialogue with colleagues, and nontraditional means for probing new dimensions of human possibility.

Lest, however, they build on the sand of messianic fervor, we suggest distilling the vintage of solid language methodology and research with the fresh nectar of humanistic perspectives and practices, straining and preserving the best of both for the

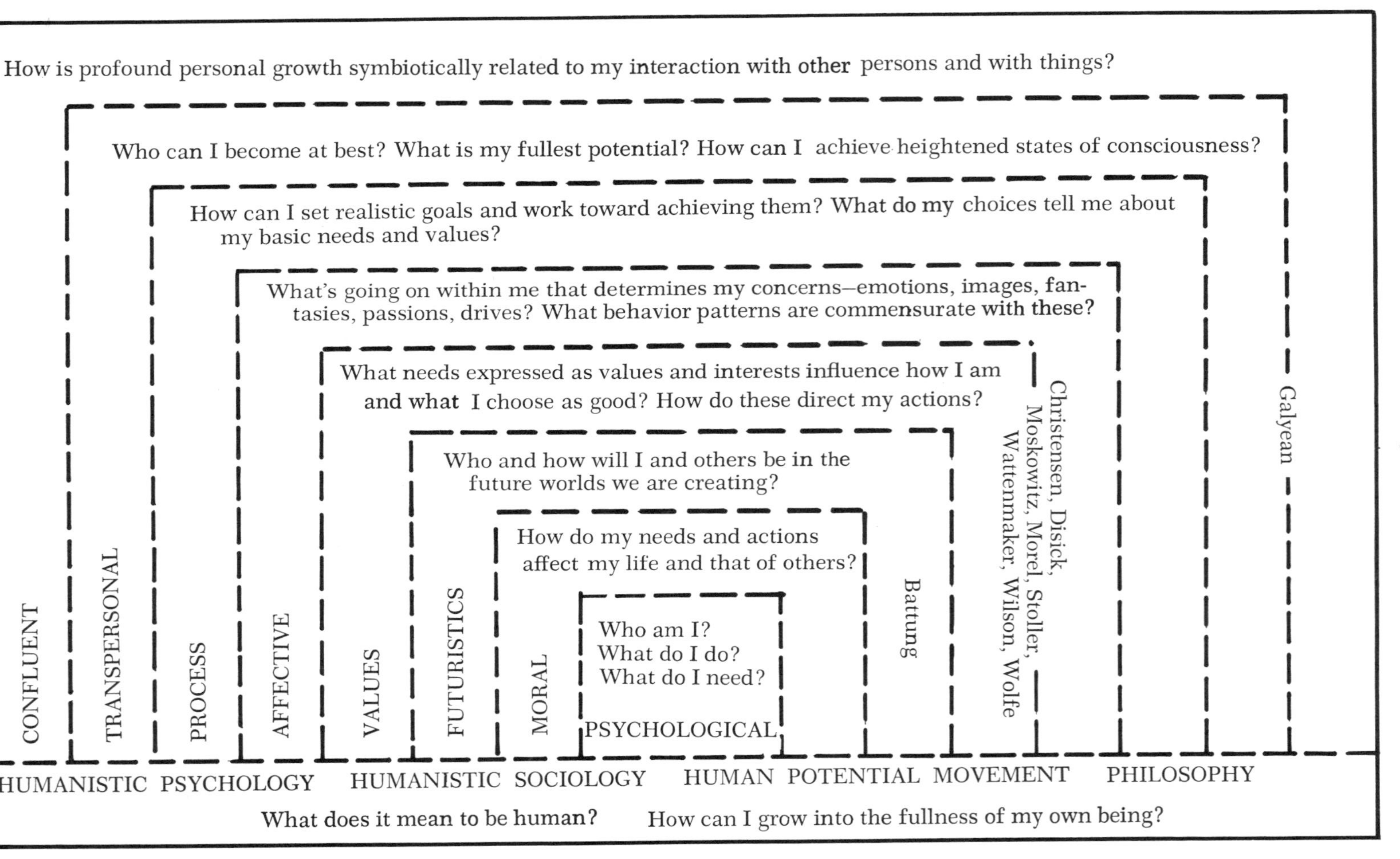
How is profound personal growth symbiotically related to my interaction with other persons and with things?
Galyean
Who can I become at best? What is my fullest potential? How can I achieve heightened states of consciousness?
How can I set realistic goals and work toward achieving them? What do my choices tell me about my basic needs and values?
What's going on within me that determines my concerns—emotions, images, fantasies, passions, drives? What behavior patterns are commensurate with these?
Christensen, Disick, Moskowitz, Morel, Stoller, Wattenmaker, Wilson, Wolfe
What needs expressed as values and interests influence how I am and what I choose as good? How do these direct my actions?
Battung
Who and how will I and others be in the future worlds we are creating?
How do my needs and actions affect my life and that of others?
Who am I? What do I do? What do I need?
CONFLUENT
TRANSPERSONAL
PROCESS
AFFECTIVE
VALUES
FUTURISTICS
MORAL
PSYCHOLOGICAL
HUMANISTIC PSYCHOLOGY
HUMANISTIC SOCIOLOGY
HUMAN POTENTIAL MOVEMENT
PHILOSOPHY
What does it mean to be human?
How can I grow into the fullness of my own being?

FIGURE 1

betterment of the whole profession. Some fears disturb our hopes. If humanistic practices are limited to "recipe" approaches, if practitioners do not seek to widen and deepen their own subjective experiences and to temper personal fervor with practical caution by providing a diversity of learning experiences for students, if careful research is not conducted to determine long-term effects and to predict the "where" and "how" of future successes, and if interested teachers are not afforded the opportunity of participating in programs for training in self-awareness, group dynamics, and humanistic curriculum development, the carefully tended theories and practices chance to become spurious.

We recognize three problem areas: 1) Claims that humanistic practices foster growth in self-identity and connectedness, language achievement, and overall positive attitudes are founded on teacher observations rather than on valid research. The question of how much affective content can be discussed in the target language lingers unanswered. We recommend research in these areas. 2) Increasing requests for enrollment in humanistic workshops indicate teacher willingness to design programs that include humanistic theories and practices; yet there is a marked paucity of available courses, workshops, and inservice training sessions. We urge colleges and universities, state departments of education, and local organizations to develop responsive programs. 3) The aggregate of humanistic materials needs ordering. Centers are needed to collate existing materials, to design new methods and strategies for dissemination, and to develop guidelines for using them. Textbook companies should consider adding humanistic components to textual materials.

Because no single teaching method works best for all, we see wisdom in Fantini and Weinstein's (48) suggestion that, to meet the varied learning styles of students, teachers should work to develop expertise in cognitive, interactive, and affective teaching skills. We concur with Brown (21) that each lesson should show learning objectives for all three domains.

The humanistic mosaic is well begun. By adhering to their own advice that solid learning emerges from reason, intuition, emotion, and interaction and by maintaining an openness to continual refinement of perspectives and practices through well-defined research in the areas of language learning, learning motivation, human behavior, and human potential, humanistic educators hope to avoid the tenuousness of housing their work in castles of sand, subject to the whim and wave of conjecture.

We conclude with an activity. Imagine yourself being the best possible teacher or administrator you can possibly be. How are you? What are you doing? How are the students growing because of you? Now become this person, understanding that you are more than you know and have potential beyond which you can conceive. And so do our students! For them and for us both we believe in the fundamentals of humanistic education and encourage its entry into language teaching. "The language teacher, above all others, ought to be a humanist" (Brown, 20, p. 30).

References, Humanistic education: A mosaic just begun

1 Alschuler, Alfred S. *Developing Achievement Motivation in Adolescents.* Englewood Cliffs, New Jersey: Educational Technology Publications, 1973.

2 ——— "Humanistic Education," 62–71 in Donald A. Read and Sidney B. Simon, eds., *Humanistic Education Sourcebook.* Englewood Cliffs, New Jersey: Prentice-Hall, 1975.

3 ——— "Psychological Education," 23–32 in Donald A. Read and Sidney B. Simon, eds., *Humanistic Education Sourcebook.* Englewood Cliffs, New Jersey: Prentice-Hall, 1975.

4 Ashton-Warner, Sylvia. *Teacher.* New York: Bantam Books, 1971.

5 Aspy, David N. *Toward a Technology for Humanizing Education.* Champaign, Illinois: Research Press Company, 1972.

6 ——— and Flora Roebuck. "The Relationship of Teacher Offered Conditions of Meaning to Behaviors Described by Flanders Interaction Analysis." *Education* 95(1975):216–22.

7 Assagioli, Roberto. *Psychosynthesis.* New York: Viking, 1971.

8 Baier, Kurt. "Ethical Pluralism and Moral Education," 100 in J. Beck, ed., *Moral Education.* Toronto: University of Toronto Press, 1971.

9 Bailey, Alice. *Education in the New Age.* New York: Lucis, 1954.

10 Bartz, Walter, Elizabeth Joiner, and Renate Schulz. *Communicative Competence: What is it? Who needs it? Ways to Approach It.* [Workshop Materials, ACTFL Conference, Washington, D.C., November 1975.]

11 Battung, Diane. *Educational Futuristics for the Second Language Classroom.* [Workshop presented at the CATESOL Spring Conference, Sacramento, California, April 1976.]

12 Bessell, Harold, and Uvaldo Palomares. *Methods in Human Development: Theory Manual.* El Cajon, California: Human Development Training Institute, 1970.

13 Bonin, Thérèse, and Diane Birckbichler. "Real Communication through Interview and Conversation Cards." *Modern Language Journal* 59 (1975):22–25.

14 Borton, Terry. *Education for Student Concerns Urban Affairs Anthology, and Making Sense.* Philadelphia: Philadelphia Public Schools, 1968–69.

15 ——— *Reach, Touch, and Teach.* New York: McGraw-Hill, 1970.

16 ——— and Norman Newberg. *Education for Student Concerns: Affective Education Research Project.* Philadelphia: Philadelphia Public Schools, 1972. [EDRS: ED 106 791.]

17 Bridges, William. *The Three Faces of Humanistic Education.* [Speech to the Association for Humanistic Psychology Conference, Squaw Valley, California, September 1972.]

18 ——— "Thoughts on Humanistic Education, or Is Teaching a Dirty Word?" *Journal of Humanistic Psychology* 13,i(1973):5–13.

19 Broudy, Harry S. "Humanism in Education." *Journal of Aesthetic Education* 7,ii(1973):67–77.

20 Brown, Charles T. "Communication and the Foreign Language Teacher," 5–35 in Gilbert A. Jarvis, ed., *The Challenge of Communication.* ACTFL Review of Foreign Language Education, Volume 6. Skokie, Illinois: National Textbook Company, 1974.

21 Brown, George Isaac. *Human Teaching for Human Learning.* New York: The Viking Press, 1972.

22 ——— Mark Phillips, and Stewart Bennett Shapiro. *Confluent Education:Integrating Intellect, Emotions, and Action*. University of California at Santa Barbara, 1976. [Unpublished paper.]
23 ——— Thomas Yeomans, and Liles Grizzard, eds., *The Live Classroom*. New York:Viking, 1975.
24 Bugenthal, J. F. T. "The Humanistic Ethic—The Individual in Psychotherapy as a Societal Change Agent," 294–306 in John F. Glass and John R. Staude,eds., *Humanistic Society:Today's Challenge to Sociology*. Pacific Palisades, California: Goodyear, 1972.
25 Buhler, Charlotte. "The Scope of Humanistic Psychology," *Education* 95,i(1974):3–8.
26 Carkhuff, Robert, and Bernard G. Berenson. *Beyond Counselling and Therapy*. New York:Holt, Rinehart and Winston, 1967.
27 Castaneda, Carlos. *Journey to Ixtlan*. New York: Simon and Schuster, 1972.
28 Castillo, Gloria A. *Left-Handed Teaching*. New York:Praeger, 1974.
29 Christensen, Clay Benjamin. "Affective Learning Activities." *Foreign Language Annals* 8(1975): 211–19.
30 ——— *Explorando*. Englewood Cliffs, New Jersey:Prentice-Hall, 1976.
31 ——— and David E. Wolfe. *Vistas Hispánicas*. Rand McNally, in press.
32 Clark, Frances. "Rediscovering Transpersonal Education." *The Journal of Transpersonal Psychology* i(1974):1–7.
33 Combs, Arthur W. "Humanistic Goals of Education," in Donald A. Read and Sidney B. Simon, eds., *Humanistic Education Sourcebook*. Englewood Cliffs, New Jersey:Prentice-Hall, 1975.
34 ——— "The Personal Approach to Good Teaching," 249–61 in Donald A. Read and Sidney B. Simon,eds., *Humanistic Education Sourcebook*. Englewood Cliffs, New Jersey:Prentice-Hall, 1975.
35 ——— Robert A. Blume, Arthur J. Newman, and Hannelore L. Wass. *The Professional Education of Teachers:A Humanistic Approach to Preparation*. Boston:Allyn & Bacon, 1974.
36 Dass, Baba Ram. *Remember Be Here Be Now*. New York:Crown, 1972.
37 Dewey, John. *The Child and The Curriculum*. Chicago:University of Chicago Press, 1956.
38 Disick, Renée S. "Teaching Toward Affective Goals in Foreign Languages." *Foreign Language Annals* 7(1973):95–101.
39 ——— and Laura Barbanel. "Affective Education and Foreign Languages," 185–222 in Gilbert A. Jarvis,ed., *The Challenge of Communication*. ACTFL Review of Foreign Language Education, Volume 6. Skokie, Illinois:National Textbook Company, 1974.
40 Dodge, James W.,ed. *Sensitivity in the Foreign Language Classroom*. [Reports of the Working Committees of the Northeast Conference on the Teaching of Foreign Languages.] New York: Modern Language Association Materials Center, 1973.
41 Dyer, Henry S. "Perspectives on Educational Accountability," 35 in Robert S. Gilchrist and Bernice R. Roberts,eds., *Curriculum Development*. Belmont, California:Fearon, 1974.
42 Ediger, Marlow. "Affective Objectives, the Pupil and Committee Work." *Education* 95(1975): 258–60.
43 Ekstein, Rudolph. "The Boundary Line between Education and Psychotherapy," 136–42 in Donald A. Read and Sidney B. Simon,eds., *Humanistic Education Sourcebook*. Englewood Cliffs, New Jersey:Prentice-Hall, 1975.
44 Etzioni, Amitai. "Basic Human Needs, Alienation and Inauthenticity," 74–95 in John F. Glass and John R. Staude,eds., *Humanistic Society*. Pacific Palisades, California:Goodyear, 1972.
45 Evans, Richard I. *Gordon Allport*. New York: Dutton, 1970.
46 Fagan, Joen, and Irma Lee Shepherd,eds., *Gestalt Therapy Now*. New York:Harper & Row, 1971.
47 ——— eds., *Life Techniques in Gestalt Therapy*. New York:Harper & Row, 1970.
48 Fantini, Mario, and Gerald Weinstein. *Making Urban Schools Work*. New York:Holt, Rinehart & Winston, 1968.
49 Fox, Thomas G., and M. Vere de Vault. "Technology and Humanism in the Classroom." *Educational Technology* 14,x(1974):7–12.
50 Frankl, Victor E. *Man's Search for Meaning:An Introduction to Logotherapy*. New York:Washington Square, 1964.
51 Freire, Paulo. *Pedagogy of the Oppressed*. New York:Herder & Herder, 1972.
52 ——— *Education for Critical Consciousness*. New York:Seabury, 1973.
53 Friedenberg, Edgar Z. *Coming of Age in America*. Toronto:Vintage, 1963.
54 Fromm, Erich. "What Does It Mean To Be Human?" 32–54 in John F. Glass and John R. Staude,eds., *Humanistic Society:Today's Challenge to Sociology*. Pacific Palisades, California: Goodyear, 1972.
55 Fryer, Bruce T. "Free to Explore:Curricular Developments," 9–46 in Gilbert A. Jarvis,ed., *Perspective:A New Freedom*. ACTFL Review of Foreign Language Education, Volume 7. Skokie, Illinois:National Textbook Company, 1975.
56 Galyean, Beverly. *Art and Fantasy:A Gestalt Approach to Counselling and Language Development*. Santa Barbara, California:Confluent Education Development and Research Center, 1973.
57 ——— "Gestalt Therapy:New Wine in Old Skins," 206–20 in George Brown, Thomas Yeomans, and Liles Grizzard,eds., *The Live Classroom*. New York:Viking, 1975.
58 ——— *Human Teaching in the Language Class: A Confluent Approach to Teaching Language*. Santa Barbara, California:Confluent Education Development and Research Center, 1976.

59 ——— *The Stranger:A Confluent Approach.* Santa Barbara, California:Confluent Education Development and Research Center, 1975.
60 ——— *Language from Within.* Santa Barbara, California:Confluent Education Development and Research Center, 1976.
61 Gardner, John W. *Self-Renewal.* New York:Harper & Row, 1971.
62 Gauthier, David. "Moral Action and Moral Education," 141 in C. M. Beck,ed., *Moral Education: Interdisciplinary Approaches.* Toronto:University of Toronto Press, 1971.
63 Gilchrist, Robert S., and Bernice R. Roberts. *Curriculum Development.* Belmont, California: Lear Siegler/Fearon, 1974.
64 Givens, Paul. "Toward a New Emphasis on Human Values in Higher Education." *Liberal Education* 60(1974):409–17.
65 Glasser, William. *Schools Without Failure.* New York:Harper & Row, 1966.
66 Glatthorn, Allan A. *Alternatives in Education: Schools and Programs.* New York:Dodd, Mead, 1975.
67 Goble, Frank G. *The Third Force.* New York: Pocket Books, 1973.
68 Gordon, Thomas. *P.E.T. Parent Effectiveness Training.* New York:Peter H. Wyden, 1970.
69 Gouldner, Alvin. "Toward a Reflexive Sociology," 171–81 in John F. Glass and John R. Staude,eds., *Humanistic Society:Today's Challenge to Sociology.* Pacific Palisades, California:Goodyear, 1972.
70 Gow, Doris T. *The PIC* (Process Individualization Curriculum) *Model:Structure with Humanistic Goals.* [Paper presented at the Annual Meeting of the American Educational Research Association, Washington, D.C., April, 1975.] [EDRS: ED 104 286.]
71 Greenberg, Herbert M. *Teaching with Feeling.* Indianapolis:Pegasus, 1969.
72 Grittner, Frank. "Barbarians, Bandwagons, and Foreign Language Scholarship." *Modern Language Journal* 57(1973):241–48.
73 ——— [Address given at the 1974 Southern Conference on Language Teaching, Atlanta, Georgia, October 11–12, 1974.]
74 Gustafson, James. "Education for Moral Responsibility," 23 in Nancy and Theodore Sizer,eds., *Moral Education:Five Lectures.* Cambridge:Harvard University Press, 1970.
75 Hancock, Charles. "Guiding Teachers to Respond to Individual Differences in the Affective Domain." *Foreign Language Annals* 6(1972):225–31.
76 Heath, Douglas. *Humanizing Schools.* New York: Hayden, 1971.
77 Heider, John. "Catharsis in Human Potential Encounter." *The Journal of Transpersonal Psychology* i(1974):1–7.
78 Hillman, Aaron. *Concepts and Elements of Confluent Education.* DRICE. Monograph No. 3. Santa Barbara:University of California at Santa Barbara, 1973.
79 ——— *Confluent Education:A Descriptive Analysis of the Concepts, Goals, and Philosophy, and the Relationship between Them.* University of California at Santa Barbara, 1973. [Doctoral dissertation.]
80 Hosenfeld, Carol. "The New Student Role:Individual Differences and Implications for Instruction," 129–67 in Gilbert A. Jarvis,ed., *Perspective:A New Freedom.* ACTFL Review of Foreign Language Education, Volume 7. Skokie, Illinois: National Textbook Company, 1975.
81 Huxley, Laura. *You Are Not the Target.* North Hollywood, California:Wilshire, 1974.
82 Jacks, L. P. *Education of the Whole Man.* New York:Harper, 1931.
83 James, Muriel, and Dorothy Jongeward. *Born To Win:Transactional Analysis with Gestalt Experiments.* Reading, Massachusetts:Addison-Wesley, 1973.
84 Jarvis, Gilbert, Thérèse Bonin, Donald Corbin, and Diane Birckbichler. *Connaître et se connaître.* New York:Holt, Rinehart & Winston, 1976.
85 Jersild, Arthur. "The Teacher as Psychologist," 133–35 in Donald A. Read and Sidney B. Simon, eds., *Humanistic Education Sourcebook.* Englewood Cliffs, New Jersey:Prentice-Hall, 1975.
86 Joiner, Elizabeth G. "Tailoring Language Instruction to Student Needs," 151–84 in Gilbert A. Jarvis,ed., *The Challenge of Communication.* ACTFL Review of Foreign Language Education, Volume 6. Skokie, Illinois:National Textbook Company, 1974.
87 Jones, Richard M. *Fantasy and Feeling in Education.* New York:Harper & Row, 1970.
88 Jourard, Sidney M. *The Transparent Self.* New York:Van Nostrand, 1971.
89 Joyce, Bruce, and Marsha Weil. *Models of Teaching.* Englewood Cliffs, New Jersey:Prentice-Hall, 1972.
90 Kirschenbaum, Howard. "Beyond Values Clarification," 92–110 in Sidney B. Simon and Howard Kirschenbaum,eds., *Readings in Values Clarification.* Minneapolis:Winston, 1973.
91 ——— and Sidney B. Simon. "Values and the Futures Movement in Education," 17–30 in Sidney B. Simon and Howard Kirschenbaum,eds., *Readings in Values Clarification.* Minneapolis: Winston, 1973.
92 Kneller, George. *Introduction to the Philosophy of Education.* New York:Wiley, 1971.
93 Koestenbaum, Peter. *Anxiety in the Foreign Language Classroom.* [Address given at the CFLTA Spring Conference, San Jose, California, April 1976.]
94 Kohlberg, Lawrence. "Moral Education, Religious Education, and the Public Schools:A Developmental View," 169 in Theodore Sizer,ed., *Religion and Public Education.* Boston:Houghton Mifflin, 1967.
95 ——— "The Child as Moral Philosopher," 49–61 in Sidney B. Simon and Howard Kirschenbaum,

eds., *Readings in Values Clarification.* Minneapolis: Winston, 1973.
96 Korzybski, Alfred. *Science and Sanity.* Lakeville, Connecticut: International Non-Aristotelian Library, 1958.
97 Lederman, Janet. *Anger and the Rocking Chair.* New York: Viking, 1973.
98 LeGuin, Ursula K. *The Dispossessed.* New York: Avon, 1975.
99 Leonard, George B. *Education and Ecstasy.* New York: Dell, 1968.
100 ——— *The Transformation.* New York: Delacorte, 1972.
101 Lewis, Howard R., and Harold S. Streitfield. *Growth Games.* New York: Bantam, 1972.
102 Lipton, Gladys. "Curricula for New Goals," 187–218 in Dale L. Lange and Charles J. James,eds., *Foreign Language Education: A Reappraisal.* ACTFL Review of Foreign Language Education, Volume 4. Skokie, Illinois: National Textbook Company, 1972.
103 Luft, Joseph. *Group Processes: An Introduction to Group Processes.* Palo Alto, California: National, 1970.
104 Lynd, Helen Merrill. "Alienation: Man's Fate and Man's Hope," in John F. Glass and John R. Staude,eds., *Humanistic Society: Today's Challenge to Sociology.* Pacific Palisades, California: Goodyear, 1972.
105 Lyon, Harold C.,Jr. *Learning to Feel—Feeling to Learn.* Columbus, Ohio: Charles E. Merrill, 1971.
106 Macnamara, J. "The Cognitive Strategies of Language Learning," 57–65 in J. W. Oller,Jr., and J. C. Richards,eds., *Focus on the Learner: Pragmatic Perspectives for the Language Teacher.* Rowley, Massachusetts: Newbury House, 1973.
107 Maslow, Abraham. *Toward A Psychology of Being.* Princeton, New Jersey: Van Nostrand, 1962.
108 ——— *Motivation and Personality.* New York: Harper & Row, 1970.
109 ——— *The Farther Reaches of Human Nature.* New York: Viking, 1971.
110 May, Rollo. *The Art of Counseling.* Nashville, Tennessee: Abingdon, 1967.
111 ——— *Love and Will.* New York: Norton, 1969.
112 ——— "Introduction to the AHP Theory Conference." *AHP Newsletter* (March, 1976): 1.
113 McCoy, Ingeborg. *Psycholinguistic Framework for a Humanistic Model of Foreign Language Acquisition.* [Paper presented at the ACTFL Conference, Washington, D.C., November, 1975.]
114 "The Meeting of East and West: A Conversation with Haridas Chaudhuri." *Synthesis* 1,ii(1975): 20–40.
115 Merleau-Ponty, Maurice. *Phenomenology of Perception.* London: Routledge and Kegan Paul, 1962.
116 Miller, Stuart. "Dialogue with the Higher Self." *Synthesis* 1,ii(1975): 122–39.
117 Morain, Genelle. "Humanism in the Classroom: A Dramatic Proposal," in Frank Grittner,ed., *Careers, Communication and Culture in Foreign Language Teaching.* Skokie, Illinois: National Textbook Company, 1974.
118 Morel, Stefano. *Human Dynamics in French.* Upper Jay, New York: Adirondack Mountain Humanistic Education Center, 1974.
119 ——— *Human Dynamics in Spanish.* Upper Jay, New York: Adirondack Mountain Humanistic Education Center, 1974.
120 Morton, Alpren. "Curriculum Significance of The Affective Domain." *Theory into Practice,* 13,i (1974): 46–53.
121 Moskowitz, Gertrude. "Training Foreign Language Teachers in Interaction Analysis." *Foreign Language Annals* 1(1968): 218–35.
122 Moustakas, Clark. *The Self: Explorations in Personal Growth.* New York: Harper Colophon, 1974.
123 ——— and Cereta Perry. *Learning To Be Free.* Englewood Cliffs, New Jersey: Prentice-Hall, 1973.
124 Narveson, J. "Method and Substance in Moral Education," 329 in J. Beck,ed., *Moral Education.* Toronto: University of Toronto Press, 1971.
125 Nebraska Department of Education. *Humanistic Language Strategies.* [Workshop conducted at the University of Nebraska, Summer, 1975.]
126 Overly, Norman V.,ed. *The Unstudied Curriculum: Its Impact on Children.* Washington, D.C.: Association for Supervision and Curriculum Development, 1970.
127 Palomares, Uvaldo. "The Key to Understanding Self and Others," *Educational Leadership* 32,i (1974): 19–21.
128 Papalia, Anthony, and Joseph Zampogna. "The Changing Curricula," 299–328 in Gilbert A. Jarvis,ed., *The Challenge of Communication.* ACTFL Review of Foreign Language Education, Volume 6. Skokie, Illinois: National Textbook Company, 1974.
129 Patterson, C. H. *Humanistic Education.* Englewood Cliffs, New Jersey: Prentice-Hall, 1973.
130 Perls, Frederick. "Four Lectures," 14–38 in Joan Fagan and Irma Lee Shepherd,eds., *Gestalt Therapy Now.* New York: Harper Colophon, 1970.
131 ——— *The Gestalt Approach and Eye Witness to Therapy.* Palo Alto, California: Science and Behavior, 1973.
132 ——— Ralph E. Hefferline, and Paul Goodman. *Gestalt Therapy.* New York: Dell, 1951.
133 Perry, Cereta. "Can Human Relations Be Taught through a Formalized Program?" *Educational Leadership* 32,i(1974): 27–30.
134 Pfeiffer, J. William, and John E. Jones. *A Handbook of Structured Experiences for Human Relations Training,* I, II, III, IV, V. La Jolla, California: University Associates, 1970.
135 Progoff, Ira. *Jung, Synchronicity, and Human Destiny.* New York: Dell, 1973.
136 Ramsey, Mark. "The OK School: A Guide to Humanizing." *NASSP Bulletin,* 59(1975): 66–71.
137 Raths, Louis E., Merrill Harmin, and Sidney B. Simon. *Values and Teaching.* Columbus, Ohio: Merrill, 1966.

138 Reinert, Harry. "Extending the Teacher: From Text to Context," 275–298 in Gilbert A. Jarvis, ed., *The Challenge of Communication.* ACTFL Review of Foreign Language Education, Volume 6. Skokie, Illinois: National Textbook Company, 1974.
139 Richards, Fred, and Anne Cohen Richards, "The Whole Person: Embodied and Disembodied Images." *Journal of Humanistic Psychology* 14,iii (Summer 1974): 21–27.
140 Roberts, Jane. *Seth Speaks.* Englewood Cliffs, New Jersey: Prentice-Hall, 1972.
141 Rogers, Carl. *Freedom to Learn.* Columbus, Ohio: Merrill, 1969.
142 ——— "A Humanistic Conception of Man," 19–37 in John F. Glass and John R. Staude, eds., *Humanistic Society: Today's Challenge to Sociology.* Pacific Palisades, California: Goodyear, 1972.
143 ——— "Bringing Together Ideas & Feelings in Learning," 39–49 in Donald A. Read and Sidney B. Simon, eds., *Humanistic Education Sourcebook.* Englewood Cliffs, New Jersey: Prentice-Hall, 1975.
144 ——— "The Interpersonal Relationship in the Facilitation of Learning," 3–19 in Donald A. Read and Sidney B. Simon, eds., *Humanistic Education Sourcebook.* Englewood Cliffs, New Jersey: Prentice-Hall, 1975.
145 ——— and Barry Stevens. *Person to Person: The Problem of Being Human.* Lafayette, California: Real People Press, 1967.
146 Rubin, Louis. "Curriculum, Affect and Humanism." *Educational Leadership,* 32,i(1974): 10–13.
147 Samples, Bob, and Bob Wohlford. *Opening.* Menlo Park, California: Addison-Wesley, 1975.
148 Sartre, Jean-Paul. *Existentialism.* New York: Philosophical Library, 1947.
149 Savignon, Sandra J. *Communicative Competence: An Experiment in Foreign Language Teaching.* Philadelphia: Center for Curriculum Development, 1972.
150 ——— *Teaching for Communication.* [Paper presented at the OMLTA/MYSAFLT IV International Conference, Toronto, February 1975.]
151 Schmuck, Richard A., and Patricia Schmuck. *Group Processes in the Classroom.* Dubuque. Iowa: Brown, 1971.
152 Schroder, Harold M., Marvin Karlins, and Jacqueline O. Phares. *Education for Freedom.* New York: Wiley, 1973.
153 Schulz, Renate A., and Walter H. Bartz. "Free to Communicate," 47–88 in Gilbert A. Jarvis, ed., *Perspective: A New Freedom.* ACTFL Review of Foreign Language Education, Volume 7. Skokie, Illinois: National Textbook Company, 1975.
154 Schultz, William C. *Joy.* New York: Grover, 1967.
155 Severin, Frank. "What Humanistic Psychology Is About." *Association of Humanistic Psychology Newsletter Supplement* (July 1974).
156 Silberman, Charles E. *Crisis in the Classroom.* New York: Random House, 1970.
157 Simon, Sidney, and Alice Carnes. "Teaching Afro-American History with a Focus on Values," 145–49 in Sidney B. Simon and Howard Kirschenbaum, eds., *Readings in Values Clarification.* Minneapolis: Winston, 1973.
158 ——— Robert C. Hawley, and David D. Britton. *Composition for Personal Growth: Values Clarification through Writing.* New York: Hart, 1973.
159 ——— Leland W. Howe, and Howard Kirschenbaum. *Values Clarification.* New York: Hart, 1972.
160 ——— and Howard Kirschenbaum. *Readings in Values Clarification.* Minneapolis: Winston, 1973.
161 Simpson, Elizabeth. *River Run Deep, River Run Strong: Confluence in Humanistic Education.* New York: Ford Foundation, 1975.
162 Simpson, C. Kenneth, with W. Jeffrey Hastings. *The Castle of You.* Dubuque, Iowa: Kendall/Hunt, 1974.
163 Slater, Philip. *Earthwalk.* New York: Bantam, 1975.
164 Stanford, Gene, and Albert Roark. *Human Interaction in Education.* Boston: Allyn & Bacon, 1974.
165 Staude, John R. "The Theoretical Foundation of Humanistic Sociology," 262–70 in John F. Glass and John R. Staude, eds., *Humanistic Society: Today's Challenge to Sociology.* Pacific Palisades, California: Goodyear, 1972.
166 Stevens, John O. *Awareness: Exploring Experimenting Experiencing.* Lafayette, California: Real People Press, 1971.
167 Stevick, Earl. "Language Instruction Must Do an About-Face." *Modern Language Journal* 18 (1974): 379–84.
168 Stoller, Phyllis, Joanne Lock, Beverly Wattenmaker, and Virginia Wilson. *Real Communication in French.* Upper Jay, New York: National Humanistic Education Center, 1974. [EDRS: ED 104 152.]
169 Sutich, Anthony. "Some Considerations Regarding Transpersonal Psychology." *Journal of Transpersonal Psychology* (1969): 11–20.
170 Timmermann, Tim, and Jim Ballard. *Strategies in Humanistic Education,* Volume 1, Amherst, Massachusetts: Mandala, 1975.
171 Toffler, Alvin, ed. *Learning for Tomorrow.* New York: Vintage, 1974.
172 Van Cleave, Morris. *Existentialism in Education.* New York: Harper & Row, 1966.
173 Wass, Hannelore, Robert A. Blume, Arthur W. Combs, and William D. Hedges. *Humanistic Teacher Education: An Experiment in Systematic Curriculum Innovation.* Fort Collins, Colorado: Shields, 1974.
174 Watts, Alan. *The Book: On the Taboo Against Knowing Who You Are.* New York: Vintage, 1972.
175 Weinstein, Gerald. "Self-Science Education: The Trumpet," 373–382 in Donald A. Read and Sidney B. Simon, eds., *Humanistic Education Sourcebook.* Englewood Cliffs, New Jersey: Prentice-Hall, 1975.

176 ——— and Mario D. Fantini. "Affect and Learning," 101–112 in Donald A. Read and Sidney B. Simon,eds., *Humanistic Education Sourcebook.* Englewood Cliffs, New Jersey: Prentice-Hall, 1975.
177 ——— and Mario D. Fantini,eds., *Toward Humanistic Education.* New York: Praeger, 1972.
178 Weisberg, Joan. *Effective Language Techniques in the Foreign Language Classroom.* [Workshop presented at the Modern Language Association of Philadelphia and Vicinity, Philadelphia, Pennsylvania, 1975.]
179 Welch, I. D., I. Richards, and A. C. Richards,eds. *Educational Accountability:A Humanistic Perspective.* Fort Collins, Colorado: Shields, 1974.
180 Wilson, Virginia, and Beverly Wattenmaker. *Real Communication in Foreign Language.* Upper Jay, New York: Adirondack Mountain Humanistic Education Center, 1973.
181 Wittmer, Joe, and Robert D. Myrick. *Facilitative Teaching:Theory and Practice.* Pacific Palisades, California: Goodyear, 1974.
182 Wolfe, David E., and Leland Howe. "Personalizing Foreign Language Instruction." *Foreign Language Annals* 7(1973):81–90.
183 ——— and Philip Smith,Jr. "Teacher Education for New Goals," 97–126 in Dale L. Lange and Charles J. James,eds., *Foreign Language Education:A Reappraisal,* ACTFL Review of Foreign Language Education, Volume 4, Skokie, Illinois: National Textbook Company, 1972.
184 Yeomans, Thomas. *Confluent Education:The Dynamics of Wholeness.* [Unpublished paper. University of California at Santa Barbara, 1974.]
185 Yogi, Maharishi Mahesh. *Transcendental Meditation.* New York: Signet, 1963.

8

Expanding the options: Curricula in many languages

Introduction

Edith Kroo Allouche
Congregation Tifereth Israel
Gerard L. Ervin
Washington, D.C.

Some foreign languages seem more foreign than others. Sanskrit, Tagalog, and Navajo, for example, are not likely to be familiar to most teachers of Spanish, French, or German. This lack of familiarity is somewhat surprising: Sanskrit, the classical language of India, belongs to the same family as the Romance and Germanic languages. Tagalog, a national language of the Philippines, has been greatly influenced by Spanish, and therefore resembles it. Navajo is the mother tongue of a significant number of Americans in the Southwest.

Some of the less familiar languages, such as Chinese, Russian, and Hindi, are national languages of major political countries, and hundreds of millions speak them. Others are spoken by much smaller numbers of people—Armenian, Basque, and Hawaiian, for example. But all together, these languages are

---

Edith Kroo Allouche (A.B.D., The Ohio State University) is Coordinator of the Hebrew High School and Assistant Administrator of the Religious School at Congregation Tifereth Israel of Columbus, Ohio. She has taught Hebrew language and prepared materials on the FLES and secondary school levels as well as at the college level. She has also taught Hebrew Education courses. Additionally, she has led workshops in language teaching throughout Ohio and has published in *Accent on ACTFL*.

Gerard Ervin (A.B.D., The Ohio State University) is currently a language teaching and methodology specialist with the United States Government. Most recently he was Coordinator for Secondary School Programs at the Center for Slavic and East European Studies, The Ohio State University. He has taught French and Spanish at the high school level and English as a foreign language, Russian, and foreign language methods courses at the college level. He is a bibliographer for the 1974 and 1975 *ACTFL Annual Bibliographies;* his other publications include a Russian songbook, a chapter in *Russian Language Study in 1975:A Status Report,* and articles in *Foreign Language Annals* and the *ADFL Bulletin*. He has conducted numerous workshops for Russian teachers in Ohio, was principal organizer of Ohio's first high school Russian language camp, and has made presentations at various national and regional AAASS, AATSEEL, and ACTFL conferences.

the mother tongues of over three fourths of the world's population. Seen in this light, the overwhelming dominance of Spanish, French, and German in American foreign language education is curious indeed. Throughout this chapter the reader is urged to keep in mind the fact that in 1970 only 2 percent of America's secondary school and college and university population was studying any of the native languages of 75 percent of the world's population.

Choosing a term: uncommonly taught

Referring to these languages when writing about them is problematic. Thompson (53) states: "these languages have been referred to alternately as neglected, unusual, uncommonly taught, exotic, hard, critical, non-Western, noncognate, and even funny (p. 279)." None of these labels is quite satisfactory, for they all have implications that are, to some extent, invalid for one or more of the diverse languages so designated. Even the word *foreign* is inaccurate to the extent that it includes Hawaiian, Navajo, and other nonEnglish languages that are spoken exclusively within the United States (Brod, 4). We follow Thompson in using "uncommonly taught" to refer to these languages as a group. Although the term is unwieldy, it quite accurately represents the status of these languages in the United States, and it provides a realistic basis upon which to build a discussion of the problems and potentials of their instruction.

An historical perspective

Not until after the launching of Sputnik I by the Soviet Union in 1957 was extensive support by the federal government for nongovernment research in the uncommonly taught languages available.

NDEA

The National Defense Education Act (NDEA) of 1958, Title VI, provided for the establishment of language and area centers as well as for institutes for the training of teachers and advanced students in foreign languages, linguistics, and methodology. Thompson (53) discusses the origin and development through 1970 of the NDEA program in language and area studies; in this chapter we update much of Thompson's material.

A part of the NDEA funds was allocated to support conferences on the uncommonly taught languages. The conferences were to help provide assessments of available materials as well as suggestions for further research and materials development for languages of specific geographic areas. The 1961 National Conference on the Neglected Languages reviewed the findings of the earliest of these conferences and set the directions for future priorities in its Fife-Nielsen Report. Similar conferences were convened throughout the 1960s and early 1970s.

Establishing priorities

The U.S. Office of Education further contributed to the classification of information about research on these languages with the establishment of the Educational Resources Information Center (ERIC). ERIC indexes include the *Current Index to Journals in Education,* which classifies journal articles from more than 720 journals, and *Research in Education,* which indexes and abstracts nonjournal materials such as research reports, conference reports, curriculum documents. ERIC may be searched by computer for comprehensive coverage of specific topics, thus enabling teachers to keep abreast of current research. Because much material of particular interest to teachers of uncommonly taught languages is not available elsewhere, ERIC represents an especially valuable resource.

ERIC

The ERIC Clearinghouse on Languages and Linguistics has been at the Center for Applied Linguistics (CAL) since June 1974. Since its founding in 1959, however, the CAL has been serving as a national clearinghouse and as a center of activity for the study and teaching of the uncommonly taught languages. The CAL's *Linguistic Reporter,* a newsletter that appears nine times per year, frequently contains information relevant to instruction in these languages.

Center for Applied Linguistics

In addition to its ERIC responsibilities, the CAL's current activities may be treated under three headings. First, it has undertaken several special projects with the support of the U.S. Office of Education. The final report of the Kittamaqundi Conference (36) and an update of the 1969 materials survey (Blass et al., 3) are of particular relevance to this chapter. Second, it has been collaborating on contrastive analysis projects in four countries of Eastern Europe (Hungary, Poland, Romania, and Yugoslavia) both to help develop the teaching of English in those countries and to further knowledge of Eastern European languages in the United States. Finally, the CAL has become increasingly involved in the development of literacy and adult basic education in the Middle East.

Selected publications

Interest in the uncommonly taught languages, as seen in reports about the historical development of their instruction, the growth of area-oriented professional associations, and programs needing further attention has continued through the 1970s (Gage, 19; Hodge, 21; Thompson, 54). These reports, however, have dealt more with broad goals and needs than with specific pedagogical concerns. The relatively few articles that have related aspects of the language to classroom practices have largely appeared in publications and conference papers issued by the professional associations concerned, or by national institutions of linguistics or international studies. Most of these articles are available through ERIC and represent a wide range of languages and topics: *Some Cultural Problems in Teaching Romanian* (Capusan, 12), *Problems of Textbooks in Teaching Chinese Poetry* (Kuo, 30), *A Survey of Commonly Used Expressions in Chinese and An Analysis of Its Possible Implications in Language Teaching on the College Level* (Lin, 33), *Hebrew for Secondary Schools* (Moskowitz, 37), and *Development of Instructional Materials in Japanese for Elementary Schools*" (Sato, 45). A 1971 publication that may be particularly useful to teachers of the uncommonly taught languages is Stevick's book (49) dealing with materials development. It includes guidelines for evaluation of existing instructional materials and suggestions for the writing of new maximally adaptable lesson plans.

Uncommonly taught languages highlighted

A look through recent volumes of *The Modern Language Journal* and *Foreign Language Annals* reveals a number of articles highlighting progress in these languages. Included are surveys, evaluations, and teaching techniques in Chinese (Leong, 32; Tsu, 55; Yang, 58), Italian (Pane, 40), Japanese (Jolly, 26), Latin (Read, 43), Portuguese (Bagby, 2), Romanian (Impey, 24), and Russian (Shane, 48). These journals have included book reviews, available materials and media listings, and announcements of professional association meetings for the Classical, Slavic, Oriental, and Middle Eastern languages.

A survey of the current status

Enrollments

Numerical perspective

Perhaps the best way to begin a survey of enrollments is to place the whole language-teaching picture in numerical perspective. In Figure 1 public secondary school and college/university enrollment figures for 1970 (the most recent year for which complete foreign language enrollment data at both levels are available) have been combined to illustrate that total foreign language enrollments were barely 20 percent of the total student population and total enrollments in the uncommonly taught languages were only 2 percent of the total student population. In other words, only one student in five was studying a foreign language in 1970, and only *one in 50* was studying an uncommonly taught language.

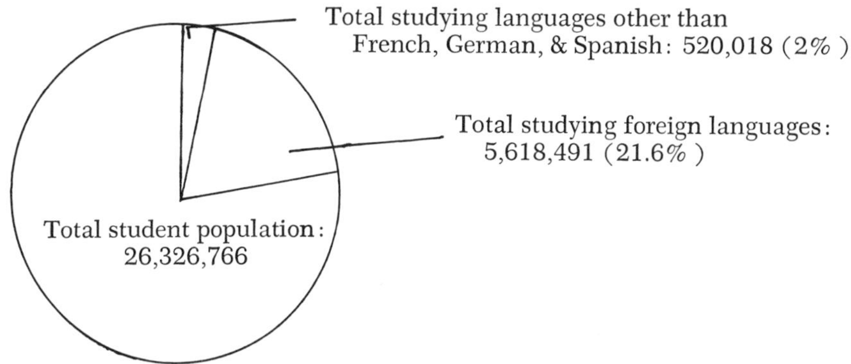

FIGURE 1. Foreign language enrollments in American public secondary schools, colleges, and universities compared with total enrollments in these institutions, 1970.

Sources of enrollment data

The secondary school and college data discussed in this section have been compiled from information gathered by the Modern Language Association of America (Brod, 4, 5, 6, 7, 8; Herslow and Dershem, 20; Kant, 28, 29; Scebold, 47; Willbern, 57). Data for the government language schools have been secured through personal communication (Hutchinson, 23; Swift, 50).

Trends in secondary enrollments

Secondary school enrollments. The term *secondary schools* is defined for purposes of this chapter to include all public secondary schools, grades 7 to 12. Because of the vast numbers of autonomous administrative units whose cooperation must be secured to survey secondary school foreign language enrollments, these figures are less complete and up-to-date than might be desired. The most recent complete data available from the Modern Language Association cover the 1970 enrollments. Key data relevant to the present chapter from the MLA surveys for 1965, 1968, and 1970 are presented in Figure 2.

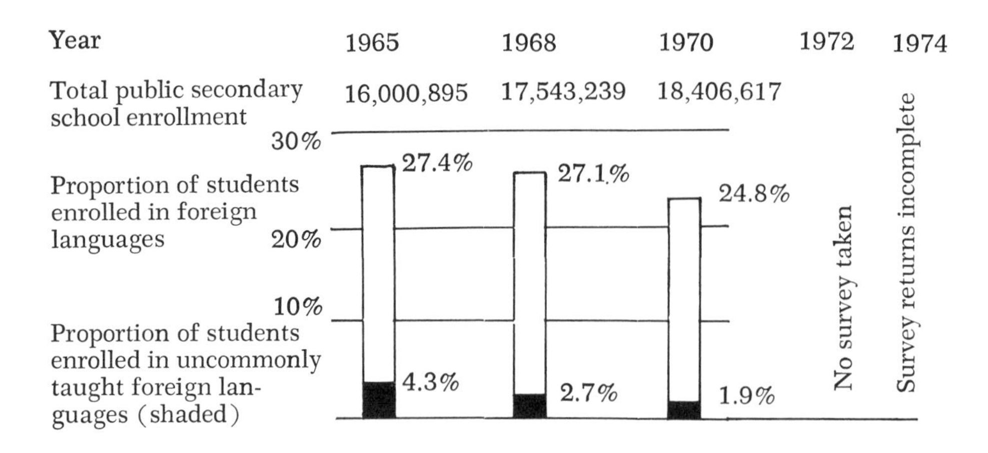

FIGURE 2. Public secondary school enrollments with proportion of students enrolled in foreign languages and proportion of students enrolled in the uncommonly taught foreign languages.

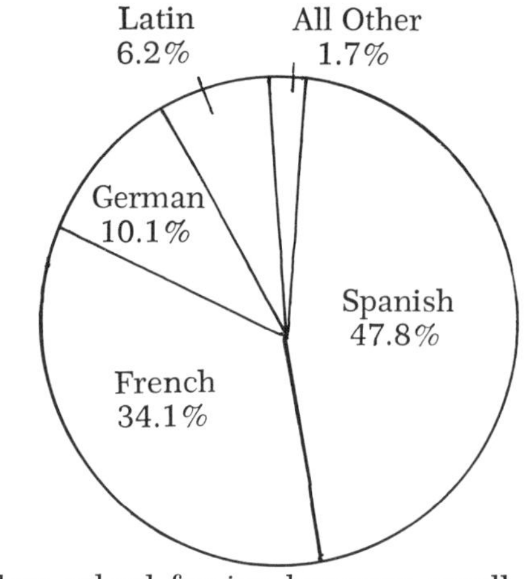

Total, top 2 languages = 82.0%
Total, top 3 languages = 92.1%
Total, top 4 languages = 98.3%

FIGURE 3. Comparative public secondary school foreign language enrollments, Fall, 1970.

From Figure 2 we can see that between 1965 and 1970 foreign language enrollments were declining, and the study of the uncommonly taught languages in secondary schools declined even more steadily. Figure 3 shows that in 1970 all of the uncommonly taught languages combined accounted for only 7.9 percent of the total 1970 foreign language enrollments, of which Latin enrollments alone accounted for 6.2 percent. Of the remaining 1.7 percent, Italian and Russian accounted for 0.7 percent and 0.4 percent respectively. A complete breakdown of secondary school enrollments in the uncommonly taught languages in 1970 is given below:

Language	Enrollment	Percent
Latin	283,230	(78.8 percent)
Italian	35,741	(9.9 percent)
Russian	23,338	(6.5 percent)
Japanese	8,511	(2.4 percent, Japanese through Navajo)
Portuguese	1,850	
Hebrew	1,454	
Chinese	1,345	
Swahili	1,011	
Polish	524	
Norse	288	
Xhosa	280	
Czech	265	
Ancient Greek	186	
Swedish	168	
Arabic	132	
Hawaiian	122	
Modern Greek	90	
Hungarian	56	
Navajo	25	
Language & level unspecified	929	
Total	359,545	(100.0 percent)

Enrollments in the uncommonly taught languages were by no means spread evenly throughout the country. In fact, among these languages only Latin, Italian, and Russian achieved any wide popularity. Few of the rest were being taught in more than five states, and many were being taught in only one or two.

Limited geographic distribution

Preliminary returns from the 1974 MLA secondary school survey (Table 1) indicate that the decline in overall foreign languages continued through the first half of the decade. There are some very strong gains, however, among the uncommonly taught foreign languages. To project any detailed figures beyond those that have been released by the MLA would be premature; in general, however, double-digit percentage gains between 1970 and 1974 are foreseen for Italian, Chinese, Ancient

Preliminary returns from 1974

Increases in uncommonly taught languages

TABLE 1. Fall 1974 MLA survey of foreign language enrollments in public secondary schools: preliminary tally of enrollments in 27 states (plus the District of Columbia) with complete returns.*

Language	1970	1974	% change
Spanish	1,609,664	1,498,173	—6.9
French	1,138,198	892,300	—21.6
German	333,354	304,131	—8.8
Latin	201,424	132,459	—34.2
Italian	34,472	49,251	+42.9
Russian	16,733	12,436	—25.7
Others	16,415	30,333	+84.8
Total	3,347,065	2,919,083	—12.8

*The states here represented are Arkansas, California, Connecticut, Hawaii, Indiana, Kansas, Kentucky, Louisiana, Maine, Massachusetts, Minnesota, Missouri, Montana, Nebraska, New Hampshire, New Jersey, New York, North Dakota, Ohio, Oklahoma, Pennsylvania, Rhode Island, South Carolina, Texas, Virginia, Washington, and West Virginia. Their enrollments in 1970 represented 73.2% of the national total of foreign language enrollments (4,569,986).

and Modern Greek, Hebrew, Hungarian, Navajo, Norwegian, Polish, Portuguese, and Swedish. In addition, a number of new languages have made their appearance in secondary schools, including Arabic, Armenian, Athabaskan, Finnish, Hindi-Urdu, Chippewa, and Tsimoshean.

College and university enrollments. The picture of enrollments in the uncommonly taught languages at the college and university level is somewhat brighter and more complete than the secondary school picture. (The figures cited include two-year colleges, four-year colleges, and graduate schools.) In comparing Figure 4 with Figure 2, one can see that although the overall percentage of college and university students enrolled in foreign languages in 1970 was far lower than the corresponding secondary school figure, fewer than one secondary school foreign language student in 12 was enrolled in one of the uncommonly taught languages, while the figure for college students was one in seven.

Furthermore, while overall foreign language enrollments in higher education decreased in 1972 and again in 1974, enrollments in the uncommonly taught languages actually showed increases. Although the size of the increases has been small, Figure 4 shows that growth in the study of uncommonly taught languages in higher education has kept pace with growth in total enrollments: In effect, enrollments in these languages have *increased* in relationship to overall foreign language enroll-

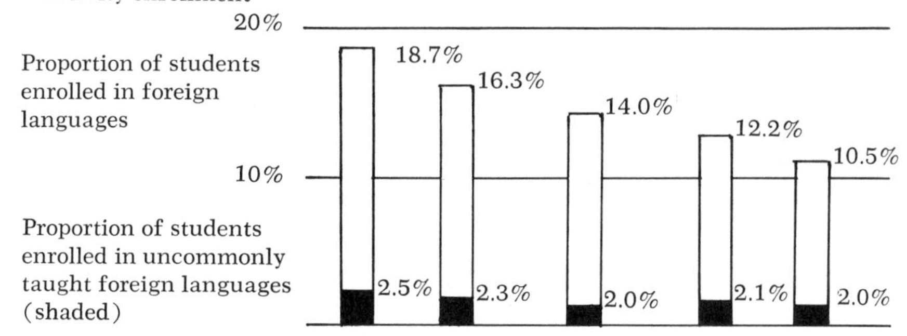

FIGURE 4. College and university enrollments with proportion of students enrolled in foreign languages and proportion of students enrolled in the uncommonly taught foreign languages.

ments, which have in turn been *decreasing* in relationship to total college and university enrollments.

Still uncommon

One should not infer, however, that the term *uncommonly taught* is soon to become inappropriate: As Figure 5 shows, even in 1974 over 80 percent of all language enrollments in higher education were accounted for by Spanish, French, and German. The remaining one fifth was divided among 113 other languages. Of these 113, only 37 had nationwide enrollments of 100 or more; 41 reported enrollments between 11 and 99; and 35 showed *nationwide* enrollments of 10 or fewer.

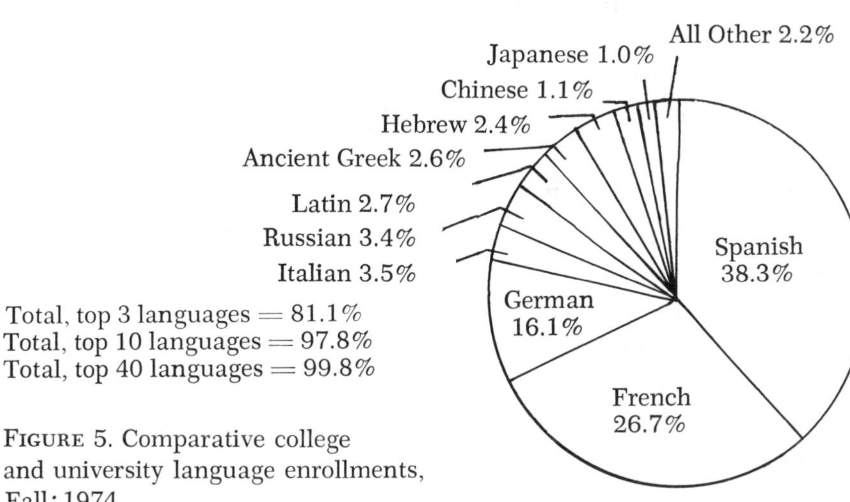

FIGURE 5. Comparative college and university language enrollments, Fall; 1974.

The 40 languages that had enrollments of 100 or more in 1974 are presented, along with other data, in Table 2. In the first group, of course, are the big three–Spanish, French, and German. They are grouped together because their enrollments are far above those of the other languages; but even among these three there is wide variation: Spanish enrollments are nearly half again as high as those in French, and are more than double those in German. Furthermore, all three of these languages showed a decline in enrollments between 1972 and 1974, though the decline in the case of Spanish was extremely slight.

Italian and Russian

Next come Italian and Russian. A slight drop in Italian enrollments and a serious drop in Russian enrollments have resulted in these two languages' exchanging places in the popularity ranking since 1972. Although studied by far fewer students than Spanish, French, and German; Italian and Russian are nonetheless widely taught, each representing about 3.5 percent of the language enrollments on college campuses.

Classical languages and Hebrew

The third group consists of Latin, Ancient Greek, and Hebrew. These languages report enrollments of between 22,000 and 26,000. The traditional classical languages, Latin and Greek, are taught in many more institutions than is Hebrew; but the last, in addition to being a language whose recent popularity may reflect a resurgence of ethnic interest, also derives strength from a large number of religious institutions–Jewish and non-Jewish alike–that offer it. (Because most reports do not distinguish between enrollments in modern and classical Hebrew, no distinction has been made here.) At this third "layer," we note recent gains in all three languages: modest in Latin and Hebrew, very strong in Ancient Greek.

Average enrollment per institution

Some additional aspects of the enrollment figures for Italian, Russian, Latin, Ancient Greek, and Hebrew are noteworthy: If one divides the number of nationwide enrollments in these languages by the number of institutions in the country offering each, the result might be called an "average enrollment per institution" figure. Such a figure is admittedly of limited use, but it does suggest that Hebrew is characterized by relatively few high-enrollment programs; Italian and Russian programs are greater in number than those in Hebrew but, in terms of average enrollment, they are of lesser strength; and the classical languages' popularity reflects a broadly based strength that may well be overshadowed at a given institution by higher enrollments in some of the uncommonly taught *modern* languages.

TABLE 2. "Top 40" foreign languages in higher education, 1972 and 1974.

	Language	1972	1974	1972–74 % Gain (Loss)	Total no. of institutions offering language, 1974
1.	Spanish	364,531	362,151	(0.7%)	1968
2.	French	293,084	253,137	(13.6%)	1912
3.	German	177,062	152,139	(14.1%)	1550
4.	Italian	33,312	32,996	(0.9%)	495
5.	Russian	36,409	32,522	(10.7%)	561
6.	Latin	24,398	25,167	3.2%	530
7.	Ancient Greek	20,584	24,391	18.5%	612
8.	Hebrew	21,091	22,371	6.1%	279
9.	Chinese	9,985	10,576	5.9%	281
10.	Japanese	8,273	9,604	16.1%	166
11.	Portuguese	4,837	5,073	4.9%	146
12.	Arabic	1,669	2,034	21.9%	81
13.	Swahili	2,322	1,694	(27.0%)	70
14.	Norwegian	1,248	1,557	24.8%	32
15.	Swedish	1,166	1,396	19.7%	46
16.	Polish	954	1,123	17.2%	51
17.	Yiddish	912	1,079	18.3%	22
18.	Navajo	273	589	115.7%	6
19.	Hawaiian	461	555	20.4%	6
20.	Modern Greek	379	533	40.6%	25
21.	Dutch	288	456	58.3%	21
22.	Sanskrit	405	402	(0.7%)	28
23.	Aramaic	496	371	(25.2%)	13
24.	Czech	231	337	45.9%	21
25.	Persian	282	278	(1.4%)	18
26.	Old Church Slavic	230	258	12.2%	17
27.	Serbo-Croatian	354	242	(31.6%)	24
28.	Hindi	329	223	(32.2%)	23
29.	Filipino	12	203	1,591.7%	3
30.	Danish	177	183	3.4%	13
31.	Akkadian	166	168	1.2%	12
32.	Hindi-Urdu	115	161	40.0%	9
33.	Turkish	186	156	(16.1%)	22
34.	Finnish	137	134	(2.2%)	9
35.	Tagalog	89	122	37.1%	4
36.	Armenian	110	121	10.0%	7
37.	Indonesian	114	121	6.1%	8
38.	Basque	–	118	–	2
39.	Ukrainian	77	117	51.9%	13
40.	Iranian	72	104	44.4%	6

The fourth group (Chinese, Japanese, and Portuguese) varies as widely from top (Chinese) to bottom (Portuguese) on a percentage basis as does the first group. Nevertheless, these three stand together, being less commonly taught than those above them, yet clearly more popular than those below. These languages exhibit a characteristic typical of the more "exotic" of the uncommonly taught languages: Their popularity seems to depend heavily, although not totally, on support from concentrations of ethnic groups who identify with them. More than one fourth of the Japanese and Chinese enrollments, for example, are located in California; Massachusetts shows a strength in Portuguese that might surprise someone who is unaware of the large Portuguese ethnic concentrations there. Like the Latin-Greek-Hebrew group, this group also posted moderate-to-strong gains in enrollment between 1972 and 1974.

Ethnic influence

The role of ethnic interest becomes even more pronounced in the fifth group (Arabic, Swahili, Norwegian, Swedish, Polish, and Yiddish). These languages are taught at comparatively few institutions; they are often a part of interdisciplinary, linguistics, or graduate programs; and with the exception of Swahili, they have posted strong gains from 1972 to 1974. One might hypothesize that Swahili, like Russian, is settling down after an initially high-attention growth spurt.

High fluctuations in enrollment

The sixth group includes the last of the languages with 1974 enrollments above 100. The sometimes mercurial percentage changes in the enrollments of these languages are, most likely, reflections of the effect of one or two schools' initiating or cancelling courses rather than of a trend in student or national interest. For many of these languages, enrollments are clearly related to the presence of ethnic concentrations near the institution(s) where they are taught: For example, 61 percent of all 1974 Czech enrollments were located in Texas; 100 percent of the Hawaiian enrollments were in Hawaii; and all of the Navajo enrollments were in the four western states of Arizona, Colorado, New Mexico, and Utah.

The seventh and last group (not shown on Table 2) comprises those languages whose reported nationwide enrollments were lower than 100 in 1974. These 73 languages account for only 0.2 percent of the college/university language enrollments, and in most cases they are taught as a kind of ancillary activity

Enrollments below 100

carried on by large language or linguistics departments, either as a matter of individual interest, in conjunction with area studies or other interdisciplinary programs, or as a result of the influence of a local ethnic population. A significant portion of the enrollment in these languages is accounted for by students engaged in independent study programs; many of these programs are affiliated with the National Association of Self-Instructional Language Programs (NASILP).

Factors affecting enrollments

Brod and Scebold (10, pp. 14–15) suggest that at least four factors are significant in an analysis of enrollments in uncommonly taught languages in higher education:

1. *Presence of ethnic identification.* This factor may affect enrollments in Hebrew, Chinese, Japanese, Polish, and Serbo-Croatian, among others.
2 *The language requirement.* Brod and Meyerson (9) report that, among the colleges responding to their surveys, the percentages reporting *entrance* and *degree* foreign language requirements have been dropping steadily over the past decade:

	Colleges with a foreign language *entrance* requirement	Colleges with a foreign language *degree* requirement
1965–66	33.6%	88.9%
1970–71	27.4%	76.7%
1974–75	18.6%	53.2%

Brod and Scebold note that, while Spanish, French, and German bear the brunt of the impact of the widespread trend toward abolition, reduction, or modification of language requirements at undergraduate and graduate levels, the trend seems to be having some effect on the uncommonly taught languages as well.
3 *Political interest.* The spurt of growth of Russian in the 1960s is paralleled in the 1970s by the spurt of growth of Chinese.
4 *Marginality.* This term refers to the permanence and ability of a program to withstand the pressures of cost accounting. Brod and Scebold suggest that marginality affects the commonly taught languages as well as the uncommonly

taught languages, though for the latter, local demand, availability of instructors, and other special factors seem more significant.

Government language schools. The government language teaching enterprise is sizable, and it is particularly significant for its efforts in the uncommonly taught languages, which consistently account for more than half of the student population at the two largest government language schools.

Interagency Language Roundtable

The government language effort is not centralized in any single administrative body. There is, however, coordination through the Interagency Language Roundtable (ILR), which was recently described in an article by Rickerson (44). Rickerson indicated that four of the agencies that participate in the ILR have training programs large and structured enough to be called "schools": the Defense Language Institute (DLI), the State Department's Foreign Service Institute (FSI), the Central Intelligence Agency, and the National Security Agency. Other agencies that are represented in the ILR—either because they have a language training component or because they are consumers or supporters of the language training services offered by the others—include the U.S. Information Agency, the Agency for International Development, the Office of Education, the Drug Enforcement Agency, the Bureau of Indian Affairs, the Foreign Agriculture Office, the Peace Corps, the Customs Bureau, the Civil Service Commission, and the FBI.

Difficulty with comparisons

Enrollment figures for government language teaching agencies are not easily interpreted. Government figures, for example, are compiled on a fiscal-year rather than an academic-year basis. Additionally, students at these schools begin and complete their training in a continual flow; the number of students in training at any given time and in any particular language varies from month to month. This flow of personnel fluctuates in response to many factors: military recruitment, changes in government linguist needs, manpower limitations, and changes in the international situation (p. 3). For example, at the FSI in fiscal year 1970 there were 362 students of Vietnamese; by 1974 this number had shrunk to 15 (Swift, 50). Furthermore, some of the government schools cannot release data on student populations because the figures are classified information.

Manner of instruction

One of the most important differences between the government and academic language teaching communities derives from the fact that virtually all teaching at the government schools is intensive small-group instruction. As a result of this approach, which is carried out by native-proficiency speakers under the guidance and supervision of a staff of linguists, a student who attends a government language school for one year or less may complete language study that would be spread over four years or more at an academic institution.

Differing goals

There are, of course, differences in goals between government and academic language schools. The listening, reading, and speaking skills are generally more important than writing in government schools. (Written foreign language duties are presumably handled by highly qualified specialists.) Culture may or may not receive particular emphasis, depending on the job the student will be doing. (At FSI, where many foreign service officers are trained, culture tends to be more important than at DLI, where the students are principally military language specialists whose duties may require high levels of listening and reading competence in specialized fields only.)

These differences in goals, methods, class size, and number of contact hours have made direct comparison between government and academic language teaching difficult. Perhaps for this reason, an evaluation of DLI and FSI courses was commissioned in 1974 by the American Council on Education so that recommendations for academic credit for individuals who had taken government courses could be made. The evaluation was carried out by members of the academic language teaching community; an excerpt from their report may give the reader an idea of the relationship between DLI courses and university courses as viewed by the evaluators:

Credit evaluations

> With regard to credit evaluations for these courses, it must be emphasized that they are conservative in the extreme. For example, a course which runs for a year (47 weeks) involves the trainee in 1,389 contact hours of class work in small groups, and 460 hours of study for a total of over 1,800 hours. The recommended credit varies from 21 to 27 hours depending on the orthography of the language. Compare this with a typical semi-intensive language course at Cornell

where classes in groups not to exceed 10 students meet 7 hours a week for 30 weeks, or a total of 210 contact hours of instruction (plus outside study and access to a language lab) for 12 credit hours. Or, at Georgetown University where intensive language classes (averaging 10 students each) with supervised individual study sessions meet 12 hours per week per student during a 30-week academic year for a total of 360 contact hours for 12 credit hours (Alatis, Cowan, van Buitenen, 1).

TABLE 3. Total enrollments, number of languages, and non-Spanish, French, and German enrollments at DLI and FSI, 1970 through 1975.

	Fiscal Year	1970	1972	1974	1975
FSI	A. Total Number of students	1,808	1,989	1,660	1,741
	B. Total number of languages taught	35	42	47	48
	C. Non-SFG students	917	928	830	813
	D. C as a % of A	50.7%	46.7%	50.0%	46.7%
DLI	A. Total Number of students	7,901	5,446	2,973	2,749
	B. Total number of languages taught	45	25	22	24
	C. Non-SFG students	6,764	4,379	2,071	1,937
	D. C as a % of A	85.6%	80.4%	69.7%	70.5%
DLI & FSI	Total number of students	9,709	7,435	4,633	4,490
	Non-SFG students	7,681	5,307	2,901	2,750
	Non-SFG students as a % of total number of students	79.1%	71.4%	62.6%	61.2%

Size comparisons

Table 3 provides DLI and FSI enrollment statistics for recent years. To gain some perspective on the size of a given year's student body at DLI or FSI, one might multiply a year's DLI or FSI student body by 3 (to allow for the concentration and intensiveness of foreign language study at government institutions) and then by 8 (to allow for the fact that only 10 percent to 12 percent of the students at a university are enrolled in a foreign language). If this is done, a DLI or FSI student body of 1,800 corresponds to the number of foreign language students one might expect to find at a university of more than 43,000!

A striking fact shown by Table 3 is that the uncommonly

taught languages consistently account for well over half of the students at DLI and FSI in any given year. Furthermore, while school and college overall language enrollments have been showing decreases year after year, government needs for civilians trained in languages, as represented by FSI enrollment figures, have remained relatively constant (though emphasis on a particular language may fluctuate widely). Nevertheless, in 1974 the combined DLI-FSI student body was less than 0.5 percent of the total foreign language enrollments reported in higher education for that year.

In summarizing the current enrollment picture, we should note that several spheres of foreign language study in the United States have not been considered in this section due to lack of information: public and nonpublic elementary schools, nonpublic secondary schools, and commercial language schools.

Available materials

1974 materials conference

The most recent national conference to survey material needs in the uncommonly taught languages was convened by the U.S. Office of Education in 1974. The conference produced recommendations on current and future priority needs for instructional materials in these languages. Eight papers, each dealing with a specific geographic area, discuss what is available and what is needed in African languages; Amerind and Creole languages in the Americas and the Caribbean; Chinese, Japanese, and Korean languages; languages of the Near and Middle East (Arabic and Persian); Slavic and East European languages; languages of South Asia; languages of Southeast Asia; and Uralic-Altaic and Inner Asian languages.

Basic tools of access

The needs in these languages are so diverse as to preclude concise summary. However, most of the papers are concerned with the availability of the so-called "basic tools of access" to a given language. One paper defines these tools as:

1 *An adequate description of the language* should include a survey of the speech area to determine geographic and stylistic variants as well as a student reference grammar.
2 *An adequate student dictionary* should include tone, where relevant, and other necessary grammatical data.
3 *Articulated pedagogic materials,* in broad terms, are: basic course, intermediate course, advanced course, which are to

> provide adequate spoken (and reading, where relevant) control of the language, with cultural understanding (Hodge and Spears, 22, p. 47).

A teacher of Spanish, French, or German may be somewhat shocked to realize that, while he is faced with the problem of choosing from an often bewildering array of texts (not to mention the vast amount of supplementary materials that are available) for his classroom, teachers of other languages—even of some widely spoken languages—are limited to one or two texts and one or two dictionaries. In some cases even these are not available.

Among languages with college and university enrollments above 1,000 (see Table 2), the reports of the 1974 conference make no mention of any materials development needs in Spanish, French, German, Italian, Latin, Ancient Greek, Hebrew, Portuguese, Norwegian, Swedish, or Yiddish. Although improvements could certainly be made in most present materials, development needs are particularly critical in Arabic.

Needs critical for Arabic

Among the languages with enrollments below 1,000, some are designed as more urgently in need of attention than others. The criterion applied in making decisions on these languages appears to reflect the contemporary economic and political "clout" of the population(s) using them. Thus, ". . . any language, whether present on the list or not, may be given appropriate priority when political or cultural changes justify such action" (Hodge and Spears, 22, p. 47).

The role of government efforts

Development of teaching materials for the uncommonly taught languages seems to have been largely dependent on federal funding in the past (Thompson, 53) and will probably continue to be dependent. The government language schools regularly develop their own language teaching materials in all languages, and for some of the uncommonly taught languages these are the *only* readily available materials. There is also considerable government support for materials development by the academic sector, made available through Section 602 of the NDEA Title VI program.

Professional organizations

While many teachers of the uncommonly taught languages

are active in their national professional organizations, the real strength of a national organization often depends on the extent of its programs at the local level. The fact that one may be "the only Russian teacher in town" or "the only Japanese teacher on campus" must have its effect. Still, for languages that have an AAT-, such organizations provide a forum in journals and at national meetings for the discussion of common problems. Semiautonomous affiliates, if any, often hold meetings also.

Local activities

An attempt was made to gather information about as many of the organizations of teachers of uncommonly taught languages as could be located. The data are presented at the end of this chapter. It would be misleading, however, to define "professional organizations" narrowly and discuss them without mentioning the wide spectrum of interdisciplinary and ethnic heritage organizations that also serve to stimulate interest in the uncommonly taught languages. Indeed, as Brod (4) pointed out in referring to the various area studies organizations, ". . . the recognition of a need for expert specialists was after all a prime force behind the passage of NDEA and still carries great weight in government and academic circles." Some of the largest and most influential of the area studies organizations were described by Thompson (53, pp. 297–302). Lambert (31) presents an even more detailed examination of the scope and status of language and area studies in the United States.

Area studies organizations

The influence of the ethnic heritage organizations should not be ignored. Their existence provides teachers and students of the uncommonly taught languages with a wealth of resources that traditional governmental and academic circles cannot offer. Some of the larger of these organizations, such as the Kosciuszko Foundation, even offer students generous financial support for language and culture study in the country of interest. Information on the activities of the area studies and ethnic heritage organizations may be obtained by writing directly to them; the addresses of many are listed by language, country, or area of interest in the continually updated *Encyclopedia of Associations* (18).

Ethnic heritage organizations

Support from the federal government

The national interest in the uncommonly taught languages

is manifested not only in government language schools, but also in Title VI of the National Defense Education Act. Both Petrov (41) and Thompson (53) present capsule histories of the NDEA program; updated NDEA data for this section were provided by the U.S. Office of Education (Thompson, 51).

NDEA Title VI

Language and area centers. This facet of the NDEA program can be divided into three phases (Twarog, 56): In Phase I (1958–73) emphasis was on training language and area specialists. Although only graduate training was originally included, undergraduate training had also become a major thrust by the end of this phase. Phase II (1973–76) saw the number of centers halved (from over 100 to approximately 50), with competition for center awards growing more and more intense and with a new emphasis on programs of community service ("outreach" programs). The competition for center awards for Phase III (1976–79) is beginning now. Unofficial guidelines for this competition indicate that "outreach" programs are to be allocated a minimum of 15 percent of proposed center budgets, which will undoubtedly result in the centers' becoming more service-oriented.

Outreach programs

In 1975–76 there were 66 NDEA language and area centers funded for a total of over $5.7 million. They are listed in Table 4 by world area of concern.

The effect that these centers have had in higher education is well illustrated by the data in Table 5, which shows the number of degrees, by geographic area, awarded at the centers between 1959 and 1973. (More recent data were not available.) These figures for total degrees granted represent many disciplines besides language. (For a breakdown by discipline of degrees awarded in a recent year, see Table 6.) Instruction in the uncommonly taught languages will benefit as more and more specialists with interest in countries where these languages are spoken are graduated. Indeed, 46,264 (61.6 percent) of the degrees shown in Table 5 were awarded in geographic areas of concern *other* than Latin America and Northwest Europe.

Tangible results

Summer intensive language programs. The U.S. Office of Education (USOE) no longer funds summer intensive language programs as such. Many institutions maintain their own summer intensive programs without federal help, and some of the language and area centers reported above may use some of their

TABLE 4. NDEA Title VI language and area centers, 1975–76.

GENERAL
Columbia University (with CUNY) (W. Europe)
University of Denver (Comparative Studies)
Duke University (Canadian Studies)
University of Hawaii (Pacific Studies)
Indiana University (Inner Asia)
Tufts University (Fletcher School)

LATIN AMERICA
University of California at Los Angeles
University of Florida
University of New Mexico
University of Texas
Tulane University
University of Wisconsin

USSR AND EAST EUROPE
University of California at Berkeley
Columbia University
Indiana University
University of Michigan
Ohio State University
University of Pittsburgh
University of Washington
Yale University
University of California at Los Angeles
University of Illinois
University of Kansas
University of Oregon
University of Vermont

AFRICA
University of California at Los Angeles
University of Illinois
Indiana University
Northwestern University
Stanford University
University of Wisconsin

SOUTHEAST ASIA
Cornell University
University of Michigan
Ohio University (at Athens)

EAST ASIA
Cornell University
Duke University
University of Texas
University of Virginia
University of Chicago
Columbia University
Harvard University
University of Michigan
Princeton University
Stanford University (with University of California at Berkeley)
University of Washington
Yale University
Amherst College (with Smith College)
Carleton College (with St. Olaf College)
University of Colorado (with University of Denver)

SOUTH ASIA
University of California at Berkeley
University of Chicago
University of Minnesota
University of Pennsylvania
University of Washington
University of Wisconsin

NEAR AND MIDDLE EAST
University of Utah
University of Washington
University of California at Berkeley
University of California at Los Angeles
University of Chicago
Harvard University
University of Michigan
University of Pennsylvania
Princeton University (with New York University)
University of Arizona
Portland State University

funds to support summer intensive language programs. There is, however, no longer any specific USOE commitment to fund summer intensive language programs.

TABLE 5. Degrees awarded at NDEA language and area centers, 1959–73, by geographic area of concern.

Area	B.A.	M.A.	Ph.D.
Asia (general)	3,884	2,001	512
East Asia	5,967	1,748	555
Inner Asia	43	78	30
South and Southeast Asia	1,480	595	266
Southeast Asia	66	227	132
South Asia	1,250	757	425
Asia and East Europe	278	150	28
Middle East	3,112	1,101	585
Soviet Union and East Europe	9,655	3,650	1,172
Northwest Europe	321	79	31
Africa	3,789	2,091	637
Latin America	19,577	6,472	2,347
TOTAL	49,422	18,949	6,720

TABLE 6. NDEA language and area studies degrees awarded, by discipline, 1972–73.

	B.A.	M.A.	Ph.D.
Language and Literature	1,352	376	173
Linguistics	142	113	59
Area studies (general)	502	280	20
American studies	23	17	3
Anthropology	424	79	54
Demography	0	0	0
Economics	254	88	56
Fine Arts	181	50	14
Geography	107	33	21
History	1,012	224	126
International relations	138	114	14
Music	7	5	1
Natural sciences	185	19	9
Philosophy and religion	181	17	8
Political science	742	170	87
Psychology	230	3	5
Sociology	309	56	23
Agriculture	21	8	14
Architecture and urban planning	20	10	2
Business	129	56	15
Education	237	114	48
Engineering	36	14	6
Health professions	23	13	5
Journalism	155	27	9
Law	23	31	10
Library science	7	37	1
Public administration	0	2	1
Social work	8	1	0
Speech	7	0	1
Theater	4	3	2
Unspecified	331	0	0
Total	6,790	1,960	787

NDFL Title VI fellowships. The National Defense Foreign Language fellowships continue to provide economic assistance *specifically for language study.* Table 7 compares the data presented by Thompson (53) on graduate NDFL awards by geographical area of concern from 1959 to 1970 with similar data from 1970 to 1974. The two time periods differ with respect to the proportion of fellowships granted for study in the various geographic areas of concern. In general, the figures show that over the entire 1959–74 period, over 85 percent of all graduate NDFL awards were made for geographic areas *other* than Western Europe and Latin America. In particular, the languages of Southeast Asia, East Asia, and Africa seem to have accounted for larger proportions during the 1970–74 period than they did during the 1959–70 period.

TABLE 7. Graduate NDFL awards by geographic area of concern.

Area	1959–70		1970–74	
Eastern Europe and USSR	2,907	(20.1%)	679	(15.1%)
Southeast Asia	602	(4.2%)	346	(7.7%)
East Asia	3,668	(25.4%)	1,250	(27.8%)
South Asia	1,460	(10.1%)	463	(10.3%)
Africa	1,130	(7.8%)	488	(10.9%)
Near and Middle East	2,211	(15.3%)	699	(15.6%)
Western Europe	182	(1.3%)	72	(1.6%)
Latin America	2,305	(15.9%)	493	(11.0%)
Total	14,468	(100.0%)	4,490	(100.0%)

Language and area research studies. Thompson (53) notes that research under this portion of NDEA is classified under six broad headings: surveys and studies, conferences, methods of instruction, specialized materials for commonly taught languages, specialized materials for uncommonly taught languages, and foreign area studies. Total expenditures during the period between 1959 and 1974 have amounted to $43.7 million (Petrov, 41). Petrov notes that

> the Research Program has supported work in 146 languages or language groups and contracted for some 49 studies in basic linguistic research, 24 linguistic analyses, 116 level-one and 38 level-two basic courses, a total of 131 graded readers, 49 reference grammars, 57 dictionaries and glossaries, 153 sets of basic or advanced recordings to accompany the printed materials, 26 bibliographies, and 26 language manuals. Sup-

> plementary materials . . . add up to some 30 additional items (p. 8).

Petrov also indicates that the level of funding for these types of programs is decreasing: "typical years in the late sixties provided an average [expenditure] of about $2.8 million. However, starting with fiscal year 1971, language research appropriations dropped to slightly under $1 million" (p. 8).

Petrov refers those interested in tangible results of the program to *List No.* 7 (Petrov, 42); this list is now somewhat out of date, but it gives some idea of the range of publications that have come from the research studies program.

Other federal support. The influence of the federal government has not been limited to providing NDEA monies. Most language teachers are aware, for instance, of the revolution in foreign language teaching inspired by the "Army Method" of the 1940s. While its descendent methods and activities were and are having wide effect 20 and 30 years later in schools and colleges across the nation, many foreign language educators are only dimly aware of the extent of the continuing federal government interest. Rickerson (44) points out:

> Since the federal government is by far the largest language-teaching establishment in the country—with a budget of over $60 million a year—it is not surprising that the government language community has a powerful interest in finding ways to teach foreign languages more effectively (p. 3). Rickerson notes that the Interagency Language Roundtable (ILR) has standing committees on Research, Materials Development, and Testing. From his description of a new course in Chinese being developed under the aegis of the ILR, we can see that the developers of the course are in tune with current trends in foreign language education:
>
> It is an innovative course, *modular* in design, and synthesizing much of what has been advocated in the professional literature of the past ten years: It relies heavily on *programmed instruction* for the input of new material, *leans away from habit-formation* to stress *communicative activities,* and consciously incorporates features that will permit *individualized instruction* (pp. 10 and 14) [emphasis added].

New course in Chinese

The National Endowment for the Humanities has recently given a grant to The Ohio State University for the development of individualized instruction programs in several foreign languages. Based on what is reported here and in other sections of this chapter, we can predict that the government will continue to play a major role in materials development and in the training of personnel in the uncommonly taught languages.

Other influential factors

The role of ethnic concentrations. Many of the uncommonly taught languages are taught at institutions that are located in communities with an identifiable ethnic tie to a given language. In attempting to determine what contribution the ethnic community makes to a given institution's language program, a questionnaire was sent to selected institutions. By far the largest portion of those responding checked "Informal Contact"; somewhat fewer checked "Cultural"; very few checked "Financial" or "Instructional." One respondent noted that the presence of an ethnic population is a mixed blessing: Although it accounts for a large enrollment, which in turn helps funding, it also creates an uneven linguistic background among students.

Informal contact

The role of the teacher supply. On the secondary school level there have been reports of administrators who were reluctant to start programs in uncommonly taught languages because of the possibility that a program, once started, would be cancelled peremptorily if the teacher were suddenly to leave (Brod and Scebold, 10; Cote, 16). Principles of supply and demand seem to indicate, however, that declining student enrollments have a more decisive effect on the existence of programs in these languages than does the teacher supply.

Teacher supply as a factor

The teacher supply does not appear to play a major role in enrollments at the postsecondary level. The majority of questionnaire respondents reported that "obtaining qualified instructors" is "not a serious problem," though 14 percent of them indicated that it is "somewhat of a problem." (Because of the relatively small number of questionnaires returned in any given language, no firm conclusions about the teacher supply in individual languages can be drawn.)

The government language schools indicate that in several languages obtaining qualified instructors *is* a problem. This is particularly true for some of the languages spoken in countries from which emigration is restricted, which undoubtedly limits the availability of teachers who meet the native or near-native proficiency level required by the government language schools.

Business world

The needs of the business world. One would suppose that major developments in the international business community tend to be accompanied by increased employment for individuals with foreign language qualifications. A recent news article, for instance, reported that at All-Language Services, Inc., a Manhattan agency that provides a wide-ranging translation service in 59 languages, the language currently in greatest demand is Arabic. The company now employs more than 30 Arabic translators, compared with two on the staff before the oil-rich Arab world flexed its economic muscle. The article also noted that, although the demand for Chinese is still limited, the number of Russian translators had climbed from 12 to 40 in six months (Liston, 34). Although such increases in the language needs of the business world are noteworthy, there is room to speculate on the extent of their *direct* effect on the school and college language enrollments. The same article pointed out that when All-Language Services assigns a team of linguists, technical personnel, lawyers, accountants, and editors to an effort such as translating an annual corporate report into a foreign language, each team member is *native* to the target language. As long as the American business world views language as an auxiliary rather than a primary skill, the business world's language needs probably will not greatly affect language enrollments here.

Some current issues

Questionnaire and interviews

To determine current concerns and trends in the teaching of the uncommonly taught languages, a questionnaire was sent to departments of Slavic, Oriental, Middle-Eastern, and Classical languages at schools and universities throughout the United States. Responses were analyzed for 1) Russian, Polish, Serbo-Croatian, Czech, and Ukrainian; 2) Chinese and Japanese; 3) Arabic and Hebrew; and 4) Greek and Latin. To supplement survey information with firsthand observations about the teaching of these languages interviews were held with instructors.

Funding

Among the responses from Slavic language departments, only 16 percent of those in Russian (the most widely taught Slavic language) indicated that obtaining funding for present courses was a "serious problem." The presence of ethnic populations and their direct or indirect financial support might offer an explanation for the fact that such funding is "not a problem" at all for 44 percent of those teaching Polish, Ukrainian, Czech, and Serbo-Croatian and was only "somewhat of a problem" for the other 56 percent. Obtaining funds was also generally not considered a problem for the Classical languages, Latin and Greek, and the Middle-Eastern languages, Arabic and Hebrew. However, responses from Oriental language departments (Chinese and Japanese) showed that for 43 percent of the instructional programs, funding for existing courses was considered a serious problem. Growth and expansion seem to be difficult for all of the uncommonly taught languages: 66 percent of total responses showed that funding for innovative courses was difficult to obtain.

Texts and supplementary materials

Acquiring good basic texts was considered to be at least "somewhat of a problem" by 76 percent of the respondents in the Slavic languages, 78 percent in Middle-Eastern languages, 57 percent in Oriental languages, and 60 percent in Classical languages. Likewise, obtaining supplementary language materials (realia, tapes, visuals) was considered to be somewhat of a problem by 59 percent, 67 percent, and 57 percent of those teaching Slavic, Middle-Eastern, and Oriental languages respectively.

Staffing

In answer to a query concerning the availability of instructors, a majority of total respondents (86 percent) indicated that obtaining a qualified staff was not a problem for them. A similar percentage felt that obtaining up-to-date information about the teaching of their specific language was not difficult.

Some methodological issues

Although considerations of materials, staff, and dissemination of current research findings were viewed optimistically by the teachers of the uncommonly taught languages, the actual classroom methodology employed sometimes seems to require extra effort and ingenuity. In response to a question concerning the difficulties that American students encounter in learning

Slavic, Oriental, Classical, or Middle-Eastern languages, broad areas of grammar, vocabulary, and pronunciation were most commonly cited, just as they would be by teachers of any foreign language. The pedagogical strategies employed to cope with these problems, as indicated by the responses on the questionnaire, were also similar to those employed by teachers of French, Spanish, or German–systematic presentation of rules, grammatical exercises, individual or small-group instruction, repetition, practice, use of the language laboratory, and sponsorship of social language houses.

Typical concerns, typical solutions

A closer look, however, reveals that these broad areas of grammar, vocabulary, and pronunciation include some very specific complexities. The Slavic, Middle-Eastern, and Classical languages have highly inflected morphological systems that require skills in analyzing the mechanism of the language as well as attention to the formation of words. This is especially true in Arabic and Hebrew, where roots containing semantic meaning, such as *k-t-v* with its implication of "writing" in Hebrew, interact with almost algebraic precision to derive related words of the same or different categories, such as *katav* (wrote) or *ktiva* (writing). Cases and verbal aspects were frequently mentioned by teachers of the Slavic languages as constituting problem areas. Japanese word order, with its placement of the verb at the end of the sentence and the use of particles to indicate topic and the direct subject of the verb, requires practice by native speakers of English. Vocabulary building, too, seems more difficult for the students of Slavic, Oriental, and Middle-Eastern languages because of the relative absence of cognates.

Unique difficulties

Japanese word order

In the area of pronunciation the sound system of the Oriental languages may be among the most difficult for American students to master. If not properly observed by the student, tones in Chinese, which signal differences in meaning of some words, and lack of vowel nasalization in Japanese (which occurs naturally and subconsciously in speaking English) can cause misunderstanding or at best an American accent. Teachers of Slavic languages other than Russian mention an area of interference in addition to transfer of English habits: They point out that because many of their students previously have studied Russian, negative transfer in both vocabulary and pronunciation is common. Teachers of Classical Latin, theoretically removed from

Chinese tones

the problems of pronunciation because their language is no longer spoken, are nonetheless frequently concerned with the oral component. They note that the full significance of some reading passages can be appreciated only by reference to its oral rendition–that is, by the melodic interplay of its consonants, stress, and rhythm.

Availability of language laboratories

As in the teaching of Spanish, French, or German, instruction in the Slavic, Middle-Eastern, and Oriental phonological systems is facilitated by the use of language laboratories in addition to careful classroom modeling. A full 100 percent of the respondents to the questionnaire indicated that they had access to language laboratories. Their usefulness (including available tape materials) was rated from extremes of poor to excellent.

Presenting a new orthography

Reading and writing represent a particularly significant area of pedagogical concern for languages that are not written with the Roman alphabet. The Cyrillic letters used in Russian, the characters in Chinese and Japanese orthography, Arabic script, and Hebrew and Greek letters are generally new to American students. Careful attention must be given to graded, sequential development of the psychomotor aspects of reading and writing, especially when a change in directionality is involved, as in the right to left reading of Arabic and Hebrew or the vertical placement of Oriental characters. Chinese and Japanese instruction in the literate skills is complicated by the fact that a character may have more than one meaning, depending on context. Thus instruction in reading generally progresses from basic sound-symbol correspondences, to word recognition, to comprehension of sentences and narratives, and finally to literature. The writing skill is also developed gradually, beginning with basic activities that relate print to script forms: These can differ significantly, as the two Hebrew forms ש (print) ש (script) of the same letter show. Then come copying activities followed by successively more complicated activities, culminating finally in free creative writing.

Interference in reading and writing

Interference from the Roman alphabet may be a problem in both reading and writing when the target language contains letters similar in form but not in pronunciation to those in the native language. Thus, the printed Russian letters *B*, *H*, and *Y*, which represent the sounds /v/ and /n/ and /u/, respectively, are often confusing for the student.

Attention to criterial attributes

With the presentation of any new alphabet, special attention must be given to the criterial attributes that serve to distinguish letters: The Hebrew *tav* ת, for instance, is written with a curved foot to the left that is absent from the otherwise identical *xet* ח. Additional complications may arise when a single letter has more than one form. In Arabic, the sound /f/ may be represented by three different shapes depending on its position in the word: ـف (final), ـفـ (medial), and فـ (initial).

The orthography of Oriental languages requires attention to the number, position, and relative length of the strokes as well as to the overall shape, composition, and spacing of the characters. The use of Chinese character sheets represents an effective means of ensuring both proper stroke order and the necessary practice obtained through repetition. A written character, color-coded to distinguish the radical from the phonetic element, is presented in various stages of completion. The student begins by tracing the completed letter and continues from left to right filling in missing strokes as the number of guidelines decreases progressively. At the end of the line there are empty spaces where, completely unaided, the student writes the character. The more complicated the character, the more times the student is required to write it. A glance at the progression of required fill-ins reveals the correct stroke order. A sample from a character sheet is presented below (Ching, 14, p. 24):

Chinese character sheets

Varied reactions to transliteration

Although teachers of languages that do not have a Roman-based alphabet indicated that transliteration was available in instructional texts, the degree of enthusiasm about the use of phonetic transcription varied. Chinese texts utilizing Romanization are used successfully to teach basic grammar and vocabulary prior to presenting the 3,000 basic characters (30 characters average each week). Many instructors of Hebrew and Russian note, however, that students sometimes become very dependent on the transcription, making transfer to the target alphabet and recognition of words that have already been used orally difficult. The instructors point out that memorization of the entire printed alphabet, involving 27 different forms in Hebrew and 32 in Russian, does not represent an awesome task. Presentation of the orthography of Hebrew may actually simplify the instructional task of highlighting lexical roots that are not obvious in oral production.

Sociolinguistic concerns

Another area of concern in the teaching of the uncommonly taught languages is the use of the language in social contexts. While polite and familiar differences affect primarily pronominal and verbal forms in the Romance and Germanic languages, for example, honorifics in Japanese affect entire sentences. Social status disparities in Japanese, male-female distinctions, and transactional relationships (who is performing the action for whom) permeate even the most objective utterances. Thus, most verbs have two forms: a neutral and a polite. Arabic, however, differentiates along social and functional lines by the use of two "dialects"; modern standard and colloquial. Modern standard Arabic is used in all written work and formally on the radio, television, and in lectures; the colloquial form is used for informal or interfamilial occasions and is not written.

Although teachers of Slavic, Oriental, Middle-Eastern, and Classical languages readily acknowledge the difficulties associated with instruction in their particular language, most are quick to point out that their language is actually quite accessible to the motivated learner. Teachers of Arabic speak of overcoming the initial reluctance of many Americans to attempt anything as foreign as a new writing system or pharyngealized consonants. Systematic and guided presentation, however, soon promotes ease and enthusiasm in learning. Teachers of Chinese, too, admit that a great deal of patience, perseverance, and sheer memorization is involved in learning the characters of the orthography; at the same time they point out that the relative simplicity of the grammar, which is not inflected for either tense or number, facilitates learning the spoken language. In the same way, teachers of Greek regard time, effort, and interest as key elements ensuring success in the mastery of a new symbol system.

Reluctance, then enthusiasm

These attitudes are most meaningfully interpreted in reference to stated goals in language instruction. While the questionnaire respondents from the Oriental languages indicated that the specified areas—listening-speaking, reading, writing, and cul-

Differential emphasis on the goals

ture—received similar emphasis in language instruction, Slavic and Middle-Eastern language respondents placed a greater emphasis on the oral skills and reading. Creative writing and culture received "little emphasis" from the majority in both groups. Teachers of the Classical languages indicated that their primary concern is with the reading and writing skills and is secondarily with the culture of the ancient societies.

Trends

The ingenuity shown by individual teachers of the uncommonly taught languages in easing the sometimes unusual demands of learning new alphabets or phonological systems is reflected in the diversity of programs offered by these teachers. From information on the questionnaire, the following types of instruction were found to be available in many Slavic, Classical, Middle Eastern, or Oriental languages.

Diverse programs

Bilingual education. Bilingual programs were reported in all of the modern languages included in the survey. Where once only French and Spanish were discussed in the context of bilingual-bicultural needs, Japanese, Chinese, Navajo, Indian, and many of the Slavic languages are receiving attention because of the large ethnic populations in the United States that speak these languages. These languages are considered native rather than foreign, however, and as such, bilingual programs are beyond the scope of the present chapter.

Career education. Questionnaire returns showed that career-oriented language courses were available in Arabic, Hebrew, Russian, Japanese, and Chinese; there are undoubtedly others as well. Many language instructors in programs without such courses expressed a need or desire for them. Responses from Russian instructors, for instance, showed that all of the programs not currently offering Russian for careers (50 percent of the respondents) listed this type of course as a high priority option in future program expansion. Significantly, none of the other Slavic languages currently have such courses. In view of the more limited business opportunities to use Czech or Serbo-Croatian, for example, such a lack is understandable.

Literature and area/culture. In both the target language and in English, literature and area/culture were the most frequent type of nonlanguage courses included in language programs, according to the survey. Such courses are given in all of the languages included in the survey; 92 percent of total respondents indicated the existence of literature courses in the target language, and 80 percent had literature courses in translation. Area/culture courses in the target language were reported by 53 percent of the respondents, and 70 percent of them reported such a course given in English.

Immersion courses. Total immersion courses, not always available even in the major languages, were reported to be available by 31 percent of the respondents. When instruction in the uncommonly taught languages is restricted by funds or staffing problems, intensive courses given during the summer and open to participants from many universities can be a viable alternative.

Independent study. This instructional description may encompass diverse types of activities such as private study of basic language materials when small enrollment precludes the opening of a regular course or pursuit of specific literary interests by advanced students. Regardless of specific definition, independent study as an option was found to be available among 80 percent of the respondents, with all languages surveyed represented in that figure.

Individualized programs. Programs with some form of individualization exist for all of the languages surveyed. The total positive response (62 percent) may include the use of programmed texts, self-pacing through traditional texts, or the use of self-instructional materials.

NASILP

A significant share of the current enrollment in the uncommonly taught languages at the postsecondary school level, particularly in languages with nationwide enrollments of 100 or fewer, is accounted for by individuals in programs affiliated with the National Association of Self-Instructional Language Programs (NASILP). Although the organization dates formally from only 1972, it had its origins in 1963. Conceived by Boyd-Bowman (currently NASILP's Executive Secretary) and funded initially by the Carnegie Corporation and the USOE's Institute for International Studies, in the spring semester of 1974 the program reported 1,345 students at 42 colleges enrolled in 38 different languages. Under the general administrative supervision of a designated campus NASILP administrator, the NASILP student utilizes a textbook, tapes, and weekly tutorials with a native speaker (who is often a foreign student at the same institution) to make progress in his chosen language at his own rate. At the end of the term NASILP-designated outside examiners in each language meet with and test students to evaluate their progress and recommend credit and grades to the local institution's administrator. The local institution, which has collected regular tuition from the student, thus grants credit to the student. Costs per student (principally for the tutor and the outside examiner) are reportedly on a par with costs per student in normal classroom instruction, thus enabling "classes" of one or two students to continue in a variety of low-enrollment languages. NASILP invites both individual and institutional inquiries about its programs. Information is available from Dr. Peter Boyd-Bowman, Center for Critical Languages, Richmond Quadrangle, SUNY at Buffalo, Amherst Campus, Buffalo, New York 14261.

NEH grant for individualized instruction

A recent four-year grant by the National Endowment for the Humanities to The Ohio State University for developing individualized instruction programs in foreign languages seems to hold promise for the future. Funds have been provided to develop materials, initiate programs, and evaluate the success of individualized study in six languages: Arabic, French, German, Latin, Russian, and Spanish. A pilot program in Latin has been functioning since September 1975, with favorable initial reactions from students and faculty (Jarvis, 25).

CALI

Computer-assisted instruction. Although only 8 percent of the respondents actually had programs utilizing a computer, computer-assisted Language Instruction (CALI) was found to be available among all of the language groups surveyed. The use of computers to guide the learning process efficiently and economically hold much promise. Nelson et al. (39) suggest that the reluctance of foreign language teachers to accept CALI is attributable in part to psychological reasons and in part to economic considerations, though the advantages of CALI have been amply described. Kalbouss (27) states that computer access for education is available on both the secondary and postsecondary levels and may be adapted for language instruction by a "time-sharing system" at a per-student cost in the same range as a library or physical education fee. Nelson and Kalbouss agree that there is a wide diversity of approaches to the computer in a wide range of languages: CALI has already been applied to the teaching of Russian (Curtin et al., 17), Latin (Scanlan, 46), and most recently, to Arabic: With the help of a computer, the task of learning the Arabic phonology and script can be accomplished in six to 20 class hours (Cadora, 11). Additionally, CALI programs for the instruction of French, Spanish, and German have been implemented and publicized (Nelson et al., 39).

A particularly well-known CALI effort is The University of Illinois Project, called PLATO (Programmed Logic for Automatic Teaching Operations), which includes programs in French, Spanish, German, Latin, Russian, Chinese, and Japanese. Considered a pioneer in the field, PLATO was unique in utilizing a special screen console, audio, and slide equipment in addition to the familiar teletype (Kalbouss, 27).

PLATO

CALI is of high interest to teachers of uncommonly taught languages because it offers a practical alternative when enrollments are small and instructional staff is limited.

Affective learning activities. The inclusion of classroom activities utilizing personal experiences of the learners as the basis for language lesson content, instead of strictly textual material, was reported by 14 percent of the respondents. Considering the newness of this attempt to humanize language instruction more fully and the relative unfamiliarity of many language teachers with the concept, this percentage of programs in the uncommonly taught languages including affective activities in the classroom is highly encouraging.

Study-abroad programs. Study-abroad programs suit virtually any age, time, goal, and expense requirements that a student of Spanish, French, or German may have. One wonders, however, to what extent a student of Serbo-Croatian or Kannada could avail himself of the language experience abroad that Carroll (13) has found so beneficial for the development of fluency. The Institute of International Education reports that the study-abroad field grew in size and scope in 1974–75 and:

> Programs are becoming more whole world oriented. Asia and Africa have grown in favor with those desiring study overseas. Europe still continues to dominate the study-abroad field

Study in Asia and Africa

as the area most popular with students, but study abroad is increasingly coming to mean semesters in Nairobi or Tokyo (Cohen, 15, p. 1).

Helpful publications

Fortunately, there are inexpensive, continually updated publications available to help foreign language teachers and students locate and compare study-abroad programs. Three publications in particular that include sections of interest to students of uncommonly taught languages are *U.S. College-Sponsored Programs Abroad* ($3.50) and *Summer Study Abroad* ($3.00), both available from the Institute of International Education, 809 United Nations Plaza, New York, N. Y. 10017; and the *Whole World Handbook* ($2.95), available from the Council on International Educational Exchange, 777 United Nations Plaza, New York, N. Y. 10017. Many of the programs described are open to high school students.

Summary

Nearly two decades ago there arose a renewed national concern about the quality of American education. In particular, great interest was expressed in the teaching of foreign languages. In the intervening years, however, foreign language instruction has attracted fewer and fewer students, despite the expenditure of considerable sums of public money to support research and development in language teaching methods and materials.

As a group, the uncommonly taught languages (languages other than Spanish, French, and German) have benefited and continue to benefit greatly from the availability of government funds and activities that support their instruction. They seem to be benefiting, as well, from a heightened ethnic awareness in the United States and from an increased awareness of the importance of the languages of nations that only recently have begun to develop their own economic and political strengths. Although in any absolute terms their enrollments are low, many of these languages have been gaining students in recent years, in sharp contrast to the overall trend in foreign language enrollments.

Teachers of the uncommonly taught languages employ a

variety of methods to acquaint American students with orthographic and phonological systems that may at first appear forbidding. Indeed, because teachers of these languages do not have the vast selection of language teaching materials that is available to teachers of Spanish, French, and German, extra demands are made on their ingenuity and energy. There is also an appreciable amount of activity among these teachers in the developing areas of bilingual education, career education, intensive/immersion courses, independent study, individualized instruction, and computer-assisted instruction.

As technological advances make the world grow smaller and as the nations of Africa, Asia, Eastern Europe, and the Middle East become more influential in world affairs, the prospects for growth in instruction in the uncommonly taught languages are enhanced. While there is no question that the traditional languages will dominate language instruction in the United States for the foreseeable future, there are signs that the role to be played by the uncommonly taught languages in foreign language education in America will expand.

References, Expanding the options: Curricula in many languages

1 Alatis, James, J. M. Cowan, and J. A. B. van-Buitenen. *Report to the American Council on Education,* 1974. [Mimeo.]

2 Bagby, Albert I.,Jr., and Nancy Rogers Bagby. "Review Article: Brazilian Literary and Bibliographical Studies Over the Last Twenty Years: Example Machado de Assis." *The Modern Language Journal* 59(1975):186–88.

3 Blass, Birgit A., Dona E. Johnson, and William W. Gage. *A Provisional Survey of Materials for the Study of Neglected Languages.* Washington, D.C.: Center for Applied Linguistics, 1969. [EDRS: ED 044 683.]

4 Brod, Richard I., Personal Communication, 1976. [Letter and telephone conversation.]

5 ——— "Foreign Language Enrollments in U.S. Colleges—Fall, 1974." *ADFL Bulletin* 7,ii(1975): 37–42.

6 ——— "Trends in Foreign Language Enrollments, 341–62 in Dale L. Lange,ed., *Individualization of Instruction.* ACTFL Review of Foreign Language Education, Volume 2. Skokie, Illinois: National Textbook Company, 1973.

7 ——— "Foreign Language Enrollments in U.S. Colleges—Fall, 1972." *ADFL Bulletin* 5,i(1973): 54–60.

8 ——— "Foreign Language Enrollments in U.S. Colleges—Fall, 1970." *ADFL Bulletin* 3,ii(1971): 46–50.

9 ——— and Jeffrey H. Meyerson. "The Foreign Language Requirement—Report on the 1974–75 Survey." *ADFL Bulletin* 7,i(1975):43–48.

10 ——— and C. Edward Scebold. "What Do Foreign Language Enrollment Statistics Show in the Uncommonly-Taught Languages?" 14–25 in *Material Development Needs in the Uncommonly-Taught Languages:Priorities for the Seventies. Arlington, Virginia:Center for Applied Linguistics,* 1975.

11 Cadora, Frederick. Personal Communication, 1976. [Interview.]

12 Capusan, Cornel. *Some Cultural Problems in Teaching Romanian.* Seattle, Washington: Washington University, 1972. [EDRS: ED 109 910.]

13 Carroll, John B. "Foreign Language Proficiency Levels Attained by Language Majors Near Graduation from College." *Foreign Language Annals* 1(1967):131–51.

14 Ching, Eugene. *Write Chinese Characters.* Columbus: The Ohio State University Department of East Asian Languages and Literature, 1975.

15 Cohen, Gail A.,ed., *U.S. College-Sponsored Programs Abroad.* New York: Institute for International Education, 1975.

16 Cote, Maureen. "You Can Promise Undying Devotion but Not Immortality." *AATSEEL's Newsletter* 16,v(1975):1–2.

17 Curtin, Constance, Douglas Clayton, Cheryl Finch, David Moor, and Lois Woodruff. "Teaching the Translation of Russian by Computer." *The Modern Language Journal* 56(1972):354–60.

18 *Encyclopedia of Associations*. Detroit:Gale Research, 1975.

19 Gage, William. *Uncommonly-Taught Languages*. ERIC Bulletin Number 17, 1970. [EDRS: ED 042 163.]

20 Herslow, Nina Greer, and James Dershem. *Foreign Language Enrollments in Institutions of Higher Education, Fall, 1965*. New York:Modern Language Association, 1966. [EDRS: ED 031 103.]

21 Hodge, Carleton T. *Response to W. Gage's Article "Uncommonly-Taught Languages."* ERIC Clearinghouse Bulletin, Washington, D.C.:Center for Applied Linguistics, 1970. [EDRS: ED 042 164.]

22 ——— and Richard Spears. "African Languages," 47–53 in *Material Development Needs in the Uncommonly-Taught Languages:Priorities for the Seventies*. Arlington, Virginia:Center for Applied Linguistics, 1975.

23 Hutchinson, Joseph C., Defense Language Institute. Personal Communication, 1976. [Letter.]

24 Impey, Michael H. "Review Article:The Present State of Romanian Studies in the United States and Canada." *The Modern Language Journal* 59 (1975):263–72.

25 Jarvis, Gilbert A. Personal Communication, 1976. [Interview.]

26 Jolly, S. Yukiko. "The Use of Songs in Teaching Foreign Languages." *The Modern Language Journal* 59(1975):11–14.

27 Kalbouss, George. *Computers and the Teaching of Foreign Languages*. Columbus:The Ohio State University Department of Slavic Languages and Literatures, 1976. [Mimeo.]

28 Kant, Julia Gibson. *Foreign Language Offerings and Enrollments in Public and Non-Public Secondary School, Fall, 1968*. New York:Modern Language Association, 1970. [Reprinted in part in *Foreign Language Annals* 3(1970):400–58.]

29 ——— *Foreign Language Registrations and Student Contact Hours in Institutions of Higher Education, Fall 1968 and Summer 1969*. New York: Modern Language Association, 1969. [Reprinted in part in *Foreign Language Annals* 3(1969): 247–304; 3(1970)459–76.]

30 Kuo, Ta-Hsia. *Problems of Textbook in Teaching Chinese Poetry*. [Paper presented at the Annual Meeting of the Chinese Language Teachers Association, 1972.] [EDRS: ED 071 526.]

31 Lambert, Richard D. *Language and Area Studies Review*. Monograph Number 17, Philadelphia: American Academy of Political and Social Science, 1973.

32 Leong, Che Kan. "A Study of Written Chinese Vocabulary." *Modern Language Journal* 56(1972): 230–34.

33 Lin, Helen T. *A Survey of Some Commonly Used Expressions in Chinese and An Analysis of Its Possible Implications in Language Teaching*, 1974. [EDRS: ED 098 784.]

34 Liston, Roz. "Foreign Language—Corporate Marketing Tool." *Columbus Dispatch* (April 5, 1976): C–5.

35 Marraro, Howard R. "Miscellaneous Notes on Italian Literature in America in the Nineteenth Century." *The Modern Language Journal* 54(1970): 324–28.

36 *Material Development Needs in the Uncommonly-Taught Languages:Priorities for the Seventies*. Arlington, Virginia:Center for Applied Linguistics, 1975.

37 Moskowitz, Solomon. *Hebrew for Secondary Schools*. Albany:New York State Education Department Bureau of Secondary Curriculum Development, 1971. [EDRS: ED 057 706.]

38 "A National Foreign Language Program for the 1970's." *ADFL Bulletin* 6,i(1974):7–19.

39 Nelson, G. E., Jean Renard Ward, Samuel H. Desch, and Roy Kaplon. "Two New Strategies for Computer-Assisted Language Instruction (CALI)." *Foreign Language Annals* 9(1976):28–37.

40 Pane, Remigo U. "Present Status of Italian Studies in the United States and Canada." *The Modern Language Journal* 54(1970):507–23.

41 Petrov, Julia A. "Foreign Language and Area Studies Research Under the National Defense Education Act:Historical Background," 3–9 in *Material Development Needs in the Uncommonly-Taught Languages:Priorities for the Seventies*. Arlington, Virginia:Center for Applied Linguistics, 1975.

42 ——— *National Defense Education Act, Foreign Languages, Area Studies and Other Aspects of International Education:Completed Research and Instructional Materials. List Number 7*. Washington, D.C.:U.S. Government Printing Office (DHEW Publication Number OE 72 194), 1972.

43 Read, William M. "Aims and Objectives of the Latin Program." *Foreign Language Annals* 8 (1975):118–22.

44 Rickerson, Earl. "The U.S. Government Interagency Language Roundtable." *Linguistic Reporter* 18,iii(1973):3.

45 Sato, Esther M. T. *Development of Instructional Materials in Japanese for Elementary and Secondary Schools*. University of Hawaii, Honolulu: Institute of International Studies, 1971. [EDRS: ED 063 826.]

46 Scanlan, Richard T. "Computer-Assisted Instruction:PLATO in Latin." *Foreign Language Annals* 5(1971):88.

47 Scebold, C. Edward. *Foreign Language Offerings in Public Secondary Schools, Fall, 1970*. New York:Modern Language Association of America, 1973. [EDRS: ED 081 262.]

48 Shane, Alex M. "An Evaluation of the Existing College Norms for the MLA-Cooperative Russian

Test and Its Efficacy as a Placement Examination." *The Modern Language Journal* 55(1971): 93–99.
49 Stevick, Earl W. *Adapting and Writing Language Lessons*. Office of Education, 1971. [EDRS: ED 053 597.]
50 Swift, Lloyd B. Personal Communication, 1976. [Letter and telephone conversation.]
51 Thompson, Richard T. Personal Communication, 1976. [Letter and telephone conversation.]
52 ——— "Defining the Task," 12–13 in *Material Development Needs in the Uncommonly-Taught Languages:Priorities for the Seventies*. Arlington, Virginia:Center for Applied Linguistics, 1975.
53 ——— "Modern Foreign Language Teaching in the Uncommonly-Taught Languages," 279–309 in Dale L. Lange,ed., *Pluralism in Foreign Language Education*. ACTFL Review of Foreign Language Education, Volume 3. Skokie, Illinois:National Textbook Company, 1973.
54 ——— *Uncommonly-Taught Languages:Another Perspective*. ERIC Clearinghouse Bulletin, 1971. [EDRS: ED 044 707.]
55 Tsu, John B. "The Teaching of Chinese in Colleges and Schools of the United States." *Modern Language Journal* 54(1970):562–79.
56 Twarog, Leon I., Personal Communication, 1976. [Interview.]
57 Willbern, Glen. "Foreign Language Enrollments in Public Secondary Schools, 1965." *Foreign Language Annals* 1(1967):239–53.
58 Yang, Winston L. Y. "Teaching Chinese Through Chinese Literature." *The Modern Language Journal* 60(1976):31–35.

Professional associations of foreign languages

Although this chapter is concerned with the uncommonly taught languages, information has been included below for AATF, AATG, AATSP, TESOL, and TESL in the interest of completeness and to facilitate comparisons. To keep this section to a manageable length, however, information concerning organizations whose membership does not include individual language teachers (for example, the Association of Departments of Foreign Languages, the National Federation of Modern Language Teachers' Organizations, the National Council of State Supervisors of Foreign Languages) or whose concerns are not *principally* those of language teachers (for example, the Linguistic Society of America, the American Philological Association, and the various ethnic heritage and area studies organizations) have not been included.

Name: American Association of Teachers of Arabic (AATA)
Address: Arabic Program, The Ohio State University, 1841 Millikin Road, Columbus, Ohio 43210
Correspondent: Frederic J. Cadora, Executive Secretary
Founded: 1964
Membership: 120
Purpose: To promote study, criticism, and research in the field of Arabic language and literature and to further the common interests of teachers of these subjects
Publications: An Nashra (semi-annual)
National meetings: Annual with two panels on linguistics and literature; in conjunction with the Middle East Studies Association

Name: American Association of Teachers of Esperanto (AATE)
Address: Apt. C-18, 445 Waupelani Drive, State College, Pa. 16801
Correspondent: Cornelius J. McKown, Corresponding Secretary
Founded: 1961
Membership: 100
Purpose: To promote the teaching of Esperanto in American schools
Publications: *Bulteno* (quarterly)
National meetings: Annual
Other information: This association is affiliated with the International League of Esperanto Instructors.

Name: American Association of Teachers of French (AATF)
Address: 57 East Armory Avenue, Champaign, Ill. 61820
Correspondent: F. W. Nachtmann, Executive Secretary
Founded: 1927
Membership: 11,000
Purpose: To serve teachers of French and to promote the study of French language, literature, and civilization
Publications: *French Review* and AATF *National Bulletin* (newsletter)
National meetings: Two years in succession during the Christmas holidays and the third year during the Thanksgiving weekend; a summer meeting in 1977 in France
Local/regional meetings: Each of the 76 chapters has from one to five meetings, according to its local preferences, during the academic year.
Other information: AATF operates a Placement Bureau, a Correspondence Bureau, a National Information Bureau, a Flights to France program, an Honorary Society (for high school students), a group insurance program—all from the National Office; a program of summer scholarships for teachers from Marblehead, Mass., a National French Contest (for high school students) from East Meadow, Long Island, N.Y.; and a traveling exhibits program from Charlotte, N.C.

Name: American Association of Teachers of German (AATG)
Address: 339 Walnut Street, Philadelphia, Pa. 19106
Correspondent: Louis F. Helbig, Executive Director
Founded: 1928
Membership: 8,500
Purpose: To encourage the study of German language and culture
Publications: *German Quarterly, Die Unterrichtspraxis,* and AATG *Newsletter*
National meetings: Annual
Local/regional meetings: 60 chapters have chapter meetings usually twice per year.

Name: American Association of Teachers of Italian (AATI)
Address: Rutgers University, New Brunswick, N.J. 08903
Correspondent: Joseph E. Laggini, President
Founded: 1924
Membership: 2,000
Purpose: A professional society of college and secondary school teachers and others interested in Italian language and culture
Publications: *Italica* (quarterly)
National meetings: Annual
Local/regional meetings: Fourteen local groups

Name: American Association of Teachers of Slavic and East European Languages (AATSEEL)

Address: Modern Language Building, Room 340, University of Arizona, Tucson, Ariz. 85721
Correspondent: Joe Malik, Jr., Executive Secretary-Treasurer
Founded: 1941
Membership: 1,600
Purpose: The advancement of the study of and the promotion of the teaching of Slavic and East European languages, literatures, and cultures on all educational levels
Publications: *Slavic and East European Journal* (quarterly); *AATSEEL Newsletter* (six issues per year)
National meetings: Annual
Local/regional meetings: 32 state chapters meet once or twice a year.

Name: American Association of Teachers of Spanish and Portuguese (AATSP)
Address: College of Holy Cross, Worcester, Mass. 01610
Correspondent: Richard B. Klein, Secretary-Treasurer
Founded: 1917
Membership: 13,500
Purpose: For teachers of Spanish and Portuguese languages and literature and others interested in Hispanic culture
Publications: *Hispania* (four per year)
National meetings: Annual

Name: American Classical League (ACL)
Address: Miami University, Oxford, Ohio 45056
Correspondent: Robert Wolverton, President
Founded: 1918
Membership: 3,000
Purpose: To improve and extend the study of the classics in the U.S., to supplement and reinforce the activities of other classical organizations, and to advance the cause of liberal education
Publications: *Classical Outlook* (monthly except July and August) and *CAUSA* (a newsletter coming out about twice a year)
National meetings: Annually in June or July

Name: American Council of Teachers of Russian (ACTR)
Address: 10 Club Road, Baltimore, Md. 21210
Correspondent: Claire Walker, Executive Secretary-Treasurer
Founded: 1974
Membership: 160
Purpose: To encourage the study and teaching of Russian language, literature, linguistics, and area studies
Publications: *ACTR LETTR* (a newsletter sent out irregularly five to 10 times in an academic year)
National meetings: In conjunction with AATSEEL, same date and place
Local/regional meetings: Specially called if occasion arises
Other information: ACTR has created the first U.S. graduate study program in Moscow, at the Pushkin Institute. ACTR's president serves as the American vice-president of MAPRIAL (International Association of Teachers of Russian Language and Literature). ACTR also selects participants for spoken Russian "Olimipadas" in Moscow and advises American competitions.

Name: American Council of Teachers of Uncommonly-Taught Asian Languages (ACTUAL)
Address: 4403 Midstone Lane, Fairfax, Va. 22030
Correspondent: David W. Dellinger, Secretary/Treasurer
Founded: 1972

Membership: 48
Purpose: The corporation is organized exclusively for educational and scientific purposes as defined under section 501(c) (3) of the Internal Revenue Code of 1954 (or the corresponding provision of any future United States Internal Revenue Law).
Publications: Working papers (annual), papers read at annual meeting; newsletter
National meetings: Once a year under the auspices of ACTFL

Name: American Council on the Teaching of Foreign Languages (ACTFL)
Address: 62 Fifth Avenue, New York, N.Y. 10011
Correspondent: C. Edward Scebold, Executive Secretary
Founded: 1967
Membership: 10,700 (including subscriptions)
Purpose: To promote and improve the teaching of all foreign languages, literatures, and cultures in American education; to provide educational services to the members of ACTFL; to publish appropriate journals and other publications; and to conduct an annual convention and other meetings
Publications: Foreign Language Annals (six per year); *Foreign Language Education Series* (annual); Materials Center
National meetings: Annual meeting and preconference workshops (Thanksgiving week, each year)
Local/regional meetings: Organized by state affiliated groups

Name: Association of Teachers of English as a Second Language (ATESL), a section of the National Association for Foreign Student Affairs (NAFSA)
Address: 1860 19th Street, N.W., Washington, D.C. 20009
Correspondent: Charles W. Gay
Founded: 1948
Membership: 400
Purpose: To serve the purposes of international education; to stimulate, guide, and sponsor research into the learning and teaching of English as a second language; to assemble, exchange, and disseminate information on teaching and research concerned with English as a second language; to provide effective liaison with other groups whose members share any of these purposes
Publications: NAFSA Newsletter and *Selected Conference Papers of the Association of Teachers of English as a Second Language*
National meetings: Annual
Local/regional meetings: ATESL sponsors regional and local workshops throughout the year.

Name: Association of Teachers of Japanese (ATJ)
Address: Department of Far Eastern Languages and Literatures, University of Michigan, Ann Arbor, Mich. 48104
Correspondent: Robert H. Brower, Chairman
Founded: 1962
Membership: 300
Purpose: To meet the common intellectual and academic needs of the membership, which includes teachers of Japanese as a second language
Publications: Journal (three per year)
National meetings: Annual

Name: Chinese Language Teachers Association (CLTA)
Address: c/o Department of Asian Studies, Seton Hall University, South Orange, N.J. 07079
Correspondent: Fred Fangyu Wang, Secretary-Treasurer

Membership: 600
Purpose: To improve Chinese language instruction in the United States by securing effective instructional materials and standard texts. The CLTA hopes to improve the professional status of every teacher below the rank of Assistant Professor and to develop general standards for the teaching of Chinese.
Publications: Chinese Language Teachers Association JOURNAL (three times per year)
National meetings: Annual

Name: Department of Foreign Languages (DFL), National Educational Association
Founded: 1961
Publications: DFL *Bulletin* and DFL *News and Notes*
National Meetings: Annually with NEA meetings
Other information: DFL has been "inactive" for the past seven years and is presently still on inactive status.

Name: Modern Language Association of America (MLA)
Address: 62 Fifth Avenue, New York, N.Y. 10011
Correspondent: William D. Schaefer, Executive Director
Founded: 1883
Membership: 29,000
Purpose: To promote study, criticism, and research in modern languages and their literatures, and to further the common interests of teachers of these subjects
Publications: PMLA (six per year), newsletter (four per year), *International Bibliography* (annual), *ADFL Bulletin* (four per year)
National meetings: Annual
Other information: Uncommonly taught languages are represented through Divisions with permanent executive committees.

Name: National Association of Language Laboratory Directors (NALLD)
Address: Box 623, Middlebury College, Middlebury, Vt. 05753
Correspondent: James W. Dodge, Executive Secretary
Founded: 1965
Membership: 1,100
Purpose: To promote more effective use and better understanding of the machine-aided language laboratory and the foreign language programs of both schools and colleges
Publications: Journal (four per year)
National meetings: Annual

Name: Teachers of English to Speakers of Other Languages (TESOL)
Address: 455 Nevils Building, Georgetown University, Washington, D.C. 20057
Correspondent: James E. Alatis, Executive Secretary-Treasurer
Founded: 1966
Membership: 5,000
Purpose: To promote scholarship, to disseminate information, to strengthen at all levels instruction and research in the teaching of standard English to speakers of other languages or dialects and to cooperate with other groups having similar concerns
Publications: TESOL Quarterly (scholarly and pedagogical journal) *TESOL Newsletter* (five per year)
National meetings: Annual convention in spring
Local/regional meetings: Twenty-four regional affiliates, often covering the area of one state, are autonomous and hold their own meetings.

9

Foreign languages in elementary and emerging adolescent education

Introduction

Dwayne Adcock
Eugene, Oregon Public Schools

Expectations for FLES

Nearly two decades have passed since the inception of a concerted nationwide effort to include the study of foreign languages in the elementary curriculum. This cold war phenomenon, hailed as a strategic weapons system in the nation's arsenal, was to become known, of course, as FLES. It took many shapes and forms in terms of the kinds of materials used, the time allotted for instruction, the staffing patterns employed, and the nature of the audiences to whom the programs were directed (McKim, 63). FLES held the promise of a bilingual nation moving out front as the uncontested leader on the international scene.

A paradox

At a time when phrases such as *multicultural curriculum, cultural pluralism, intercultural education,* and *global interdependency* are familiar entries in the lexicon of those who are designing and implementing curricula for the middle 1970s the difficulty of finding even mention of FLES in print must seem paradoxical. Not only is the word missing from the vocabulary of educational decision-makers and curriculum designers, but it is conspicuously absent in the journals and newsletters of the foreign language profession.

The purpose of this chapter is not to conduct a postmortem of the profession's nationwide attempt in the Sputnik-NDEA era

---

Dwayne Adcock (M.A., University of Oregon) is Regional Curriculum Director for the Eugene, Oregon, Public Schools. He is a candidate for the Ph.D. degree in Foreign Language Education at The Ohio State University. Previously he taught Latin and served as department chairman at the high school level, taught Spanish at the elementary level, and served as district coordinator of foreign languages for seven years. He was president of the Oregon Association of Foreign Language Teachers and represented the State of Oregon as a member of the ACTFL Constituent Assembly for three years. In 1976 he served as program chairman of the annual conference of the Pacific Northwest Council on Foreign Languages. He is a member of ACTFL, PNCFL, and ASCD.

to make foreign language education an integral part of the elementary curriculum. Rather, its purpose is to update the profession on the legacy of the FLES movement, including both the identification of representative programs across the nation that are still viable and a description of new approaches to foreign language education in the elementary school, which may well serve as prototypes for another attempt to make FLES an integral part of the elementary curriculum.

FLES legacy

The chapter also includes a review of foreign languages in emerging adolescent education (programs for students in grades 5–8 or 6–8 that are housed in a middle or junior high school). One reason for including a review of programs at this level is the existence of a variety of age groupings in many elementary and middle schools throughout the country. What might be called an elementary program in one district may be identified as a middle school program in the other. In addition, such a review is timely; for there is a national effort directed toward an intensive study of emerging adolescent education, an area of human development that has been neglected (Thornburg, 84).

Emerging adolescent education

Any analysis of foreign language education in grades K–8 must be based on a clear understanding of curriculum trends, characteristics of individual learners, and the realities of the classroom. Hence, the first part of this chapter will identify the major curriculum trends of the 1970s and describe both the nature of the elementary and emerging adolescent learner and the kind of curriculum that should be developed for students at these levels. The second part of the chapter brings the reader up to date on what is currently happening at the elementary and middle school levels. Finally, an assessment is made of foreign language programs at these levels, and prospects for the future are discussed.

Major curriculum trends

Freedom, relevance, openness, learner-centered school, individualized instruction, open classroom, school within a school, the nongraded school, modular scheduling, cultural pluralism, individually prescribed instruction, core-curriculum, activity, self-expression, and alternative schools are terms that, from varying perspectives, reflect the dominant trend of the curriculum movement of the middle 1970s—the primacy of the nature and development of the individual learner in the design and implementation of curriculum. There is a growing reaffirmation of the personal benefit theory which originated with the Progressive Movement of the 1930s. The hallmarks of this theory are:

Personal benefit theory

> . . . individuality and diversity in terms of needs, skills, and preferences. In response to this diversity, the school is charged with creating a differentiated educational program designed to foster individual interests and maximize individual potential (Doyle, 29, p. 255).

To say, however, that the personal benefit theory of education, with its focus on relevance, openness, individuality, and diversity, represents the cutting edge of the curriculum movement today is not to say that in practice formal education in the middle 1970s embodies this theory. In reality, formal elementary and secondary education can generally be characterized as still committed to using commonly agreed upon means to reach common goals (Goodlad, 44). Nevertheless, there has been a considerable change in attitude toward identification of a series of alternative means to commonly agreed-upon ends. The parameters of what constitutes acceptable alternatives have been extended, and there are numerous signs indicating that formal education is on the threshold of translating words into action. Goodlad, whose opinion is that "the days of entrenched resistance to the idea of more alternatives, greater openness, and universal humaneness in the conduct of education are largely behind us despite stubborn pockets of resistance" (p. 25), has categorized most of the reforms of the past two decades as instructional, institutional, and societal alternatives to common ends. Programmed instruction, diagnosis and prescription, learning centers, small-group instruction—all of these are indications of the profession's renewed interest in the importance and uniqueness of the individual learner and his or her learning style.

Alternative means

Instructional alternatives

The various attempts at pupil-teacher mix (multigrading, multiage grouping, team teaching), the development of a variety of models for curriculum organization (multidisciplinary,

Institutional alternatives

interdisciplinary, school within a school), and flexible time arrangements (modular scheduling, off-campus experiences) are examples of institutional alternatives provided by the public school system. Examples of societal and systemwide alternatives can be found in the movement toward decentralizing the decision-making process, opening up the access to resources, and performance contracts with outside agencies.

Societal alternatives

Multicultural curriculum: A recognition of individuality and diversity

One manifestation of the emphasis on individuality and diversity in curriculum development that is of particular interest to foreign language educators is the growing realization of the role education must play in helping Americans live effectively with other cultures, both domestic and international. This realization is not new to the foreign language profession. What is new is that national educational organizations, the leaders of curriculum development in the elementary and secondary schools, have joined their voices to the increasing demand for a multicultural curriculum to meet the needs of a culturally pluralistic society. In an editorial published in *Educational Leadership,* the organ of the Association for Supervision and Curriculum Development, Arciniega (6) states:

Demand for multicultural curriculum

> Schools will have to openly affirm cultural, ethnic, and linguistic differences as good and positive resources that are worthy of preserving and enhancing. Since cultural diversity is recognized as a fact of life in American society, its schools need to insist on the reorganization of programs and the reorientation of teaching staffs and to capitalize and build on basic differences which heretofore they had been so committed to wipe out (p. 163).

Cultural diversity a fact

The AACTE has taken the following position:

> Education for cultural pluralism includes . . . the encouragement of multiculturalism, multilingualism, and multidialectism. If cultural pluralism is so basic a quality of our culture, it must become an integral part of the educational process at every level (70, p. 264).

One of the 1975 ASCD resolutions calls for multilingual/multicultural legislation:

A call for legislation

> In order to meet some of the challenges of the twenty-first century, it is desirable that all students, including monolingual and bilingual, have the opportunity to study a multicultural curriculum. The accomplishment of this goal will be determined by the degree of federal, state, and local assistance. It is recommended that the ASCD Board of Directors take a positive position supporting national legislation relative to multilingual/multicultural legislation and that all state affiliates do the same in support of state and local efforts (7, p. 10).

The National Commission on the Reform of Secondary Education (69) analyzed goals obtained from 37 states and reports that cultural pluralism is high on the list of emerging curriculum development in the schools that responded.

In addition to the emphasis on the need for a multicultural curriculum reflecting our culturally pluralistic society, the international dimension of intercultural education is being stressed in national educational forums. The National Commission on the Reform of Secondary Education makes the following recommendation about global education in encouraging transnational and crosscultural experiences:

International dimension

> The education of the nation's adolescents must be superior to that of their parents. Part of this superiority must be an enhanced sense of the globe as the human environment, and instruction to this end must reflect not only the ancient characteristics of the world, but emerging knowledge of biological and social unity. All secondary school students should receive a basic global education (p. 16).

Global interdependence

The call for a recognition of global interdependence is eloquently stated by Commager (23) in the preamble of the *New Declaration of Interdependence:*

> To establish a new world order of compassion, peace, justice, and security, it is essential that mankind free itself from

> the limitations of national prejudice and acknowledge that the forces that unite it are incomparably deeper than those that divide it . . . that all people are part of one global community, dependent on one body of resources, bound together by the ties of common humanity, and associated in a common adventure on the planet Earth (p. 8A).

Optimism tempered by reality

The optimism that the above comments about a multicultural curriculum may have engendered in the hearts of foreign language educators may wisely be tempered with the reality that although there seems to be an increasing awareness of a need for domestic and international intercultural education, the specific role that foreign language education should play is not so clear in the minds of the national curriculum leaders. For example, the National Commission on the Reform of Secondary Education fails to make a case for the role of a foreign language in the development of interglobal dependency. And most of the articles published by the Association for Supervision and Curriculum Development are not so specific about foreign language study as Arciniega's (6) statement:

> All students upon completion of the school program would be able to speak, read, and write in two languages; and more importantly, they would be able to learn academic conceptual material in either language. One of the most beautiful benefits to be derived from such a system is the creative ability to approach problem-solving activities with a built-in repertoire of bicultural perspectives (p. 167).

A second opportunity

Nevertheless, a second opportunity exists for foreign language educators. The climate is right for making a convincing case that foreign languages have an important and vital role to play in a multicultural curriculum. An opportunity is provided to relate foreign language study to a curriculum movement rather than to a state of panic caused by the growing fear of America's inability to compete with Russia in science and technology. The time is particularly right to make a new case for foreign languages in childhood education, emphasizing both the role of intercultural education in child development and the relationship to foreign language study to intercultural education.

Let us take a look first at the role intercultural education plays in child development. Carpenter and Torney (21) stress the importance of cultural pluralism in the cognitive development of the child.

Intercultural education and child development

> We need to recognize that cultural pluralism is a positive force for the psychological development of the individual. Piaget has noted that the major thrust of cognitive development is realized when one comes into contact with ideas or experiences that challenge one's present way of viewing the world. Information gained from the environment conflicts with the child's existing ideas, resulting in an accommodation of these schema. In this manner, exposure to cultures other than one's own assists in a continuous personal growth (pp. 17–18).

Personal growth

Piaget identifies three stages through which a child passes as he makes distinctions between his group and other groups:

Stage I Cognitive and affective egocentricity (ages 6–7)
Stage II Sociocentricity (ages 7–9)
Stage III Reciprocity (ages 9–12)

Piaget and Weil (74) conclude that "the child's discovery of his homeland and understanding of other countries is a process of transition from egocentricity to reciprocity" (p. 578). The challenge of intercultural education is to "discover how to develop that reciprocity in thought and action which is vital to the attainment of impartiality and affective understanding" (p. 578).

Egocentricity to reciprocity

Yerxa (91) identifies the 7–10 age span as critical for the development of cultural pluralism and suggests that role-playing may be an important factor in the development of reciprocity.

Seven–10 age span crucial

> Piaget's Stage II (7–8–9–10 years) seems to be a particularly important time for the introduction of information since children are curious and receptive at these stages and since Stage II is particularly critical to the development of the attitude of reciprocity. The exposure to such information should en-

> able the child to discover the similarities among all people. . . . Elementary education's most important goal, in the pursuit of international understanding, should be to help children develop reciprocity, that is, the ability to identify with people of other countries and visualize oneself in their place and vice-versa. Perhaps role-playing in which children at Stage II and older spontaneously enact the role of persons from other countries would be one means by which to develop reciprocity (p. 32).

Importance of role-playing

Research conducted by Lambert and Klineberg (58) indicates that after the age of 10, social attitudes of children are more rigid, and stereotypes begin to develop:

> The 10-year age period seems to be the critical one, for at this age children are most ready to consider other people as similar and are particularly friendly. By age 10 the readiness to like people who are dissimilar also reaches its maximum, for in none of the national groups studied is there a reliable increase in affection for dissimilars from 10 to 14 years. In fact, this tendency typically decreases after age 10 (p. 6).

Language and intercultural attitudes

The findings of Lambert and Klineberg are supported by the research of Masangkay et al. (64) who conducted a study of the attitudes of members of Philippino families towards Chinese people who lived in the Philippines. They concluded that "in times of the socialization of generalized attitudes, it seems that by the age of 10 years, children have adopted ethnic attitudes similar to those expressed by the adult community" (p. 267).

Having discussed the role of intercultural education in child development, the next issue to be addressed is the role a second language has in developing a child's intercultural attitudes. Carpenter and Torney (21) report an interview in which children were asked how other countries differed from their own.

> Children, when asked how other countries differ from their own country, placed great stress upon language. This factor was mentioned spontaneously by more than 70 percent of the children interviewed at all ages from six to 12. For example, these responses came from an eight-year-old boy:

I: How are people in other countries different from you?
S: Most talk Mexican.
I: Anything else?
S: Most talk different from us.
I: Do you think it would be better if everyone in the world were American?
S: Yes, because I want them to talk normal, the way we do (pp. 19–20).

Intercultural competency

Carpenter and Torney conclude that there may be a direct relationship between speaking and learning languages and one's own attitudes, and hence suggest that children should be exposed to a second language "to become interculturally competent" (p. 20).

More positive attitudes

Finally, the research of Riestra and Johnson (76) conducted under the auspices of the University of Illinois and underwritten by a research grant from the United States Office of Education, concluded that FLES pupils had significantly more positive attitudes toward the Spanish-speaking peoples they had studied than did the non-FLES group.

The elementary school setting

The movement toward open education in this country originated in the elementary school system, and openness is recognized as "the most powerful and germinal idea on the scene today" (Frazier, 40, p. 1). The open school or the open classroom can be characterized as a free and humane environment for children in which the use of flexible scheduling, team teaching, and individualized instruction is maximized.

Education-by-choice model

Openness can be identified as a compelling force in the alternative school movement with its focus on teaching and learning styles. The education-by-choice model has been actualized by the establishment of alternative schools within a school district, a school within a school, and alternative classrooms within a school. Fantini (34) has classified the variety of organizational structures present in elementary education by placing the structures on a continuum (free-open-modified-standard) based on "how much freedom the student has to choose the teacher, content, methodology, time, and place for learning" (p. 139).

Types of organizational structures

Free	Open	Modified	Standard
Learner-directed and controlled; learner has complete freedom to orchestrate his own education; teacher is one resource.	Learner has considerable freedom to choose from a wide range of content areas considered relevant by teacher, parent, and student; resource centers in major skill areas made available to learner.	Prescribed-content is made more flexible through individualization of instruction; school is ungraded; students learn same thing but at different rates. Using team teaching, teachers plan a differentiated approach to the same content.	Learner adheres to institution requirements uniformly prescribed: what is to be taught—how, when, where, and with whom. Teacher is instructor-evaluator. Student passes or fails according to normative standards.
Opening of school to the community and its resources	Opening of school to the community and its resources	Teacher and programmed course of study are the major sources of student learning.	
Learner-centered	Teacher-centered	Subject-matter-centered	Institution-centered (p. 141).

The concepts of openness, freedom, and humanness and the emphasis on the importance of the nature of the learner and his unique learning style, in addition to fostering the "education by choice" model that is growing in popularity within the public school system, have had, in one way or another, a substantial impact on elementary classrooms across the nation. The approach to freedom that perhaps has had the most influence on American education comes from the British Primary with its emphasis on freedom with controls. Although the British version is not adopted on a broad basis, the development of numerous options and alternatives within a fixed curriculum is a serious attempt to meet the demands of freedom and openness and to recognize the uniqueness of individual learners (Frazier, 40).

Freedom with controls

In general, elementary education has been characterized through the years as a setting in which integration of curriculum is really happening. This wholeness-in-learning approach as contrasted with the compartmentalization of knowledge in discrete disciplines so characteristic of the secondary schools, can make learning more relevant and hence more readily identifiable with life learning. If there is not an arbitrary division of time for the separate disciplines, an integrated-day model be-

Wholeness in learning

Integrated-day model

comes more feasible, and flexible scheduling may facilitate the use of independent study.

Teacher as facilitator

The teacher's role is perceived as that of a guide, a facilitator. This is an active, not a passive role; for active learning demands active teaching. There is an important place for differentiated staffing in the elementary school. It should be viewed, however, as a redefinition of staff roles in terms of "the nature of teaching and learning rather than the nature of the teacher" (Frazier, 40, p. 37).

Foreign language educators must have an awareness and understanding of the elementary school curriculum and the organizational structure. But even more important, they must have knowledge about and an understanding of the nature and development of the school's client, the student. The focus of any foreign language program at the elementary level must be the learner. Although generalization should be avoided in speaking of individuality, certain developmental characteristics of the eight-to-eleven-year-old child can be related to language learning.

Focus on the learner

Johnny's high energy level is readily transmitted to the competitive aspect of learning a foreign language, but he also realizes that he is putting himself on public view every time he solos. He constantly needs teacher reinforcement and approval rather than criticism as he takes the public risk involved in language skill development.

Thinking-language development

In terms of thinking-language development, Johnny has the following characteristics:

1 Thinking
   Capable of prolonged interest; often makes plans and goes ahead on own
   Sees similarities because two things share observable features or abstract attributes
   Can apply logical thought to practical situations
   Beginning to understand the relationship between cause and effect
   Understands concept of time; has ability to plan ahead
2 Language
   May vary greatly from others in reading abilities and language skills

> Using language to exchange ideas; much time spent in talk and discussion
> Beginning to use more abstract words (Tyler et al., 85, p. 1)

The elementary foreign language teacher can capitalize on Johnny's appreciation of the utilitarian aspect of language and should build on his interest in talking and discussing. Although Johnny's concept of time permits him to plan ahead, it is not sufficiently developed to give him an historical perspective; consequently, contemporary rather than historical cultural referents should be used.

Piaget's stages of mental development

Piaget has identified three stages of mental development through which all children pass in a fixed sequence, though they do not do so at the same age. The eight-to-eleven year olds, according to Piaget, are entering and exiting Stage II, which he identifies as that of concrete operations. In this stage the children "always think in terms of real (concrete) objects, not abstractions. . . . Thought grows from actions, not words. . . . Knowledge cannot be given to children. It must be discovered and constructed through the learners' activities. . . . children learn best from concrete experiences" (Charles, 22, p. 45).

Importance of concrete experiences

Ausubel (9) underscores the position taken by Piaget:

> Many features of the activity program are based on the premise that the elementary school child perceives the world in relatively specific, concrete terms and requires considerable firsthand experiences with diverse concrete instances of a given set of relationships before he can abstract genuinely meaningful concepts (p. 107).

Child as active agent

Any foreign language program developed for elementary students must provide a rich variety of concrete experiences. The program must encourage the child to be an active agent; for his cognitive development is dependent on the quality of his interaction with his environment. The use of discovery and inquiry, the providing of unstructured time, the movement away from group instruction toward independent study, the development of individualized learning packets, and the establishment of learning centers are sample descriptors of elementary foreign language programs that are truly focused on the individual learner.

Emerging adolescence—The middle school

As in foreign language education at the elementary level, programs in the middle and junior high schools, which are offered either for students who are continuing an elementary program or for those who are being exposed to foreign language study for the first time, must be developed with a clear understanding both of the school setting and the nature and development of the emerging adolescent. In reality, the division into elementary and junior high or middle school is artificial and can create unnecessary barriers and conflicts. To the students the elementary and middle school are only points on their continuum. We should think not in terms of an elementary or middle school program, but in terms of programs for childhood and emerging adolescence.

Artificial division

Individual differences in terms of physical, social, emotional, and intellectual development are nowhere more obvious than in the 10–14 age group. At the national, state, and local levels the reorganization of the educational experience for this group of youngsters is an item listed high on the agenda for action. In 1974 the Association for Supervision and Curriculum Development charged a committee with the responsibility of identifying the kinds of middle school programs that should be developed for the emerging adolescent learners. There are now an estimated 4,000 to 5,000 middle schools across the country, and 47 of the 50 states have officially recognized middle schools.

A national study

The real issue is not whether we refer to the organizational structure for the emerging adolescent years as a middle school or a junior high school. The main concern is not whether a middle school is defined either as a 5–8 or a 6–8 model. The principal challenge is to design a program specifically tailored to the needs of transescents and early adolescents that will provide "a critical link in the chain of continuous progress education" (Alexander, 2, p. viii).

Middle years a critical link

What are some of the developmental characteristics of the emerging adolescent? In particular, what do we need to know about the mental and intellectual growth characteristics of this age level to develop programs that are truly responsive to their unique needs?

The emerging adolescent

Energetic, negative, dynamic, rebellious, imaginative, anxious, inquisitive, and *frightened* are adjectives frequently employed to describe the emerging adolescent. Other descriptions come readily to mind. Peer pressure is paramount, and the desire to conform may result in intolerance of others' lack of conformity. Emotional stress is increased by rapid physical changes, which in turn influence the development of self-concept. There is a strong desire for approval, and a lack of achievement quickly causes discouragement (Tyler et al., 85).

Stage of formal operations

In terms of mental and intellectual development, the 11–14 year old is entering and exiting the stage of development Piaget refers to as that of formal operations. In this stage "students can think using abstractions. They form theories about everything and are very concerned with the possible as distinct from the actual" (Charles, 22, p. 3). In this final stage of intellectual development which is preparatory to adult thinking:

> . . . the student can begin to hypothesize and can go beyond what might be—that which may be discovered as true. A high degree of intellectual curiosity also is generally characteristic of this developmental state.

Preference for active involvement

Importance of immediate goals

> They prefer active involvement to passive recipiency. Intellectual activity is especially interesting when related to their immediate goals or purposes. They tend to be intellectually uninhibited. They like to discuss some of their experiences with adults, have a tremendous potential range of creative expression and appreciation in the arts and humanities, and can evaluate rather critically.

Personal responsibility for learning

> Transescents can see relationships among similar concepts and experiences and make inferences therefrom. . . . Middle school students are capable of exploring and selecting learning materials and experiences on their own. To an increasing degree they can be trusted to assume personal responsibility for their own learning, independent of teacher control (Gatewood and Dilg, 43, pp. 10–11).

Foreign language programs at the middle and junior high school levels must take into account the unique developmental characteristics of the emerging adolescent, especially keeping in mind that the rate of cognitive growth differs greatly from student to student. A simple extension of a senior high program down into the middle and junior high school has been done frequently in the past, with little or no regard for the special characteristics of the learners. The uniqueness of the middle school's clients demands a unique curriculum, and that includes the foreign language curriculum.

Difference in cognitive growth

A curriculum for the emerging adolescent

A middle school curriculum that is truly child-centered provides "an environment where the child, not the program is most important and where the opportunity to succeed is insured for all students" (Gatewood and Dilg, 43, p. 7). The curriculum takes into account the great diversity found in youngsters from ages 11–14. There is a need for a variety of learning experiences to account for the full range of students who are functioning at different levels of concrete and formal operations. These learning experiences should be so structured that a student can progress in an individualized manner based on continuous progress.

Child-centered curriculum

Variety of learning experiences

Given the individual differences among emerging adolescents, the use of individualized instruction at the middle school level is not an option but a requirement. The middle school is challenged "to make a reality of the long-held ideal of individualized instruction" (Alexander and Williams, 3, p. 32). Both the individualization of pace and learning modalities are necessary.

Individualized instruction a requirement

The middle school should provide a curriculum "in which all areas are taught to reveal opportunities for further study, to help students learn how to study, and to help them appraise their own interests and talents" (Gatewood and Dilg, 43, p. 11). Consequently, a variety of exploratory programs should be available.

All areas

Because "the innate complexities of the early adolescent demand a program of education that is fully integrated and geared to the individual needs of the student" (Harvey, 50, p. 47), emphasis should be on an integrative approach to curriculum in which areas are combined, and an attempt is made to break down the artificial divisions of curriculum content. Eichhorn (32) suggests that "subject matter from the humanities, arts, and sciences will form the basis of the integration. This approach will have a thematic base out of which a whole range of interrelated topics will emerge" (p. 43).

Team teaching

The formation of teams of teachers from a variety of disciplines will facilitate the integration of curriculum, and the teaming of students and teachers provides large blocks of time in which to bring about this integration. There is certainly a place for the foreign language teacher on an interdisciplinary team. Such an arrangement permits the development of specific foreign language skills while fostering at the same time an integrated approach to the development of learning processes and the acquisition of knowledge.

FLES–The state of the art

My recent survey of state foreign language supervisors and editors of state newsletters and journals confirms the observation of Kunkle (56) that "there seems to be no question that FLES . . . spawned in most communities by the Sputnik-NDEA events is an almost completely defunct creature" (p. 417). The 1974 ACTFL workshop entitled "Exploratory Foreign Language Programs in the Middle School" was predicated on the fact that the FLES programs that filled the exploratory function had disappeared and that this role was now to be filled by the middle and junior high schools (Fearing and Grittner, 37). The observation that "the present state of foreign language instruction for elementary students is rather dim, rudderless, and debilitating of precious learning time and resources in an already overcrowded elementary curriculum" (Thompson and Blackwell, 83, p. 543) is generally representative of the views of the FLES movement held by educators outside the foreign language profession.

Current FLES programs

Although FLES has become a relatively isolated phenomenon in the elementary school and is often the first program to feel the impact of school levy defeats, some FLES programs throughout the country are alive and well. The Latin FLES program in Philadelphia has grown to include 12,000 elementary students who receive 20 minutes of instruction daily (Masciantonio, 65).

A similar program continues to flourish in Washington, D. C. Lipton (61) reports a thriving program in French, German, Hebrew, Italian, and Spanish in New York City. In Texas approximately 58,000 students are enrolled in FLES programs (García, 42).

In the Des Plaines, Illinois, elementary schools all fifth and sixth grade students receive Spanish instruction from specialist teachers as part of the regular curriculum. The fifth grade classes meet 20 minutes per day, and the sixth grade classes meet for 30 minutes per day five days per week (Hubbard, 52). Some FLES programs—for example, that in the Allentown, Pennsylvania school district—are directed toward the academically gifted students. In this program the students take German in the fourth grade, Spanish in the fifth grade, and French in the sixth. Specialist teachers offer 30 minutes of daily instruction (Bruni, 19). Durden (31) reports that in Akron, Ohio, all sixth graders (approximately 4,000) are enrolled either in French, German, or Spanish. FLES specialists conduct 20-minute sessions daily.

Programs for the gifted

Television was used by many of the school districts throughout the country in the early 1960s as the primary medium of instruction with follow-up provided by language specialists and classroom teachers. Alabama is typical of most states that have abandoned instructional television, and for the majority of the 3,500 students who remain in the FLES program, instruction is provided by specialist teachers (Crane, 25). Some FLES programs, however, do still use instructional television. In Milwaukee, Wisconsin, Gradisnik (45) reports that 5,500 fifth and sixth graders voluntarily participate in a televised Spanish program in which the studio teacher also makes class visitations. Classroom teachers are provided with a teacher guide, visual display cards, records containing the dialogue of each lesson, and student take-home and song recordings. There are 24 lessons for each grade level (15 minutes in length). The Robbinsdale, Minnesota, elementary schools offer a multimedia program in German for grades 4, 5, and 6 (Fearing, 36).

Use of television

In Atlanta, Georgia, 8,200 students are enrolled in the four levels of the Spanish TV program *Viva nuestra amistad* produced by the Georgia ETV network (McClure, 62). The classroom teacher, Spanish teacher, and TV teacher work as a team to present, teach, and expand activities in skill development and cultural insights of the target language culture. The 4,000 students in French participate in the *Parlons Français* television program in the fourth grade and receive daily teaching in the remaining grades by specialist teachers.

The ITFS Spanish program in the Jefferson County, Kentucky, Public Schools (Elliott, 33) is designed for students of all levels of ability in grades 3 through 6. Two 15-minute programs are telecast twice weekly. Each classroom teacher is provided with a curriculum guide that contains a set of illustrations to accompany many of the TV lessons and daily lesson plans. The Spanish program is integrated with social studies, science, music, and art. An interesting feature of the fifth and sixth grade program is the use of a "Spanish commercial" that serves both as a transition between the major segments of the program and as a reinforcement of new words and phrases.

In addition to the ITFS Spanish program in the Jefferson County Public Schools, approximately 1,550 students (grades 2–8) are enrolled in an advanced program for academically gifted students. A Spanish specialist conducts these classes for 30 minutes each day.

Radio lessons

Sherman (79) reports that radio lessons in French, German, and Spanish are broadcast over WCBE-FM in Columbus, Ohio. Although the programs are directed to the fifth and sixth grade levels, they are used by almost every grade level within the elementary school. Participation is voluntary, and the language to be studied is chosen by the classroom teacher. Teachers' manuals and supplementary tapes are provided. The foreign language supervisor makes class visitations and does demonstration lessons upon request. A number of schools in Columbus participate in this program and utilize volunteers from the community as resource persons.

All sixth graders in Wauwatosa, Wisconsin's 11 elementary schools must study a modern foreign language as a part of their curriculum (Meyer, 67). They may choose to study French, German, Russian, or Spanish. Daily 30-minute classes are conducted by specialists. The classroom teacher is not involved in the teaching of the second language. Enrollment figures for the past seven years indicate that consistently 50 percent of all students in grades 7–12 continue in a second language.

The FLES program in West Hartford, Connecticut, begins at the fourth or fifth grade level, depending upon the organizational pattern of the individual school. Because foreign language study is considered an integral part of the curriculum, all students are required to participate (Barry, 12).

A new program

Although many FLES programs across the country have been recent victims of the budget cutters' knife, the community of Hennessey, Oklahoma, inaugurated a grade 1–6 FLES program in the fall of 1975 (Britton, 17). Using specialist teachers, instruction is given for 20 minutes a week in grade 1 and is increased to 40 minutes per week in grade 2. The program has received strong administrative and community support.

An individualized approach

Juan, María y Pepe is a locally developed, individualized, self-instructional Spanish language program in which approximately 1,000 elementary students, grades 4–6, in Tucson, Arizona, are enrolled (Valencia, 86). The supervision and consultation services for the program are provided by native-speaking paraprofessionals. Due to limitations in terms of personnel, materials, and time, the program is operated on a selective basis. On an average of three times per week participating students leave their classrooms for a period of 30 minutes to study Spanish in groups of three in an open-spaced environment. The success of the individualized/independent learning mode depends on the successful functioning of a variety of interrelated components: printed programmed material; correlated recorded cassettes; cassette playback units; native-speaking paraprofessionals; open-space learning environment that stimulates oral interaction among students; and the supportive role played by the classroom teachers, administrators, and parents.

Use of paraprofessionals

For evaluation there is a system of internal checks initiated by the student on cue from the program and a system of external checks initiated by the native-speaking paraprofessionals. Through these and other controls the programmed materials are self-instructional and permit the students to pace their own progress.

"Spanish through Folk Music"

Supplementing *Juan, María y Pepe* is an enrichment program entitled *Spanish Through Folk Music*. Capitalizing on the medium of music, the program offers students an opportunity to learn about the Hispanic world in general and about neighboring Mexico in particular. *Spanish Through Folk Music* is not performance-oriented, nor is it a substitute for Spanish language learning programs.

FLEX

Rundell (78) reports that pilot programs, which are exploratory in nature and are referred to as FLEX, are currently in progress at the fourth grade level in three elementary schools in Topeka, Kansas. At McClure Elementary School the program consists of two-week blocks in each of six languages: Spanish, German, French, Russian, Chinese, and Latin. Each lesson consists of 20 minutes of language study and 10 minutes of cultural involvement. There is a two-week interval between each of the languages studied. Spanish and Chinese are offered at Rice and Bishop Elementary Schools. In the latter, the fourth grade students are divided into two groups, one group studying Chinese and the other Spanish. After their 30-minute classes, both groups get together to share their learning experiences with each other for a period of 15 minutes. When the students change languages, teachers anticipate a faster learning experience as a result of the previous interchange.

The district foreign language specialist has recently presented a proposal to the administration for the next school year that recommends an implementation of a FLES program in all fourth grades in the district. The proposal specifies that 30 minutes per day for 10 consecutive school days be devoted to the study of each of four languages and cultures and that the instruction be carried out by certified language specialists.

Total immersion

The Ottawa Roman Catholic Separate School Board program is representative of the successful total immersion programs conducted in Canada (Game, 41). At the kindergarten level in which 50 percent of the instruction is conducted in French, 15 thematically based modules have been developed. These modules essentially reflect the second language element within the total kindergarten program.

In grades 1–5 certain elements of the second language approach are retained. In practice, lessons include syllabification exercises, basic linguistic structures, and creative language activities. Conversations and dialogues are emphasized and natural intonation is stressed. All other subjects (mathematics, environmental studies, music, art, physical education, and family life education) are taught in French in Grades 1, 2, and 3.

Religious education is taught in English by an English-speaking teacher at all four levels, and 75 minutes of English language arts are taught in grade 3. In grades 4 and 5, 50 percent of the time is allotted to instruction in French and 50 percent to English.

School within a school

Using the school within a school approach, the Cincinnati, Ohio, Public Schools have developed a K–6 bilingual/bicultural program in German, French, and Spanish for students who almost exclusively speak English (Met, 66). Using the French program as an example, the following goals have been identified.

1 To teach children to understand, speak, and eventually read and write French
2 To develop an understanding of and appreciation for the French people and their culture
3 To recognize the contributions of the French people and culture to American life

In the kindergarten programs French is used for all instruction except in language arts and reading. In the first grade French is taught formally for 70 minutes each day and is integrated informally throughout the rest of the day. Children count and compute in French and use metric measurements by the third grade level. Science is taught in French at the fourth grade level; and by grade 5, 50 percent of the instruction is in French.

There is an emphasis on listening skills prior to the development of speaking skills. Communicative rather than linguistic competence is stressed and no repetition drills are used. Many of the concepts and vocabulary words are taught through the telling and reenactment of familiar fairy tales.

Approximately 95 children are enrolled in this bilingual/bicultural program in each of three elementary schools. The programs are open to children living in all parts of the Cincinnati school district. Because of the voluntary nature of the program, parental support has been reported as outstanding. Although a specialist teacher is used in addition to the classroom teacher in this program, the potential is present in a school within a school context to employ a bilingual classroom teacher and hence substantially reduce the cost of the program.

The Milwaukee, Wisconsin, Spanish K–6 bilingual/bicultural program which began in 1969 is open to both the Spanish-dominant and English-dominant child whose parents would like to have him develop both skills in two languages and an appreciation for more than one culture (Gradisnik, 45). The alternative school design, which is now operational in six elementary schools in Milwaukee, is consistent with the options-for-learning concept because it provides parents with a choice of alternative schooling for their children. The Milwaukee program is developmental. Each year one bilingual grade is added vertically until the school has a continuous bilingual/bicultural program from K–6. A bilingual classroom teacher conducts the program in a self-contained classroom setting.

"Options-for-learning" concept

An adaptation of the alternative school concept is the magnet learning center which has been developed in the St. Paul, Minnesota, Public Schools (Jorstad, 55). A foreign language magnet learning center has been established in four elementary schools in St. Paul. Students spend half days for a quarter at a time in which they have an intensive experience in crafts, drama, and a foreign language. The program is open to all elementary students in the city, and the success of the program is reflected in the waiting lists for the FLES program.

Magnet learning center

A bilingual program in French, German, and Spanish is being developed for K–3 and 7–8 in the Saint Louis, Missouri, Public Schools. The program will be similar to that of Cincinnati (Fay, 35).

In Dade County, Florida, 31,000 students are enrolled in a bilingual/bicultural program (Alonso, 5). Federal funds enable a teacher to be assigned to each of six administrative areas to help coordinate the program. A team of four to seven itinerant teachers and five paraprofessionals works in each of the areas. Under a Title VII grant the Spanish Curriculum and Development Center has produced SCDC kits consisting of a Spanish second language strand for grades 1 and 2.

Second language strand

Individualization and FLES

A survey of existing FLES programs indicates that no new materials have been published within recent years by the major textbook companies. Many of the programs that have survived over the years are continuing to use locally produced materials.

Little evidence of individualization

The survey also confirms Phillips' (73) observation that there is little evidence of a concerted attempt to individualize foreign language instruction at the elementary level. There are, however, several examples of approaches to individualization of programs. As mentioned earlier, *Juan, María y Pepe,* developed by the Tucson, Arizona, Public Schools, uses programmed materials that permit self-pacing and utilize independent learning.

Small-group process

Stewart (81) developed a small-group process approach to beginning Spanish instruction in the elementary school (K–2). The manuals contain eight Spanish lessons intended for use in small heterogenous groups of no more than six children for 20-minute instruction periods. Emphasis is placed on developing information-seeking skills by stressing the asking of questions.

A review of the professional literature reveals only a few articles about individualized instruction at the elementary level.

LAPs

Larew (60) suggests how Learning Activity Packages (LAPs) can be used in the elementary classroom for primary instruction as well as for remedial and enrichment activities.

The following is a sample LAP which is to be used in conjunction with a cassette or tape recorder.

Days of the Week

General Objective: To learn to express the days of the week in Spanish both orally and in writing. At the end of this unit, you must be able to answer questions, both orally and in writing, on the days of the week.

Procedure

1 Listen to the tape and recite each day of the week in Spanish after the model.
2 When you are able to say the seven days correctly in Spanish, look at how they are written below and now READ the days of the week.

lunes	*miércoles*	*viernes*	*domingo*
martes	*jueves*	*sábado*	

3 Write each day of the week three times in your notebook, paying close attention to the spelling of each one and saying each one aloud as you write it.

4 Listen to segment two of the tape and repeat the question you hear and the model answer. Let's find out what today is.

¿Qué día es hoy?	*Hoy es martes.*
¿Qué día es hoy?	*Hoy es jueves.*
¿Qué día es hoy?	*Hoy es domingo.*
¿Qué día es hoy?	*Hoy es lunes.*
¿Qué día es hoy?	*Hoy es sábado* (p. 115).

Methods class

In a proposed syllabus for a FLES methods class Ford (38) stresses as a chief feature of the course the preparation and implementation of individualized learning packets. During the tenth week of the course the student teacher field-tests a LAP as an example of how to individualize instruction at the elementary level.

Activity versus instruction

Hunter (53) addresses individualizing FLES programs from a theoretical point of view. She points out that in developing individualized programs for elementary students, the distinction between individualized activity and individualized instruction must be kept in mind. Because of a lack of skills to sustain himself for a period of time without adult support, a teacher cannot assume that the young learner will instruct himself.

Self as instrument

While recognizing the importance of individualizing the learning task in terms of learning rate and respecting differences in terms of preferred learning modalities, Hunter (53) emphasizes the role of the teacher as a facilitator of learning as the most important component of individualization, especially at the elementary level. "It is in his use of self as instrument that the teacher further individualizes his instruction" (p. 497) whether in a group or one-to-one situation.

Research and FLES

No negative impact

Past studies indicate that the addition of a second language does not impair the general achievement or the native language progress of children (Donoghue, 28). For example, Smith (80) states that second language study in the fourth grade does not interfere with achievement in basic skills. Studies by Johnson (54) and Potts (75) support this finding.

Divergent thinking skills

The recent research of Landry (59) points out a unique contribution that FLES makes to the cognitive development of children. The research demonstrates that the study of two languages during the elementary school years is an enriching experience resulting in the development of divergent thinking abilities such as fluency, flexibility, and originality. Children in this investigation who studied a second language at the elementary school level were significantly better divergent thinkers at the sixth grade level than children who had studied only their own language.

The area of the long-term effects of FLES on the development of language skills is a controversial one. Vocolo (87) reports that FLES students who had four years of language prior to high school did significantly better than the control group (who were in their second year of foreign language study) in listening, speaking, and writing. Brega and Newell (16) reported similar findings with students who had six years of FLES compared with the control group that was in its third year of language study.

Excluding the area of second language pronunciation, research in the field of psycholinguistics gives little support to the argument that children learn a second language better or with more ease than adolescents or adults (Oller and Nagato, 71). Asher and García (8) and Grider, Otoma, and Toyota (46) conclude that, with the exception of pronunciation, adolescents and adults usually do better and perform more easily while learning a second language.

A research project studying the long-term effects of FLES in a private elementary and secondary school system for girls in Japan was conducted by Oller and Nagato (71). The FLES students had studied English for six years before they entered junior high. A cloze test (which requires the student to supply the words deleted from a prose passage) was used to measure the long-term effect of FLES. The control group, which began the study of English in junior high, was able to overtake the FLES students by the eleventh grade. The researchers conclude that "there is no evidence students with a FLES background will progress more rapidly . . . under certain conditions they will not even maintain their initial advantage over non-FLES students" (p. 18).

Foreign languages in emerging adolescent education

With the demise of FLES programs across the nation, the middle or junior high school is generally the first place a student has the opportunity to begin the study of a foreign language. While most beginning programs at these levels are designed to constitute all or part of a Level I sequence that can be directly articulated with a senior high program, there is a definite trend throughout the country toward the development of exploratory foreign language programs.

Trend toward exploratory programs

Fearing and Grittner (37) identify four kinds of exploratory foreign language programs. In what is referred to as The Language Potpourri, three to five different languages are offered over short periods of time within a given academic year. This is an opportunity to expose all students to the languages that will be available for further study at the high school level.

Language potpourri

In the General Language Course the emphasis is on the nature of language and deals with the history, etymology, and cultural facets of several languages. Proponents of the general language course insist that skill-development activities in a specific language be built into the course to avoid a theoretical approach to language study.

General language course

The Single Language Exploratory Offering is usually offered in a six- or nine-week block or may be offered on alternate days for a semester. The program is not necessarily sequential with the high school and in fact the language that is taught may not be available at the high school. While some proponents argue that this course should be available immediately prior to the high school experience, others would argue that because of the exploratory nature of the program, the time gap is not a serious problem. A variation of this approach is the Required Elective Program in which a student has to take one of the languages that will be offered at the high school level for a nine-week period.

Single language exploratory offering

Required elective program

Identifying an exploratory program as an experience that is worthwhile in itself and that provides the basis for decisions about further language study, Grittner (47) makes the following distinctions between an exploratory and nonexploratory program:

Characteristics of exploratory program

1 The program is self-sufficient; that is, there is no attempt

whatever to make it fit sequentially with subsequent foreign language instruction in the senior high school.

2 The emphasis is on breadth; that is, the program offers a bona fide sampling of many aspects of foreign language learning.

3 The program is nonselective; that is, its purpose is to provide a language learning experience for all students. Therefore, such things as I.Q., grade-point average, vocational aspiration, and other alleged predictors of success are considered to be irrelevant.

4 The atmosphere in the class is "low pressure." While each unit of work is covered thoroughly, there is no compulsion to cover a specified amount of material within an allotted period of time.

5 Homework is minimal in such a program (although some students may choose to participate in certain out-of-class project activities or may wish to do outside reading in areas of interest) (pp. 74–75).

The Language Potpourri approach to foreign language exploration was the one most frequently reported in a national survey conducted by this writer. Baker (10) reports that Johnson Park Junior High in Columbus, Ohio, offers the Seventh Grade Survey Program. Seventh grade students in the school have a class once a week so that they receive nine sessions in each of four languages. This program was initiated to give all students an insight into another language and culture and to acquaint them with the process involved in learning a second language.

The exploratory program at the Burns Middle School in Owensboro, Kentucky, requires all seventh grade students to take nine weeks of each of the following languages: French, German, Spanish, and Russian. At the Daviess County Middle School, also in Owensboro, Kentucky, all students in the sixth grade take an exploratory course composed of four and one-half weeks of French and four and one-half weeks of Spanish. Seventh and eighth graders may take nine weeks of each subject. In the Bedford City Schools in Cleveland, Ohio, three languages are offered to eighth grade students for 12 weeks each (Harmon 49).

The Washoe County School District in Nevada requires all sixth graders to take three nine-week exploratory classes in each of three languages: French, German, and Spanish. In these classes two to three weeks are spent on history, two to three weeks on culture, and the remaining weeks explore the art and music of the culture and offer a limited opportunity for some skill development in the language (Abrams, 1).

Bourque and Chehy (15) describe a successful program in the Stratford, Connecticut, Public Schools that can be categorized as an example of a General Language Course. This interdisciplinary and intercultural program is a requirement for all seventh graders. It stresses the nature of language in general and introduces as many specific languages as possible to the students. Listed below are the specific student objectives of the course.

Objectives of general language course

The student will:

1 Be able to count to 10 in several different foreign languages
2 Recite from memory, and with understanding, a brief dialog in several different languages
3 Identify elementary differences between American and other cultures
4 Do independent research on cultural areas of particular interest to him
5 Do personal research on his own ethnic background and on the origin of his own name
6 Keep notes on and ask questions about cultural and linguistic facts presented to him by the teacher and by numerous guest speakers (p. 11)

There is no fixed scope and sequence for the course. Each class adapts itself to variables such as student interest, availability of community resources, teacher strengths, and ethnic composition. Although there is no basic text, there is a wide variety of supplementary materials including passport units on cultural themes, culture capsules, letters from foreign pen pals, worksheets, tapes and records, and realia from the various countries. Evaluation strategies include the use of listening and speaking tests; written tests about language and culture; and reports, research papers, and projects.

"Language and Man"

Language and Man is an exploratory foreign language program for grade 6 developed by the Monroe County Community Schools in Bloomington, Indiana, and is available from the ACTFL Materials Center (Bartos et al., 13). Following the introductory units on how language operates and on the importance of gestures, there is a brief introduction to both Spanish and French. This includes a review of Spanish and French elements in our culture, an introduction to the French and Spanish sound system, and a unit on gestures.

Career education focus

An exploratory program with a career-education focus has been prepared by the Prince George's County Public Schools in Maryland (39). The course is intended primarily for sixth or seventh graders who are not ready to enroll in a sequential structured program of language study. The objectives include cultural contrasts and similarities, language awareness and enhancement by noting relationship to English, language exploration-readiness, awareness of foreign visitors, and career awareness.

Scheduling models

German career packet

Die Kinder Auf Dem Flugplatz is a career learning packet designed for a middle school exploratory German program (Kurovsky, 57). The objectives are:

1 To investigate some careers related to the air industry and to find out through observations and interviews how knowledge of a foreign language aids these careers.
2 To learn the names in German of some careers that are related to the air industry and that have been identified by the students through observations and interviews.
3 To learn the German words for the names of the careers of the students' relatives (p. 4).

Suggested activities include the making of a booklet listing occupations in English and German, the preparation of an occupational bulletin board, and the writing of an original dialogue simulating an experience at an airport. Materials provided in the career learning packet include an overview of the airport, vocabulary of airport terms, conversations, student worksheets, and tests.

At the middle school level there are examples of foreign language teachers working as members of an interdisciplinary team. *Living Arts—a Humanities Course* is a program offered at the Carl Sandburg Middle School in Freeport, Illinois, for all seventh graders. Six specialist teachers meet with 300 students for three 55-minute classes per day. The following subject areas are included: art, music, drama, creative writing, home economics, and foreign language. The foreign language component consists of a survey of French, Spanish, and German. "According to the course description, 'The basic rationale of the course is to homogenize rather than to specialize; to seek an overall view of the arts with the student, not the subject at the center' " (Brown and Brown, 18, p. 12).

Interdisciplinary approach

Carney (20) reports that the foreign language program in the middle schools of the Tulsa, Oklahoma, Independent School District is also organized as part of a humanities program. At the Carver Middle School, social studies concepts are taught through a foreign language and the foreign language teacher team teaches with the other members of the humanities team including representatives from the areas of drama, art, literature, and social studies. An extensive use is made of community resources. In addition to exposing the students to the four skills, emphasis is placed on relating language to culture, historical events, self-concept, art, drama, and literature.

Success story

A success story exists at the Anwatin Middle School in Minneapolis. The middle school (grades 5–8), which opened in the fall of 1976, enrolls 65 percent of its seventh and eighth graders in French, German, Spanish, and Latin. This is the highest percentage of enrollment in the city of Minneapolis, although the school is located in the lowest socio-economic area. In addition, 600 fifth and sixth graders are also studying a foreign language (Hoye, 51).

An Assessment

New FLES prototypes

Although the FLES Movement, which began in the 1950s, can be characterized as a rather isolated phenomenon in the 1970s, there are examples of programs in various parts of the country that have survived and are flourishing. In addition, there are some exciting prototypes of new dimensions in FLES programs that provide the opportunity for the foreign language profession to choose among some options. That these new prototypes are being developed in an educational climate that is more committed to a multicultural curriculum and intercultural education than that of the 1950s is a portent of a renewed commitment to foreign language education in the elementary curriculum.

New organizational patterns

The alternative school or school within a school concept based on the education-by-choice model can provide a truly bilingual/bicultural experience for those who desire it. Either by establishing a magnet school that is open to all students in a school district on a part-time or full-time basis or by identifying one classroom for each grade level within one building for the clients of that particular school, programs can be offered that will eventually lead to conducting all of the instruction in the target language. The number of alternative schools within available schools and the variety of languages offered in a school district is limited only by the demand of the clients. There will be no additional cost to the program over and above the cost for regular classroom instruction if the staffing plan calls for the utilization of an elementary classroom teacher who is fluent in the target language. This approach to staffing makes the addition of an elementary foreign language program more realistic within the context of an economy-minded public.

Differentiated staffing

An exploratory type of foreign language program that is aimed at all students in a school or school system can be staffed in a number of ways in addition to the utilization of a FLES specialist. An elementary school that uses differentiated staffing can utilize the strengths of individual staff members to conduct the language classes. Such an arrangement has the additional advantage of using the integrated-day model based on the integration of curriculum. A regular member of a school staff who is responsible for the foreign language instruction, working as a member of a team, can effectively bring about this integration.

Ancillary resources

Peer teaching, cadet teaching, and the use of paraprofessionals and community volunteers (Barnett, 11; Biehn, 14; Hall and Sturm, 48) are examples of other options available when considering the problem of staffing an elementary foreign language program. For example, an individualized program based on a multimedia approach and designed for student-initiated learning with paraprofessionals or volunteers in an ancillary role is a viable approach. The increasingly common practice of multiage grouping of students affords an excellent opportunity for students to teach each other. Staffing is obviously an important consideration in establishing an elementary foreign language program, whether it be total immersion in the language or exploratory. But no matter how ingeniously human resources might be employed, little is really gained if the program is not designed with the child as the central focus. A child-centered language program translates into a learning environment rich in concrete experiences that permits the learner to be an active agent. The emphasis is on learning, not on teaching (Weber, 89). Individualized instruction, both in terms of pace and learning modality, is maximized. Historically, individualized instruction has not been the hallmark of elementary foreign language programs. If anything, they have been generally characterized as models of lockstep instruction. That great strides have been made toward individualization of language programs at the secondary but not at the elementary level is ironic; for the movement toward individualization of instruction in the United States was generated in the elementary school.

Emphasis on learning, not teaching

More individualized instruction

At the middle school level (grades 6–8) the development of exploratory programs and the integration of foreign languages with other disciplines, though certainly not widespread, are encouraging indications that the profession is becoming aware of the unique character of the middle school environment and is responding to the developmental characteristics of the emerging adolescent learner. While there are those who argue that the middle and junior high school program should serve as a downward extension of the senior high school curriculum and that exploratory programs are a waste of time, effort, and money, there is a growing realization in the profession that the emerging adolescent years are a time for exploring and a time for the discovery of one's interests and talents within the context of short-range goals that can be related easily to reality.

Encouraging signs

For some middle school students an intensive language program sequentially structured so that it leads into Level II or III at the senior high is desirable. But for many this is not a viable option. No wonder the middle and junior high schools have historically been battlegrounds with high mortality rates. Students should have the option to choose a low-pressure program and to enter and exit that program at various times during the school year.

Options necessary

The integrative aspect of learning is emphasized when an interdisciplinary team approach is used, and the integration of foreign languages with other disciplines helps to focus on the student rather than on the subject matter. Focusing on the student is what education is about. Because of the wide range in skills, interests, and abilities, and the great variation in the cognitive growth rate, individualized instruction becomes a requirement, not an option, in emerging adolescent education. The foreign language profession must join with other educators to meet the challenge of developing a truly individualized program.

Integrative aspect emphasized

Conclusion: A call to action

In 1970 McKim (63), summarizing the state of FLES programs at that time, observed that "there is little doubt that FL instruction will continue to play an important role in American elementary education. Perhaps it will be stronger in the future than it is today" (p. 9). Six years later the number of FLES programs has been substantially reduced from those in existence in 1970. But perhaps we are on the threshold of "the future" to which McKim refers. The emphasis on cultural pluralism, intercultural education and global interdependency in curriculum development today may help to usher in a new era of foreign language education, especially at the elementary level. "One of the educational tasks of the 1970s is to change the curriculum of the elementary school so as to bring the children to a high level of international understanding and empathy" (Donoghue, 27, p. 1059). Foreign language education has a vital role to play in this educational task.

On the threshold

The questions before us are simple and direct. Given the failures and disappointments of the recent past, is the profession psychologically prepared to launch another national effort to make FLES an integral part of the elementary curriculum? Is the profession ready to capitalize on the curriculum trends and the prototypes of new dimensions in FLES that are developing in various parts of the country? Are editors of professional journals and state newsletters and conference chairpersons willing to return FLES to the lexicon?

Questions to be answered

Any attempt, of course, to revitalize foreign languages in the elementary curriculum must be done within the perspective of history. The FLES movement of the 1950s and 1960s came to the elementary schools with little interest in or knowledge of the elementary curriculum and the developmental characteristics of the learner. The interest did come, but unfortunately it came too late. The National Invitational Work Conference sponsored by the Indiana Language Program and ACTFL in 1968 focused on the elementary school setting. While there is a need to update some of the information, its publication *New Dimensions in the Teaching of FLES* (4) is required reading for school district administrators who are considering a FLES program.

The lesson of research

The lesson to be learned from the review of research in FLES is that the making of unsubstantiated claims about what FLES can do serves only to undermine the credibility of its substantiated contributions. There is a continuing need for research in FLES as well as in other levels of foreign language education.

Need to assess emerging adolescent education

At the middle and junior high school levels, the profession needs to become a part of the national movement to assess in depth the curriculum for emerging adolescent education, an area which has been long neglected. Although there are encouraging signs that there is a breakthrough in designing exciting curricula for this age group, for too long the program for sixth through eighth graders has been viewed as simply an extension of the senior high program.

The foreign language profession, the wiser for its mistakes, more knowledgeable about developmental learning theory, and as beneficiaries of a curriculum trend toward intercultural education, has the opportunity to bring about the restoration of foreign language study to the elementary curriculum. A rebirth of FLES, coupled with meaningful reforms of the middle school and senior high curriculum, can well lead to a new era in foreign language education as our nation enters its third century.

References, Foreign languages in elementary and emerging adolescent education

1 Abrams, William G. Personal Communication, 1976. [Letter.]

2 Alexander, William M. "The Middle School Emerges," vii–ix in Robert R. Leeper,ed., *Middle School in the Making:Readings from Educational Leadership.* Washington, D.C.:Association for Supervision and Curriculum Development, 1974.

3 ——— and Emmett L. Williams. "Schools for the Middle Years," 30–36 in Robert R. Leeper,ed., *Middle School in the Making:Readings from Educational Leadership.* Washington, D.C.:Association for Supervision and Curriculum Development, 1974.

4 Allen, Virginia Garibaldi, and F. André Paquette,

eds., *New Dimensions in the Teaching of FLES.* Bloomington: Indiana Language Program, 1969.
5 Alonso, Elizabeth B., "Spanish and Portuguese in the Elementary Schools: Promising Practices." *Hispania* 59(1976):118–20.
6 Arciniega, Tomás A. "Thrust Toward Pluralism: What Progress?" *Educational Leadership* 33 (1975):163–67.
7 "ASCD Resolutions." *News Exchange* 17,ii(1975): 10–11.
8 Asher, J. J., and R. García. "The Optimal Age to Learn a Foreign Language." *Modern Language Journal* 53(1969)334–41.
9 Ausubel, David P. "Viewpoints from Related Disciplines: Growth and Development," 99–108 in Glen Hass, et al.,eds., *Curriculum Planning: A New Approach.* Boston: Allyn & Bacon, 1974.
10 Baker, Reid. Personal Communication, 1976. [Questionnaire.]
11 Barnett, Harriet. "Peer Teaching." *Hispania* 56 (1973):635–38.
12 Barry, Doris. Personal Communication, 1976. [Letter.]
13 Bartos, Marilyn, et al. *Language and Man: An Exploratory Foreign Language Program for Grade Six.* Bloomington, Indiana: Monroe County Community Schools, 1972.
14 Biehn, Aubrey. "Peer Teaching in The Valley of the Genesee." *Hispania* 58(1975):929–31.
15 Bourque, Jane, and Linda Chehy. "Exploratory Language and Culture: A Unique Program." *Foreign Language Annals* (1976):10–16.
16 Brega, E., and J. M. Newell. "High School Performance of FLES and Non-FLES Students." *Modern Language Journal* 51(1967):408–11.
17 Britton, Barbara. Personal Communication, 1976. [Letter.]
18 Brown, Mary S., and Beverly L. Brown. "Communications, Social Science and Humanities." *NASSP Bulletin* 58,ccclxxxi(1974):6–15.
19 Bruni, Thomas G. Personal Communication, 1976. [Questionnaire.]
20 Carney, Helen. Personal Communication, 1976. [Questionnaire.]
21 Carpenter, John A., and Judith V. Torney. "Beyond the Melting Pot," 14–23 in Patricia Maloney Markun,ed., *Childhood and Intercultural Education: Overview and Research.* Washington, D.C.: Association for Childhood Education International, 1974.
22 Charles, C. M. *Teacher's Petit Piaget.* Belmont, California. Fearon, 1974.
23 Commager, Henry Steele. "New 'Declaration of Interdependence.'" Eugene *Register-Guard* (17 February 1976):8A.
24 Cook, Ruth C., and Ronald C. Doll. *The Elementary School Curriculum.* Boston: Allyn & Bacon, 1973.
25 Crane, Joanna. Personal Communication, 1976. [Questionnaire.]
26 Davis, O. L.,Jr.,ed., *Perspectives on Curriculum Development 1776-1976.* Washington, D.C.: Association for Supervision and Curriculum Development, 1976.
27 Donoghue, Mildred R. "FLES and International Understanding." *Hispania* 56(1973):1059–65.
28 ——— *Foreign Languages in Elementary School: Effects and Instructional Arrangements According to Research.* ERIC Focus Reports on the Teaching of Foreign Languages, Number 3, 1969. [EDRS: ED 031 980.]
29 Doyle, Walter. "Educational Opportunity—A National Commitment." *Educational Leadership* 33 (1976):252–56.
30 Dunfee, Maxine, and Claudia Crump. *Teaching for Social Values in Social Studies.* Washington, D.C.: Association for Childhood Education International, 1974.
31 Durden, John D. Personal Communication, 1976. [Questionnaire.]
32 Eichhorn, Donald H. "The Emerging Adolescent School of the Future—Now," 35–52 in J. Galen Saylor,ed., *The School of the Future Now.* Washington, D.C.: Association for Supervision and Curriculum Development, 1972.
33 Elliot, Maxine R. Personal Communication, 1976. [Letter.]
34 Fantini, Mario D. "Alternatives within Public Schools," 132–42 in William Van Til,ed., *Curriculum: Quest for Relevance.* 2d ed. Boston: Houghton Mifflin, 1974.
35 Fay, Eloise. Personal Communication, 1976. [Questionnaire.]
36 Fearing, Percy. Personal Communication, 1976. [Questionnaire.]
37 ——— and Frank Grittner,eds. *Exploratory Foreign Language Programs in the Middle School.* [Curriculum report prepared in ACTFL Preconference Workshop for Foreign Language Consultants and Supervisors, Denver, Colorado, November 27, 1974.] [EDRS: ED 104 174.]
38 Ford, James F. "FLES Methods: A Proposed Course Syllabus." *Hispania* 57(1974):301–04.
39 *Foreign Language Exploratory: Resource Guide and Handbook.* Upper Marlboro, Maryland: Prince George's County Public Schools, 1975.
40 Frazier, Alex. *Open Schools for Children.* Washington, D.C.: Association for Supervision and Curriculum Development, 1972.
41 Game, Adrienne. Personal Communication, 1976. [Letter.]
42 García, Inés. Personal Communication, 1976. [Questionnaire.]
43 Gatewood, Thomas E., and Charles A. Dilg. *The Middle School We Need: A Report from the ASCD Working Group on the Emerging Adolescent Learner.* Washington, D.C.: Association for Supervision and Curriculum Development, 1975.
44 Goodlad, John I. "A Typology of Educational Alternatives," 3–27 in John I. Goodlad, et al.,eds., *The Conventional and the Alternatives in Education.* Berkeley, California: McCutchan, 1975.
45 Gradisnik, Anthony. Personal Communication, 1976. [Letter.]

46 Grider, R. E., A. Otomo, and W. Toyota. *Comparison between 2nd, 3rd, and 4th Grade Children in the Audio Lingual Learning of Japanese as a Second Language.* Honolulu: University of Hawaii, 1961.
47 Grittner, Frank M. "Foreign Languages and the Changing Curriculum." *NASSP Bulletin* 58,ccclxxxiv(1974):71–78.
48 Hall, Marian, and Dorothy Sturm. "Spanish Cadet Teaching—Its Own Excuse for Being." *Hispania* 56(1973):110–11.
49 Harmon, Brenda J. Personal Communication, 1976. [Letter.]
50 Harvey, Philip J. "Teacher Attitudes: Subject Matter and Human Beings," 46–51 in Robert R. Leeper,ed., *Middle School in the Making: Readings from Educational Leadership.* Washington, D.C.: Association for Supervision and Curriculum Development, 1974.
51 Hoye, Almon. Personal Communication, 1976. [Letter.]
52 Hubbard, Maxine. Personal Communication, 1976. [Questionnaire.]
53 Hunter, Madeline. "Individualizing FLES." *Hispania* 57(1974):494–97.
54 Johnson, C. E., F. P. Ellison, and J. S. Flores. "The Effect of Foreign Language Instruction on Basic Learning in Elementary Schools: A Second Report." *Modern Language Journal* 47 (1963):8–11.
55 Jorstad, Helen. Personal Communication, 1976. [Questionnaire.]
56 Kunkle, John F. "Now That FLES is Dead, What Next?" *Educational Leadership* 29(1972):417–19.
57 Kurovsky, Gina H. *Die Kinder auf dem Flugplatz: A Career Learning Packet Designed for Middle School German Exploratory Language Programs.* St. Paul: Minnesota State Department of Education, Division of Instruction, Elementary and Secondary Section, 1975.
58 Lambert, Wallace E., and Otto Klineberg. *Children's Views of Foreign People.* New York: Appleton-Century-Crofts, 1967.
59 Landry, Richard G. "A Comparison of Second Language Learners and Monolinguals on Divergent Thinking Tasks at the Elementary School Level." *Modern Language Journal* 58(1974):10–15.
60 Larew, Leonor A. "LAPS for FLES in Individualized Instruction." *Hispania* 56(1973):114–16.
61 Lipton, Gladys. "New York City's Foreign Language Elementary Schools in Good Health." *Inside Education* 60(1974):6.
62 McClure, Martha G. Personal Communication, 1976. [Questionnaire.]
63 McKim, Lester W. *FLES: Types of Programs.* ERIC Focus Reports on the Teaching of Foreign Languages, Number 16, 1970. [EDRS: ED 043 268.]
64 Masangkay, Z. S., F. F. Villorente, R. S. Somico, E. S. Reyes, and D. M. Taylor. "The Development of Ethnic Group Perception." *Journal of Genetic Psychology* 121(1972):263–70.
65 Masciantonio, Rudolph. Personal Communication, 1976. [Questionnaire.]
66 Met, Myriam. Personal Communication, 1976. [Interview.]
67 Meyer, Gertrud E. Personal Communication, 1976. [Letter.]
68 Mussen, H., and John J. Conger. *Child Development and Personality.* New York: Harper & Row, 1974.
69 National Commission on the Reform of Secondary Education. The *Reform of Secondary Education: A Report to the Public and the Profession.* New York: McGraw Hill, 1973.
70 "No One Model American: AACTE Statement on Multicultural Education." *Journal of Teacher Education* 24,iv(1973):264–65.
71 Oller, John W.,Jr., and Naoko Nagato. "The Long-Term Effect of FLES: An Experiment." *Modern Language Journal* 58(1974):15–19.
72 Perkins, H. *Human Development and Learning.* Belmont, California: Wadsworth, 1974.
73 Phillips, June K. "Individualization and Personalization," in Gilbert A. Jarvis,ed., *Responding to New Realities."* ACTFL Review of Foreign Language Education. Volume 5, Skokie, Illinois: National Textbook Company, 1974.
74 Piaget, J., and A. M. Weil. "The Development in Children of the Idea of Homeland and of Relations With Other Countries." *International Social Science Bulletin* 3(1951):561–68.
75 Potts, M. H. "The Effect of Second Language Instruction on the Reading Proficiency and General School Achievement of Primary Grade Children." *American Educational Research Journal* 4(1967): 367–73.
76 Riestra, M. A., and C. E. Johnson. "Changes in Attitudes of Elementary School Pupils Toward Foreign Speaking Peoples Resulting from the Study of a Foreign Language." *Journal of Experimental Education* 32(1964):65–72.
77 Rogers, Vincent R., and Bud Church. *Open Education: Critique and Assessment.* Washington, D.C.: Association for Supervision and Curriculum Development, 1975.
78 Rundell, George M. Personal Communication, 1976. [Letter.]
79 Sherman, Susy. Personal Communication, 1976. [Letter and questionnaire.]
80 Smith, Wayne H. "Linguistic and Academic Achievement of Elementary Students Studying a Foreign Language." *Dissertation Abstracts* 27 (May, 1967):3882A.
81 Stewart, Adela Artola. *Mini-clases de español: A Small Group Process Approach to Beginning Spanish Instruction in the Elementary School.* Phoenix: Wilson School District 7, 1972. [EDRS: ED 058 801.]
82 Thatcher, David. *Teaching, Loving, and Self-Directed Learning.* Pacific Palisades, California: Goodyear, 1973.
83 Thompson, Richard A., and Janet M. Blackwell.

"FLES: To Be or Not To Be." *Elementary English* 51(1974):541–43.

84 Thornburg, Hershel. "Learning and Maturation in Middle School Age Youth," 364–70 in Glen Hass et al.,eds., *Curriculum Planning:A New Approach.* Boston:Allyn & Bacon, 1974.

85 Tyler, Bonnie B., Charles H. Flatter, E. Joan Hunt, and Robert F. Marcus. *Developmental Characteristics of Children and Youth.* Washington, D.C.: Association for Supervision and Curriculum Development, 1975.

86 Valencia, Felizardo. Personal Communication, 1976. [Questionnaire.]

87 Vocolo, J. M. "The Effect of FLES on Achievement in the Same Foreign Language in the High School." *Modern Language Journal* 51(1967): 463–69.

88 Vollmer, J. H. *Evaluation of the Effect of FLES upon Achievement in the High School Final Report.* Somerville, New Jersey:Board of Education, 1962.

89 Weber, Lillian. *The English Infant School and Informal Education.* Englewood Cliffs, New Jersey:Prentice-Hall, 1971.

90 Wilson, L. Craig. *The Open Access Curriculum.* Boston:Allyn & Bacon, 1971.

91 Yerxa, E. J. "Attitude Development in Childhood Education Toward Foreign People." *Journal of Education* 152(1970)23–33.

10

Pursuing continuing education as a foreign language teacher: An overview

Roland Goddu
New England Program in Teacher Education

Introduction

In a nation committed to equality and quality in all aspects of society, a foreign language teacher is faced with a continuing problem: Having overcome the throes of disinterest and neglect by peers in choosing a distinctly unpopular undergraduate major and having moved into a highly specialized and often isolated segment of the teaching profession, most practicing foreign language teachers have developed very strong personalities, opinions, values, and visions of society that are different from those of their colleagues. This difference has developed not through neglect but through exposure, choice, and education. Reading in German, Russian, Latin, French, Spanish, Portuguese exposes one to ideas that are formulated and valued differently from those in English. Growing up in or learning about different cultures while living in the United States exposes one to diverse lifestyles and norms.

To teach in a different tongue, about other peoples, about cultural advances, and about the greatness of ancestors requires a special self-image as a person, as a professional, and as a member of society. It also requires particular sensitivity and skill in challenging, supporting, and nurturing the dominant tongue, people, culture, and tradition in order to accept rather than reject the valuable and the different that comes from elsewhere. This is not an easy task. It is even more difficult for persons in a specialty that has been considered a remnant

Roland J. B. Goddu (Ed.D., Harvard University) is Chief Administrative Officer of the New England Program in Teacher Education, Inc. He has taught French and served as consultant for the Organization for Cultural and Economic Development in Paris, France. He has served as Dean of the School of Education, The Catholic University of America, and Director of the Master of Arts in Teaching Program, Trinity College, Washington, D.C. His publications have appeared in the *Journal of Teacher Education* and *Teachers College Record*.

from ruling classes' interests or a residue from excitement about the arcane and precious or considered a concession to those unable or unwilling to melt into the dominant language, culture, and tradition. Only a strong person can maintain equanimity and perspective under the charges of elitism, frill, and foreign when the bases for the charges seem to be quality, return to basics, and protectionism. I hope this chapter will serve as a support for a small speciality group in the teaching profession, assuming, however, that foreign language teachers have the will to reach out to influence what is vital in the profession and in the teaching of all language: reading, writing, speaking, and listening.

The foreign language teacher is different; challenged by knowledge and rejection—knowledge that language is the key to culture, to history, and to human understanding; rejection based on the charge of elitism—and isolated by subject matter and by the small number of practitioners in a profession itself seeking power and identity.

The chapter is organized to help chart some paths. It explicates apparent assumptions about the content of continuing education and observable patterns for the inservice education of foreign language teachers, patterns for adult learning that should be considered, and opportunities that are being offered.

The content and patterns of continuing education

Assumptions about content and patterns

If one examines the extensive literature related to the idea of the continuing education of teachers, and in particular foreign language teachers, one is struck by the following perceptions:

Perception I: There are many different hypotheses about what the focus of continuing education for teachers and foreign language teachers should be. For example:

1 Improve methods in order to use existing innovative approaches to teaching learners (39)
2 Change the content of instruction (Karp et al., 27)
3 Change the process of instruction including the place where it occurs (Papalia, 37)
4 Focus on language proficiency (Mazon and MacRae, 30; O'Connor and Twaddell, 34)

5 Change the patterns of instructing teachers (Beckerman, 3; Coste, 11)
6 Change the control and governance that determines the nature of continuing education and certification (Devaney and Thorn, 13; 23)

Perception II: A range of training patterns is utilized for providing instruction. The patterns can be organized as follows:

	Environment of training	*Time of training*	*Sanction of result*
Level I	academic	credit course	degree
Level II	pedagogic	module	professional advancement
Level III	practice	apprenticeship	certification
Level IV	materials	workshop	professional effectiveness

After the demise of the NDEA Institutes, much of the activity in inservice education was focused on the pedagogical and materials levels. One finds an extensive literature of efforts in microteaching (Carver and Wallace, 9), individualized instruction (Bockman and Gougher, 6), and syllabus development (Forbes, 19)—all of which are concerned with development of teaching pedagogical skills. There is also an extensive literature describing efforts in the improvement and revision of textbooks, tests, and other materials (Stansfield, 43), the development of Learning Activity Packages (LAPs) (28; 29), and the evaluation of available teaching materials (39).

Perception III: Many of the programs developed to provide training tend to be developer-rationalized rather than trainee need-responsive. Much of the literature is devoted to the logic of various teacher-development approaches. There is little discussion of the value of a particular pattern in energizing different kinds of learners to acquire more language competence, more linguistic competence, more cultural competence, and more professional competence. It is difficult to identify training programs that demonstrate the immediate connection between what content is to be taught to students in a classroom and the inservice training procedures (Rush and Fifer, 41) or between the inservice training offering and the MLA recommended qualifications for teachers of modern foreign language (Ollman, 36).

Perception IV: There is an on-going confusion between the terms *advanced academic education, continuing education, adult education,* and *inservice education.* Whatever the category or terminology used, the following types of programs are offered for practicing classroom teachers.

Program I (Mulhauser, 32)
- Language competency development
- Cultural background improvement
- Techniques and skills development

Program II (Karp et al., 27)
- Principles and methods of learning languages
- Principles and methods of teaching sounds, words, and structures
- Techniques of language teaching

Program III (Nedler, 33)
- Immersion in language
- Immersion in culture
- Analysis of materials
- Analysis of culture

Program IV (Coste, 11)
- Knowledge development
- Pedagogic development
- Self-image development
- Professional development
- Institutional development

Program V (Jakobovits, 26)
- Communications for teaching
- Problem-solving in teaching
- Strategy development for teaching
- Materials development for teaching

These programs are offered for academic credit, and sometimes are part of an academic degree program. Some are arranged to provide recertification credit and lead to salary increase. Others are designed simply as responses to a teacher or school system need and provide neither credit nor certification.

Perception V: Foreign language teacher education for beginning or experienced teachers tends to be university dominated and initiated. Foreign language classroom teachers rarely initiate the design of their training programs. Few, if any, serve on teacher planning groups that design the mainstream of inservice teacher education. In few instances have practicing classroom teachers accepted or sought the power to determine solutions to their educational needs.

Academic development

Graduate programs

A preponderance of training programs emphasizes graduate education as the basis for the continuing education of foreign language teachers. Program design begins from internalizing a concept of what knowledge is–knowledge about language, about how one does teaching. Such a conceptualization is the basis in many institutions for the Master of Arts program, the Master of Arts in Teaching program, the Doctor of Arts in Foreign Language program (Benseler, 4), or other advanced academic degrees in foreign languages. If one looks at the National Defense Act institutes, fellowships, and programs, one finds that most of them were conceptualized on this basis (Walsh, 46). The assumptions and patterns were that the practicing teacher went back to school to learn about language, to learn about the teaching of language using the most advanced research about language and linguistics, and to advance knowledge about language or about teaching language. Mulhauser (32) provides an articulate version of this point of view:

> May we rather arbitrarily categorize the professional qualifications of a good foreign language teacher under three headings, leaving aside all personality considerations which are, of course, extremely important but not pertinent to this discussion. The three categories are: 1) language competency–oral, aural, reading, and writing; 2) cultural background in the broadest sense, including civilization, linguistics, and literature; 3) techniques and skills specific to teaching of a foreign language. All three of these categories are particularly dynamic today with the rapid evolution of knowledge placing new demands on even the best and most active professional teacher (p. 140).

This approach to training is associated with immersion-type institutes in foreign lands which seek to increase language competence while acknowledging the limits of learning in what become primarily social environments. "The Fulbright teacher exchange program and all the summer schools abroad deserve full honor and attention" (p. 141). They should indeed receive continuing honor and attention if foreign language teachers are to transmit values, norms, and knowledge across language barriers. In any event, and in spite of extraordinary inflationary pressures, the foreign travel portion of this approach continues to expand and to receive particular sanction through the NEA International Institute in cooperation with the Inter-University International Teacher Education Council (47).

Reading focus

Traditional training

As the knowledge development movement continues, the tradition of language training based on *examination de textes* continues to disappear in favor of anthropological or humanistic studies. Much evidence remains, however, that high school teachers continue to use readers as a significant portion of the classroom activity for learning civilization, literature, and advanced composition. Guidelines for "foreign language learning experiences" prepared in California suggest the following proportional emphases upon the four language skills (39, p. 50).

	9th %	*10th* %	*11th* %	*12th* %
Listen	15	15	15	10
Speak	40	25	25	25
Read	25	35	35	40
Write	20	25	25	25

One wonders whether experienced teachers will be able to develop new approaches if reliance on reading rather than speaking continues to characterize their instruction. This is of particular concern if one acknowledges these observations by Gaarder (22):

> Carroll's data show that . . . majors would speak and comprehend the language at a level somewhere between a "limited

working proficiency" and a "minimal professional proficiency." . . . The Carroll data are confirmed by other data on the competence of experienced teacher participants in the National Defense Education Act Institutes. . . . In general the averages of the means of the institute *posttests* . . . for the three years are substantially lower for the experienced teachers than for the foreign language majors studied by Carroll (pp. 9–10).

Integrated learning

Theory and practice

We are thus left with a tradition that has high prestige and heavy logic, where teachers learn ideas but do not change their practice. One suspects that teachers as individuals and as researchers rather than as teachers learn more about language and culture. They may gain a stronger grasp of the discipline of language. Certainly, this has value in the continuing education of a teacher and in the academic development of a professional. But classroom teaching requires learning about teaching and learning. Inservice education must nurture the intellectual development of a teacher, both to assure that the young, in emulating their teachers learn to respect knowledge (Coste, 11) and to assure that teachers remain informed about the content they transmit with and through language (Nedler, 33). Teachers must also remain proficient in teaching in the language to be learned (O'Connor and Twaddell, 34).

The academic dimension may not have been conceptualized to extend much beyond the college years. One complete design for teacher education has been prepared by Bush (8) and is represented in Figure 1.

Teacher requests

Although learning about subject matter continues to be a major portion of the continuing education of teachers, there is a dearth of conceptual frameworks that integrate pedagogy with this content, even in the MLA standard. At the same time the foreign language teacher continues to request urgently supportive inservice programs (Hudet et al., 25) that: "provide methods courses taught by experts that are realistic, innovative, and effective in demonstrating the teaching of all of the skills at all levels and which correlate the use of audiovisual aids" (p. 12).

FIGURE 1.
A design for teacher education.

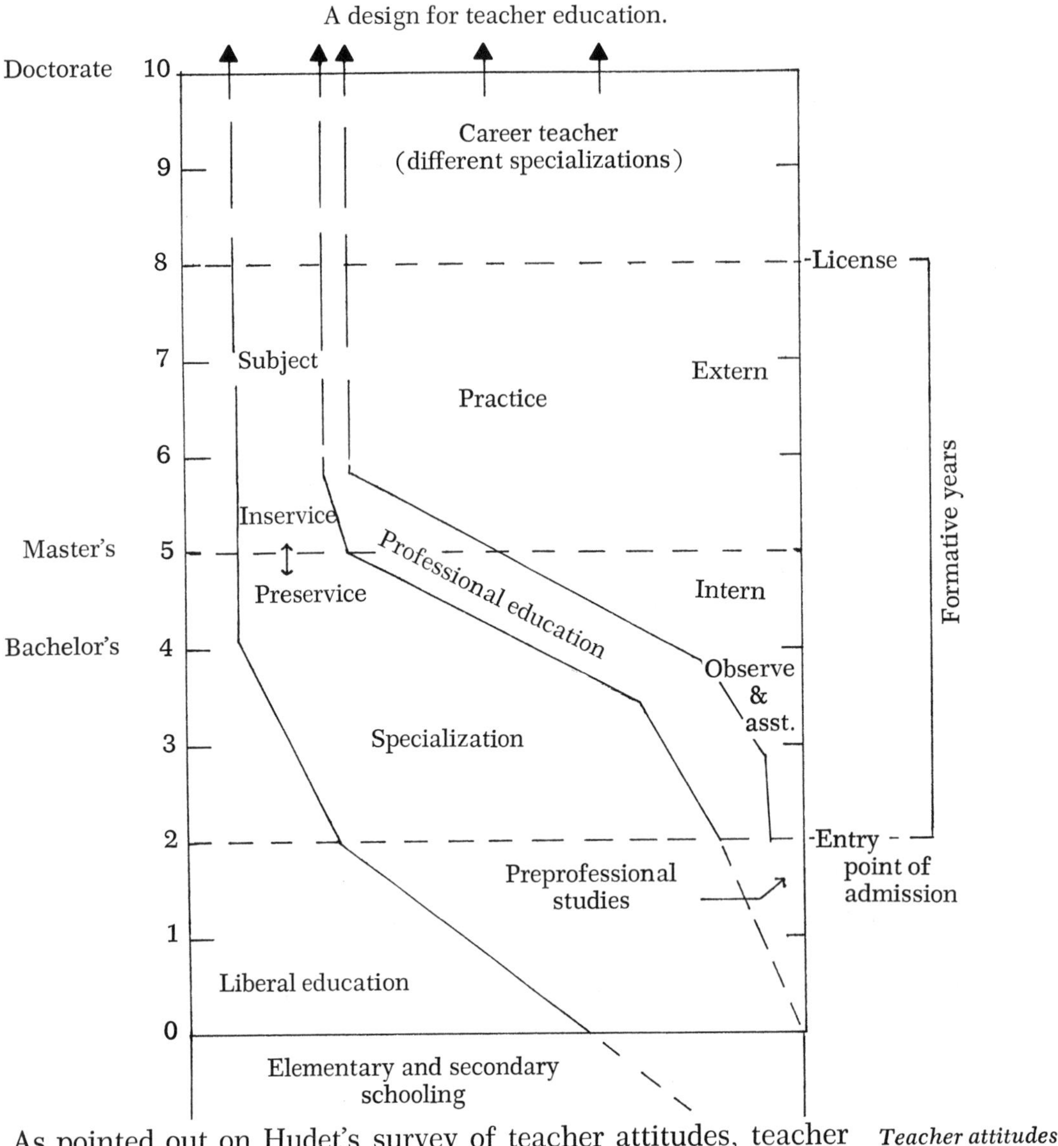

As pointed out on Hudet's survey of teacher attitudes, teacher interest is in courses on techniques and expanded contacts with practitioners. Little interest is shown in integrated sequential patterns that put the pieces of teaching into a coherent whole.

Teacher attitudes

Learning about new developments in education

Probably due in large part to the enormous federal investment in foreign language teacher training through the NDEA institutes from 1959 to 1969, many experienced foreign language teachers have been exposed to the innovations of the 1960s.

NDEA effects

TABLE 1. Ratings of courses and activities taken by credential holders*

Course or activity	Percent of responses Most helpful	Least helpful
Observation of Experienced teacher	79	8
Practice teaching	69	8
Methods	66	20
Advanced grammar	61	15
Phonetics	60	12
Civilization	52	18
Linguistics	51	21
Advanced composition	50	26
Literature	39	38
Audiovisual and laboratory training	37	34

*Hudet, 25, p. 10

With the continued influx of dollars to some foreign language teachers through the bilingual education act, pedagogic improvement does continue. Innovations such as microteaching, individualized instruction, learning activity packages, and minicourses have at least been pilot tested in classrooms.

Learning about teaching-related skills

Competency-based field-centered programs that focus on classroom skills may connect the pedagogical framework and the quality practice through the development of written learning prescriptions called modules. Not many programs exist beyond those leading to provisional certification (Meyer, 31). More detailed listings of abilities and skills in pedagogy could provide the beginning of the needed framework that would place methodological innovations in a coherent perspective. This effort may be reinforced if the Teacher Corps effort to develop inservice education programs includes foreign language teachers. Because Teacher Corps projects must serve minorities, some will certainly touch bilingual-bicultural environments.

Learning about language

As foreign language teachers explore the content of teaching language, they may find commonalities in foreign language, bilingual, and language instruction. Thus, examination of the validity of various methods for foreign language instruction, particularly in the area of oral language development and listening comprehension improvement, may lead to more systematic

Validity of methods

application of procedures for analyzing the actions that make up teaching and learning activities (Brent, 7). An advance beyond the various inservice patterns proposed as pedagogical instruction in linguistics is certainly needed (Feldman and Kline, 18; Forbes, 19; Haden, 22; O'Hare, 35). All of these are limited to content presentation followed by prescriptions for action without a significant distinction between the logic by which a researcher found knowledge and the often intuitive patterns by which teachers help students learn.

Improving practice

Learning by observing

We know that teachers learn from observing other practitioners and by the trial-and-error evolution of their own experience. Microteaching and simulations speed somewhat the process of learning new patterns (Bartley, 2), but actual experience in a classroom, often called field experience, remains a somewhat random, often fortuitous event for teacher development (12). A handbook for selecting quality field-experience sites and field practitioners has not been developed. As a result, internships, apprenticeships, or practice teaching are negotiated ideosyncratically. This is not to say that rigorous, and often intuitively valid criteria are not applied to the selection of good schools or great teachers. What is lacking, though, is a checklist that would allow comparison. The checklist should not be limited to the quality of classroom practice. It should include observable environmental characteristics and decision patterns; existing analytical (planning and evaluation) patterns; an available inventory of learner-usable materials; articulated mission and management objectives; and articulated learning outcomes for students, community, teachers, and the school. Such school- and classroom-specific checklists would provide the context for identifying what can best be learned from experiences in school settings. Thus, one could develop a framework of content to be learned in practice and identify patterns or practices that were not learnable in a given site or classroom.

Classroom checklists

Practicing teachers not only want to know more and new things about language and language teaching, but also want to learn more and new things about how to act as better professionals and how to develop methods and materials that are effective.

Learning about changing education

The content of practice in education is distinct from methods and materials. It goes beyond the techniques by which a teacher transmits knowledge about language. Certain stages in education assure that a learner does integrate the target language. The stages have been identified as stages through which each learner must progress:

Learner stages

1 Awareness
2 Interest
3 Pilot testing
4 Evaluation
5 Development
6 Installation (Havelock, 24)

Evidence in organization research indicates that individuals or organizations go through these stages cyclically at their own pace. The pace is not increased by pressure or repetition; it is increased only by awareness on the part of the teacher (process helper) and the learner (person to be changed) of the order of the stages. The acceptance (on the part of both) of definition of the stages and appropriate response at each stage make growth possible. The explicit agreement by both parties is what makes practice more professional (Jakobovits, 26).

In applying this approach to education, one finds persons talking of education as innovation development (Havelock, 24) rather than the installation of innovations, of teachers in support and implementation roles (Beckerman, 3) rather than project implementation, and of teaching as strategy (Argyris and Schön, 1) rather than craft. Improving practice of teachers becomes a search for the more coherent and modern patterns. One examines the patterns in use that are effective and proposes patterns for reaching some future expectation. One makes explicit the habits and intuitions used as the basis for lesson plans rather than the lesson plan itself. One provides a plan for performing a class rather than an identification of the materials and activities. The plan includes awareness, interest, pilot test, evaluation, development, and installation. Only at the end (installation) does learning become consolidated and integrated. Teachers are being challenged to describe publicly what they do in class. Foreign language teachers are challenged to move their articulation of practice beyond opinion, habit, and emotion to planned intervention to bring learners to a humane and comprehensive vision of personhood in modern society.

Changing training

The challenge belongs to those who educate teachers. Continuing education is needed of foreign language teachers who are seen as powerful agents of social articulation and change and as systematic practitioners of enlightened, empowering, and nurturing activities. Teacher centers (Bissex, 5; Chiapetta, 10; Devaney and Thorn, 13; Ducharme et al., 14; Ether, 17), teacher development centers (Bissex, 5), staff development cooperatives (39), and school-based staff developers (Ollman, 36) increase the possibility of using actual classroom experience as a systematic learning opportunity. Thus, patterns are provided for describing the levels and dimensions of teaching practices as they occur, and the approaches that help experienced teachers learn ways of doing things are documented.

Documenting change in practices

One way of organizing explicit practices and the patterns of practice in a classroom is the following checklist:

TABLE 2. Checklist for practices development

	Stages for integrating a practice					
Types of activity used	Awareness	Interest	Pilot test	Evaluation	Development	Installation
1 Exposure	x	x			x	
2 Review	x			x	x	
3 Analysis		x		x	x	
4 Simulation	x	x	x		x	
5 Modeling		x	x	x	x	
6 Practice			x			x
7 Adaptation				x	x	x
8 Invention					x	x
9 Consolidation				x		x
10 Recording			x			x
11 Reporting		x	x	x	x	x

Facilitating learning

A teacher discovers what kinds of teaching and learning activities are needed to move a student to a different stage in development. For example, a student who has barely been exposed to the history of France cannot be expected to invent a report on the culture of French people, but one can expect a student who can model (repeat) the linguistic patterns of sentences to adapt the new words and sounds to these patterns. Similarly, the teacher seeking to learn new techniques, language, or culture can trace the reasonable choices for courses or activities for continuing education. A teacher who has minimal speaking ability should probably choose modeling (language laboratory drill work) activities rather than invention (curriculum development), which is based on the ability to integrate techniques, language, and culture.

Using such frameworks allows program developers to organize the multiple types of learning activities for continuing education with certain caveats:

> What any listing of potential professional development activity for experienced staff will show is the geometric for novices. . . . Because experienced teachers are doing many of the things on the list in the normal course of employment . . . the list may suggest . . . the great range of activity that is legitimately professional development. The challenge lies in developing theory of practice around the 49 or more ways that experienced teachers grow (Bissex, 5, introduction).

Materials development

Significant and insightful efforts in materials development exist in bilingual education and may have implications for foreign language education. USOE has created bilingual education materials development centers, resource centers, and dissemination and assessment centers (44) with the following responsibilities:

Bilingual materials

Materials development centers (MDCs)

1 To develop instructional and testing materials for use in programs of bilingual education
2 To develop instructional materials for use by institutions of higher education in preparing persons for vocations in the field of bilingual education

Resource centers (RCs)

1 To provide training for teaching personnel in the use of bilingual educational methods and materials
2 To conduct pilot and field testing of bilingual materials and to train personnel in this area
3 To develop procedures for the selection and use of appropriate instruments for measuring the educational performance of children with limited English-speaking ability
4 To provide means for involving parents and community organizations in programs of bilingual education and incorporating into such programs the use of available cultural and educational resources
5 To develop procedures to evaluate the impact of programs of bilingual education

Dissemination and Assessment Centers (DACs)

1 To publish and distribute instructional and testing materials for use in programs of bilingual education and by institutions of higher learning personnel in preparing students in bilingual education courses of study
2 To assess the effectiveness and applicability of bilingual educational and teaching materials
3 To assess the need for instructional and testing materiials for children of limited English-speaking ability

Materials development efforts have resulted in various types of products:

1 Handbooks for teachers (Freire, 20)
2 Evaluative or annotated listings of curriculum materials (Ollman, 36)
3 Resource listings (40)
4 Teacher training bibliographies (Eddy, 15; Svlis et al., 45)
5 Specialized listings of learning activity packages (28)
6 Specialized listing of diverse curriculum materials and sites where the materials are in use (Chiapetta, 10)

There even exist very pragmatic descriptions of steps to follow to develop foreign language materials (Bockman and Gougher, 6).

Teacher-originated materials

Teacher-made materials

Present practice seems to see materials development and modifications mainly as the job of the publishers or the research and development groups and not the domain of practicing teachers. Teachers should assure that efforts are made to validate and collect materials adaptations and developmental efforts of practicing teachers. Many such efforts have increased the individual teacher's effectiveness, have facilitated departmentwide and community cooperation, or have developed common standards. The creative handbook developed by the Foreign Language Special Interest Committee (39) in California must be supplemented and enriched by specific systematic materials exemplars based on the handbook. One would expect the efforts of educational change agents to lead to such concrete products that could be shared. Producing a document that is the reorganization of written, oral, and audiovisual materials should be a basis for gaining inservice or continuing education credit. If such an effort were undertaken, teachers could have catalogues of teacher-adapted and tested learning materials and processes, and the profession would be a step closer to a systematic, coherent, interrelated teacher-development program. A promising step in this direction is the Materials Center of ACTFL Headquarters (62 Fifth Ave., New York, N.Y. 10011).

Perspectives on programs

Reviewing the assumptions about content and patterns for continuing or inservice education, one finds a preponderance of the published effort focusing on:

1 The creation of academically related programs that are designed to be logical and systematic
2 The development of training programs to install new practices in classrooms
3 The preparation of annotated listings of materials

Clearly, if a coherent program for experienced-teacher development is to be provided, some significant gaps must still be filled:

1 The statement of a comprehensive theory of pedagogy

2 The establishment of criteria and standards for effective practice in a school and for creating (and changing) school environments
3 The production of catalogues of teacher-developed curricula and the documentation of the patterns used to reinvent the wheel in a more relevant fashion

Characteristics of programs

Lack of teacher input

How and when education is provided often becomes a confusing factor in the continuing education of teachers. That a teacher wants credit for participation in training or education does not in and of itself influence the time or mode of delivery. Inservice education occurs and credit or certification is added on. As teachers move to control their own training, some alternative resources other than academic training are developing. Professional Development Centers answer the need for "materials, guidelines, career information, workshops, enrollment figures, identification of special types of programs, and consultant [help]" (Chiapetta, 10).

Content and pattern for providing service are two interrelated vectors that training institutions have to contend with. The value of a response tends to be negotiated between the training institution and the trainee. There is little evidence as to a consistent norm for whether a given activity shall carry credit or no credit and whether the credit will be counted toward an academic degree, toward recertification and/or toward salary increment. Could this be because the training need is of more importance to a practicing teacher than its coinage? One should at least ask first, "What training need do experienced teachers want addressed?" Then, "How and under what conditions do they want the training program designed and delivered?"

Patterns of adult learning

The most intriguing questions to consider when one examines the continuing education of teachers is whether teachers as adults learn in a particular way and, in the case of foreign language teachers, whether they learn foreign languages in a particular manner. Because almost all of the programs reported in the literature do perceive continuing education or inservice education programs as a continuation of an undergraduate education pattern, the practice at best ignores the question. Instruction that is organized around a didactic information-giving approach, even in workshops, is not directed toward an active adult learning pattern. Experienced teachers are a new learner population; these new students need new patterns for learning.

How teachers learn

Developmental stages

Microteaching and communications approaches are primitive examples of providing a new organization of experiences for adults. One of the few comprehensive theories developed for adults is articulated by Freire (20), whose experience is with a more primitive and less educated population than teachers, but an approach that emphasizes raising consciousness for deliberate programmatic action is applicable. The stages Freire articulate relate significantly to Havelock's (24) pattern for development of a revised program or Erickson's stages (16) for human development and integration with reality.

Varied approaches

Stages of language learning

Language learning may well follow distinct stages for a teacher who, by profession, is assumed to be a competent speaker,

Nature of learning

TABLE 4.

Content of Training	Freire stages	Erickson stages	Havelock stages	Content of Training
Institutional and social analysis	Describes problem as they see it existing	Hope	Define problem as it is now in contrast to what it should be like	Institutional and social analysis
Ego-development	Accepts that some change is possible	Will	Build relationship among those assigned to solution	Communications
Social and cultural background and expectations	Awareness of the way things should be	Purpose	Diagnose problem	Problem identification and clarification techniques
Commitment	Awareness of role in solving problem	Competence	Acquire relevant resources	Cataloging and networking
Problem-solving	Accepts to solve problem and to pursue its solution	Fidelity	Choose a solution	Problem solving techniques
Institutional analysis	Decides limits about what can be done	Have	Gain acceptance of solution	Communications and political processes
Communications and confrontation skill	Faces conflict where necessary	Care	Stabilize the innovation	Techniques for practice
Techniques for practice	Adapts solution to environment	Wisdom	Generate process for self-renewal	Decision-making

reader, and writer, but who in reality has limited exposure to enough foreign language to maintain the level of competence attained. Some examination of the stages of adult language learning is certainly needed in evaluating the effectiveness of any form of oral, aural, or other language approach when applied to teachers. Language learning for teachers may require different patterns for each content area as well as for each level of need (exposure, understanding, familiarity, reinforcement). The correct approach may vary according to whether the language to be learned is new or already learned; learned correctly or learned incorrectly; and whether the technique to be learned is new, already learned, learned correctly, or learned incorrectly. Choices on these dimensions will influence the kind of offering when the adult learning process has reached a stage where the specific content, technique, program, or approach meets a felt need. Such needs tend to respond to pressures from several sources:

Need responsiveness

1 Institutional (school) need (usually results from outside of the teacher and is required because of the school's vision of what its program should be)
2 Learner (child) need (usually results from lack of response by a child to the normal program or from pressure to provide all learners with all learning opportunities)
3 Research patterns and products needs (usually results from a theory or product designed in a specific manner that requires a given sequence of teaching or learning arts)
4 Teacher needs relating to effectiveness as a teacher (usually results from the teacher seeking to implement more efficiently a known practice or to expand the repertory of teacher skills), relating to effectiveness as a professional (usually results from the teachers seeking to increase the concept he has of his role in the institution of education and to be recognized as competent), relating to effectiveness as a person (usually results from a teacher realizing that his/her own ego development or communications patterns are not as sophisticated as role or teaching demands).

These needs tend to be deeper than the visible need simply to learn a skill, knowledge, or attitude. By specifying and recognizing these levels of needs, inservice education programs can have more impact on the learning of teachers as adults. The specification of all types of needs-response makes possible the development of more systematic quality control of inservice experiences.

Types of inservice opportunities

Opportunities for experienced teachers are extensive but not catalogued in a standard format; information reaches teachers in a random fashion. As a result, participation depends either upon teachers' own interests and self-motivation (which for foreign language teachers seems high for new technologies) or upon pressures or bribes from the establishment (which seems high for tested products and degree programs).

Opportunities available

The major types of available inservice opportunities nationwide are:

1 Courses, which are usually offered on-campus and as an integral part of a degree program sometimes scheduled at times convenient for teachers. Practicing teachers have a limited access because of their full-time employment, travel distances involved, and energy needed.
2 Workshops, which are usually offered during the summer or in addition to the regular work day for teachers. High participation is evident in peer-association-sponsored activities or in school-system-sponsored (and required) workshops. The latter tend to be quite general and lack specific relevance to foreign language teachers.
3 Study groups, which are usually task forces or curriculum committees assigned to revise or update existing guides or standards. Some of these efforts expose teachers systematically to much of what is the state of the art in foreign language instruction.
4 Projects, which are usually problem-solving efforts utilizing federal funds, usually lead to renewal of process or products of instruction.
5 Travel programs, which are usually organized for social as well as academic reasons. Academic credit usually requires extensive analysis and writing.

6 TV and film series, usually a course on film offered by expert informants, requires special motivation by teachers to reinforce their learning by trying suggested change in practice.
7 Teacher centers, which are an arrangement of materials and programs designed by practitioners to examine, explore, and document practice. Emphasizes peer learning and peer support.
8 Staff development programs, which exist in a few states, are comprehensive interrelated programs for improving instruction in a school or school system. Sometimes connected directly to recertification, they usually emphasize integrated training for all members of a school staff at the same time.
9 Alternative programs are human-relations programs (usually emphasize learning about communication and collaborative decision-making with concern and respect for the affective as well as the cognitive), behavior-modification programs (usually emphasize systematic linear learning patterns with known and specified-in-advance objectives, often organized into modules), best-practice programs (usually the observation of or description of the practice of recognized effective practitioners).

These opportunities are often offered through institutions. Teachers should be sure that the additional advantages they seek—credit, certification, or salary increment—are provided.

Teacher centers

An examination of a few teacher center programs suggests that foreign language teachers seem to participate in a limited number of these opportunities. The small number of foreign language teachers in a given geographic area is probably why. However, foreign language teachers should develop the complete repertory for their specialty if they desire equality in opportunity.

Quality control of inservice experiences

Traditionally, the quality of an educational program for teachers has been vouched for by the granting of academic credit and academic degrees and then by certification. In most instances, the degree carried certification, and the two were seen as synonymous. In fact, major energy continues to be spent in some places on maintaining control of the degree in order to control the quality of teachers.

Credit and certification

The advent of a significant increase in inservice education for practicing teachers places pressure on the degree-equals-certificate syndrome. In some states teachers are approved for certification by a competency approach; in a few states certification is granted or credit is given for programs that may be totally nonacademic (23). The reality of nonacademic recertification of teachers has led to the development of different evaluative standards, and some explicit dimensions of teaching, such as community-related and school-related competencies (Pitman, 38) that have been ignored in academic programs.

The purpose of language instruction and standards

Quality control for inservice training requires establishing academically validatable characteristics of quality foreign language teaching as well as dimensions of practice that take into account methods, materials utilization, and development of institutional or social impact. If foreign language teachers are to "see their work as . . . the transmission to their students of a powerful perspective on the student's own language and life, and intimate access through another language (that unrivaled exteriorization and manifestation of the self) to the way of life, the wisdom of the beauty of an entire people" (Gaarder, 21, p. 14), they must articulate standards for classroom practice as well as for academic learning. Purpose translated to standards should form the criteria for measuring the results of a training event. The need to document the productive effect of a training event in classroom practice may be more important. What one can do differently in a classroom as a result of a training event is of more importance to institution, learner, and teacher than other measures that respond to research or knowledge development needs. The more documentation of what teachers do in the classroom and of the effect of training on this practice, the more patterns for targeted response to learner needs and to teacher needs will emerge. Perhaps foreign language teachers can take leadership in filling this critical gap.

The professional and standards

Teacher development should be forward-looking. If the teacher is an influencer of learning and a learner in the classroom, programs for continuing education or inservice education should provide teachers with new skills or at least reinforce their skills as language developers, knowledge developers, and profession developers. As language developers, foreign language teachers must identify and document patterns and stages of language development for adolescents and adults. Teachers help students learn sounds or language patterns in the student's individual style. The description of the characteristics of different categories of learners who pick up sounds in distinct sequences could form a basis for more systematic language development. Language teachers can also serve as informants about the stages of learning a foreign language because they are more aware of when students learn some new language fact. Tracking language development is a clear area where language teachers can, by professional expertise, assist the profession.

As knowledge developers, foreign language teachers must identify and document patterns of effective language pedagogy, patterns of effective classroom practice and schooling, patterns of effective curriculum and materials adaptation and development, patterns of socialization, patterns of acculturation, and so on. As profession developers, foreign language teachers must model the characteristics of a systematic experienced-teacher development program and document the examples of practice that empowers learning by teacher and students.

The profession and standards

Quality control can come from effective practitioners or can be imposed from without. Task forces and committees on standards can be influenced by documents of effective practice. If these are lacking, the vision of quality they suggest for the profession will suffer. Planning groups or inservice program developers can be influenced by examples of practice and needs. If these are lacking, logic and systems will direct their design. The evidence in this chapter suggests that, at least for foreign language teachers, the pieces of the humane comprehensive teacher development program do exist. The experienced teachers themselves face the challenge of putting it together.

Conclusion

Foreign language teachers hold a special affection for machinery and technology. Quick to accept and utilize language laboratories and audiotapes, they now face the challenge of building a theory of pedagogy for language learning that is as creative as the excitement and insight they create in learners who see through a foreign tongue into a distant land. To make a practice into a science requires systematic documentation and persistent reporting, shorn of rhetoric and emotion, capped by patient observation and creative insight. To develop a unique specialty in a profession requires exploration of the differences among self-growth, professional growth, knowledge development, and cultural transmission with deep sensitivity to equality and open communication. To share discovery with a learner is a kind of learning that a true teacher seeks. To find as an adult a pattern of learning that challenges the boundaries of known practice will break open new paths in helping all to grasp the fundamental key to human growth and language development. Then in contact with a common language, culture, and vision, the students and the teacher can reach into their past to build the future. "The object of action is the reality to be transformed by them together . . ." (Freire, 20, p. 17). Teachers must develop the ability to "see, name, analyze, and collaboratively transform reality . . ." (Smith, et al., 42, p. 17).

Lifelong learning

References, Pursuing continuing education as a foreign language teacher: An overview

1 Argyris, Chris, and Donald A. Schön. *Theory in Practice:Increasing Professional Efficiency.* San Francisco:Jossey-Bass, 1974.

2 Bartley, Diana E. *Practice Centered Teacher Training for TESOL.* Portland:Pacific Northwest Conference on Foreign Languages, 1973.

3 Beckerman, Marvin M. "Educational Change Agents:An Inside-Outside Team." *Educational Leadership* 30(1973):530–32.

4 Benseler, David P. "Is there Life After Death? New Perspectives on the Doctor of Arts in Foreign Languages." *Bulletin of the Association of Departments of Foreign Languages* 6,iv(1975):5–8.

5 Bissex, Henry. *Methods of Staff Development.* Newton, Massachusetts:Newton North High School, 1975.

6 Bockman, John F., and Ronald L. Gougher,ed. "Individualized Instruction." *Foreign Language Annals* 5,ii(1971):240–45.

7 Brent, G., et al. *Module Cluster:Applied Behavior Analysis Principles.* Glassboro, New Jersey:Glassboro State College, 1975.

8 Bush, Robert N. "The Formative Years." *The Real World of the Beginning Teacher.* Washington, D.C.:NEA National Commission on Teacher Education and Professional Standards, 1965.

9 Carver, David, and M. J. Wallace. "Some Applications of Micro-Teaching to TESL." *English Language Teaching Journal* 29,iii(1975):184–90.

10 Chiapetta, Michael. *Professional Development Center for Teachers.* Bloomington:Indiana University, 1976.

11 Coste, Daniel. "Vers une redéfinition de la formation initiale des professeurs de français?" *Le français dans le Monde* 113(1975):13–23.

12 "Designing Field Experiences." *Teacher Education in Practice* 1,i(1975):1–2.

13 Devaney, Kathleen, and Lorraine Thorn. *Explor-*

ing Teacher Centers. San Francisco: Far West Laboratory for Educational Research and Development, 1975.

14 Ducharme, Edward, et al. "Retrospective Report on NERCOM Funded Projects." *NEPTE Working Papers.* Durham, New Hampshire: New England Program in Teacher Education, 1974.

15 Eddy, Peter A. *A Selected Bibliography of Films and Videotapes on Foreign Language Teacher Training.* Arlington, Virginia: ERIC Clearinghouse, 1975.

16 Erickson, Erik H. "Reflections on Dr. Borg's Life Cycle." *Daedalus* 105,ii(1976): 1–28.

17 Ether, John A. *Teacher Education Development Service.* Albany: SUNY, 1975.

18 Feldman, David M., and Walter D. Kline. *French: Contemporary Methodology.* Denver: Colorado Department of Education, 1967.

19 Forbes, Margaret. *A Syllabus: An Inservice Course in the Teaching of Latin.* Austin: Texas Education Agency, Division of Program Development, June 1969.

20 Freire, Paulo. *Pedagogy of the Oppressed.* New York: Herder & Herder, 1972.

21 Gaarder, A. Bruce. *Elitism, Teacher Training, and Other Forbidden Topics.* Washington, D.C., 1975. [Author in private capacity.] [Mimeo.]

22 Haden, Ernest F. *A Syllabus for an Inservice Course in Applied Linguistics in French.* Austin: Texas Education Agency, 1971.

23 "Handbook for Staff Development." *New Hampshire Education Resource Catalog.* Concord, New Hampshire: State Department of Education, 1974.

24 Havelock, Ronald G. *The Change Agent's Guide to Innovation in Education.* Englewood Cliffs, New Jersey: Educational Technology Publications, 1973.

25 Hudet, Claude L., et al. *Teacher Training Practices in Foreign Language Instruction.* Sacramento: California State Department of Education, 1970.

26 Jakobovits, Leon A. "The Encounter—Communication Workshop." *Interim Report: A Longitudinal Study of the Use and Effects of Affective Techniques in the Preparation of Teachers.* Bath, Maine: Mid Coast Education Development Center and Colby College, 1972.

27 Karp, Theodore B., et al. *Principles and Methods of Teaching a Second Language.* Washington, D.C.: Center for Applied Linguistics of the Modern Language Association of America, 1963.

28 *LAP Catalog.* New Haven, Connecticut: ACES/ Education Resources Center, 1975.

29 *Learning Package, Bilingual-Bicultural Education: An Overview.* Salem: Oregon State Department of Education, 1974.

30 Mazon, M. Reyes, and Susan C. McRae. *Bilingual Education: Oral Language Assessment as a Prerequisite.* Pueblo, California: California Institute for Cultural Pluralism, San Diego State University, 1975.

31 Meyer, John C. "CBTE: Potential Inservice Help for Teachers." *Teacher Education* 10,ii(1975): 27–33.

32 Mulhauser, Ruth. "Upgrading the Inservice Teacher," 140–44 in Marjorie C. Johnston,ed., *Modern Foreign Language in the High School.* Washington, D.C.: Office of Education, 1958.

33 Nedler, Shari. "Language, the Vehicle: Culture, the Content." *Journal of Research and Development in Education* 4,iv(1971): 3–10.

34 O'Connor, Patricia, and W. F. Twaddell. *Intensive Training for an Oral Approach in Language Teaching.* St. Louis: National Federation of Modern Language Teachers Associations, 1960.

35 O'Hare, Thomas J. *A Syllabus for an Inservice Course in the Teaching of German.* Austin: Texas Education Agency, 1971.

36 Ollman, Mary J.,ed., *MLA Selective List of Materials for Use by Teachers of Modern Foreign Languages in Elementary and Secondary Schools.* New York: Modern Language Association, 1962.

37 Papalia, Anthony. *A Competency Based and Field Centered Teacher Education Program in French.* Buffalo: Faculty of Educational Studies, SUNY, 1974.

38 Pitman, John C. "Competency Based Certification: What are the Issues?" *NEPTE Working Papers.* Durham, New Hampshire: New England Program in Teacher Education, 1973.

39 *A Practical Handbook for Implementation of Foreign Language Programs.* Hayward: California Association for Supervision and Curriculum Development, 1967.

40 *Publications available from the MLA Publication Center.* New York: Modern Language Association, 1974.

41 Rush, Donald E., and Fred L. Fifer. *In-Service Education Based on Program Evaluation: An Assessment of the Immediate Perceived Benefits Resulting from an Evaluative Process.* Nashville: George Peabody College for Teachers, 1973.

42 Smith, William, et al. "Critical Consciousness." *ME Forum.* (Spring 1975): 12–18.

43 Stansfield, Charles. *Teachers' Attitudes Toward Publishers' Tests.* Boulder: University of Colorado, Department of Spanish and Portuguese, 1976.

44 *A Study of the State of Bilingual Materials Development and the Transition of Materials to Classrooms.* Washington, D.C.: Office of Planning, Budgeting, and Evaluation, U.S. Office of Education, 1976.

45 Svlis, Juan D., et al. *Teacher Training Bibliography: An Annotated Listing of Materials for Bilingual Bicultural Teacher Education.* Austin, Texas: Dissemination Center for Bilingual Bicultural Education, 1975.

46 Walsh, Donald D. "NDEA Institutes, Summer 1961, A Survey." *The Modern Language Journal* 48,iv(1964).

47 *The Year of the Experience.* Washington, D.C.: NEA International Institute, 1976.

11

Directions of research in the 1970s

Introduction

Ernest A. Frechette*
Florida State University

Educators have always sought solutions to classroom problems. At the same time researchers have attempted to furnish educators with knowledge to help them to achieve their goals. Yet, somehow, many of the research findings never reach the classroom teacher. Perhaps this lack of communication can be attributed to the teacher's disregard of professional journals or to the fact that reports, replete with technical jargon, have generally not been written with a teacher audience in mind. This chapter is *not* a summary of research results, nor is it an examination of the quality of the research efforts. It is, instead, a compilation of more than 300 studies, completed since 1970, in an effort to determine and analyze the topical areas that have interested researchers, the designs and methodologies they have utilized, and the educational milieu in which research is being done. These studies are suggestive of what has been happening in research, how investigators are proceeding, the constraints under which they are working, and the trends that appear to be developing. Based on this overview, some judgments are made about the relevancy of research to the teacher, what is needed, and what the teacher can do.

---

*With the collaboration of Sherrod Braxton, Roy Pinto, and James Williams.

Ernest A. Frechette (Ed.D., Boston University) is Professor of Foreign Language Education at the Florida State University, where he teaches courses in methodology, research, reading, FLES, bilingual education, and the teaching of culture. He has taught French and Latin in secondary schools and foreign language methodology at Boston University and Southeastern Massachusetts University. He was State Foreign Language Supervisor for the Massachusetts Department of Education. He has conducted numerous inservice teacher workshops and spoken to teacher groups in many parts of the country and abroad. Dr. Frechette is Head of the Testing Section of the *ACTFL Annual Bibliography* and Editor of the Florida Foreign Language Association Newsletter. His works have been published in various modern language and classical journals. His professional affiliations include AATF, ACTFL, NABE, ATESOL, TESOL, NALLD, ACL, CAMWS and FFLA.

Birkmaier's (27) review of research on teaching foreign languages furnishes an excellent summary of studies for the period prior to 1970 and can also serve as background for this synthesis.

What is research?

A definition

The term *research,* widely used in educational circles, means many things to many persons. As used in this chapter it is simply a deliberate search for facts, a search for the truth. More formally, it is "the careful, unbiased investigation of a problem, based insofar as possible upon demonstrable facts and involving refined distinctions, interpretation, and usually some generalization" (Good, 111, p. 346).

Educational research in our field involves special studies whose purpose is to determine either what has been done or what could be done to improve the teaching and learning of foreign languages. The process is therefore one conducive to change for the better.

Research in education has become more systematic and scientific as better techniques have been developed for planning research studies, delineating the steps to be taken by an investigator, and implementing the collection and analysis of data that will lead to possible solutions to a problem.

Steps in conducting research

These steps (labeled differently in a variety of situations) become the following sections in research articles or reports:

1 A statement of the question, topic, or problem to be researched
2 A review of the literature
3 A prediction or statement of an hypothesis
4 A description of the methods and procedures used
5 The collection and analysis of the data
6 A discussion of the results
7 A summary and conclusions or recommendations

If the steps are followed, systematic inquiry will result. This inquiry must be done in an unbiased manner—that is, with accuracy, an open mind, and intellectual honesty. Once the research has been completed one should ask what inferences can be drawn and what implications there are for the teaching and learning of foreign languages.

Types of research

Many systems of classification have been introduced, but the types that appear regularly in the literature are historical, descriptive, and experimental studies.

Historical

Historical research deals with the past. The investigator searches for information about what has existed—collecting, analyzing, synthesizing, and interpreting that information for the purpose of generating a new understanding of the facts in question. Descriptive research is concerned with the present. Many different types can be identified, including observational studies, surveys, case studies, developmental studies, and content analysis. As in the historical study, the collected data is examined and interpreted. Experimental research involves comparison under controlled conditions. Here, the hypotheses that are formulated are tested by systematically varying or manipulating one or more of the elements in order to observe the effects of that manipulation.

Descriptive

Experimental

What kinds of research are being done?

To determine what has been done, a review was made of a number of studies that have appeared in 1) Educational Resources Information Center (ERIC); 2) professional journals that are easily accessible to teachers such as *Foreign Language Annals, Modern Language Journal, TESOL Quarterly, French Review, Hispania, Language Learning, International Review of Applied Linguistics, Audio-Visual Language Journal;* and 3) *Dissertation Abstracts.* Personal comments and information regarding current studies forwarded to us by several colleagues were also examined.

Views of colleagues

Approximately 150 colleagues were asked, "What kinds of research are being done?" Their responses were highly varied.

Chastain (55), for example, believes that efforts are being made to deal with individual differences and the interaction or relationship between instruction and student learning styles and strategies. Papalia (260) views much research as being directed at individuals' learning profiles, at error analysis in relation to both second language learning and its implications for writing student-centered materials. He also has the impression that some advances are being made regarding the effects of second language learning on ethnocentricity and empathy. Lipschutz (198) observes that studies are dealing with the primacy of culture as the basis of new programs, with greater student involvement and input, and with human dynamics.

Experience with research leads some persons to be somewhat negative, not only about the type of research being done but also about its value. Mladenka (212) believes that most studies are irrelevant and that colleges and universities are ignoring findings of experiments on methodology at the secondary school level. Grittner (121) asserts that a great deal of the "same old thing" is going on; people are continuing to play statistical games with classical research procedures. He states that there is a great deal of the experimental versus control-group type of study, but this design is often misused. Needs assessments are being attempted but not very scientifically.

Research in progress

Personal correspondence has provided us with a sampling of the varieties of studies *currently* in progress. Among research efforts recently completed, for example, is Carroll's (48) International Study of Educational Achievement (IEA) which is an attempt to determine students' achievement in French in various countries. It represents the largest research effort ever conducted in foreign language education—approximately 30,000 students were involved. Testing has interested many others. At Cornell University, Jones (172) is working on the development of testing models that are reliable, valid, and efficient. Basically, he is trying to adapt the Foreign Service Institute model so that it can be used in a university situation. At Indiana University Gradman (113) is continuing his research on reduced redundancy and noise distortion. In Dade County, Florida, Rothfarb (287) and colleagues are currently engrossed in the development of a series of Criterion-Referenced Unit Achievement Tests in Spanish for Spanish-English Bilingual Programs, Grade 1–6, in the assessment of the impact of the Spanish Curricula Development Center instructional materials on pupil achievement, in validating the Spanish Language Arts and Reading Criterion-Referenced Unit Achievement Tests for Grades 1–3, and in the classification of students using the Dade County Aural Comprehension Test Development of a 5-Category Scale Describing Areas of Functioning in English. Cloze tests have interested Oller at the University of New Mexico, who has been doing a great deal of work in English as a Second Language (Hanzeli, 133); Hanzeli (133) at the University of Washington, who is replicating Oller's experiments in French; and Lange at the University of Minnesota, who is doing a major project in German, examining two ways of determining which words to delete and two ways of scoring responses (Jorstad and Lange, 174). At the University of Minnesota researchers are also involved in the comparison of multiple-choice versus normal (fill-in) cloze tests, in the testing of teacher proficiency, and in exploring the use of interview techniques for establishing teacher proficiency. A group of educators, made up of two representatives from each teacher-preparing institution in the state, is validating the rating scales.

Other work in progress at the University of Minnesota includes studies on:

The influence of syntactic factors in reading comprehension in German

A character count of Chinese texts correlated to the count in modern Chinese (Communist) newspapers and magazines

Curriculum development for the middle and junior high schools

Attitudes toward foreign language study, the attitudes of parents and teachers toward FLES, the attitudes of foreign language students, and language dropouts (Jorstad and Lange, 174).

The Deutsch-französisches Institut, Ludwigsburg, West Germany, will soon publish a volume of bibliographical essays on contemporary French institutions, literature, and so on, in an attempt to be helpful to teachers (Nostrand, 230). Rothfarb and her colleagues are engaged in a pilot study consisting of an integrated oral-language-development approach to teaching ESOL to limited-ability and nonstandard English-speaking students in kindergarten and first grade; and Fernandez, at the Center for Bilingual Education in Portland, Oregon, has been collecting data and information on language dominance and the language proficiency of children who are bilingual and multilingual (Rothfarb, 287). Krashen, University of California, is developing a new comprehensive theory of the performance of second language learners (Hanzeli, 133).

A survey of research completed

In this segment, which covers studies that have been completed, an attempt has been made to group the various studies under headings that reflect the nature of the different types of investigations. Those of a general nature are within a general category; others are under linguistics, curriculum and development, physiology and psychology of language learning, teacher education and certification, methods, testing, and bilingualism and bilingual education.

General

Surveys

Several broad surveys were conducted: Alden (1) sought to determine the number of students enrolled in French in United States high schools and colleges; Brod (35, 36) presented a comprehensive view of foreign language course registrations in higher education and reviewed foreign language entrance and graduation requirements in colleges; and Klayman (180) solicited high school teachers' opinions on foreign language requirements in colleges. Two other studies attempted to show what career opportunities existed for the student in foreign languages (Fuller, 105; Honig and Brod, 155). The surveys, except for the one on career opportunities, mirror the profession's concern for numbers, possibly as a result of declining enrollments and reduced language requirements.

Linguistics

Research in problems of linguistics as it relates to foreign languages falls into three categories: sociolinguistics, phonology, and vocabulary and grammar.

Sociolinguistics

Sociolinguistics problems were an area of prime interest to researchers. Among the topics investigated were the following:

The use of *tu* and *vous* among French *lycée* students (Bustin-Lekeu, 42)

The linguistic, personal and social development of immigrant children in Sweden (Stockfelt-Hoatson, 322)

The use of nonstandard English by blacks and whites in Alexandria, Virginia (Bachmann, 7)

The speech characteristics of black and Mexican-American children (Natalicio and Williams, 227)

The role of cultural conflict in the classroom (Suiero-Ross, 324)
An analysis of social distance as a factor in the evaluation of writing proficiency in ESL (Reeback, 283)
Ability of speakers of Standard English versus children who speak a black dialect to hear final consonant stops (Johnson, 168)

Phonology

Among the studies dealing with phonology, Olson and Samuels (249) examined whether younger children have a natural advantage over adults. Baird (9) used phonological procedures to test the hypothesis that morphophonemic rules have psychological reality in children.

Vocabulary and grammar

Several studies were identified in the general area of vocabulary and grammar:

The collection of data for the creation of word-frequency lists (Richards, 285)
The frequencies of verb forms and noun phrases in English for ESL instruction (White, 347)
The effect of new-word density on efficiency of vocabulary learning and reading comprehension (Holley, 153)
The effect of glossing in foreign language reading materials (Holley and King, 154)
An error analysis of lexical and structural mistakes in the written French of Nigerian students (Obanya, 231)
Lexical and grammatical items in French literature, as analyzed by computer (Willis, 349)
The deep structures of Italian-English bilingual children (Kessler, 177)
The use of the articie in English by speakers of English as a second language (Oller and Redding, 245)
An analysis of prepositions and prepositional patterns (Ghadessy, 107)
English register characteristics (Chiu, 57)
Spelling errors among learners using a Roman script versus learners using a non-Roman script (Oller and Ziahosseiny, 247)
The unpredictability of four contrastive analyses (Whitman and Jackson, 348)

Thus, it appears that linguistics is an area of moderate interest. Furthermore, many of the studies appear to have methodological implications for the teacher. Unfortunately, much research in this area is too esoteric or technical to be interpreted by many teachers.

Curricular problems and development

Research interest in curricular problems and development ranges over a wide variety of topics. The following studies dealt with curriculum at the elementary and secondary levels:

Elementary and secondary levels

The effect of TESOL classes at both the elementary and secondary levels (Hale and Budar, 129)
The long-term effects of FLES programs (Oller and Nagato, 244)
The effect of the Philadelphia 1970–71 Latin FLES program (Offenberg et al., 232)
The effect of a program specifically designed to cut attrition (Molina, 216)
A comparison of three programs of individualized instruction (Berwald, 23)
A study of the merits of ability grouping (Papalia, 259)
The factors that influence the development of school district policy in an Indian area (Spolsky, 316)
The goals of foreign language instruction in the light of the attitudes of students, parents, and teachers (Papalia, 262)
The factors responsible for foreign language attrition in Utah (Lima, 197)
A survey of curricular problems in New York—the use of the Regents examination, language laboratory installations, enrollments, and the status of foreign language in the secondary schools of New York (Teitelbaum, 331)

Undergraduate level

At the undergraduate level, data were sought in one study to determine whether there was a need for differentiated materials for black and white students in a remedial composition class (Sternglass, 321), while another study compared the efficiency of intensive versus regular English as a foreign language by examining results of foreign language students in two differently paced courses (Mason, 207).

Surveys and evaluations of special types of programs received more attention from researchers than other areas of curricular problems at the undergraduate level:

Surveys and evaluations of special programs

The status of Rumanian studies in the United States and Canada (Impey, 161)
The status of Italian studies in the United States and Canada (Pane, 256)
The status of the teaching of Chinese in United States schools (Tsu, 336)
The success of private language schools and its implications for public school foreign language instruction (Marottoli, 205)

Other programs assessed were:

The effect of a special letter, slide, and realia exchange program to increase interest and motivation (Jonas, 171)
The efficacy of the use of Adelante (Clarke, 59)
The effectiveness of the Southwest Regional Laboratory English language concepts program for a variety of Spanish-speaking children (Molina, 215)
The comparison of the results of an intensive one-month foreign language course with those achieved in the regular semester course (Wallace, 343)
An investigation into possible sources of disaffection of teachers, superintendents, and administrators in two Adult Basic Education programs (Perlman, 266)

Evaluations of programs abroad

Three studies examined programs abroad. One assessed the effect of a homestay and tour program in France on students' acculturation, language skills, and attitudes (Hoeh and Spuck, 150); a second French-abroad program, the Carlton-Pau Experiment, was evaluated by Monnot and Monnot (217). The achievement of beginners studying Spanish abroad for one semester was compared to that of their counterparts studying Spanish in the United States for three semesters (Stansfield, 319).

The emphasis of the evaluations has been primarily on French and Spanish programs here and abroad, but there was some interest in the effects of ESL and Latin FLES programs. Objectives and instruction attracted researchers in a moderate way, and programs have been the center of attention; but administration, organization, and theory have been dealt with only superficially in areas such as attrition, grouping, and policy. The evidence points to a lack of coordinated and guided research; therefore, a need may exist for some central bureau for identifying topics or areas requiring some study.

Lack of coordinated effort

Physiology and psychology of language learning

In the interest of readability, we have endeavored to use a rather limited number of subcategories: teaching and learning methods, bilingualism, student factors, and psycholinguistics.

Teaching and learning methods

An investigation of applied generative-phonology-inspired methodology (Schnitzer, 294), the relative efficacy of systematic production training (Catford and Pisoni, 52), and the effect of teaching methods and attitudes on black speakers of nonstandard English (Politzer and Hoover, 273) were the only identified studies on teaching and learning methods.

Bilingual studies

Research studies on bilingual factors in the psychology of language learning were only slightly more numerous. Formation of concepts in second language prior to first language concept formation was discussed by Stern and Ruble (320). Another study dealt with inter- and intro-lingual associations of English and German students (Riegel and Zivian, 286). Three studies by Landry were focused on some facet of possible cognitive enhancement for the second language learner. The studies probed these three questions:

1 Is there a difference between monolinguals and second language learners in divergent thinking tasks (Landry, 189)?
2 Is verbal creativity enhanced through second language learning (Landry, 191)?
3 Is figural creativity enhanced through second language learning (Landry, 190)?

Student factors

The importance of individual differences as a factor in language learning drew the attention of a rather large number of researchers. Attitudes were also an area of interest. About one third of all studies concerning student factors focused on the relationship between students' attitudes and foreign language study and achievement. They were:

- A survey of studies on attitudes toward foreign language learning in general (Ford, 99)
- Attitudes toward foreign language study in Utah (Wood, 350) and in Virginia (Warriner, 345)
- The effects of various attitudinal factors on foreign language achievement (Mueller, 223; Mueller and Miller, 225; Lukmano, 200; Guiora et al., 123)
- Attitudes of black high school students toward other black persons who speak standard English and nonstandard Negro English (Hensley, 143)
- Teacher behavior as a factor in student attrition in foreign language classes (Papalia and Zampogna, 264)
- The relationship between students' ethnolinguistic attitudes and the teaching method for the second language (Tang, 327)
- The influence of ethnocentric attitudes on second language acquisition (Dulay and Pepe, 85)
- The effects of cultural differences on performance in language learning (Ramsey and Wright, 281)
- The effects of affective techniques in teaching a foreign language (Bergen, 19)
- The reliability of measures of intelligence, previous study, and so on as predictors of success in foreign language learning (Green, 118)
- The use of measurable personality traits to identify under- or overachievers in college French (Smart et al., 310)
- Issues in attitude theory in Jerusalem and their role in relationship to sociolinguistic study (Cooper and Fishman, 68)
- The implications of social psychology on student attitudes (Cooke, 67)
- Problems of individual learning styles (Lepke, 193; Papalia, 257, 261; Zampogna et al., 351)
- A comparison of attitudes of students in an individualized program with attitudes of students in a standard program (Creed, 73)

Psycholinguistics

Studies in psycholinguistics were numerous and covered a wide spectrum of language-learning problems in both first and second language acquisition. They dealt with:

Error analysis in communicative competence (Politzer and Ramirez, 275; Powell, 278)
Error analysis in writing (Bhatia, 24; Buteau, 43)
Comparison of first language acquisition with second language acquisition (Asher, 5; Boyd, 33; Cook, 66)
Cognitive processing strategies (Birckbichler, 26; Knorre, 181)
Second language acquisition through commands (Asher et al., 6)
Modalities of syntactic choice and productivity (Titone, 334)
Adult ESL students' acquisition of grammatical morphemes outside the communication situation (Freeman, 102)
Natural sequence in second language acquisition (Bailey et al., 8)
The acquisition of English auxiliaries by native speakers of Spanish (Cancino et al., 46)
Retention of the second language over varying intervals such as summer vacation (Smythe et al., 313)
The relation of language and thought and its implications for teaching (Lado, 186)
Specific competencies that an English-speaking learner must possess to read a French sentence (Phillips, 270)
Transfer of students' perception of suprasegmental features to normal language behavior (Feldman, 96)
The importance of sound discrimination for second language oral production (Dreher and Larkins, 80)
The acquisition of inflections (Bellamy and Bellamy, 17; Solomon, 314)
ESL students' speech patterns (Bertkua, 22)
Child versus adult judgment of sound/symbol correlations (Read, 282)
Phonological interference in learning English as a third language (Chamot, 53)
The role of interlanguage in second language acquisition (Dickerson, 78)

First language development

First language development in the child was treated by Jakobovits and Gordon (165) in an empirical study of a two-and-one-half-year-old child's conversational rules in an effort to develop a model of transactional engineering competency, by Krashen

(182) in an examination of lateralization as a factor in first language acquisition after puberty, and by Oller (235) in a study of the existence of a unitary proficiency factor underlying language performance in all four skills.

Studies in psycholinguistics seemed to stress the acquisition of the oral skill, perhaps due to the influence of the audiolingual goals of the 1960s.

Teaching materials

Basic texts

Studies on teaching materials were mainly concerned with inquiries about some aspect of basic texts and readers:

A survey of elementary and intermediate basic texts in Latin (Scanlan, 292)
A survey of elementary and intermediate basic texts in French (Frechette, 101)
Readers' reactions regarding good style in German texts (Frey, 103)
The study of noun genders in high school level beginning French texts (Jorstad, 173)
The vocabulary range of elementary Chinese school children as a basis for materials development (Long, 192)

Readers

A survey of elementary and intermediate French readers (Frechette, 100)
The effectiveness of a programmed reader (Henning, 142)
The design of EFL reading materials (Cowan, 71)
The development of English prevocational literary materials for Spanish-speaking students (Smith, 312)
The effectiveness of *Spanish Curricular Kits* by the Spanish Curricula Development Center (Rothfarb and Cahill, 288)

We found no studies in the Germanic or Slavic languages. Our research also revealed no special investigations of conversational texts, culture and civilization texts, integrated programs, and literary texts. There was a conspicuous absence of research relating to audio and visual materials; this lack of interest in software probably reflects a decline in the favor that language laboratories enjoyed in the 1960s and the rising costs of such materials.

Teacher education and certification

Certification

Research in this area dealt primarily with preservice training and surveys of teacher attitudes and backgrounds. A study on competency-based certification (Eddy, 88) was the only one specifically addressed to certification *per se*. Of three program evaluations, one dealt with the effectiveness of Foreign Language Institutes abroad on the training for leadership in the teaching profession (Eddy, 87); the other two were concerned with ESL: Bruck et al. (40) examined the effectiveness of the NDEA Philippine Institute for TESOL teachers, and Horst et al. (156) evaluated a stateside program preparing ESL teachers. Preservice teacher training studies consisted of:

Program evaluations

Preservice training

An evaluation of student teachers by means of teacher performance tests (Herold, 146)
Techniques for English oral skill training for nonnative speakers of English who plan to become ESL teachers (Fukuda, 104)
The use of simulation in foreign language teacher training to help sensitize teachers to individual differences among students (Hancock, 132)
The importance of innovative instructional approaches in teacher preparation (DeLorenzo, 77)
The merits of microteaching as a teacher-training technique (Beattie and Teather, 16)

Inservice training

Inservice training included a report on a workshop to show teachers how to evaluate themselves realistically with a view toward developing possibilities of individualized instruction (Bockman and Gougher, 29) and another on the preparation of graduate teaching assistants and an evaluation of the effectiveness of such preparation (Gilbert and McArthur, 109). The role of the native paraprofessional and an evaluation of his effectiveness was the subject of yet another teacher preparation study (Hammelman and Nielsen, 130).

Teacher attitudes

Teacher attitudes received a great deal of attention in proportion to other teacher factors. Studies found were:

Background and attitudes of teachers (Elmquist, 89; Papalia, 258)

A comparison of the attitudes of prospective foreign language teachers with those of teachers of other disciplines toward linguistically and culturally different learners (Ford, 99)
Attitudes of English teachers toward speakers of non-standard English (Hewett, 147)
A survey of the attitudes of West Texas teachers toward Southwestern Spanish and English language varieties (MacIntosh and Ornstein, 203)
Factors that influence the attitudes of Florida foreign language teachers toward foreign language methodologies (Pinder, 271)

Methods

A number of studies have been concerned with methods and techniques of teaching foreign languages; they seem to fall into the broad categories of instructional techniques, comparison of methodologies, the use of media in instruction, and individualized instruction. This diversity of investigation may be interpreted positively as a result of the wide-ranging concerns of foreign language education researchers, but it may also be indicative of lack of direction in the profession. Few of the studies can be easily interrelated except in a most artificial way; this must surely perplex the teacher who is trying to identify findings in the research area for possible use in the classroom.

A variety of studies

No visible direction

In the category of instructional techniques we found the following studies:

A survey of foreign language teaching methodology (Levinsky, 195)
The introduction of cultural material and its effect on student motivation (Lewald, 196)
The value of Hispanic folk music for creating crosscultural understanding and improving student motivation (Griffin, 120)
The effectiveness of planned dramatic scenes in creative linguistic experiences (Tiefenbrun, 333)
The development of ESL teaching techniques for specific populations (Beardsmore and Lee, 15)
The value of a learning for mastery approach to the teaching of foreign literature (Fadil, 93)

Most studies appeared to focus on more effective ways of involving students in the language-learning process.

Instructional techniques

Of interest to researchers was the general question of how best to foster the development of particular language skills. These include:

The effects of time-expansion on the listening comprehension of French students (Flaherty, 97)
The teaching of speed reading in Spanish (Carsello and Braun, 51)
A description of the specific procedures involved in teaching Spanish-speaking children to read Spanish (Herbert, 145)
A comparison of intensive written practice versus intensive oral practice to determine which is more beneficial for beginning second language learners (Postovsky, 277)
The relative effectiveness of oral and orthographic stimuli in the presentation of dialogues (Lado et al., 187)
The effectiveness of training beginning foreign language students for communicative competence (Savignon, 291)
The value of repetition in oral learning (Locke, 199)
An evaluation of a course designed to teach children to form correct speech habits in French (Olsen, 248)
The extent to which a student's errors can be corrected without inhibiting his oral expression (Fanselow, 95)
The effects of delayed versus immediate introduction of foreign language script (Hawkins, 138)
The value of written assignments as reinforcement for speaking and understanding (Pfister, 268)
The effectiveness of a bidialectical approach to the teaching of written composition (Bruder and Hayden, 41)

Language skills

The researchers considered several techniques for teaching and learning the four skills; but the focus was on the introduction of oral and written stimuli.

Effect of Latin study on English

There has been mild interest in Latin. Masciantonio (206) reported some studies on the effect of Latin instruction on the development of English language skills:

The Philadelphia Public Schools examined the effect of the study of Latin on all the English language skills.
The District of Columbia examined the effect of the study of

Latin on sixth grade students' reading abilities in English, Spanish, and French.

The Indianapolis Public Schools have researched the effect of the study of Latin and civilization on the verbal functioning of sixth grade pupils in English, on the broadening of cultural horizons, and on the interest in humanities.

The Easthampton, Massachusetts, Public Schools and the Classics Department of the University of Massachusetts attempted to determine whether the study of Latin stimulated and strengthened pupils' reading skills in English.

Comparison of methodologies

Some work has centered around the comparison of methodologies. A concentration of such studies has been focused on the relative effectiveness of the audiolingual versus the cognitive learning strategies (Mueller, 221; Oskarsson, 253; von Elek and Oskarsson, 339, 340). Others have been more diverse:

A comparison of traditional methods with those emphasizing oral communication and functional grammar (Tamarkin, 326)

The effectiveness of a communicative-competence-based method (Joiner, 170)

A comparison of structural versus situational methods of teaching (Hauptman, 137)

A comparison of contextual versus drill practice (Jarvis and Hatfield, 167)

A comparison of immersion type foreign language instruction versus traditional approaches (McGowan, 208)

The use of CAS strategy (Keuleers, 178)

A comparison of the achievement of teacher-directed versus non-teacher-directed groups of foreign language learners (Gibbons, 108)

A comparison of the results of teaching Spanish through team teaching and supervised independent study versus traditionally taught classes (Boyd-Bowman et al., 34)

A comparison of the achievement of college students in audiolingual classes versus those in classes utilizing audiovisual materials (Reilley and Oakes, 284)

The variety alone in the studies should be of interest to teachers, but the results of the effectiveness of the methods examined should be of some benefit to those seeking change and innovation.

Language laboratories

In the category of media as aids to instruction, language laboratories were the most commonly investigated. They were:

The effectiveness of voice reflectors and audioactive language laboratories in foreign language programs (Brown et al., 38)
Student attitudes toward the language laboratory (Schotta, 295)
Students' varying abilities to recognize and correct mistakes in the language laboratory (Higgins, 148)
A comparison of the effects of delayed versus immediate correction of errors made in the language laboratory (Sisson, 308)
A survey of the use of language laboratories in British foreign language classrooms (Green, 119)
The effectiveness of the listen-and-respond mode versus a comparison mode in college classes (Perelle, 265)
An examination of five different language laboratory treatments and their most effective use with visuals (Chomei and Houlihan, 58)

In general, the studies in this area revolved around the effective utilization of the language laboratory to help students develop proficiency.

Videotape

Videotape as a teaching medium was also studied in relation to its use in advanced conversation classes (Santoni, 290), its possible use in language laboratories and classrooms (Huberman and Medish, 157), and as an aid to oral language skill development through instant replay (Sisk, 307). Two other studies were found in which Mohr and Lally (214) looked at the possible role of shortwave radio in the teaching of German, and Hammerly (131) studied visual aids as a means of presenting meaning without recourse to the native language.

Individualized instruction

Individualized instruction received its share of attention as several studies considered its effectiveness in relation to conventional or standard techniques (Clausing et al., 60, 61; Ponchie, 276; Prince and Casey, 279). Mueller (224) examined its effect upon attrition in foreign language classes; others concerned themselves with ways of developing programs of individualized instruction at various levels of foreign language instruction (Cuddington, 75; Everett, 92; Schwab, 299; Teichert, 330). Berwald (23) compared three individualized instruction programs in an effort to determine the most effective format. Other suggested ways to improve individualized instruction include its enhancement through small-group interaction (Papalia and Zampogna, 263) and the introduction of peer teaching to increase practice in conversation (Semke, 305).

There is ample evidence that methods have been on the minds of researchers and that their attention has been drawn more to individualized instruction, perhaps due in part to the avalanche of literature, workshops, and convention speakers who have kept this topic very much alive.

Testing

Measurement techniques

In an area that is of concern to many, the research on testing reflected two categories of special interest: measurement techniques and standardized tests. Specific questions appeared to revolve around effectively measuring various aspects of student learning—how to measure them and with what tests.

The topics examined under the general heading of measurement techniques were quite varied. They were:

The minimum number of times needed to establish reliability on minitests (Blatchford, 28)

Developmental sentence scoring as a means of measuring skill development (Politzer, 272)

Syntactic fluency measures as tests of French language skills (Monroe, 218)

Syntactic fluency measures for the testing of German language development (Cooper, 69)

The possibility of objective assessment of a pupil's EFL pronunciation through an examination of interrater reliability (Dimitrijevic and Djordjevic, 79)

The possibility of an oral communication ability not presently tested and how it might be measured (Palmer, 255)

Dictation as a measure of oral comprehension (Brodkey, 37)

The relative usefulness of discrete versus communicative competency evaluative techniques (Schulz, 296)

The interrelationships of linguistic competence, grade point average, personality measures, and other variables, with communicative competence in second language learning (Bartz, 14)
Sentence imitations by black and Mexican-American children as a basis for language evaluation (Natalicio and Williams, 226)
The proficiency of black children in standard and nonstandard English (Politzer et al., 274)
The English reading skills of nonnative speakers in relation to native speakers' proficiency levels (Oller, 240)
Error analysis of Swedish students learning English (Olsson, 250)
Factors involved in the prediction of success of Americans learning Japanese (Jacobsen and Imhoof, 163)

The trend is towards increased research in the development of tests to measure the language proficiency of cultural and linguistic minority groups.

Cloze tests

Of particular moment during the early 1970s have been cloze tests. Stubbs and Tucker (323) used cloze procedures to evaluate English proficiency; Gould and Spencer (112) examined cloze tests in relation to the differences between exact and acceptable words; others have studied cloze procedures with audience response to films (Lynch, 201) and with reading comprehension of Anglo-American and Mexican children (Crawford, 72).

Much has been done by Oller, who has looked at these tests as a device for measuring ESL proficiency (Oller, 240; Oller and Conrad, 242) and has compared the performance of native and nonnative English speakers (Oller et al., 241).

Noise tests

Another procedure given some attention has been that of noise tests. Gradman and Gaies (115) examined the signal-to-noise relationships and error trends in selected performances on noise tests. Other studies include the revision and perfection of noise tests to increase their face validity in actual usage (Gaies et al., 106), reduced redundancy tests (Gradman, 114) and controlled distortion for the more effective teaching and testing of language skills (Gradman and Spolsky, 116).

There apparently is a developing corpus of testing instruments to measure second language factors; Oller (237) has reviewed the literature related to pragmatics and language testing and discussed questions that must be investigated to shed light on language testing as an integral part of applied linguistics.

Standardized tests

Standardized tests that have been considered by researchers include:

The power of the Modern Language Aptitude Test (MLAT) and the Pimsleur Language Aptitude Battery (PLAB) in the prediction of performance in high school foreign language classrooms (Cloos, 62)
An examination of the norms for the MLA Cooperative Russian Test (Shane, 306)
The effectiveness of the Test of English as a Foreign Language (TOEFL) as a predictor of success in graduate study (Gue and Holdaway, 122)
A comparison of TOEFL scores by native and nonnative English speakers (Angoff and Sharon, 4)
A multinational program of testing achievement in French (Carroll, 49)
An assessment of the validity of the Advanced Placement French Examination (Modu et al., 213)
The development of the Graduate School Foreign Language Tests (GSFLT) for colleges (Harvey, 136)
A comparison of the results of the Dade County Aural Comprehension Test with evaluations given by experienced teachers after prolonged contact with students (Rothfarb, 287)
An aural comprehension test administered in the language laboratory through contextualization (Seliger and Whiteson, 304)

Testing, including cloze testing, noise tests, factors in the construction of tests, and the evaluation of standardized tests, has received its share of interest. There is promise particularly in the testing of bilinguals and in better future measures of student aptitude and performance.

Bilingualism and bilingual education

Research in bilingualism and bilingual education has been concentrated in three areas: surveys, testing, and program evaluation. One of the most comprehensive profiles to date is Andersson's (2) survey of bilingual education in the United States. On a much smaller scale the following were identified:

Surveys

A study of English-Spanish proficiency in relation to socioeconomic status, social status, and intelligence among preschool Mexican-American children (Carrow, 50)
An examination of the performance and types of bilingualism among Navajos (Stafford, 317)
A study of the relationship between Spanish listening comprehension, language proficiency, and cultural attitudes of native and nonnative Spanish speakers (Bockman and Videen, 30)
A study of the role of the Hispano in the spread of Anglicisms in Spanish (Teschner, 332)

Testing

Three studies examined aspects of testing: Spector (315) assessed the errors of Mexican-American children in oral English performance; Dubois (81) evaluated the written communicative competence of undergraduate Chicanos; and Orvik (252) compared the English vocabulary of Eskimo children with that of native English-speaking children.

Program evaluations

The emphasis has certainly been on the evaluation of ongoing bilingual programs, and this is illustrated by such evaluations as the Elgin Project (Barik and Swain, 11), the St. Lambert Project (D'Anglejan and Tucker, 76), the Ottawa Study (Barik and Swain, 12), the programs in Albany, New York (Morel, 219), Pontiac, Michigan (Smith, 311), and in Connecticut (Zirkel, 352). Others noted were Skoczylas' (309) comparison of the linguistic, academic, cognitive, and affective growth of children in a bilingual program with children in the regular school program; Cohen's (63) study of the performance of English-speaking students in Spanish, English, and content subjects in a bilingual program; and Cordova's (70) investigation of the effect of an English-as-a-second-language program on the English proficiency, school success, and self-image of Spanish-speaking children.

Teacher views

Teachers were not ignored, for Campbell et al., (45) surveyed teacher views of immersion-type bilingual education programs for teachers of French and English, and McRae (209) looked at the relationship between teacher proficiency in Spanish and

English and their attitude toward the Carrascolendas bilingual television program.

What designs and methodologies are being used?

Although no attempt is made in this chapter to evaluate individual research efforts, we should recognize the wide variability in the quality of both the conceptualization and presentation. In some studies the problem, hypotheses, and procedures are clearly stated; in others, only a careful reading permits identification of the problem or hypothesis. Many studies claim significant results but fail to provide adequate information about the statistical procedures used. Several studies even fail to identify the type of design employed, give but a fragmentary description of the procedures followed, and enter into an analysis of the data either too perfunctorily or in such depth and complexity that readability is impaired.

Lack of organization and clarity

If the researchers wish to disseminate the results of their efforts to the classroom teacher, we would suggest that future research reports utilize simpler language and a format that includes statements of the problem and hypothesis and a description of the procedures to be used in obtaining the data—that is, of the design as well as how the data were used to test the hypothesis. We have encountered page after page of technical data which can be understood and interpreted only by experienced researchers or a few persons knowledgeable in methods of research. Perhaps a course in writing for professional publications, such as the one offered at The Ohio State University, should be required of Ph.D. candidates in an effort to help develop writing skills.

Suggestions for writers of research reports

Descriptive research

Most educational research is descriptive in nature—that is, the investigator looks at a situation and reports what he finds there. In the research reviewed we observed 204 studies, or about 70 percent, in this category distributed among the subcategories of surveys, interrelationship studies, and growth studies. Some consider historical research to be a subcategory of descriptive research. We do not. Moreover, only one study of this type (Andersson, 2) was identified.

Historical study

School surveys

Surveys. School surveys are a search for information about the educational process and the nature and the needs of the pupil and teacher. This variety of descriptive research is the one most frequently conducted by the foreign language researchers surveyed; we found 33 examples within our review. Several models of school surveys treating the educational process were made by Bockman and Videen (30), Harvey (136), and Teitelbaum (331). Mueller and Miller (225), Olsson (250), Papalia (261), and Stockfelt-Hoatson (322) surveyed the needs or nature of the pupil, and studies by Fanselow (94), Herold (146), Papalia (258), and Pinder (271) were focused on the teacher.

Documental analyses

Another type of survey, documentary analysis, in which books, texts, or other documents are examined, is illustrated in the works of Frechette (100), Jorstad (173), Sternglass (321), and White (347). There were 11 opinion surveys, exemplified by Eddy (87), Frey (103), Offenberg et al., (232), and Papalia (259). In addition, a very small number of job analyses and community surveys were noted.

Opinion surveys

Interrelationship studies. There were 96 interrelationship studies, the type most often found in this survey. These are an effort to discover how different factors interact or are interrelated. Such studies include case studies, where the investigator makes an intensive inquiry into a social unit (Chamot, 53; Dulay and Burt, 82; Lima, 197; Suiero-Ross, 324); correlational studies (there were 22 of these), such as those of Guiora et al. (123), Irvine et al. (162), Lukmano (200), and Stubbs and Tucker (323); and correlational-predictor studies, illustrated in the works of Gue and Holdaway (122), Ilyin (159), Saegert et al. (289), and Smart et al. (310). Interrelationship studies can also be comparative (Markman et al., 204; Oller, 233; Skoczylas, 309; Titone, 334); causal-comparative, sometimes termed *ex post facto* (Marik and Swain, 11; Hewett, 147; Politzer and Ramirez, 275; Taylor, 329); and crosscultural comparative (Carrow, 50; Oller et al., 241; Orvick, 252; Ramsey and Wright, 281).

Case studies

Correlational studies

Correlational-predictor studies

Comparative studies

Causal-comparative studies

Crosscultural comparative studies

Growth studies. The subcategory of growth or developmental studies are investigations of how a social unit changes over a period of time. A study may be longitudinal, where time and resources are big factors, as in Barik and Swain (12), Bruck et al., (39), Hakuta (128), and Smythe et al., (313), or cross-sectional, where the investigator samples across elements of a pop-

Longitudinal studies

Cross-sectional studies

ulation, as in Bellamy and Bellamy (17), Dulay and Burt (83), Oller and Nagato (244), and Ramirez and Politzer (280). There were also a small number of trend studies.

Experimental research

The next major type of research found was that of the experimental study which is characterized by a rigorous control over variables that may affect the results.

Types of designs

To achieve the desired control the methodology of research offers several designs that help the researcher in the organization and procedures of his study. The most used design, which we noted in 33 studies, was characterized by the selection of two groups, one an experimental group and the other a control group—usually two different classrooms of students. The subjects were not selected at random, but all were tested before and after the experiment. We have labelled the groups in the traditional sense in that the control group does not receive the experimental treatment, but there are those who hold that, because the two groups are being compared, both groups receive treatments, though they are different; therefore, both may be considered as experimental groups (Kerlinger, 176).

In 14 of these studies the experimental group received an experimental treatment, and the control group did not (Brown et al., 38; Prince and Casey, 279; von Elek and Oskarsson, 339). In some instances we found a variation of the above design in which either the control group also received an experimental treatment or there were two different experimental groups (Chomei and Houlihan, 58; Hauptman, 137; Jarvis and Hatfield, 167; Schulz, 296).

The second favored design (there were 15 applications) consisted solely of an experimental group that was given a posttest (Hammerly, 131; Locke, 199; Menting and Pouw, 210: Smith, 312).

A third design (used 11 times) had only an experimental group that received a pretest as well as a posttest (Carsello and Braun, 51; Mohr and Lally, 214; Molina, 215; Olsen, 248). Ten studies used two groups, an experimental group and a control group; group equivalency was not established and they received only a posttest (Catford and Pisoni, 52; Huberman and Medish, 157; Papalia and Zampogna, 263; Postovsky, 277).

There were other designs used but they were insufficient in number to warrant discussion. For a more detailed explanation of research design (including limitations and deficiencies of all the above designs) the reader is referred to Campbell and Stanley (44).

The educational climate for research

What are the current constraints upon research?

Lack of money

Money is the primary factor restricting both the quantity and scope of research efforts today (Grittner, 121; Lipschutz, 198; Lepke, 194; Stansfield, 318). Large-scale studies are generally prohibitive in cost, and only large school systems have research departments capable of such undertakings. Universities are being increasingly limited in their capacity to do research (Andersson, 3). According to Grittner (121), too many studies have been largely unproductive and too little has been learned in relation to the amount of money expended. A second factor is that many teachers know little about research; they fear it because they have not had research training. They may have negative attitudes because they have too often been asked to implement new procedures on Monday morning, simply because on Friday afternoon an administrator has read a research summary that appealed to him. Often no adequate assessment of the need for the change has been made prior to the decree. Another reason teachers may fear research is that if they attempt to do some work independently, their efforts may be denigrated by "ivory-tower" educators (Lipschutz, 198).

Lack of training

Classroom teachers at the elementary and secondary levels and most faculty members in both two- and four-year colleges have been assigned teaching loads and other activities that prohibit research endeavors. At times a teacher is willing to do research but he is unable to find knowledgeable persons to help him.

Teaching loads

Bennett (18) reminds us that "controlled experiments are prone to impose experimental design at the expense of an account of learning" (p. 25). One should also consider that existing methods of data analysis may not be sufficiently developed to give us all the insight we hope for in the system of second language learning. Many of the findings from studies are restricted to a given situation, and some findings may not be translatable into classroom use (Tarone et al., 328). Much of the research in our field is done today by graduate students in dissertation studies; we must therefore recognize that most of our research is apprenticeship work (Jarvis, 166).

School rules

A most recent constraint, now the rule in many schools, is that students must consent to participate in research efforts (Lepke, 194). One must also consider the parental view: Some parents feel that there has been too much experimenting and not enough teaching and they would prefer a return to the basics "without frills." The reader should also bear in mind that our vision of what constitutes research is not always in harmony with the time and expertise required to complete the research (Chastain, 55).

Parental views

Has FL research been relevant to the classroom teacher?

Much of little relevance

By and large, observation of classroom practices and talks with classroom teachers have revealed that many feel a large portion of research efforts are of little relevance to them. Perlman (267), for example, believes that complex statistical data create a communication gap between researchers and teachers. The average classroom teacher has not had the preparation needed to understand the technical language employed. How, then, can the teacher determine whether the findings of research are relevant to his teaching? Tarone et al., (328) offer the view that, in the area of second language acquisition, research "cannot yet provide the classroom teacher with the kind of valid and reliable guidelines needed to effect curriculum change" (p. 1). Teachers interested in implementing research results should be aware there are still many gaps in the knowledge structure about second language acquisition. Studies to date have provided the teacher with some answers, but they "are at best tentative and must be interpreted with caution" (p. 3) because much of the research has been limited in scope, the methodologies for the collection or analysis of data are still being developed or formulated, and too few studies have been replicated. Tarone et al., (328) point out that there has been some relevant research on 1) the development of the interlanguage of second language learners (that is, in phonology, morphology, syntax, and semantics), though much remains to be

Findings tentative and limited in scope

done "before applications can confidently be made to classroom teaching" (p. 6); 2) learner strategies and the cognitive processes; and 3) the influence of individual variables. Relevant findings have been reported for other areas as well, but the view of Tarone et al., is that "the most immediately 'relevant' research for the classroom should be research done *in* the classroom" (p. 11). Many educators in the teacher training field also believe that teachers should be more involved in doing studies because they are the ones who will implement change as a result of research.

Need for more teacher involvement

What seems to be needed?

For Jorstad and Lange (174), the major need is for better communication regarding graduate student research in progress. They suggest that a number of institutions training Ph.D. students might consider working together on a "needs assessment" for the field, identifying broad areas in which graduate students might do research. Cooperation among institutions with doctoral programs in foreign language education might help to focus attention on major areas.

Better communication

Cooperation

Extreme caution must be exercised in disseminating the results of research based on abstracts or summaries. The detailed reports should be carefully read in addition to their reviews. Preliminary data and results should be reviewed by specialists before they are circulated. When such materials are then distributed to the consumer they should be readable. Reports that are too esoteric, mystical, and jargonistic are generally not read (Perlman, 267).

Readable material

Carroll (48) believes that the time is at hand for the profession to review current research to clarify the aspects of teaching methodology that may be precipitating declining enrollments. He is also of the opinion that other factors, such as the apparent decline in student motivation and the elimination of the college requirement, might be explored. Related to the subject of enrollments, the reasons students elect foreign languages in the junior and senior high school might warrant further study (Hilaire, 149).

The study of the attitudes and feelings involved in interethnic situations has been somewhat neglected, and there seems to have been a lack of interest in the empirical findings of colleagues in the areas of attitude theory and sociolinguistics. There are also unanswered questions regarding teacher attitudes toward dialectical differences: How can we best measure language attitudes? Cultural attitudes? Attitudes related to students' and teachers' classroom behavior (Ford, 98)? How are we training teachers to deal with these problems? There are unanswered questions about the best way to teach bilinguals at different levels: What are we doing for the bilinguals in our regular foreign language classes? Are any modifications being made to accommodate them? If so, what success have we had (Bernal, 21)? What is the relationship between bilingualism and intellectual development (Jakobovits, 164)? Stansfield (318) argues that we need to develop an established body of research findings to clarify issues dealing with bilingualism; the lack of such knowledge is the probable reason that so much argument and debate over something as fundamental as the definition of bilingual education still continues today.

Needed research

Research in Adult Basic Education (ABE) has been largely neglected. There is a demand for solutions to problems such as the prediction of an adult's success in learning ESL, the correlation of classroom success and student or employer-perceived success, and the administrative structure conducive to success. Does the teacher-competencies model hold promise for ABE-ESL? Is there a valid purpose for using the bilingual approach in ABE-ESL (Perlman, 267)? What are the classroom implications of the entire lifelong education movement? To date, researchers have been mainly occupied with students of college age or younger.

Teachers want to know more about the learner and second language acquisition. They are interested in the learning sequence as it compares to that of the native speaker, in learning styles, and in learning environment. Why do some learners have greater difficulty than others in learning a second language? The steps taken by learners without the usual administrative and teacher interventions should be studied. Is there an optimal sequence of learning linguistic structures? To what extent do such variables as age and background affect language learning? Teachers are wondering if there is a relationship between learning styles and the way students interact with instructional environments (Lepke, 194). They are asking which errors are made at the different developmental stages, which errors represent the final stages of a learner's competence (Scott and Tucker, 301), what types of learner errors can be predicted, and how to deal with errors once they are made. They are seeking ways and means to improve and enhance communicative competence (Chastain, 55). How does one acquire competence? Bartz (13) sees the need to develop more communication activities for the classroom. He has tried to identify the basic grammatical and structural content necessary to achieve communication goals and to ascertain how much grammar detail can be ignored in the high school classroom. Hanzeli (133) sees a great need for developmental research in the area of writing pedagogical grammars, textbooks, workbooks, and laboratory materials based on a grammar of communicative acts rather than on a formal linguistic grammar. Echeverria (86) calls for studies relating to learning strategies, quality of instruction, and criteria evaluation in the areas of linguistic-rule acquisition, error analysis, teaching method, and language testing. In the area of reading comprehension investigations of "the ability to choose correct summary statements about a context" are needed (Henning, 140, p. 14).

Another important area for research is testing. We lack instruments for facilitating the diagnostic process (Phillips, 269) and we need measures for testing the oral and aural skills. Stansfield (318) urges an update of norms on all standardized foreign language tests, indicating that most are over a decade old, and some are based on samples that are too small. Today's student is taught differently and uses materials that make the tests obsolete.

Some research on career education regarding industrial needs for foreign language competencies should be considered (Noble, 228).

We need much more cultural information along with language knowledge; we need to focus on the processes of second language learning; we need studies in the classics; in short, we need information about almost everything. But, once we have the information, the major task remains to translate research findings into innovative language curricular ideas and to provide a challenge to both researchers and teachers (Tarone et al., 328). The information must be practical and useful; if not, we shall continue to have the situation exemplified by the following remark, "I am a classroom teacher and my colleagues rank it (research) right next to the plague" (Bergen, 20).

What can the classroom teacher do?

Teachers should not look at researchers as gods and accept all their pronouncements; they should take the responsibility of selecting those findings that will help their students learn. But first, they must acquaint themselves with the current research and examine it critically; for this, training in reading and interpreting research is a necessity. Moskowitz (220) has made some practical suggestions for classroom teachers who may permit themselves to be swayed by research and faulty reasoning; she also adds an eleventh commandment, "Thou shalt not quote from any research thou hast not read thyself." Bowen (32) also cautions against unrealistic promises and expectations, research too hastily or politically motivated, or searching for fresh ideas simply for the sake of novelty. Phillips (269) feels that it is essential for teachers to attempt to implement specific practices and to evaluate them in terms of how they work in the classroom. Yet, there are others who believe that the teacher can do very little (Andersson, 3; Enwall, 90), not only because of lack of training but also because of the system that wears out the teacher day after day with a combination of curricular and extracurricular activities. Likewise the "establishment reaction" often prohibits or inhibits change.

Need for making research meaningful

Implementing research findings in the classroom

If, because of research findings, teachers consider making changes, they should do so because of genuine need and not "band-wagonism." Furthermore, if teachers try new practices or engage in small-scale studies (such as determining the effect of repeated practice in taking cloze tests or dictations), they should report their results to the journals. Oller (233) believes that there is a great deal to be done in classroom situations on questions such as these. Information relating to grassroot research must be disseminated. Grittner (121) suggests that teachers use opinion polls or other somewhat formalized instruments for gaining feedback from students.

Need for reporting results

Foreign language education programs and research

Some foreign language education programs offering a research course(s) for their graduate students are briefly described below. The Second Languages and Cultures Education area at the University of Minnesota has three courses dealing with research: 1) Testing and Evaluation in Second-Languages; 2) Research in Second-Language Education, a course in which students critically analyze published studies in the field and design a project of their own, thus providing an opportunity to work with the tools of educational research; and 3) a Ph.D. Seminar held on a weekly two-hour basis throughout the year, in which students' research proposals are discussed and refined for presentation and approval by the Graduate Advisory Committee as well as the Graduate School. Research in progress is discussed; selected professors from on campus are invited to speak about areas of concern, such as child development, first language acquisition, and pressing issues in second language education. In addition, Ph.D. students generally enroll in a minimum of five courses in the Psychological Foundations Department (Introductory Statistics, Probability Statistics—for example, t tests, F tests, Chi-Square—Analysis of Variance, and General Testing and Evaluation—a prerequisite for the foreign language education course in testing and evaluation mentioned above. Many (if not most) students take one or two additional statistics courses as well as an advanced testing course (Jorstad and Lange, 174).

University of Minnesota

The Ph.D. program of Foreign Language Education at The Ohio State University is composed of a basic core of courses in foreign language education plus one or two "satellite" areas. Within the basic core 17 quarter hours of courses are entirely devoted to research skills. A two-quarter seminar deals with both findings of research within the field and an evaluation of the research methodology utilized. A subsequent Foreign Language Education Research course involves the planning and carrying out of research projects. Students take a five-hour course in Statistics Applied to Foreign Language Education and a four-hour course in Foreign Language Testing. The statistics course is an elementary course requiring no previous background. Attention is given to the typically negative attitudes of many language educators toward quantitative information; examples and procedures are applied to variables utilized in foreign language education. Many students elect to do additional work in statis-

The Ohio State University

tics and research design—either as elective courses or as an entire satellite area (Jarvis, 166).

The Florida State University

At The Florida State University the Ph.D. program, somewhat like that of Ohio State, consists of a group of core courses plus others in different area emphases—for example, linguistics, ESL, bilingual education, and others outside the program. Within the core group, students are required to register in the course entitled Research in Foreign Languages, which concentrates on three focal points: locating research (including ERIC, bibliographic, and other sources) evaluating research (major and other important studies are discussed by the whole class, while other research of interest to individual students is reported to the class and evaluated), and conducting research (all students carry out a research study). In addition, research, analyses, and discussions are carried out in the student's area of emphasis. Most students generally take two or more courses in testing and evaluation, statistics, and research methodology.

Of the three programs cited, the University of Minnesota requires the most background courses in statistics, but, on the whole, the three appear to require and focus on the same aspects. If this small sample is representative, Ph.D. specialists will be increasingly prepared to deal with and conduct research.

Summary

1 In general there is evidence of a major effort having been made in the direction of language acquisition, the learner, attitudes, test development, program evaluation, bilingual education, ESL, curricular problems, teaching and learning methods, cognitive processing, teacher training, and use of the language laboratory.
2 The research has been preponderantly of a descriptive nature, but controlled experimentation, though limited in scope, has been gaining momentum.
3 Many researchers have put emphasis on the problems of minority linguistic groups in their sociological context.
4 We have seen a minor interest in phonology, vocabulary, and grammar with no indication of any clear trend.
5 In the curriculum area variety was manifest, but surveys and program evaluations received the most attention.

Problems relating to student factors, teaching and learning methods, and bilingualism were also the object of some research.

6 There were numerous studies in first and second language acquisition. Other aspects investigated included error analysis, cognitive processing, and language development.
7 Little notice seems to have been given to audiovisual materials, but there was concern with basic texts and readers.
8 A distinct interest in the preservice training of teachers was observed, but interest was also evident in inservice training, teacher attitudes, and background.
9 Diverse methods of instruction were examined to determine their effectiveness; several methods were compared.
10 Media received their share of consideration, but the emphasis was on language laboratories.
11 A good number of researchers concerned themselves with individualized instruction with emphasis on assessing its effectiveness and on the development of such programs.
12 Measurement techniques studied were varied, but cloze tests, noise tests, and error analysis got the most attention.
13 Interest in standardized tests was related to the evaluation of their appropriateness, validity, norms, and usefulness as predictors.
14 Bilingual education research was devoted mainly to program evaluations, but surveys were made, especially one very important one on bilingual education in the United States. Some studies were involved with the testing of bilinguals.
15 The most obvious constraints in research are lack of money, time, and knowledge, as well as prohibitive school regulations.
16 Much of the published research has been too complex in its reporting and in its statistical data to be of relevance to the classroom teacher. The findings have lacked generalizability and have been tentative at best.
17 There is need for new and continued research in all areas. The profession should consider needs assessments in research, setting priorities, and establishing a body of pertinent research findings; reviewing teaching methodology

and its effects on the learner, learner errors, ways to achieve communication goals, learner strategies, and the quality of instruction; interethnic attitudes, teacher attitudes, and how to measure attitudes toward language; adult education; and industrial needs.

18 Teachers should acquaint themselves with research, examine it carefully, select, and evaluate it in terms of how it works in the classroom. In addition, they must do research themselves and report their results.

It is hoped that from the research we will eventually discover facts about language learning which can be used to improve language teaching. However, a great deal more work is necessary before this contribution can be made. In the meantime the strictest caution should be exercised in attempting to apply . . . findings . . . to second language teaching. Careful articulation between researchers and teachers will insure that the results of research . . . will be appropriately incorporated into second language teaching (Schumann, 297, p. 422).

References, Directions of research in the 1970s

1 Alden, Douglas W. "The Status of French." *French Review* 48(1974):7–16.

2 Andersson, Theodore. "Bilingual Education:The American Experience." *Modern Language Journal* 55(1971):427–40.

3 ——— Personal Communication, 1976. [Letter.]

4 Angoff, William H., and Amiel T. Sharon. "A Comparison of Scores Earned on the Test of English as a Foreign Language by Native American College Students and Foreign Applicants to U.S. Colleges." *Teachers of English to Speakers of Other Languages Quarterly* 5(1971):129–36.

5 Asher, James J. "Children's First Language as a Model for Second Language Learning." *Modern Language Journal* 56(1972):133–39.

6 ——— Jo Anne Kusudo, and Rita De La Torre. "Learning a Second Language through Commands:The Second Field Test." *Modern Language Journal* 58(1974):24–32.

7 Bachmann, James K. "Field Techniques in an Urban Language Study." *Teachers of English to Speakers of Other Languages Quarterly* 4(1970): 255–60.

8 Bailey, Nathalie, Carolyn Madden, and Stephen D. Krashen. "Is There a 'Natural Sequence' in Adult Second Language Learning?" *Language Learning* 24(1974):235–43.

9 Baird, Raymond. "Children's Phonological Rules: A Failure to Replicate." *Language Learning* 23 (1973):223–30.

10 Barik, Henri C., and Merrill Swain. *Bilingual Education Project:Evaluation of the 1974-75 French Immersion Program in Grades 2-4, Ottawa Board of Education and Carleton Board of Education.* Toronto:The Ontario Institute for Studies in Education, 1975.

11 ——— "English-French Bilingual Education in the Early Grades:The Elgin Study." *Modern Language Journal* 58(1974):392–403.

12 ——— "Three-Year Evaluation of a Large Scale Early Grade French Immersion Program:The Ottawa Study." *Language Learning* 25(1975): 1–30.

13 Bartz, Walter H. Personal Communication, 1976. [Letter.]

14 ——— *A Study of the Relationship of Certain Learner Factors with the Ability to Communicate in a Second Language (German) for the Development of Measures of Communicative Competence.* Columbus:The Ohio State University, 1974. [Doctoral dissertation.]

15 Beardsmore, H. Baetens, and Eric J. Lee. "Teaching English as a Foreign Language for Special Purposes." *Modern Language Journal* 57(1973): 343–48.

16 Beattie, N. M., and D. C. B. Teather. "Micro-

teaching in the Training of Teachers of Modern Languages: Some Preliminary Comments." *Audio-Visual Language Journal* 9(1971):117–21.

17 Bellamy, Martha M., and Sidney E. Bellamy. "The Acquisition of Morphological Inflections by Children Four to Ten." *Language Learning* 20 (1970):199–211.

18 Bennett, William A. "The Nature of Research into Second Language Learning." *Audio-Visual Language Journal* 13(1975):23–26.

19 Bergen, James R. *The Development of a Rationale and a Taxonomy for Teaching Foreign Languages in the Affective Domain.* Columbus: The Ohio State University, 1974. [Doctoral dissertation.]

20 ——— Personal Communication, 1976. [Letter.]

21 Bernal, Ernest M. Personal Communication, 1976. [Letter.]

22 Bertkua, Jana S. "An Analysis of English Learner Speech." *Language Learning* 24(1974):279–86.

23 Berwald, Jean-Pierre. "Three Innovative Programs: Comparisons and Conclusions." *Foreign Language Annals* 8(1975):200–10.

24 Bhatia, Aban T. "An Error Analysis of Students' Compositions." *International Review of Applied Linguistics* 12,iv(1974):337–50.

25 *Bilingual Education Project Research Documents.* Toronto: Modern Language Center, Ontario Institute for Studies in Education, 1975. [Mimeo.]

26 Birckbichler, Diane W. *The Effects of Orienting Tasks Requiring Different Types and Levels of Cognitive Processing on Measures of Student Achievement in Beginning College French.* Columbus: The Ohio State University, 1975. [Doctoral dissertation.]

27 Birkmaier, Emma M. "Research on Teaching Foreign Languages," 1280–1302 in Robert M. W. Travers,ed., *Second Handbook of Research on Teaching.* Chicago: Rand McNally, 1973.

28 Blatchford, Charles H. "A Theoretical Contribution to ESL Diagnostic Test Construction." *TESOL Quarterly* 5(1971):209–15.

29 Bockman, John F., and Ronald L. Gougher,eds., *Self-Analysis and Introspection: Final Report of the Workshop on Individualizing Foreign Language Instruction.* West Chester, Pennsylvania: West Chester State College, 1972. [EDRS: ED 070 362.]

30 ——— and Darleen A. Videen. *A Study to Determine the Relationship between Spanish Listening Comprehension Proficiency and Cultural Attitudes of Various Groups of Native and Non-Native Students of the Spanish Language in Three High Schools: Cholla, Pueblo, and Tucson.* Tucson: Tucson Public Schools, 1971. [EDRS: ED 057 674.]

31 Bouton, Lawrence F. "Meeting the Needs of Children with Diverse Linguistic and Ethnic Backgrounds." *Foreign Language Annals* 8 (1975):306–16.

32 Bowen, J. Donald. "TESOL Research for the Classroom." *TESOL Quarterly* 6(1972):351–62.

33 Boyd, Patricia A. "The Development of Grammar Categories in Spanish by Anglo Children Learning a Second Language." *TESOL Quarterly* 9 (1975):125–35.

34 Boyd-Bowman, Peter, Bonnie Flickinger, Anthony Papalia, and Kenneth Rasmussen. "A Comparative Study in the Teaching of Spanish thru Team-Teaching and Supervised Independent Study." *Modern Language Journal* 57(1973): 199–204.

35 Brod, Richard I. *Survey of Foreign Language Course Registrations and Student Contact Hours in Institutions of Higher Education, Fall 1970 and Summer 1971. Final Report.* New York: Modern Language Association, 1972. [EDRS: ED 062 837.]

36 ——— *Survey of Foreign Language Entrance and Degree Requirements for the Bachelor of Arts Degree in United States Institutions of Higher Education.* New York: Modern Language Association, 1972. [EDRS: ED 066 099.]

37 Brodkey, Dean. "Dictation as a Measure of Mutual Intelligibility: A Pilot Study." *Language Learning* 22(1972):203–20.

38 Brown, James W., et al. "A Testing of the Audio-Active Voice Reflector in the Foreign Language Classroom." *Modern Language Journal* 56(1972): 144–47.

39 Bruck, Margaret, Wallace E. Lambert, and G. Richard Tucker. "Bilingual Schooling through the Elementary Grades: The St. Lambert Project at Grade Seven." *Language Learning* 24(1974): 183–204.

40 ——— Wallace E. Lambert, G. Richard Tucker, and J. Donald Bowen. "The 1968 NDEA Philippine Institute for TESL Teachers: A Follow-Up Evaluation." *Foreign Language Annals* 8(1975): 133–37.

41 Bruder, Mary N., and Luddy Hayden. "Teaching Composition: A Report on a Bidialectal Approach." *Language Learning* 23(1973):1–15.

42 Bustin-Lekeu, Francine. "Tutoiement et vouvoiement chez les lycéens français." *French Review* 46(1973):773–82.

43 Buteau, Magdelhayne F. "Students' Errors and the Learning of French as a Second Language: A Pilot Study." *International Review of Applied Linguistics* 8(1970):133–45.

44 Campbell, Donald T., and Julian C. Stanley. *Experimental and Quasi-Experimental Designs for Research,* Chicago: Rand McNally, 1963.

45 Campbell, Russell N., Donald M. Taylor, and G. Richard Tucker. "Teachers' Views of Immersion-Type Bilingual Programs: A Quebec Example." *Foreign Language Annals* 7(1973):106–10.

46 Cancino, Herlinda, Ellen J. Rosansky, and John H. Schumann. "The Acquisition of the English Auxiliary by Native Spanish Speakers." *TESOL Quarterly* 9(1975):421–30.

47 Capco, Clemencia, and G. Richard Tucker. "Word Association Data and the Assessment of Bilin-

gual Education Programs." *TESOL Quarterly* 5(1971):335–42.

48 Carroll, John B. Personal Communication, 1976. [Letter.]

49 ——— *The Teaching of French as a Foreign Language in Eight Countries.* New York: Halsted, 1975.

50 Carrow, Elizabeth. "Comprehension of English and Spanish by Preschool Mexican-American Children." *Modern Language Journal* 55(1971): 299–306.

51 Carsello, Carmen J., and Lucille V. Braun. "Rapid Reading Spanish Material." *Modern Language Journal* 56(1972):148–50.

52 Catford, J. C., and David B. Pisoni. "Auditory vs. Articulatory Training in Exotic Sounds." *Modern Language Journal* 54(1970):477–81.

53 Chamot, Anna U. "Phonological Problems in Learning English as a Third Language." *International Review of Applied Linguistics* 11(1973): 243–50.

54 Chastain, Kenneth. "Affective and Ability Factors in Second-Language Acquisition." *Language Learning* 25(1975):153–61.

55 ——— Personal Communication, 1976. [Letter.]

56 Chau, Tran-Thi. "Error Analysis, Contrastive Analysis, and Students' Perception: A Study of Difficulty in Second-Language Learning." *International Review of Applied Linguistics* 13(1975): 119–43.

57 Chiu, Rosaline K. "Measuring Register Characteristics: A Prerequisite for Preparing Advanced Level TESOL Programs." *TESOL Quarterly* 6 (1972):129–41.

58 Chomei, Toshiko, and Robert Houlihan. "Comparative Effectiveness of Five Language Laboratory Methods in Relation to Visuals." *International Review of Applied Linguistics* 12(1974): 327–36.

59 Clarke, R. P. "Stands Spanish Where It Should?" *Audio-Visual Language Journal* 11 (1973–74): 190–92.

60 Clausing, Gerhard, Klaus A. Mueller, and Wilfried M. Voge. "Individualized German Instruction at the College Level—A First Appraisal." *Foreign Language Annals* 6(1972):73–87.

61 ——— Klaus A. Mueller, and Anneliese S. Stein. "Individualized German Instruction at the College Level—A Follow-Up Report." *Foreign Language Annals* 7(1973):237–42.

62 Cloos, Robert I. "A Four-Year Study of Foreign Language Aptitude at the High School Level." *Foreign Language Annals* 4(1971):411–19.

63 Cohen, Andrew D. "The Culver City Spanish Immersion Program: The First Two Years." *Modern Language Journal* 58(1974):95–103.

64 ——— "The Culver City Spanish Immersion Program: How Does Summer Recess Affect Spanish Speaking Ability?" *Language Learning* 24 (1974):55–68.

65 ——— "Forgetting a Second Language." *Language Learning* 25(1975):127–38.

66 Cook, Vivian J. "The Comparison of Language Development in Native Children and Foreign Adults." *International Review of Applied Linguistics* 11(1973):13–28.

67 Cooke, Madeline A. "Social Psychology and Foreign Language Teaching." *Foreign Language Annals* 7(1973):215–23.

68 Cooper, Robert L., and Joshua A. Fishman. *Some Issues in the Theory and Measurement of Language Attitude.* [Paper presented at the International Seminar on Language Testing, San Juan, Puerto Rico, May 1973.] [Mimeo.]

69 Cooper, Thomas C. *The Acquisition of Written Syntax by College Students of German.* Tallahassee: The Florida State University, 1972. [Doctoral dissertation.]

70 Cordova, Joe E. *English Proficiency and Behavioral Change in Spanish-Speaking Children.* Pueblo: Southern Colorado State College, 1972. [EDRS: ED 066 996.]

71 Cowan, J. R. "Lexical and Syntactic Research for the Design of EFL Reading Materials." *TESOL Quarterly* 8(1974):389–99.

72 Crawford, A. N. *The Cloze Procedure as a Measure of the Reading Comprehension of Elementary Level Mexican-American and Anglo-American Children.* Los Angeles: University of California, 1970. [Doctoral dissertation.]

73 Creed, Carol L. "Student Attitudes and Individualized Instruction." *Foreign Language Annals* 7 (1973):256–59.

74 Crymes, Ruth. "The Relation of Study about Language to Language Performance: With Special Reference to Nominalization." *TESOL Quarterly* 5(1971):217–30.

75 Cuddington, Martha A. "Individualization for First-Year Students." *French Review* 48(1974): 357–67.

76 D'Anglejan, Alison, and G. R. Tucker. "Academic Report: The St. Lambert Program of Home-School Language Switch." *Modern Language Journal* 55 (1971):99–101.

77 DeLorenzo, William E. "Rationale, Description and Feasibility of a Partially Programmed Foreign Language Methods Course." *Foreign Language Annals* 7(1973):224–30.

78 Dickerson, Lonna J. "The Learner's Interlanguage as a System of Variable Rules." *TESOL Quarterly* 9(1975):401–07.

79 Dimitrijevic, Naum R., and Dusan Djordjevic. "The Reliability of the Subjective Assessment of the Pupils' Pronunciation of English as a Foreign Language." *International Review of Applied Linguistics* 9(1971):245–65.

80 Dreher, Barbara, and James Larkins. "Non-Semantic Auditory Discrimination: Foundation for Second Language Learning." *Modern Language Journal* 56(1972):227–30.

81 Dubois, Betty L. "Written English Communicative Competence of UTEP Chicanos: A Preliminary Report." *System* 2,ii(1974):49–56.

82 Dulay, Heidi C., and Marina K. Burt. "Errors and

Strategies in Child Second Language Acquisition." *TESOL Quarterly* 8(1974):129–36.

83 ——— "Natural Sequence in Child Second Language Acquisition." *Language Learning* 24 (1974):37–53.

84 ——— "Should We Teach Children Syntax?" *Language Learning* 23(1973):245–58.

85 ——— and Helene Pepe. *The Influence of a Social Setting on Second Language Learning,* 1970. [EDRS: ED 071 472.]

86 Echeverria, Max S. "On Needed Research in Second Language Learning in the Light of Contemporary Developments in Linguistic Theory." *International Review of Applied Linguistics* 12 (1974):69–77.

87 Eddy, Frederick D. "Institute Training Abroad for Leadership in Foreign Languages: A Preliminary Survey of Results." *Modern Language Journal* 55(1971):164–77.

88 Eddy, Peter A. "Competence-Based Certification of Foreign Language Teachers: The Bellevue-Western Experience." *Modern Language Journal* 59(1975):432–39.

89 Elmquist, Anne M. "The Foreign Language Teacher: Background and Attitudes." *Foreign Language Annals* 6(1973):490–99.

90 Enwall, Beverly. Personal Communication, 1975. [Letter.]

91 Ervin-Tripp, Susan M. "Is Second Language Learning Like the First?" *TESOL Quarterly* 8 (1974):111–27.

92 Everett, Aaron B. "Individualized Instruction for Intermediate French." *French Review* 45(1972): 988–98.

93 Fadil, Virginia A. "More Understanding and Appreciation: Learning for Mastery in a Literature Course." *TESOL Quarterly* 9(1975):367–77.

94 Fanselow, John F. *Selected Behaviors of Experienced and Inexperienced Language Teachers—A Descriptive Analysis.* [Paper presented at the TESOL Convention, Los Angeles, California, 1975.]

95 ——— *The Treatment of Error in Oral Work.* [Paper presented at the TESOL Convention, Denver, Colorado, 1974.]

96 Feldman, David M. "Measuring Auditory Discrimination of Suprasegmental Features in Spanish." *International Review of Applied Linguistics* 11(1973):195–209.

97 Flaherty, Sister Etienne. *The Effect of Time-Expansion on Listening Comprehension of High School Students in Second-Year French Classes.* Columbus: The Ohio State University, 1975. [Doctoral dissertation.]

98 Ford, James F. "Language Attitude Studies: A Review of Selected Research." *Florida Foreign Language Reporter* 12(1974):53–54,100.

99 ——— *The Prospective Foreign Language Teacher and the Linguistically and Culturally Different Learner: An Attitudinal Study.* Columbus: The Ohio State University, 1974. [Doctoral dissertation.]

100 Frechette, Ernest A. "A Critical Survey of Elementary and Intermediate Level French Readers, 1968–1973." *Modern Language Journal* 59 (1975):3–7.

101 ——— "A Critical Survey of Elementary and Intermediate French Textbooks, 1968–1973." *Modern Language Journal* 58(1974):309–14.

102 Freeman, Diane E. "The Acquisition of Grammatical Morphemes by Adult ESL Students." *TESOL Quarterly* 9(1975):409–19.

103 Frey, Eberhard. "What Is Good Style? Reader Reactions to German Text Samples." *Modern Language Journal* 56(1972):310–23.

104 Fukuda, Shohachi. "The Four-Year Teacher-Training Project: Its Operation and Achievements." *TESOL Quarterly* 9(1975):15–22.

105 Fuller, Carol S. "Language-Oriented Careers in the Federal Government." *Modern Language Journal* 59(1975):153–60.

106 Gaies, Stephen J., Harry L. Gradman, and Bernard Spolsky. *Toward the Measurement of Functional Proficiency: Contextualization of the 'Noise Test.'* [Unpublished paper.]

107 Ghadessy, Mohsen. "Prepositions and Prepositional Patterns." *International Review of Applied Linguistics* 12(1974):307–16.

108 Gibbons, Michael J. *A Comparison of Learning Outcomes in Teacher-Directed and Non-Teacher-Directed Groups in Elementary College-Level Language Courses.* Columbus: The Ohio State University, 1975. [Doctoral dissertation.]

109 Gilbert, Claire P., and James F. McArthur. "In-Service Teacher Preparation of French Graduate Assistants: Design and Evaluation." *French Review* 48(1975):508–21.

110 Gonzales, Eileen, and Juan Lezama. "The Dual Language Model: A Practical Approach to Bilingual Education." *TESOL Quarterly* 8(1974): 153–60.

111 Good, C. V. *Dictionary of Education.* New York: McGraw-Hill, 1945.

112 Gould, Judith, and Jayme Spencer. *Critical Evaluation of the Cloze Test Procedure.* Cairo, Egypt: American University, 1974. [Unpublished manuscript.]

113 Gradman, Harry. Personal Communication, 1975. [Letter.]

114 ——— "Reduced Redundancy Testing: A Reconsideration," 41–48 in M. E. Concannon O'Brien, ed., *Testing in Second Language Teaching: New Dimensions.* Dublin, Ireland: Dublin University Press, 1974.

115 ——— and Stephen J. Gaies. *Reduced Redundancy and Error Analysis: A Study of Selected Performances on the 'Noise Test.'* [Paper presented at the Fourth International Congress of Applied Linguistics at Stuttgart, Germany, August 1975.] [Mimeo.]

116 ——— and Bernard Spolsky. *Progress and Prospects for Controlled Distortion as a Measure of Overall Language Proficiency.* [No date.] [Mimeo.]

117 Graham, Richard T., and Edwin H. Rudorf. "Dialect and Spelling." *Elementary English* 67(1970): 363–76.

118 Green, Peter. "Aptitude Testing—An On-Going Experiment." *Audio-Visual Language Journal* 12 (1974–75):205–10.

119 ——— "A Study of the Effectiveness of the Language Laboratory in School, Conducted at Archbishop Holgate's Grammar School, York, 1967–1970." *International Review of Applied Linguistics* 10(1972):283–92.

120 Griffin, Robert J. *Teaching Hispanic Folk Music as a Means to Cross-Cultural Understanding.* Columbus: The Ohio State University, 1973. [Doctoral dissertation.]

121 Grittner, Frank. Personal Communication, 1976. [Letter.]

122 Gue, Leslie R., and Edward A. Holdaway. "English Proficiency Tests as Predictors of Success in Graduate Studies in Education." *Language Learning* 23(1973):89–102.

123 Guiora, Alexander Z., Robert C. L. Brannon, and Cecelia Y. Dull. "Empathy and Second Language Learning." *Language Learning* 22(1972):111–30.

124 ——— Maria Paluszny, Benjamin Bait-Hallahmi, John C. Catford, Ralph E. Cooley, and Cecilia Y. Dull. "The Effects of Experimentally Induced Changes in Ego States in Pronunciation Ability in a Second Language: An Exploratory Study." *Comprehensive Psychiatry* 13(1975):421–28.

125 ——— "Language and Person Studies in Language Behavior." *Language Learning* 25(1975): 43–61.

126 Gulliksen, Harold. "Intercultural Attitude Study." *Foreign Language Annals* 5(1971):249.

127 Guskin, Judith T. *The Social Perception of Language Variation: Black and White Teachers' Attitudes towards Speakers from Different Racial and Social Class Backgrounds.* Ann Arbor: University of Michigan, 1970. [Doctoral dissertation.]

128 Hakuta, Kenji. "Prefabricated Patterns and the Emergence of Structure in Second Language Acquisition." *Language Learning* 24(1974):287–97.

129 Hale, Thomas M., and Eva C. Budar. "Are TESOL Classes the Only Answer?" *Modern Language Journal* 54(1970):487–92.

130 Hammelman, William M. R., and Melvin L. Nielsen. "The Native Paraprofessional: Identifying His Role in the Foreign Language Program." *Foreign Language Annals* 7(1974):346–52.

131 Hammerly, Hector. "Primary and Secondary Associations with Visual Aids as Semantic Conveyors." *International Review of Applied Linguistics* 12(1974):119–25.

132 Hancock, Charles R. "Guiding Teachers to Respond to Individual Differences in the Affective Domain." *Foreign Language Annals* 6(1972): 225–31.

133 Hanzeli, Victor. Personal Communication, 1976. [Letter.]

134 Harper, Jane. "A Behavioral Learning System in Foreign Languages at Tarrant County Junior College." *Foreign Language Annals* 8(1975): 327–34.

135 Harris, David P. "Report on an Experimental Group-Administered Memory Span Test." *TESOL Quarterly* 4(1970):203–13.

136 Harvey, Philip R. *Survey of Graduate Schools Regarding the Use of the Graduate School Foreign Language Tests, 1969–70.* Princeton, New Jersey, 1970. [EDRS: ED 040 679.]

137 Hauptman, Philip C. "A Structural Approach vs. a Situational Approach to Foreign-Language Teaching." *Language Learning* 21(1971):235–44.

138 Hawkins, Lee E. "Immediate versus Delayed Presentation of Foreign Language Script." *Modern Language Journal* 55(1971):280–90.

139 Heien, L. G. "Language Teaching in Different Keys." *Modern Language Journal* 54(1973): 185–89.

140 Henning, Grant H. "Measuring Foreign Language Reading Comprehension." *Language Learning* 25(1975):109–14.

141 ——— "Remembering Foreign Language Vocabulary: Acoustic and Semantic Parameters." *Language Learning* 23(1973):185–96.

142 Henning, William A. "A Study of the Effectiveness of a Programmed Reader." *French Review* 48(1975):522–25.

143 Hensley, Anne. "Black High School Students' Reactions to Black Speakers of Standard and Black English." *Language Learning* 22(1972):253–59.

144 Henzl, Vera M. "Linguistic Register of Foreign Language Instruction." *Language Learning* 23 (1973):207–22.

145 Herbert, Charles H.,Jr. *Initial Reading in Spanish for Bilinguals.* Quebec: Laval University, 1971. [EDRS: ED 061 813.]

146 Herold, William R. "Evaluating Student Teachers by Means of Teacher Performance Tests." *French Review* 48(1975):1009–12.

147 Hewett, Nancy. "Reactions of Prospective English Teachers toward Speakers of a Non-Standard Dialect." *Language Learning* 21(1971):205–12.

148 Higgins, John J. "Problems of Self-Correction in the Language Laboratory." *System* 3,iii(1975): 145–56.

149 Hilaire, Paul. Personal Communication, 1976. [Letter.]

150 Hoeh, James A., and Dennis W. Spuck, "Effects of a Three Phase Acculturation Process on Language Skill Development and Social and Personal Attitudes of High School French Students." *Foreign Language Annals* 8(1975):221–26.

151 Holley, Freda M. *The Acquisition of German Reading Vocabulary in the Advanced Foreign Language Class.* Austin: University of Texas, 1970. [Unpublished master's thesis.]

152 ——— *The Effects of Immediate Testing and*

New-Word Density in German Reading Materials upon Vocabulary Learning and Other Selected Variables. Austin: University of Texas, 1971. [Doctoral dissertation.]

153 ——— "A Study of Vocabulary Learning in Context: The Effect of New-Word Density in German Reading Materials." *Foreign Language Annals* 6(1973):339–47.

154 ——— and Janet K. King. "Vocabulary Glosses in Foreign Language Reading Materials." *Language Learning* 21(1971):213–19.

155 Honig, Lucille J., and Richard I. Brod. "Foreign Languages and Careers." *Modern Language Journal* 58(1974):157–85.

156 Horst, Donald P., et al. *Experimental Evaluation of the ELS Teacher Education Program. Final Report.* Pittsburgh: American Institute for Research, 1970. [EDRS: ED 042 073.]

157 Huberman, Gisela, and Vadim Medish. "Spanish Multi-Channel Instruction: A Progress Report." *Foreign Language Annals* 8(1975):49–52.

158 Hunt, Kellog W. "Do Sentences in the Second Language Grow Like Those in the First?" *TESOL Quarterly* 4(1970):195–202.

159 Ilyin, Donna. *Assessing Oral Communication in Adult Program English Second Language Classes,* 1975. [Unpublished paper.]

160 ——— *More on Developing ESL Placement Tests for Adult Programs in California.* [Paper presented at the TESOL Convention, New York, March 1976.]

161 Impey, Michael H. "The Present State of Romanian Studies in the United States and Canada." *Modern Language Journal* 59(1975):262–72.

162 Irvine, Patricia, Parvine Atai, and John W. Oller, Jr. "Cloze, Dictation, and the Test of English as a Foreign Language." *Language Learning* 24 (1974):245–52.

163 Jacobsen, Morris, and Maurice Imhoof. "Predicting Success in Learning a Second Language." *Modern Language Journal* 58(1974):329–36.

164 Jakobovits, Leon A. "Freedom to Teach and Freedom to Learn." *TESOL Quarterly* 7(1973):117–26.

165 ——— and Barbara Gordon. *The Context of Foreign Language Teaching.* Rowley, Massachusetts: Newbury House, 1974.

166 Jarvis, Gilbert A. Personal Communication, 1976. [Letter.]

167 ——— and William N. Hatfield. "The Practice Variable: An Experiment." *Foreign Language Annals* 4(1971):401–10.

168 Johnson, Kenneth R. "A Comparison of Black Dialect-Speaking Children and Standard English-Speaking Children and Their Ability to Hear Final Consonant Stops." *TESOL Quarterly* 8 (1974):375–87.

169 Johnson, Nancy A. "Zombies and Other Problems: Theory and Method in Research on Bilingualism." *Language Learning* 24(1974):105–33.

170 Joiner, Elizabeth G. *Communicative versus Non-Communicative Language Practice in the Teaching of Beginning College French: A Comparison of Two Treatments.* Columbus: The Ohio State University, 1974. [Doctoral dissertation.]

171 Jonas, Sister Ruth. *African Studies in French for the Elementary Grades: Phase II of a Twinned Classroom Approach to the Teaching of French in the Elementary Grades. Volume I, Technical Report.* Mt. St. Joseph, Ohio: College of Mt. St. Joseph-on-the-Ohio, 1972. [EDRS: ED 066 994.]

172 Jones, Randall. Personal Communication, 1976. [Letter.]

173 Jorstad, Helen. "Treatment of the Gender of Nouns in Selected High School Beginning French Textbooks." *French Review* 48(1975):499–507.

174 ——— and Dale L. Lange. Personal Communication, 1976. [Letter.]

175 Kalivoda, Theodore B., Genelle Morain, and Robert D. Elkins. "The Audio-Motor Unit: A Listening Comprehension Strategy That Works." *Foreign Language Annals* 4(1971):392–400.

176 Kerlinger, Fred. *Foundations of Behavioral Research.* New York: Holt, 1973.

177 Kessler, Carolyn. "Syntactic Contrasts in Child Bilingualism." *Language Learning* 22(1972): 221–33.

178 Keuleers, Alfons. "Insight, Automatization and Creativity in F-L Learning." *System* 3,iii(1975): 164–84.

179 Khampang, Phon. "Thai Difficulties in Using English Prepositions." *Language Learning* 24 (1974):215–22.

180 Klayman, Norma E. "Views of Secondary School Educators on the Foreign Language Requirement in Higher Education." *Modern Language Journal* 59(1975):168–73.

181 Knorre, Martha L. *The Role of Cognitive Processing in Second-Language Learning: A Study of the Effects of Depth Processing and Task Type on Measures of Student Learning in Elementary College Spanish.* Columbus: The Ohio State University, 1975. [Doctoral dissertation.]

182 Krashen, Stephen D. "Lateralization, Language Learning, and the Critical Period: Some New Evidence." *Language Learning* 23(1973):63–74.

183 ——— "Mental Abilities Underlying Linguistic and Non-Linguistic Functions." *Linguistics* 115 (1973):39–55.

184 ——— and H. Seliger. "The Role of Formal and Informal Environments in Second Language Learning: A Pilot Study." *International Journal of Psycholinguistics,* in press.

185 ——— H. Seliger, and D. Hartnett. "Two Studies in Adult Second Language Learning." *Kritikon Litterarum,* in press.

186 Lado, Robert. "Language, Thought, and Memory in Language Teaching: A Thought View." *Modern Language Journal* 54(1970):508–85.

187 ——— F. Aid, and M. Kruvant. *Massive Vocabulary Expansion, Phase II: The Effect of Oral and Orthographic Stimuli on the Memorization and Pronunciation of Basic Dialogs. Final Report.* Washington, D.C.: U.S. Office of Education, Bureau of Research, 1970. [EDRS: ED 047 594.]

188 Lambert, Wallace E., and G. Richard Tucker. *Bi-*

lingual Education of Children:The St. Lambert Experiment. Rowley, Massachusetts: Newbury House, 1972.

189 Landry, Richard G. "A Comparison of Second Language Learners and Monolinguals in Divergent Thinking Tasks at the Elementary School Level." *Modern Language Journal* 58(1974):10–19.

190 ——— "The Enhancement of Figural Creativity through Second Language Learning at the Elementary School Level." *Foreign Language Annals* 7(1973):111–15.

191 ——— "The Relationship of Second Language Learning and Verbal Creativity." *Modern Language Journal* 57(1973):110–13.

192 Leong, Che Kan. "A Study of Written Chinese Vocabulary." *Modern Language Journal* 56 (1972):230–34.

193 Lepke, Helen S. *An Exploratory Study of Cognitive Style as an Aspect of Prediction of Achievement in Individualized and Conventional Instruction in Beginning College German.* Akron, Ohio: University of Akron, 1975. [Doctoral dissertation.]

194 ——— Personal Communication, 1976. [Letter.]

195 Levinsky, Frieda L. *Research on Language Methodology.* 1971. [EDRS: ED 053 627.]

196 Lewald, H. Ernest. "Theory and Practice in Culture Teaching on the Second-Year Level in French and Spanish." *Foreign Language Annals* 7(1974:) 660–67.

197 Lima, Marilynne. *A Comparative Study of Foreign Language Programs in Two Adjacent School Districts in the State of Utah and Their Effects on the Dropout Rate.* 1973. [EDRS: ED 071 512.]

198 Lipschutz, Rachel R. Personal Communication, 1975. [Letter.]

199 Locke, John L. "The Value of Repetition in Articulation Learning." *International Review of Applied Linguistics* 8(1970):147–54.

200 Lukmano, Yasmeen M. "Motivation to Learn and Language Proficiency." *Language Learning* 22 (1972):261–73.

201 Lynch, F. D. *Clozentropy:A Technique for Studying Audience Response to Films.* Iowa City: University of Iowa, 1972. [Doctoral dissertation.]

202 Lyne, A. A. "A Word-Frequency Count on French Business Correspondence Based on a Corpus of Approximately 80,000 Running Words." *International Review of Applied Linguistics* 13(1965): 95–110.

203 MacIntosh, Roderick, and Jacob Ornstein. "A Brief Sampling of West Texas Teacher Attitudes toward Southwest Spanish and English Language Varieties." *Hispania* 57(1974):920–26.

204 Markman, Barbara R., Irene V. Spilka, and G. Richard Tucker. "The Use of Elicited Imitation in Search of an Interim French Grammar." *Language Learning* 25(1975):31–41.

205 Marottoli, Vincent. "The Success of the Private Language Schools:A Lesson to Be Learned." *Foreign Language Annals* 6(1973):354–58.

206 Masciantonio, Rudolph. *Appendix II—Summary of Recent Research on the Value of Latin in Upgrading the Basic Skills of Pupils.* [No date.] [Mimeo.]

207 Mason, Charles. "The Relevance of Intensive Training in English as a Foreign Language for University Students." *Language Learning* 21 (1971):197–204.

208 McGowan, Sister Jean P. *Measurement and Evaluation of Immersion-Type Teaching in Secondary Schools versus the Traditional Teaching Existent Today.* Wilmette, Illinois: Regina Dominican High School, 1972. [EDRS: ED 066 097.]

209 McRae, Susan. *Relations between Teacher Bilingualism in Spanish and English and Attitudes toward a Bilingual Television Program.* 1972. [EDRS: ED 066 033.]

210 Menting, J. P., and A. Pouw. "Entraînement de l'élocution à l'aide d'un modèle dans le laboratoire de langues." *International Review of Applied Linguistics* 13(1975):145–51.

211 Milon, John P. "The Development of Negation in English by a Second Language Learner." *TESOL Quarterly* 8(1974):137–43.

212 Mladenka, Alois C. Personal Communication, 1975. [Letter.]

213 Modu, Christopher C., Mariette Reed, and Robert L. Coon. "How Valid Is the Advanced Placement French Language Examination?" *French Review* 48(1975):1013–22.

214 Mohr, William, and Dale Lally. "Teaching German via Short-Wave Broadcasts." *Modern Language Journal* 27(1973):119–24.

215 Molina, Huberto. "The SWRL English Language and Concepts Program for Spanish-Speaking Children:1971–1972 Tryout." *System* 2,ii(1974): 57–68.

216 ——— "Evaluating the Effectiveness of a Program Used in School Situations Characterized by High Pupil Absenteeism and Attrition." *System* 3,i(1975):48–53.

217 Monnot, Michel, and Janice. "Second-Year French:The Carleton-Pau Experiment." *French Review* 48(1974):368–76.

218 Monroe, James H. "Measuring and Enhancing Syntactic Fluency in French." *French Review* 48 (1975):1023–31.

219 Morel, Stefano. *Total Immersion Language Program:A New Approach to Foreign Language Instruction. Technical Report.* Albany: New York State Education Department, 1971. [EDRS: ED 053 586.]

220 Moskowitz, Gertrude. "Read Research . . . Who? Me?" *Foreign Language Beacon* 4(1969):12–13.

221 Mueller, Theodore H. "Could the New Key Be a Wrong Key?" *French Review* 44(1971):1085–93.

222 ——— Personal Communication, 1975. [Letter.]

223 ——— "Student Attitudes in the Basic French Courses at the University of Kentucky." *Modern Language Journal* 55(1971):290–98.

224 ——— "Student Withdrawals in an Individualized French Course." *International Review of Applied Linguistics* 12(1974):248–51.

225 ——— and Richard I. Miller. "A Study of Stu-

dent Attitudes and Motivation in a Collegiate French Course Using Programmed Language Instruction." *International Review of Applied Linguistics* 8(1970):297–320.
226 Natalicio, Diana S., and Frederick Williams. *Repetition as an Oral Language Assessment Technique*. Austin, Texas: University of Texas, 1971. [EDRS: ED 051 680.]
227 ——— "What Characteristics Can 'Experts' Reliably Evaluate in the Speech of Black and Mexican-American Children?" *TESOL Quarterly* 6(1972):121–27.
228 Noble, A. Candace. Personal Communication, 1975. [Letter.]
229 Norton, Harriet S. Personal Communication, 1976. [Letter.]
230 Nostrand, Howard L. Personal Communication, 1976. [Letter.]
231 Obanya, P. A. I. "Lexical and Structural Errors in the Written French of Nigerian Pupils." *Audio-Visual Language Journal* 12(1974):29–32.
232 Offenberg, Robert M., et al. *Evaluation of the Elementary School (FLES) Latin Program 1970–71*. Philadelphia: School District of Philadelphia, 1971. [EDRS: ED 056 612.]
233 Oller, John W.,Jr. "Assessing Competence in ESL: Reading." *TESOL Quarterly* 6(1972):313–23.
234 ——— "Cloze, Discourse, and Approximations to English," 345–70 in Marina K. Burt and Heidi C. Dulay,eds., *New Directions in Second Language Learning and Bilingual Education*. Washington, D.C.: Teachers of English to Speakers of Other Languages, 1975.
235 ——— "Evidence for a General Language Proficiency Factor: An Expectancy Grammar." [No date.] [Reprint.]
236 ——— "Language Testing: Arguments, Findings, and Future Directions, in H. Douglas Brown, ed., *A Survey of Applied Linguistics,* in press.
237 ——— *Pragmatics and Language Testing*. Albuquerque: University of New Mexico. [No date.] [Mimeo.]
238 ——— "A Program for Language Testing Research." [No date.] [Reprint.]
239 ——— *Research with Cloze Procedure in Measuring the Proficiency of Non-Native Speakers of English: An Annotated Bibliography*. CAL ERIC/CLL Series on Languages and Linguistics: Number 13. Arlington, Virginia: Center for Applied Linguistics, 1975.
240 ——— "Scoring Methods and Difficulty Levels for Cloze Tests of Proficiency in English as a Second Language." *Modern Language Journal* 56(1972):151–58.
241 ——— J. Donald Bowen, Ton That Dien, and Victor W. Mason. "Cloze Tests in English, Thai, and Vietnamese: Native and Non-Native Performance." *Language Learning* 22(1972):1–15.
242 ——— and Christine A. Conrad. "The Cloze Technique and ESL Proficiency." *Language Learning* 21(1971):183–95.
243 ——— and Nevin Inal. "A Cloze Test of English Prepositions." *TESOL Quarterly* 5(1971):315–26.
244 ——— and Naoko Nagato. "The Long-Term Effect of FLES: An Experiment." *Modern Language Journal* 58(1974)15–19.
245 ——— and Elcho Z. Redding. "Article Usage and Other Language Skills." *Language Learning* 21 (1971):85–95.
246 ——— and James R. Tullius. "Reading Skills of Non-Native Speakers of English." *International Review of Applied Linguistics* 11(1973):69–80.
247 ——— and Seid M. Ziahosseiny. "The Contrastive Analysis Hypothesis and Spelling Errors." *Language Learning* 20(1970):183–89.
248 Olsen, Carroll L. "A Course in Corrective Phonetics." *French Review* 46(1973):573–83.
249 Olson, Linda L., and S. Jay Samuels. *The Relationship between Age and Accuracy of Foreign Language Pronunciation*. [EDRS: ED 060 702.]
250 Olsson, Margareta. *Intelligibility: A Study of Errors and Their Importance*. Gothenburg, Sweden: Gothenburg University School of Education, 1972. [EDRS: ED 072 681.]
251 Ornstein, Jacob. "Language Varieties along the U.S.-Mexican Border." 349–62 in G. E. Perren and J. L. M. Trimm,eds., *Applications of Linguistics: Selected Papers of the Second International Congress of Applied Linguistics*. Cambridge, England: Cambridge University Press, 1971.
252 Orvik, James M. *A Study of English Vocabulary Comparing Eskimo and Caucasian Children. Final Report*. Fairbanks: Alaska University, Center for Northern Educational Research, 1973. [EDRS: ED 072 705.]
253 Oskarsson, Mats. "Assessing the Relative Effectiveness of Two Methods of Teaching English to Adults: A Replication Experiment." *International Review of Applied Linguistics* 11(1973):251–62.
254 Ott, C. Eric, David C. Butler, Rowland S. Blake, and John P. Ball. "The Effect of Interactive-Image Elaboration on the Acquisition of Foreign Language Laboratory." *Language Learning* 23 (1973):197–206.
255 Palmer, Adrian S. "Testing Communication." *International Review of Applied Linguistics* 10 (1972):35–45.
256 Pane, Remigio U. "Present Status of Italian Studies in the United States and Canada." *Modern Language Journal* 54(1970):507–23.
257 Papalia, Anthony. "Assessing Students' Learning Styles and Teaching for Individual Differences." [Unpublished paper.]
258 ——— "An Assessment of Attitudes and Behaviors of Foreign Language Teachers." *Foreign Language Annals* 7(1973):231–36.
259 ——— "Attitudes of Students, Teachers, and Administrators toward Ability Grouping for Individualized Instruction." *Foreign Language Annals* 8(1975):54–55.
260 ——— Personal Communication, 1975. [Letter.]
261 ——— "Students' Learning Styles in Ascribing

Meaning to Written and Oral Stimuli." *Hispania* 58(1975):106–08.
262 ——— "Students, Parents, and Teachers as Data Sources for Determining FL Instructional Goals." *Foreign Language Annals* 7(1973):117–19.
263 ——— and Joseph Zampogna. "An Experiment in Individualized Instruction through Small Group Interaction." *Foreign Language Annals* 5 (1972):302–06.
264 ——— "An Experimental Study on Teachers' Classroom Behaviors and Their Effect on FL Attrition." *Modern Language Journal* 56(1972): 421–24.
265 Perelle, Ira B. "Level II vs. Level III Language Laboratories:An Investigation of Their Relative Efficiencies." *System* 3,iii(1975):157–63.
266 Perlman, Alice. *OPINION-AIRING:A Practitioner's Alternative to Formal Evaluation.* Brooklyn: New York City Board of Education. [No date.] [Mimeo.]
267 ——— Personal Communication, 1975. [Letter.]
268 Pfister, Guenter G. "Written Assignments—Valid Reinforcers of Speaking and Understanding." *Foreign Language Annals* 7(1974):421–24.
269 Phillips, June K. Personal Communication, 1976. [Letter.]
270 ——— *A Study of the Applicability of Task Analysis Methodology and Learning Hierarchies to Second Language Reading.* Columbus:The Ohio State University, 1974. [Doctoral dissertation.]
271 Pinder, William W. *Factors Influencing Attitudes of Florida Teachers toward Modern Foreign Language Teaching Methodology,* 1972. [EDRS: ED 069 192.]
272 Politzer, Robert L. "Developmental Sentence Scoring as a Method of Measuring Second Language Acquisition." *Modern Language Journal* 58 (1974):245–50.
273 ——— and Mary R. Hoover. "On the Use of Attitude Variables in Research in the Teaching of a Second Dialect." *International Review of Applied Linguistics* 12(1974):43–51.
274 ——— Mary R. Hoover, and Dwight Brown. "A Test of Proficiency in Black Standard and Nonstandard Speech." *TESOL Quarterly* 8(1974): 27–35.
275 ——— and Arnulfo G. Ramirez. "An Error Analysis of the Spoken English of Mexican-American Pupils in a Bilingual School and a Monolingual School." *Language Learning* 23(1973):39–61.
276 Ponchie, Jean-Pierre. "Individualizing and Personalizing Instruction in the Advanced Conversation-Composition French Class." *Foreign Language Annals* 7(1974):599–601.
277 Postovsky, Valerian A. "Effects of Delay in Oral Practice at the Beginning of Second Language Learning." *Modern Language Journal* 58(1974): 229–39.
278 Powell, Patricia B. "Moi Tarzan, Vous Jane?:A Study of Communicative Competence." *Foreign Language Annals* 8(1975):38–42.
279 Prince, Marilyn M., and John P. Casey. "Programmed Instruction Helps Teach Spanish Grammar." *Modern Language Journal* 56(1972):491–92.
280 Ramirez, Arnulfo G., and Robert L. Politzer. "The Acquisition of English and the Maintenance of Spanish in a Bilingual Education Program." *TESOL Quarterly* 9(1975):113–24.
281 Ramsey, C. A., and E. N. Wright. *Language Backgrounds and Achievement in Toronto Schools.* Toronto, Ontario:Toronto Board of Education, 1970. [EDRS: ED 078 698.]
282 Read, Charles. "Children's Judgments of Phonetic Similarities in Relation to English Spelling." *Language Learning* 23(1973):17–38.
283 Reeback, Robert T. "Range of Effectiveness as a Comprehensive Measure of Communication Skill" *Language Learning* 21(1971):97–106.
284 Reilly, John H., and William F. Oakes. "A Comparison of Two Modern Methods of Foreign Language Teaching." *French Review* 44(1971):730–37.
285 Richards, Jack C. "A Psycholinguistic Measure of Vocabulary Selection." *International Review of Applied Linguistics* 8(1970):87–102.
286 Riegel, Klaus F., and Irina W. M. Zivian. "A Study of Inter- and Intralingual Associations in English and German." *Language Learning* 22 (1972):51–63.
287 Rothfarb, Sylvia H. Personal Communication. 1976. [Letter.]
288 ——— and Robert Cahill. *Classification of Students Using the Dade County Aural Comprehension Test.* [No date.]
289 Saegert, Joel, Sue Scott, John Perkins, and G. Richard Tucker. "A Note on the Relationship between English Proficiency, Years of Language Study and Medium of Instruction." *Language Learning* 24(1974):99–104.
290 Santoni, Georges V. "Using Videotape in the Advanced Conversation Class." *Foreign Language Annals* 8(1975):233–38.
291 Savignon, Sandra J. "Teaching for Communicative Competence:A Research Report." *Audio-Visual Language Journal* 10(1972/3):153–62.
292 Scanlan, Richard T. "A Critical Survey of New Elementary and Intermediate Latin Textbooks, 1969–1973." *Modern Language Journal* 58 (1974):322–25.
293 Schachter, Jacquelyn. "An Error in Error Analysis." *Language Learning* 24(1974):205–14.
294 Schnitzer, Marc L. "Applied Generative Phonology:A Methodology for Teaching Pronunciation." *International Review of Applied Linguistics* 12 (1974):289–305.
295 Schotta, Sarita G. "Student Evaluation and Foreign Language Programs—A Case Study." *Foreign Language Annals* 6(1973):500–17.
296 Schulz, Renate A. *Discrete-Point versus Simulated Communication Testing:A Study of the Effect of Two Methods of Testing on the Development of Communicative Proficiency in Beginning*

College French Classes. Columbus:The Ohio State University, 1974. [Doctoral dissertation.]

297 Schumann, John H. "Techniques for Analyzing Second Language Acquisition Data—A Report from the 1974 TESOL Convention." *TESOL Quarterly* 8(1974):417–23.

298 ——— and Nancy Stenson. *New Frontiers in Second Language Learning.* Rowley, Massachusetts:Newbury House, 1974.

299 Schwab, Gisela. *Individualized Instruction at Levels I and II.* 1972. [EDRS: ED 074 825.]

300 Scoon, Annabelle R. "Affective Influences on English Language Learning among Indian Students." *TESOL Quarterly* 5(1971):285–91.

301 Scott, Margaret S., and G. Richard Tucker. "Error Analysis and English-Language Strategies of Arab Students." *Language Learning* 24(1974): 69–97.

302 Seliger, Herbert W. "Inductive Method and Deductive Method in Language Teaching:A Reexamination." *International Review of Applied Linguistics* 13(1975):1–18.

303 ——— Merrill Swain, and Guy Dumas. "The Interlanguage Hypothesis Extended to Children." *Language Learning* 25(1975):139–52.

304 ——— and Valerie Whiteson. "Contextualizing Laboratory Administered Aural Comprehension Tests." *System* 3,i(1975):10–15.

305 Semke, Harriet D. "Peer-Teaching Helps!" *Foreign Language Annals* 8(1975):123–27.

306 Shane, Alex M. "An Evaluation of the Existing College Norms for the MLA-Cooperative Russian Test and Its Efficacy as a Placement Examination." *Modern Language Journal* 55(1971):93–99.

307 Sisk, Karin R. "The Use of Instant Replay Television as a Tool for Teaching Oral Language—A Research Study." *Foreign Language Annals* 8 (1975):187–88.

308 Sisson, Cyrus R. "The Effect of Delayed Comparison in the Language Laboratory on Phoneme Discrimination and Pronunciation Accuracy." *Language Learning* 20(1970):69–88.

309 Skoczylas, Rudolph V. *An Evaluation of Some Cognitive and Affective Aspects of a Spanish-English Bilingual Education Program,* 1972. [EDRS: ED 066 990.]

310 Smart, John C., Charles F. Elton, and Collins W. Burnett. "Underachievers and Overachievers in Intermediate French." *Modern Language Journal* 54(1970):415–20.

311 Smith, Merle. *Pontiac Title VII Bilingual Education Program 1970–71. Final Evaluation Report.* 1971. [EDRS: ED 061 840.]

312 Smith, Philip D.,Jr. *A Project to Develop Pre-Vocational Literary Materials for Spanish-Speaking Students.* West Chester, Pennsylvania:West Chester State College, 1972. [EDRS: ED 074 824.]

313 Smythe, P. C., G. C. Jutras, J. R. Bramwell, and Robert C. Gardner. "Second Language Retention over Varying Intervals." *Modern Language Journal* 57(1973):400–05.

314 Solomom, Martha. "Stem Endings and the Acquisition on Inflections." *Language Learning* 22 (1972):43–50.

315 Spector, Sima. *Patterns of Difficulty in English in Bilingual Mexican-American Children.* 1972. [EDRS: ED 066 083.]

316 Spolsky, Bernard. "Speech Communities and Schools." *TESOL Quarterly* 8(1974):17–26.

317 Stafford, Kenneth R. *Types of Bilingualism and Performance of Navaho Children in School, Phase II.* Tempe:Arizona State University, 1972. [EDRS: ED 072 706.]

318 Stansfield, Charles. Personal Communication, 1975. [Letter.]

319 ——— "Study Abroad and the First-Year Student." *System* 3,iii(1975):198–203.

320 Stern, Carolyn, and Diane Ruble. "Teaching New Concepts to Non-English Speaking Preschool Children." *TESOL Quarterly* 7(1973):309–17.

321 Sternglass, Marilyn S. "Close Similarities in Dialect Features of Black and White College Students in Remedial Composition Class." *TESOL Quarterly* 8(1974):271–83.

322 Stockfelt-Hoatson, Britt-Ingrid. "Linguistic, Personal and Social Development of Immigrant Children." *System* 2,iii(1974):67–77.

323 Stubbs, Joseph B., and G. Richard Tucker. "The Cloze Test as a Measure of English Proficiency."

324 Suiero-Ross, Carmen. "Cultural Characteristics in Teacher-Pupil Interaction." *System* 2,ii(1974): 39–48.
Modern Language Journal 58(1974):329–41.

325 Swain, Merrill. *Bibliography:Research on Immersion Education for the Majority Child.* Toronto: The Ontario Institute for Studies in Education. [No date.] [Mimeo.]

326 Tamarkin, Toby. Personal Communication, 1976. [Letter.]

327 Tang, Benita T. "A Psycholinguistic Study of the Relationships between Children's Ethnic-Linguistic Attitudes and the Effectiveness of Methods Used in Second-Language Reading Instruction." *TESOL Quarterly* 8(1974):233–51.

328 Tarone, Elaine, Merrill Swain, and Ann Fathman. "Some Limitations to the Classroom Applications of Current Second Language Acquisition Research." *TESOL Quarterly* 10 (1976):19–32.

329 Taylor, Barry P. "The Use of Overgeneralization and Transfer Learning Strategies by Elementary and Intermediate Students of ESL." *Language Learning* 25(1975):73–107.

330 Teichert, Herman U. "An Experimental Study Using Learning Packages in Beginning College German." *Modern Language Journal* 56(1972): 488–90.

331 Teitelbaum, Sidney L. *Foreign Language Practices:A Decade of Change?* Fifth Annual Survey. New York:Foreign Language Association of Chairmen and Supervisors of Long Island, 1971. [EDRS: ED 050 637.]

332 Teschner, Richard V. "Exploring the Role of the United States Hispano in the Dissemination of Anglicisms in Spanish." *Foreign Language Annals* 7(1974):681–93.

333 Tiefenbrun, Susan W. "The Use of Planned Dramatic Scenes with the Audio-Lingual Method." *French Review* 45(1972):855–59.

334 Titone, Renzo. "On Some Modalities of Syntactic Productivity and Choice." *International Review of Applied Linguistics* 8(1970):227–46.

335 Travers, Robert M. W.,ed. *Second Handbook of Research on Teaching.* Chicago:Rand McNally, 1973.

336 Tsu, John B. "The Teaching of Chinese in Colleges and Schools of the United States." *Modern Language Journal* 54(1970):562–79.

337 Valdman, Albert, and Joel Walz. *A Selected Bibliography on Language Learners' Systems and Error Analysis.* CAL ERIC/CLL Series on Languages and Linguistics, Number 21. Arlington, Virginia:Center for Applied Linguistics, 1975.

338 Veidt, Frederick P. "The Dialogue:An Aid to Oral Production in Beginning Language Study." *Modern Language Journal* 57(1973):3–8.

339 von Elek, Tibor, and Mats Oskarsson. "An Experiment Assessing the Relative Effectiveness of Two Methods of Teaching English Grammatical Structures to Adults." *International Review of Applied Linguistics* 10(1972):60–72.

340 ——— *A Replication Study in Teaching Foreign Language Grammar to Adults.* Gothenburg, Sweden:Gothenburg School of Education, Department of Educational Research, 1973. [EDRS: ED 094 551.]

341 Wagner-Gough, Judy. *Comparative Studies in Second Language Learning.* CAL ERIC/CLL Series on Languages and Linguistics, Number 26. Arlington, Virginia:Center for Applied Linguistics, 1975.

342 Walker, John L. "Opinions of University Students about Language Teaching." *Foreign Language Annals* 7(1973):102–05.

343 Wallace, John A. "Three Weeks Equals Thirty Weeks?—A Report on an Experimental Intensive January Language Course." *Foreign Language Annals* 6(1972):88–94.

344 Walz, Joel C. *A Longitudinal Study of the Acquisition of French Pronunciation.* Bloomington: Indiana University, 1975. [Doctoral dissertation.]

345 Warriner, Helen. *Student Attitudes toward Foreign Language Study:Results of a Survey.* Richmond:Virginia State Department of Education, 1972. [EDRS: ED 072 682.]

346 White, Ronald V. "Activating Advanced ESL Students:A Problem and a Solution." *TESOL Quarterly* 5(1971):231–38.

347 ——— "The Concept of Register and TESL." *TESOL Quarterly* 8(1974):401–16.

348 Whitman, Randall L., and Kenneth L. Jackson. "The Unpredictability of Contrastive Analysis." *Language Learning* 22(1972):29–41.

349 Willis, Clodius. "Computer Analysis of Literature and the Teaching of French." *International Review of Applied Linguistics* 10(1972):247–61.

350 Wood, Lynn T. *A Study of Student Attitudes toward Foreign Languages in Public Secondary Schools of Utah.* 1972. [EDRS: ED 073 711.]

351 Zampogna, Joseph, Ronald J. Gentile, Anthony Papalia, and Gordon Silber. *A Study of the Relationship between Learning Styles and Learning Environments in Selected Modern Language Classes.* Buffalo:SUNY at Buffalo, 1975. [Mimeo.]

352 Zirkel, Perry A. *An Evaluation of the Effectiveness of Selected Experimental Bilingual Education Programs in Connecticut.* West Hartford, Connecticut:University of Hartford, 1972. [EDRS: ED 070 326.]

Index to Persons Cited

Index to Topics and Institutions Cited